SWM Faculty and first class, 1965 with President Hubbard.

Part of the 1966-67 class with faculty. Left to right front row: Winter, Tippett, McGavran, and J.T. Seamands, an adjunct that year. Peter Wagner, a future faculty member, is at right end of back row.

Front row: Winter, Orr and Seamands. Back row: Tippett and McGavran

Kraft and McGavran, early 70s.

1986 Convocation when Tippett returned from Australia for a few days. This was the last time he and McGavran were together.

Three deans (Pierson, McGavran and Glasser) about 1987 when McGavran was 90.

Faculty early 80s: back row: Betty Sue Brewster, Viggo Sogaard, Carl George (adjunct), Pat Harrison (adjunct), Don McCurry (adjunct), Roberta King (adjunct), Edwin Orr. Front row: Tom Brewster (with Jed), Charles Kraft, Dan Shaw, Art Glasser, Paul Pierson, Bobby Clinton, Che Bin Tan, Dean Gilliland, and Peter Wagner.

A future dean and Jana, November 1982.

Mid-80s
faculty:
Front row
Clinton, Tan,
Shaw, Kraft,
Gilliland,
Back row
Wagner,
Woodberry,
Pierson,
Hiebert,
Gibbs, and
Glasser.

Late 80s faculty: Kraft, Elliston, Gilliland, Gibbs, Glasser, Hiebert, Wagner Pierson, Brewster, Tan, Clinton, Shaw and Woodberry.

Wagner after an earthquake.

Five Deans. From left to right: Lingenfelter, Woodberry, McConnell, Pierson, and Glasser.

Secretaries and Administrative Assistants. Top: Nancy McRae. Middle: Doris
Wagner and Marilyn Clinton. Bottom: Denise Shubert and Betty Ann Klebe.

Class of
1974-75

Class of
1978-79

Class of
1981-82

Class of
1985-86

Class of
1990-91

Class of
1994-95

Class of
2000-01

Class of
2004-05

SWM/SIS at Forty:
A Participant-Observer's View
of Our History

Charles H. Kraft

William Carey Library
Pasadena, CA

Cover design: Joseph Gil

Book design: Corinne Kershaw

Published by William Carey Library
1605 E. Elizabeth Street
Pasadena, California 91104
www.WCLBooks.com

William Carey Library is a Ministry of the U.S. Center for World Mission, Pasadena, California.

ISBN 0-87808-349-9

Printed in the United States of America

Kraft, Charles H.
  SWM/SIS at forty : a history / Charles H. Kraft.
      p. cm.
  Includes bibliographical references (p.   ) and index.
  ISBN 0-87808-349-9 (pbk. : alk. paper)
  1. Fuller Theological Seminary. School of Intercultural Studies--History.   2. Missions--Study and teaching--California--Pasadena--History. I. Title.

  BV2093.F84K73 2005
  230'.071'179493--dc22

2005050819

Contents

Foreword

Seldom are we able to listen to the story of a school that has so greatly impacted world mission. As we contemplated how to record the first forty years of the School of World Mission, now School of Intercultural Studies, it was obvious that the best way was to capture the memory of one who lived it. While many of our faculty can claim deep roots in the school, no one compares to Chuck Kraft who, apart from the first four years, has been a vital part of every development.

At the outset, Kraft made every attempt to listen to the stories of others and to record them as part of the text. We are also thankful to Ralph Winter who was a great help in refining and even challenging our memory. So as you read this volume, remember that it is not so much a history as the memory of the ultimate insider or as Kraft taught us all to think, it is the emic perspective of a participant-observer!

Written as a chronological memory, each chapter introduces the participants and their stories allowing the events to support the contributions to our school. The major emphasis is on the early years, which is an encouragement to all of us who have participated in the later years. After setting the foundation, Kraft remembers the years through the eras of each successive Dean. Introducing each new faculty member, he weaves their stories into the character of the school with the skill of a loving older brother. Although we wanted to hear from all of our graduates, we have selected a few to represent the amazing story of impact that is part of our school.

Finally, in a style that we have come to appreciate, Kraft takes the time to reflect on the past and project into the future. His call to center our vision on the incarnation of Christ is a worthy challenge to our faculty, students, and graduates alike. Founded in service to Christ and His Church, SWM/SIS turns forty with a renewed commitment to the *panta ta ethne*, the lost world that were so often in McGavran's thoughts and on his lips. We owe a debt of gratitude to Chuck Kraft; this is a memory worth sharing.

By C. Douglas McConnell
Dean, Fuller School of Intercultural Studies

Introduction

What follows is a story or, rather, a set of stories within a larger Story, each with its own integrity but each merging with the others at some point in time to make up the broader Story that was the School of World Mission. I say *was*, not because SWM has ceased to exist but because it now continues under another name—The School of Intercultural Studies. We will find out later why that change was made.

This is a story of the Hand of God working in the affairs of men, women and an institution. He started this story ages ago. We will not go back that far. We will, however, go back to the early and middle decades of the twentieth century—to a missionary son of a missionary working diligently in India, using methods that were not effective under a Church that had given up on the Gospel. His was the major story. It merged, however, with that of an Australian Wesleyan missionary who felt his time was up in Fiji and was looking for what the Lord had next for him. And these two stories merged first with that of a small Bible College and then with the quest of Fuller Seminary to fulfill a dream of its founder to initiate an institution to train missionaries.

One stream of the story of the School of World Mission begins with the vision of Charles E. Fuller, a pioneer radio evangelist of the 1930s, 40s and 50s. As early as the 1940s Fuller spoke of his desire to establish a school to train evangelists and missionaries. Fuller saw this as a logical extension of his own efforts at evangelism and a worthy legacy of his life's commitment to winning the lost.

Toward this end, Fuller consulted with a variety of people, including notably his friend Harold John Ockenga, pastor of Park Street Congregational Church in Boston. These friends influenced Dr. Fuller in a different direction, convincing him that what was needed was a theological seminary with quite a different purpose from the vision of Dr. Fuller. That purpose, valid though different, was "for a theological institution committed to a high level of scholarship while retaining a conservative commitment to biblical truth" (Works 1974:309). The major aim, then, came to be to prove to theological Liberals that Conservatives could think.

With the establishment of Fuller Theological Seminary in 1947, then, Dr. Fuller's plan for a school to train evangelists and missionaries was delayed. Perhaps to gain Dr. Fuller's favor, he was promised (according to rumor) that he could count on half of the graduates of the seminary entering missionary service. This, of course, never occurred since the concern that the new institution prove to Liberals that Evangelicals could carry out high level academic work is not the kind of concern that produces missionaries. However, Professor William LaSor, an Old Testament professor and strong supporter of missions has stated that "in the early years of the Seminary, there was a heavy emphasis on missions in almost every class" (Works 1974:309).

Whatever the degree of emphasis, the concern for a missionary training institution was not entirely abandoned. It was resurrected under interesting circumstances in the early 60s and became a reality in 1965. It is at that time that the four stories merge to produce the School of World Mission and Institute of Church Growth.

But the SWM story has a Prehistory and to that we will turn first. This Prehistory, then, is followed by 40 years of History, divided into six Eras superintended by six Deans. The body of our book will cover the Prehistory plus those six Eras, followed by three appendicies and a Bibliography. In the appendicies I present a Timeline, outlining the major events of these 40 years as recorded in the Text (Appendix A), followed by Student Testimonials (Appendix B) and a listing of Church Growth and Missiology Lecturers (Appendix C).

In the body of the book, I have chosen to focus on the persons who have made up the history—the faculty and higher-level administrators who have made our operation go. The story of SWM/SIS, as I see it, is their/our story with the invisible Hand of God in every event, sometimes obviously, often unseen.

From the original mandate to write this book until its completion, I have had the cooperation of many. Except for the Prehistory and the sections on McGavran, Tippett and Orr where I had to depend on written accounts, I have had greater or lesser personal interaction with those whose stories fill these pages. I thank each of them for their assistance and encouragement. Where I have

Introduction

portrayed them accurately it is to their credit. Where I have missed things or otherwise been inaccurate, the fault is mine.

Special thanks goes to Marilyn Clinton and Deb Hannaford who helped in all kinds of ways, including finding pictures and the gathering of the student testimonials and to Corinne Kershaw who did the finishing-up detailed work and shepherded the book through to publication. I thank Ralph Winter, Paul Pierson, Wilbert Shenk and Doug McConnell for going over the manuscript and picking up many of the inaccuracies in early drafts. The input of former deans Pierson and Woodberry and present dean McConnell have been invaluable in providing insight into the details of their administrations. And I appreciate greatly the cooperation of each of those whose stories are included here. Bless you all.

South Pasadena
August 2005

Dedication

Dedicated to the Memory
of the
Founders
of the
School of World Mission/
School of Intercultural Studies
Fuller Theological Seminary

Donald A. McGavran
and
Alan R. Tippett

and to
the Deans who followed them

Aurthur F. Glasser
Paul E. Pierson
J. Dudley Woodberry
Sherwood G. Lingenfelter
C. Douglas McConnell

Part I
Prehistory

Chapter 1

Donald A. McGavran
(1897-1990)

At Fuller: 1965-1983

Youth and Education

The McGavran story begins in India where he was born on December 15, 1897 and brought up the son and grandson of missionary parents and grandparents working under the United Christian Missionary Society of the Christian Church (Disciples of Christ). His father was an American of Scotch-Irish descent and his mother British, a woman who "never lost the poise and queenly bearing learned in her land of birth" (Middleton 1989:1). The influence of his mother and of British colonialism marked the way McGavran interacted with people for his entire life, leading to accusations of arrogance by his critics. Another of McGavran's lifetime characteristics likely came from his father who was known in his college days as, "Fighting Mac" (ibid.:5).

The story continues through largely informal schooling in India up to age 13 when, in 1910, his family moved to the United States for his father to spend a year doing an M.A. degree in Ann Arbor, Michigan. Donald and his three siblings found this resettlement to be "a time of deep cultural adjustment, since almost all their schooling had been home studies and their worldview was very much that of village India" (ibid.:8). This year was followed by a year and a half in a pastorate in Tulsa, Oklahoma and then a move to Indianapolis where his father took a post in the newly created College of Missions as Professor of Indian Studies. During the time in Oklahoma, McGavran gave his life to Jesus Christ.

Enrolling in Butler University in Indianapolis in 1915, he was able to graduate with a B.A. in 1920, in spite of the fact that he spent two years (1917-19) in the Army. Germane to the way he later

approached and defended Church Growth Missiology was the ability
to discipline himself that he learned in the army and especially the
fact that when he returned to Butler he became an accomplished
debater.

In his final year at Butler (1919), McGavran had a major
spiritual experience at a YMCA camp where the great missionary
statesman, John R. Mott was a speaker. Up to this time McGavran
had determined that he was to go into some money-making
occupation such as law, geology or forestry, feeling that "my family
has done enough for the Lord." At the camp, however, he was
challenged every day to surrender completely to the Lord and finally
gave in, saying,

> Very well, Lord. It is clear to me; either I give up all claim
> to being a Christian, or I go all the way. Since that is the
> situation I choose to go all the way . . . From then on I was sure
> that if God called me to the ministry or the mission field I would
> go (ibid.:11).

At the beginning of his final year at Butler, McGavran met
Mary Elizabeth Howard, a student from Muncie, Indiana whose
parents had dedicated her to the Lord for missionary service. Together
they attended the quadrennial Student Volunteer Movement
Convention in Des Moines, Iowa, led by missionary statesmen Robert
E. Speer, John R. Mott and Robert Wilder. At those meetings, they
both dedicated themselves to missionary service. They were engaged
in the spring of 1920 but were apart for two years while Donald
attended Yale Divinity School and Mary completed her B.A. work at
Butler.

At Yale, he majored in religious education and received a B.D.
in 1922. Though he was strongly attracted to the theologically more
conservative of his professors, he was not unaffected by the liberal
theology of the majority of the Yale faculty. Middleton states, "The
impact of the theological environment of Yale led McGavran to
emphasize Christianization and gradualism over evangelism
throughout his first term in India" (ibid.:14).

Donald and Mary were married in 1922 and together attended
the Disciples of Christ College of Missions in 1922-23. This College
was one of the first schools of mission in the United States. This
school, as well as the Kennedy School of Mission in Hartford,
Connecticut, was established as a result of the large Edinburgh
Missionary Conference of 1910. It became a part of Kennedy in 1928

but withdrew in 1941 to become the College of Missions Foundation at Yale Divinity School. In 1956, it became the College of Missions at Crystal Lake, Michigan, in which from 1957-61 McGavran was the main (sometimes only) professor. In 1961, the library of this school was given to McGavran's Institute of Church Growth in Eugene, Oregon and thence, in 1965, transferred to Fuller Seminary. But we are getting ahead of our story.

Donald had argued with the mission board that he should continue on at Yale for a Ph.D., rather than take special mission studies, since he had been brought up in India. This was not allowed. Instead, he took courses on India, religion and the science of missions at the College of Missions and graduated with an M.A. in 1923. He apparently missed studying under his father who had returned to India in 1922.

During the summer of 1923, he and Mary were ordained together for missionary service. This, for its time, was quite an unusual approach to partnership in ministry and helps explain McGavran's openness to women in ministry. He always saw Mary as a partner in ministry, nothing less.

Back to India

The McGavrans sailed for India in September 1923, arriving in November. They were assigned first to learn (or for Donald relearn) Hindi followed by an assignment to be principal over a group of the mission's schools in central India. As he carried out these duties, he became very upset over the secularization that had taken place in the schools. This concern led to the writing of his first book, *How to Teach Religion in Mission Schools* (1928). In that book, which was widely distributed and used, he contended that mission schools were not bringing students into Christianity. Though his view of the purpose of the schools at this time in his career was short of seeking a radical encounter with Christ, we can see here the seeds of dissatisfaction with the usual approach to mission.

In 1928, McGavran was appointed Director of Religious Education, a position in which he was expected to "upgrade the standard of Bible teaching and instruction in spiritual matters in all of the schools administrated by the Disciples of Christ" (Middleton 1989:25). There were 25 of these schools, from primary to vocational. In this capacity, he began to formulate the approach that would characterize his later missiology. He saw his job as "appraisal, training and improvement through research."

> It is very significant that these three principles would form the backbone of church growth. Thus in his first term God was preparing him to discover and apply these principles to the educational task. Later this was applied to his understanding of the central missionary task (ibid.:26).

McGavran's first term lasted to 1930, seven years, followed by a two-year study leave at Columbia University. Works describes this study period as follows:

> Immediately upon their arrival in the States for furlough in May, 1930, McGavran applied to Union Theological Seminary in New York City for admission and was granted a fellowship of $750 for the 1930-31 academic year. At the end of a year, McGavran applied for a year's extension of furlough, in order to complete work on his degree program. In the spring of 1932, he completed requirements for a Ph.D. degree in religious education from Columbia University. The degree was conferred in 1936 when his dissertation was published. Its title was *Education and the Beliefs of Popular Hinduism* (1974:61).

During this time we see the seeds beginning to sprout of his later work at the Institute of Church Growth and the School of World Mission. He went out a traditional colonial missionary with a theology leaning toward liberalism but began to change, especially toward the end of that seven year period.

> Throughout his first term McGavran's focus was on proclamation and presence. There was little concern for persuasion of men and women, boys and girls to receive Christ as Lord and Savior of their lives. In a 1925 report he wrote, "our task is not to conquer heathenism, but to lift up Jesus in the midst of heathenism. The contrast does the rest" (Middleton 1989:31).

A major tragedy in his family had much to do with his change of attitude toward what mission is to be about. In early March 1930, as Donald, Mary and the four McGavran children were about to leave for the States on furlough, the oldest child, Theodora, age 7, suffered a burst appendix and died. This left Donald and Mary "stricken and numb," virtually immobilizing Donald for days. When he recovered, however,

> From this point on a very detectable change in the spiritual life of McGavran is evident. Reason gave way to a growing spiritual relationship with Christ. His letters over the months

and years that followed contain clear evidence of his growing love and commitment to his Lord and Savior.

As a direct result of his renewed relationship with Christ he was concerned with the issue of the excessive institutional preoccupation of the India field. "I personally think that the whole present distribution of mission forces needs to be reconsidered in an attempt to put more of our force into direct persistent evangelism [he wrote in 1931] (ibid.:35).

During McGavran's second term (1932-35), he was elected by his colleagues to be Secretary-Treasurer (Executive Secretary) of the Mission and thrust into administration. This made him responsible to represent the Mission with the government of India and to be liaison with the Home Board. Among the effects of this assignment on McGavran was the keen sense he developed of the lopsidedness of the expenditure of funds between the schools and evangelistic work. He became a strong advocate for a greater proportion of funds to be devoted to evangelism.

Other changes occurred during this second term as well. Middleton writes:

> Thus his second term was one of radical transition. There was a geographical shift from Harda to Jabalpur and then on to Chattisgarh. He left much of his educational ministry and took up administration and evangelism with a passion. The focus of his ministry switched from the classes to the masses. He became a champion for the rights of the Untouchables. His apologetics changed from a Christianizing through the gradual transformation of the basic concepts of nations and tribes to that of direct discipling through multi-individual conversions of groups of receptive castes. He changed from a ministry which essentially challenged philosophic Hinduism to a thrust which confronted popular animistic concepts at the village level (ibid.:52-53).

A major factor in these changes was his relationship with J. Waskom Pickett who had been authorized by the National Christian Council of India to conduct research on mass movements in India, culminating in the publication in 1933 of Pickett's *Christian Mass Movements in India*. McGavran in 1935 hailed that book as "the most significant missionary publication of the twentieth century."

The three years McGavran spent in administration served to wean him from his involvement with schools and to set him on a new course. For

During these years, McGavran, the administrator, was also McGavran, the learner, seeing for the first time the dynamics of church growth in India and considering what those dynamics meant for the Churches and Missions all across India. His mind shuttled rapidly between administering a mission where large sums of money and personnel were producing limited results and observing rapidly multiplying congregations in many parts of India (Works 1974:66-67).

This new perspective is reflected in his annual report of 1934, where he spoke of the current situation of the mission under his direction as follows:

> The attention of the entire force is being turned to the redemption from sin offered through the sacrifice of Jesus our Lord, to the power of the indwelling Christ and to the gift of the Holy Spirit. Our message is not education . . . our message is not medicine . . . our message is not rural uplift. But our message is Jesus Christ, the power of God unto salvation (ibid.:57).

A major change occurred at the end of 1935 when McGavran was voted out of his administrative position as Executive Secretary of the Indian mission. He was hurt by this but it looks as if the hand of God was in it. For he was assigned to a tribal area where he labored for the next 17 years, putting his theories into practice. He worked hard to bring about a people movement during these years with less than expected results. However,

> McGavran's years as a village evangelistic missionary should not be understood as a time when he applied church growth theory to a population in a laboratory-type situation. Rather, he was groping forward largely in the dark, finding out how to work, what to do, what mistakes to avoid, what priorities to observe, what methods accomplished desired ends, and how to persuade the mission to act in the most effective ways. He was exposed in a village situation, as he had never been in the cloistered atmosphere of an educational institution, to the realities of Indian life in the midst of which the missionary must work (Works 1974:74-75).

Though he had many responsibilities in the rural situation, including supervising village schools, dispensaries, a hospital, a leprosy home and keeping the accounts, he was able to focus more of his energy and creativity on evangelism than previously. He also was able to take part in research in other areas, often with Pickett, to write, largely for periodicals in India, and to do occasional lectures and seminars on church growth. And through his contacts and his position on the Executive Council of the Mission, he was enabled to be "God's instrument to initiate an unprecedented growth in church planting and evangelism in the Mission" (Middleton 1989:64).

New insight came but so did failures. On one occasion he dismissed a pastor for sexual immorality "only to have the whole small church revert, not because of the pastor's sin, but because it had become public as a result of his dismissal" (Works 1974:76). Another mistake was paying preachers when it would have been better to develop an unpaid clergy. And they experimented with presenting the Gospel through drama but found that the people treated the dramas merely as entertainment rather than witness. And the expected people movement was frustrated when the people turned to politics rather than to Christ for salvation.

Out of India—1954-1961

The years 1954 to 1960 were stretching years for McGavran. He

> had not been fully satisfied with his India work. In spite of his assignment to an area with high church growth potential, he had not been successful in generating a people movement . . . However, his furlough, in the spring of 1954, provided an opportunity for him to explore new directions for his influence and ministry (Works 1974:128).

To his delight, the Missionary Society had agreed to McGavran's request that he spend three months in Africa on his way to America. He was anxious to compare what was going on in Africa, especially any people movements, with what he had observed in India. In addition, he felt it important to include African examples and insights in his forthcoming book, *Bridges of God*, lest that book by being so India-specific suffer the same fate as Pickett's books had. So, he left India for Africa in April 1954 while Mary waited to leave until the children finished school in June. McGavran was able to visit Kenya, Uganda, Burundi, Congo, Nigeria and Ghana on that trip. He found several small scale people movements but missionaries who by and large "neither recognized the dynamics involved nor believed that the 'group movement' approach to conversion was a valid means of church growth" (ibid.:129).

> The three month period McGavran spent in Africa was significant in its influence on his thinking. He began to recognize the complexity of church growth, as it existed in

cultures radically different from those of India. He could see that some of the convictions he had developed out of his India experience would have to be modified before they would be true in other societies. His basic concepts, however, were reinforced by his observations in Africa. He later described the changes he had to make in the manuscript of *Bridges of God* after his African trip as a "manicuring" process, rather than one of severe modification (ibid.:131).

As early as 1951, McGavran had retreated to a secluded place in the hills to begin the writing of *Bridges of God* (1955). His intention was to bring all of his previous insights into an integrated whole and, in addition, "to place a biblical foundation under the new concepts, validating them not only from successful experience in the field, but from evidence of people movements from the Old and New Testaments as well" (ibid.:93).

McGavran had been granted a research fellowship at Yale, so he and the family went directly to New Haven to live in a house maintained there by the Missionary Society. This was to be their home from 1954 to 1957 while doing various things for the United Christian Missionary Society (UCMS). His research year at Yale exposed him to new audiences and enabled him to write *How Churches Grow*. This manuscript was turned down by six American publishers before being accepted and published in England by World Dominion Press in 1959. McGavran's American contacts were largely in ecumenical circles where his ideas were not favorably received. This may explain why the American publishers he approached would not publish his work.

Soon after arriving at Yale, McGavran wrote to at least 20 key professors of missions setting forth his concerns concerning the state of missions. In doing so, he identified himself "as one who hoped to give the balance of his life 'to focusing the attention of the Churches and their missionary societies on the growth of the Church as the central business of missions'" (ibid.:132-133).

> The letter then defined a growing church (50 percent per decade or more), and appealed for students of missions to inaugurate, under the guidance of the professors to whom the letters were addressed, studies of growing churches. The responses to McGavran's appeal were not recorded, but the letter served to place his name before missions leaders of stature and possibly to introduce *Bridges of God* when it appeared one year later (ibid.:133).

Providentially, by the end of McGavran's research year at Yale, the UCMS had committed itself to a new strategy of world missions that required someone to go to various fields to do surveys. McGavran was available, willing and anxious to do these surveys. Furthermore, he had had experience in doing similar research and Mary and the family could stay on in Missions House in New Haven while McGavran traveled. He was, therefore, sent first to Puerto Rico for six weeks and then for much shorter periods to Japan, Taiwan, the Philippines, Thailand and Orissa, India. Later he returned to the Philippines and did a trip to Jamaica. Works states concerning these surveys,

> The greatest value of the surveys lay in the broadening influence they had on McGavran's church growth thinking. Just as his African trip had served to confirm his basic convictions about how the church grows, these surveys similarly strengthened the foundation on which he was building his church growth principles. In his later lectures and writings, he illustrated church growth principles from many lands. . . . Out of [these surveys] McGavran developed a world-wide theory of missions. While strengthening the fundamental concepts, McGavran's studies in widely divergent cultures modify specific elements of his thought, so that the principles might be more and more universally applicable (ibid.:141-142).

Peripatetic Professor of Missions

McGavran's status during this time was as a missionary on furlough assigned to special tasks such as the surveys. With the completion of the surveys, then, the question arose as to his future. A return to India was a possibility. There was also discussion of his becoming Field Secretary for UCMS missions in Africa. He was attracted, however, to a proposed two year experiment in which he would become a roving professor of the revived College of Missions in which he had once studied but which had become defunct after breaking away from the Kennedy School of Missions. His responsibilities would be to conduct brief, pre-field orientation sessions for outgoing missionaries at Crystal Lake, Michigan and to teach courses on missions in several Christian Church institutions. He then became what Works calls a "peripatetic professor of missions" for the next three and a half years (1957-60)

> his time was occupied with three to six month periods as visiting lecturer on missions and related fields on various Christian

Church-related seminary and college campuses. These periods were interspersed with specific lectures and addresses delivered to churches and missionary conventions spread across the United States. In addition, the McGavrans served as host and hostess during the summer session of the College of Missions at Crystal Lake, Michigan, and as hosts for the Missions House there during the summer. As a part of the faculty, McGavran taught in these summer sessions of the College of Missions (ibid.:145).

This was a difficult time for the McGavrans. They spent six months each at Butler University (Indianapolis), Drake University (Iowa), Phillips University (Oklahoma), Northwest Christian College (Oregon), a year at Bethany College (West Virginia), and three months at Berkeley's Pacific School of Religion. The UCMS provided salary and travel expenses but they had to live in quite a variety of accommodations. Though their needs were taken care of salary-wise and accommodation-wise, and he was able to get acquainted with a lot of different people, McGavran was impatient with the whole setup and very glad when his cry for an institute for graduate training of missionaries was heard by Dr. Ross Griffeth at Northwest Christian College, Eugene, Oregon.

An official invitation came to McGavran in June 1959 from Dr. Griffeth. At the same time, however, it looked as though an invitation would be coming from Dean Stephen J. England of the Graduate Seminary at Phillips University in Enid, Oklahoma. Though McGavran wanted to be in a place more centrally located in the States than NCC and also one that could offer graduate degrees, he feared that what England was really interested in was not the proposed Institute, but his services as a missions professor. Also, when he presented to England the dimensions of his vision, including the costs, Dean England cooled off.

At the Denver Convention of the Disciples of Christ, then, in August of 1959, McGavran and Griffeth sat down and made final plans, including a formal written invitation and a brief acceptance letter. McGavran then returned to do his teaching stint at Bethany College in West Virginia where he received a letter from Griffeth setting out the details of their arrangement. The Institute was to begin on January 1, 1961 at Northwest Christian College after McGavran finished up his "peripatetic professor" duties at Bethany College and Pacific School of Religion.

The Institute of Church Growth—1961-1965

The Institute of Church Growth thus became a reality. At last McGavran's dream of an Institute in which experienced missionaries could study the growth and nongrowth of the churches in which they worked had come into existence. McGavran's friend Ross Griffeth, the president of NCC had gone way out on a limb to sponsor the new Institute even though there was no clear "fit" between the Institute and the rest of what was going on at NCC. For one thing, the Institute was to train at a graduate level whereas NCC was totally undergraduate. McGavran did, however, allow certain advanced students from NCC's regular programs to attend certain of the Institute's classes.

The question of where the new Institute was to be housed at NCC was solved by the fact that a portion of the recently built library building was not being used. A very large desk was obtained and installed in one corner as McGavran's office and the rest of the space became classroom and study space for the anticipated students. The classes were held around a large oak table and several small carrels were made from the bookshelves. "There was no telephone, no secretary, no 'executive washroom'" (Works 1974:176).

As for library, the books McGavran had been carrying to his various teaching posts became the core. This collection ultimately grew to 2,500 to 3,000 volumes before the move to Fuller. Students also made much use of the library of the nearby University of Oregon and borrowed through interlibrary loan.

McGavran admitted students unilaterally, often without consulting the Registrar until after the student had arrived. Registration and other administrative matters were handled by the staff without any additions to the staff or other facilities. McGavran and Griffeth built good relationships with the Dean of the Graduate School of the University and especially with the Anthropology Department.

Getting the word out concerning the new Institute was a challenge. McGavran and Griffeth did their best to inform the NCC constituency (e.g. through the NCC Bulletin) and the world at large (e.g. through the *International Review of Missions*). McGavran's major means of publicizing the Institute was, however, through correspondence. In the days before email, McGavran was a prolific letter writer. Middleton says he wrote an average of ten to twelve letters a day! (ibid.:276). In testimony to this fact, the McGavran archives at Wheaton's Billy Graham Center house over a hundred boxes of his letters! A large part of his correspondence during the late 50s was devoted to inviting prospective missionary students to come study with him. Much of the correspondence started even before the Institute had begun operations, as he became aware of any given missionary, whether through personal contact or through something he read written by the missionary.

McGavran's awareness of Alan Tippett, for example, started when he read a 1960 article by him in the *International Review of Missions*. He then wrote from his teaching post at Bethany College to Tippett in Fiji urging him to come to the fledgling Institute in Oregon to pursue study of the growth of the church in his field. Tippett, an Australian Wesleyan missionary with eighteen years of ministry in Fiji, was totally unknown to him at that time, but something in the article caught his eye. So he wrote a letter urging Tippett to come study with him at Eugene and offering him the usual scholarship. As we will read in Tippett's story, he and his family had just decided that their work in Fiji was completed and were moving back to Australia to look for something else to commit themselves to. Tippett had read *Bridges of God* and *How Churches Grow* and was both acquainted with and impressed by McGavran's insights, so he took him up on his offer, arriving in Eugene in late December of 1961 to begin study in January of 1962.

McGavran was a recruiter. He was constantly on the lookout for students. When he read something that impressed him he routinely wrote to the missionary inviting, and even pressuring, him/her to come study with him at the Institute or, before that, at whatever place he was teaching. He also wrote repeatedly to mission executives, encouraging them to send their missionaries.

In the unpublished autobiography of Alan Tippett who was to become McGavran's first faculty associate, we read,

> McGavran's basic plan was to contact missionaries in the field and guide them in data-collecting so that they brought in research material of certain types to the institute, there to be instructed in how to evaluate and use it, write-up, etc., after testing it against other Fellows in the I.C.G. The idea of exposing us to each other was in the plan from the start. The basic qualifications were field experience, knowledge of the language, wide knowledge of the field, its mission and indigenous churches (Tippett 1985:279).

The motivation for the Institute of Church Growth had come from McGavran's conviction that the growth of Christian churches worldwide could be enhanced by the scientific study of the conditions under which churches grow and the application of the insights gained in such study. The experienced missionaries invited to ICG were to study the "principles of Church Growth" and do research into the growth or nongrowth of their own missionary situation.

The first missionary student to come to ICG was Keith Hamilton, a Methodist missionary superintendent working in Bolivia. He was to come in January 1961 and was the only student that first semester. However, in reality, due to McGavran's mentoring through letters, his church growth education began a full seven months before he arrived in Eugene (Middleton 1989:279). Things picked up after that, though, with some outstanding missionary researchers coming early on. In addition to Keith Hamilton there were James Sunda, Roy Shearer, William Read and, of course, Alan Tippett. Many of the earlier publications (see below) were done by these men or were done by McGavran with much important input from these early students.

Between 1961 and 1965, 61 students attended the ICG, including research fellows, other furloughing missionaries and the pre-field undergraduates from NCC who made up approximately one-third of the total. Of the other two-thirds, about half were from evangelical groups and half from conciliar denominations (Works 1974:196). Works records, "thirty-nine . . . were active missionaries . . . Thirteen were candidates with firm plans for a specific field, but ten had no definite plans for field service" (1974:198).

Each of those chosen as research fellows was offered a $1,000 scholarship (sometimes more) with the assumption that they would continue to receive their regular missionary support while at ICG and use such funds for research and publication. They were expected to develop what came to be called "church growth eyes" under McGavran's tutelage and to write for publication an analysis of the situation on their own field. McGavran was able to arrange with Eerdmans the publication of several of these studies in a Church Growth series. See below.

The Vision versus Reality

As the Institute at NCC took shape, McGavran's vision of what could happen sometimes led to an overestimation of what the ICG had to offer. The ICG brochure promised an M.A. degree based on 30 hours of coursework and a thesis (Tippett 1985:279). A major disappointment, both for McGavran and for the students, however, was the fact that the accrediting agency refused to allow either NCC or ICG to award an M.A. due to a lack of library holdings.

Tippett himself nearly bolted over this disappointment, since he had expected to be able to use an M.A. in missions (in addition to the M.A. he already had in history) to gain entrance into a program in missions and comparative religions back in Australia. In the face of this disappointment, however, McGavran insisted that Tippett do a Ph.D. at the University of Oregon. This further upset Tippett and led him all the more to consider returning to Australia. But, he says, "Once I resigned to having been hoodwinked into a doctoral program, I determined to utilize the resources [of the university] to the utmost and to make the most of my course work" (Tippett 1985:279). One result of this decision was, however, that he was away from his family for two and a half years instead of the nine months he had planned on.

Tippett records the following insightful impression of the ICG in his unpublished autobiography:

> The Institute of Church Growth, at the Northwest Christian College, Eugene, Oregon had been established by Donald McGavran with the strong support of Dr. Ross Griffeth, President of N.C.C., from his institutional budget. Although the institute operated as an academic and research body, and we had our titles and very nice letter-heads, in point of fact, the institute had no constitutional existence. Donald McGavran was Director and I was a Research Fellow but our affairs were merely accounts somewhere in the books of the N.C.C. This all came as a great surprise to me, because I had received the institute brochures, and the course lists, and on their official letter-heads had been informed of my research fellowship and even its monetary amount. The brochures had depicted the N.C.C. buildings, and these I had assumed were institute establishments. Dr. McGavran had a small section like an office off the end of the library (upstairs) and I had a library carrel. A large table and a blackboard had been set between two stacks, where seminars or classes could be held (1985:276).

ICG was part substance and part dream. Tippett, who had come so far to take advantage of the promises and who would play such an important part in the Church Growth Movement provides this description of what he found when he arrived:

We all did McGavran's courses and after the required number of credits had been passed an I.C.G. Certificate would be awarded. McGavran had prepared a list of Courses and these had been advertised in the brochure. I imagine he intended in time to supply all these courses, but they were not being given and a number of them never were because the whole program developed as we went along. The main course was Principles and Procedures of Church Growth which ran through each term and covered the methodology of research and was an intensely practical coverage. Jointly with this he had a series of Case Studies in various mission fields, the Philippines, Ghana, Liberia, Jamaica, Mexico, Orissa and other places. They were all operative in 1962, and I myself did them all. They were really stimulating and alerted me to many things in my own field.

The first brochure also listed courses at the University of Oregon and N.C.C. where appropriate. They looked, to the reader, to be a much wider coverage than was so ... McGavran was in the process of expanding in the area of theory and theology of mission but there was no [course in] theology when I arrived. When it came it was very much geared to his own slant on theology and the theological battles in which he personally wanted encounter ... Most of what I learned from McGavran fell into that year 1962. He gave me directions as to where I should be heading myself, and once I had my own momentum we interacted more as colleagues, although he was never any less than the Director (Tippett 1985:278).

Anthropology

From the start, McGavran recognized that he would need courses dealing with culture and religions. At first, he advised his students to depend on the University of Oregon for such courses but "he was very much aware that he had to have a lecturer in anthropology and the primal religions and he wanted these courses from a Christian viewpoint that could get him beyond too great a dependence on a secular university" (Tippett 1985:278). So McGavran turned to Tippett who had several years before (1956) done an M.A. in history and anthropology at American University. By the end of his first year at ICG, then, Tippett was teaching a course in anthropology and one on religion.

In so doing, McGavran demonstrated his knack for seeing the broad picture, whether or not he understood the details. McGavran did not understand anthropology very well and objected to much of what he thought he understood. But Tippett was impressive, an amazing intellect who soon proved his ability to integrate theological and anthropological insight into McGavran's church growth perspective. So McGavran quickly came to view Tippett as a potential teaching colleague and strongly encouraged him to enroll in the University of Oregon to earn a Ph.D. in anthropology. This Tippett did and became McGavran's "right hand man" as the ICG continued and eventually moved to Fuller.

McGavran needed Tippett's help for he made many enemies as well as many friends. He was intensely committed to what he saw as a scientific approach to missions and called Church Growth Theory and Practice— teaching it, writing it, researching and stimulating research, looking for facts on which to base his theories. His singlemindedness, however, was not always appreciated, even by those who basically agreed with his positions. Tippett writes,

> Both at the podium and on paper McGavran was an extremely aggressive person. Psychologically he expected opposition and to some extent looked for it. He was always at his best when he was most threatened. On the platform his style was oratorical and by repeated presentation, well honed. He developed metaphoric phrases and punchlines. His thirty years on the mission field within colonial structures and dealings with missionary bureaucracy had left him ready to "enter the ring to spar" with any who would—bishops, scholars or board administrators. (The "top brass" he called them.) He "pulled no punches" and sometimes his punches really hurt. As a result of this he made enemies and critics, and many there were who would have been glad to see him brought down. These critics I felt to be of two types: those who feared the effect of attacks on strategy, policy, vested interests, etc; and others who were ready to pull items out of his contexts just to score points against him. The real battle lay with the former but the latter were like a pack of little dogs always snapping at your heals as you went by.

> The issue of deployment based on McGavran's harvest theology, and supported by statistics, brought hostile reaction from Boards with vested interests in resistant areas, especially in Islamic lands . . .

> There were also critics who hated the idea of statistics as being man-oriented instead of dependence on the Spirit of God. [They] implied that church growth had no doctrine of the sovereignty of God, which was completely untrue. Granted we opposed the theological defensiveness based on the notion that God, being in control, would give growth when and where He

would. All we had to do was to be faithful. I myself . . . [developed] a biblical doctrine of stewardship under God [to counter this criticism] . . . (ibid.:283).

Such criticisms led to the calling of a consultation by the Department of World Mission and Evangelism of the World Council of Churches "in order to examine our viewpoint, discuss the problems it raised, and make a statement for the world Church" (ibid.:284). This was the Iberville Consultation of 1963 dealt with in more detail in the chapter on Tippett. It is likely that the underlying (and unspoken) issue leading to the calling of this consultation was McGavran's intransigence in advocating his positions rather than the positions themselves. The result, however, was a positive demonstration of the ability of McGavran, with Tippett's considerable help, to not only advocate but to effectively defend his positions. This, of course, led to some further animosity on the part of those who were unable to effectively counter McGavran.

Evangelical Acceptance of Church Growth Theory

McGavran's schooling, missionary experience and, therefore, his personal relationships and contacts had been largely within the conciliar (ecumenical) movement. Though there were many in World Council circles who were evangelical theologically, conciliar missiology and missiologists, though often polite to McGavran, were not usually "on the same page" with him. For example, their interest in converting the lost, if it was there at all, was often submerged under social gospel concerns. So, though these were McGavran's natural contacts, as a group they were not really with him.

On the other hand, there was a growing acceptance of what came to be known as "Church Growth Theory" by evangelical missionaries and mission administrators. As evangelicals became more aware of McGavran, their attitudes varied from cautious to enthusiastic. With the visibility of the Church Growth emphasis increasing through the establishment of the Institute of Church Growth, "his speaking engagements and involvements were steadily increasing among the EFMA-IFMA circle of missions. Several conservative evangelical leaders of denominational and interdenominational missions played a major role in this reorientation" (Middleton 1989:302) and became McGavran's natural support.

Professor Cal Guy of Southwestern Baptist Seminary, for example, wrote a very positive review of *How Churches Grow* in the *Southwestern Journal of Theology*, exposing McGavran's work to the Southern Baptist denomination. Following this review, McGavran "began to include many conservative evangelical mission executives in his monthly mailings" requesting, among other things, that they send missionaries to study at ICG (ibid.:303). Conservative Baptist Missions leader Edwin Jacques, Louis King of the Christian and Missionary Alliance, Kenneth Strachan of the Latin American Mission and Melvin Hodges of the Assemblies of God were among the early evangelical mission leaders to favor McGavran. And they sent students to ICG.

The most helpful of these leaders was Norman Cummings who used his positions as leader of Overseas Crusades and President of EFMA to support McGavran and advocate Church Growth Theory. He both sent OC missionaries to Eugene and in 1964 responded to McGavran's desire to have a bi-monthly *Church Growth Bulletin* by agreeing to produce and underwrite it. This OC did for 22 years, until 1986. Cummings also served on the Fuller committee that invited McGavran to Pasadena.

By 1962 and especially 1963, evangelical mission leaders were inviting McGavran to speak at seminars, conferences and retreats for mission executives. In September of 1962, he was invited to make several presentations at the EFMA Missions Executives Retreat at Winona Lake, Indiana. This retreat marked a turning point as McGavran moved from almost exclusive attempts to influence conciliar leaders to giving major attention to his natural theological allies—the evangelicals. This change was not without its problems, however. After the EFMA Retreat, Middleton records,

> Although the evangelical leaders were appreciative of McGavran's principles of church growth, they were disturbed by his terminology and ecumenical vocabulary. Because of this a few leaders even questioned his conversion experience. At that point, men like Jacques, King and Cummings drew along side of McGavran and encouraged him to express his ideas with a vocabulary more consistent with conservative evangelical thinking (ibid.:303).

After one of these speaking engagements, involving six two-hour lectures to Christian and Missionary Alliance missionaries in Phoenix in May 1963, their leader, Louis King announced that CMA was going to follow church growth principles with the aim of trebling their membership over the following ten years. Such invitations evolved into a series of Church Growth Seminars, at first put on by McGavran alone, then by McGavran and his faculty associates. One of these was with the Assemblies of God missionaries in June of 1963.

The first "official" Church Growth Seminar was held at Winona Lake in September 1963, sponsored by EFMA. As an indication of how support for Church Growth thinking had expanded into evangelical circles we find that the major movers behind this seminar were Edwin Jaques, head of the Conservative Baptist Board and Byron Lamson, Executive Secretary of the Free Methodist Board. The Conservative Baptists began to require all their missionaries on furlough to attend the Winona Lake seminars. "There were sometimes as many as fifty Conservative Baptist missionaries there" (Works 1974:239). Ninety missionaries from 18 boards and 25 countries attended that first Winona Lake seminar. McGavran reported to Griffeth that

> Opinions were changed during the Seminar and at least two students for I.C.G. were secured. . . . the board executives present were insistent that this be repeated next year . . . They also listened favorably to my proposal that the E.F.M.A. boards give regular cash support to I.C.G. (ibid.:240).

After this, invitations for seminars came from the Evangelical Covenant Church, the Conservative Baptist Foreign Mission Society, Overseas Crusades and the Presbyterian Church in the U.S. At the September 1964 Winona Lake Seminar, 135 missionaries attended from 16 boards, working in more than 20 countries.

> The Church Growth Seminars at Winona Lake became one of McGavran's most effective means of reaching the evangelical segment of Protestantism. He could impart his concepts there, promote church growth publications, recruit students effectively for the Institute of Church Growth, and seek financial support for the cause (ibid.:241).

One effect of the Winona Lake seminars and these other opportunities on the ICG was to increase the number of students from evangelical boards. Unlike the first two and a half years, the final two years of the ICG at Eugene involved twice as many from evangelical boards as from conciliar boards.

By 1974 when Works wrote up his research EFMA-sponsored seminars included a West Coast seminar held each spring at Biola and a seminar held at Jaffray School of Missions at Nyack, NY. The Winona Lake seminar was merged into the Wheaton Summer School of Missions (ibid.:241).

In spite of the success of these seminars and speaking engagements in winning people to the church growth point of view, McGavran had but limited success in attempting to get evangelical missions to add ICG to their budgets. While working in ecumenical circles, McGavran had been relatively successful in getting financial support. Though evangelicals were accepting his message and their Boards began sending students to ICG, only Overseas Crusades provided much to support the program. "Thus in the period from 1960-1965 McGavran's ministry to the EFMA related missions was often at considerable expense to himself," though he was often able to piggyback on an ecumenically-sponsored trip to conduct a seminar for evangelicals in a nearby location (ibid.:306).

Publications

In addition to the teaching program of ICG, McGavran engaged in two major publishing ventures and a Church Growth lectureship. It was his mentor, J. Waskom Pickett who was chosen as the lecturer in 1961. His topic was "The Dynamics of Church Growth" and the results were published under that title by Abingdon Press in 1963. In 1962, then, the lectureship consisted of a panel of speakers in interaction with each other with the title "Crucial Issues in Church Growth Today." The speakers were Calvin Guy, Professor of Missions at Southwestern Baptist Seminary, Melvin Hodges, Field Secretary for Latin American and the West Indies of the Assemblies of God, Eugene Nida, Translations Secretary of the American Bible Society and McGavran. These presentations were published by Harper and Row in 1965 entitled, *Church Growth and Christian Mission*. The third and following Church Growth Lectures took place at Fuller.

In each of the publishing ventures, McGavran was committed to publishing the findings of a scientific approach to research into the "hard bold facts" of missionary and church life. He sought in this way to disseminate as widely as possible the findings of the research done by ICG students. The first of these was the publishing of several of the early church growth studies by students at ICG.

Among the early church growth studies published by ICG in Lucknow, India, were

> *Church Growth in the High Andes* (1962) by Keith Hamilton,
> *God's Messengers to Mexico's Masses* (1962) by Jack Taylor,
> *Church Growth in West New Guinea* (1963) by James Sunda,
> *Church Growth in Jamaica* (1962) by McGavran.

Church Growth studies published by Eerdmans included,

> *Church Growth in Mexico* (1963) by Huegel, Taylor and McGavran,
> *New Patterns of Church Growth in Brazil* (1965) by William Read,
> *Church Growth in Central and Southern Nigeria* (1966) by John Grimley and Gordon Robinson,
> *Wildfire: The Growth of the Church in Korea* (1966) by Roy Shearer,
> *God's Impatience in Liberia* (1968) by J. C. Wold.

The second publishing venture was the *Church Growth Bulletin*, launched in September 1964 as a bimonthly, costing $1.00 per year. McGavran had dreamed of a newsletter and some of the early students pushed for it.

> McGavran's dream began to be realized with the offer from Overseas Crusades, an interdenominational missionary society in Palo Alto, California, to publish the *Bulletin*. The moving force in the project was Norman L. Cummings, Home Director of Overseas Crusades, who came to Eugene and studied at I.C.G. for a month in 1964. Cummings . . . agreed to give the *Bulletin* its form, supervise its printing, and provide for distribution and mailing (Works 1974:242).

This periodical was to serve as the public voice of the Church Growth Movement for the next decade. The CGB provided the movement with the opportunity to state positions such as The Principles of Church Growth and the Theological Basis of Church Growth. It also enabled McGavran and others to reply to criticism, to review and advertise books and articles, to comment on writings and happenings and to communicate news concerning events related to the movement. For many, the CGB provided support for innovation in missionary work, stimulus that enabled them to try new approaches and challenges to look more carefully at what they were doing to see if it was really producing what it was supposed to produce.

McGavran's Dream in Danger

To all outward appearances, by 1964 The Institute of Church Growth was well on its feet at Northwest Christian College. As mentioned above, though, the foundation of the Institute was anything but firm. It existed at NCC purely by the grace of one man, Dr. Ross Griffeth, the President of the school. And it cost the school money that many felt ought to be spent in other ways—ways more in keeping with the school's main calling rather than for an Institute that seemed to be tangential to the purposes for which NCC existed.

On the horizon, however, was retirement for Dr. Griffeth. This raised the specter of a situation in which a new president would not be supportive of the Institute, joined to which was the probability that support for the Institute on the part of the Board and the Faculty would be slim. In addition, the expense of the Institute would be increased by virtue of the fact that Alan Tippett had been appointed to the faculty of the Institute as of September 1965. This would incur for NCC an additional faculty salary not adequately covered by a modest increase in the number of students.

Into this scenario, then, came the beginning of a sequence of events that would change the story dramatically. It seems clear to me that God's hand was on the Institute of Church Growth. Most of the time, though, God seems to be working in the background. At this point in the history, though, God's working becomes very obvious.

In 1964, Fuller Theological Seminary in Pasadena, California began looking for someone to head up a new school of mission to be started under the Fuller Seminary administration parallel to the new School of Psychology and the continuing School of Theology. A faculty committee was set up to search for a Dean to head up the new school. The ICG moved to Fuller Seminary over the summer of 1965 with classes starting in September.

See the following chapters for details about the move of the ICG to Fuller Seminary. In summary of the years up to the move in 1965, Middleton writing in 1989 neatly concludes,

The move of the ICG to Fuller ended one of the most creative periods in McGavran's life. The Eugene years were a period of growing *acceptance* of church growth principles by many and the development of theological barriers to McGavran's ideas by others. These were also days when the missionaries who gathered around the Oak table at NCC literally became disciples of McGavran. Those privileged to be a part of those early days in the church growth movement created an esprit de corps which still continues in the School of World Mission (ibid.:321).

Chapter 2

Alan R. Tippett
(1911-1988)

At Fuller: 1965-1977

The Early Years

Alan Tippett's story began as a pastor's son in a small mining town in Victoria, Australia. As he put it,

> It was on [9th November, 1911] . . . in a hot, dusty mining town named St Arnaud, in . . . a little weatherboard cottage where all my aunts and uncles in the Dower line had been born, that the torpid peace was suddenly disturbed by a mighty yell all because either a midwife or my grandmother . . . had given me a resounding slap on my tender butt. With this my first experience of man's inhumanity to man I entered this hard, cruel world (Tippett 1985:20).

He was the first child of a Wesleyan pastor who served several congregations in rough mining towns before Alan was born and, except for a few years in a city mission in South Melbourne, thereafter. The young Tippett grew up in a context where he had to constantly defend himself and his pastor father among godless classmates and, later, as a pastor himself, among teammates and opponents on the Aussie-rules football teams he played for. Growing up was not a pleasant experience for him and his consciousness of enemies and the need to fight them was something that stayed with him all his life. He worked hard, becoming a perfectionist, never confident that he had done well enough, and always seeking to prove himself to someone.

He was, however, very intelligent and capable, a self-starter who could, even as a boy, take a project and do it so well his teachers would not believe he did it without adult help. This happened twice when, as a child, he displayed his botanical knowledge in school projects. For, stimulated by his father's interest in botany, Tippett recalls that "at the age of ten I knew all the flower families by their botanical names, before I could pass a sixth grade spelling test." He continues, "somewhere about my ninth or tenth year I entered the Maldon Show with an entry of Australian flora from the local area, all arranged in categories and marked with botanical names. The judges disqualified it as not the work of a child" (ibid.:25). A few years later a similar thing happened with an essay on "Australian Wildflowers."

Tippett continued on in school with a chip on his shoulder, attempting to prove himself to whoever was in charge. He speaks especially of the agony of his relationships with a French teacher and the junior high headmaster. The French teacher, Miss Lightfoot, kept sending him to detention for not doing his assignments well. He says, "Night after night I stayed behind until I got so utterly frustrated, and further and further behind the class, in which I was the youngest child anyway" (ibid.:31). When Miss Lightfoot passed Alan on to the Headmaster, Mr. Charles, his way of disciplining Alan was to set him to "weeding the school flower garden on sports afternoons."

These experiences so affected young Alan that a theme of his life, as recorded in his autobiography whenever he refers to a significant academic achievement became, "I wonder what Miss Lightfoot and Mr. Charles would say about this?" In contrast to those teachers and the great difficulties he had in mastering academic subjects during his schooldays, not to mention the constant physical battles with bullies, was his relationship with his father. He adored his father and, from what he recalls about him, his father deserved the adoration. William Tippett was an encourager. He it was who had taken young Alan into the wonderful world of nature. He it was who comforted, understood and supported Alan when either bullies, teachers or his own rebelliousness did him in. His father was his sponsor in life and to honor him, Alan in retirement wrote an unpublished biography of him entitled, *The Wells of My Father*.

In a particularly poignant passage concerning his decision to leave school, Tippett writes,

> The year ended. I knew I had to make some kind of a new start. Eventually I went to my father and told him that for me that school was no longer of any use. I wanted to leave and get a job somewhere as a messenger boy or whatever. . . . My father was obviously surprised. . . . He knew I refused to admit defeat. . . . He knew me as utterly pig-headed in every way. . . .

He knew I wanted to get on, to learn new things, and he had expected me to hang on to school as long as I could. And here I was suddenly wanting to throw it all overboard. . . .

Then he did what neither Miss Lightfoot nor Mr. Charles had done: he opened the door for me to share it all. At many points he might well have rebuked me, but he did not. He might have reasoned with me to continue at school, but he did not. He must have seen my flood of confession . . . for what it indeed was—a state of utter dejection. As I recall the episode, he did not reason, or dictate, or comfort, or discuss my teachers (ibid.:33).

This was just what Alan needed. His father, in counseling him, was even able to put aside his own extreme disappointment over the fact that he himself had not been able to complete his ministerial training "and he never felt he could ever compensate for what he had been deprived of." In response to his father's gentleness, then, Alan eventually enrolled in Geelong College, a church secondary school where his parents had to pay fees. The awareness of this sacrifice on the part of his parents plus his desire to get a new start "without the Ugly Witch [Miss Lightfoot] and the Big Bad Wolf [Mr. Charles] made me determined to do my very best," he recalls.

This admiration of his father as his sponsor figures into our story in his relationship with McGavran. So does his difficulties with Miss Lightfoot and Mr. Charles—but I'll develop that later. McGavran became his sponsor when no one in Australia seemed interested in him, respecting him when his own countrymen felt no need for what he had to offer and giving him a chance to perform and believing in him even though McGavran had to work hard to provide the finances. Tippett worked hard during his time with McGavran to earn the latter's favor and trust.

From the secondary school in Geelong, where he had quite a good experience, he was given a scholarship to Wesley College in Melbourne, his father having been appointed to a charge in North Melbourne. The depression came, however, and he had to drop out after only a year, taking a job as a junior clerk at the Orient Steam Navigation Company. Though he was doing well at his job, after four years he gave it up to return to school, having proved to himself his ability both in the job and in football (Aussie Rules) and cricket. But it was his spiritual growth, mostly through Christian Endeavour in North Melbourne that had the greatest impact. He says,

My life as a junior shipping clerk, the sporting life and this kind of religious development are really like three completely different stories and certainly widely separated world views, but I had no intention of living in three different compartments. They had to hold together somehow. Life had to be "all of a piece." Sooner or later I knew I had to come to terms with this kind of compartmentalization. . . .

In my religious life I had been thinking more and more of my place in the program of the Lord. . . . The weight of Jesus' "Great Commission" fell on me heavily. Even the Orient Line itself had made me look seaward. The intense evangelism of the C.E. pressed on my soul the needs of the wider world. . . .

Then suddenly it became a clear call to Christian mission. I was ready there and then to go to China or New Guinea or wherever, just as I was. I told my father.

He gave me the support I needed, but insisted that in this event I should enter the Church and do the full ministerial training course. I was horrified . . . In the end he told me plainly that I was not ready. . . . My father said I should serve a term in a pastorate at home as part of my training. . . . He was certainly right in pointing up my immaturity and my unreadiness. Very reluctantly I bowed to his greater wisdom (ibid.:44-45).

Tippett was examined by the Church leaders, chosen to pursue studies and entered Queens College (university level) where he studied first arts and then theology for the next three years, coming out with an L.Th. certificate, a program focused on practical ministry. He calls himself "an ordinary student. He did the best in practical subjects. His professor said his "potential was in the pulpit ministry and popular religious writing, but that [he] did not have the capacity for a language" (ibid.:53). This latter prediction proved to be very wrong. He says, "I passed my first, second and third years Fijian exams in two years on the field with an honour mark."

During these school and university years, Alan learned much about preaching from his father and exegesis from his time at Queens. He also learned how to pick fruit during four years' worth of long vacations to earn money for his schooling. On occasion, then, he would go on holiday with a friend of his who was courting a girl who was one of six daughters of a local farmer. There Alan met Edna, the third daughter of the farmer affectionately known as "Pop Deckert." This resulted in a friendship that involved the spending of most of

Alan's fruit picking savings on an engagement ring and blossomed into a life-long marriage relationship.

The next three years Alan served as a ministerial probationer in a series of churches in out of the way places in Victoria State. In his first year as a probationer the pressures he felt were so great he had an emotional breakdown. During these years, though, he continued his athletic career, playing on football and cricket teams with and against the roughneck inhabitants of the mining towns in which were the churches he served. In these relationships, he frequently found himself forced to defend himself physically against those who considered preachers to be sissies. My impression is that his defensiveness in academic circles in later years was cultivated on the football field where there was likely to always be someone coming up from behind to do damage.

In 1938, then, he was ordained, not without serious misgivings on his part—a typical Alan Tippett attitude when faced with an honor or a challenge. He also married Edna, survived a camping honeymoon and, with her, moved to the first church he served that provided a parsonage. His first daughter Lynette was born before the first year was out but, sadly, his father died that year as well, at age 60 during surgery. His ministry to the youth was the most productive part of these years. They lived in abject poverty. The church was not faithful in paying them and he frequently had to sell parts of his stamp collection to pay for expenses incurred. He had been collecting stamps from age eight and, as usual, became quite expert at it. In later years he was regarded as an expert collector and exhibiter with probably the best Fiji collection in Australia.

Fiji

In early May of 1941, with the Second World War already affecting Pacific travel, he, Edna and two year old Lynette headed for the Fiji islands where they would work (not counting furloughs) for the next twenty years. In registering his impressions of their arrival at Suva on May 6, Tippett records a series of frustrations that were to mark his approach to missiology throughout his later career:

> I grant that the actual fact of "arrival" was itself an exciting thing, and especially sweet after the delays and frustrations along the very long journey. My missionary call had been formulated under the influence of the Christian Endeavour Movement during 1929, 1930 and 1931, and was still as strong

as ever. A third of my life lay between those years and my eventual arrival in Fiji, and I was a much older person at 30 than at 20, very much more tried, and more disillusioned. Although I had escaped some of the more bitter experiences I was still frustrated at a number of points—first the length and time of the journey itself to the field (I am now prepared to accept this as a needed discipline but I did not see it that way then); there was a general dissatisfaction with my training course in Queens because of its slight relevance (which I accepted grudgingly as the wisdom of the "Fathers & Brethren" of the Conference), my utter inability to get any anthropology or cross-cultural instruction at all in Queens or at the Melbourne University, the Board's denial of even two or three weeks of specific missionary training before my departure for the field (which I thought was my missionary right and the Church's obligation), and one or two other aspects about the shortcomings of my spiritual and missionary formation, which had not even ten minutes space in any of my years of preparation, except what I sought on my own initiative (ibid.:110).

These frustrations, felt early on in Tippett's career, fed into his later commitment to missionary training. He felt keenly his lack of preparation for the task of cross-cultural witness and determined, as did the rest of us who came together at the Fuller School of World Mission, that the missionaries and candidates who came to us would not go away as ignorant as we had been. One of Alan's greatest frustrations was, however, that Australian church leaders did not seem to feel the need for such training. It always rankled on him that he had to attempt to supply missiological training in the U.S. because there was no opportunity to do so in Australia.

Tippett was intimidated by the authority thrust upon him, complaining that "a system placing such authority and decision-making demands on a new worker who could not yet even speak the language was manifestly wrong" (ibid.:112). But such was the colonialist approach to mission that he set himself to overcome both from within during his time in Fiji and through instructing missionaries and candidates in post-colonialist missiology at the Institute of Church Growth and School of World Mission after he left Fiji in 1961.

In an attempt to get beyond dependence on translators, Tippett set himself to learn the language and culture as quickly as possible for, he writes, "when the home Church fails to attend to missionary formation in training it has to come on the field itself" (ibid.:113).

The frustrating experiences of the past ten years weighed heavily on him as he started his new ministry but he responded to the challenge of "a different people, different language," different challenges, with the recognition that "God had cleaned the slate for me, as it were. The food was new, the life-style, and even the problems I felt would be new" (ibid.:113). So, in typical Tippett style, he launched into the work of his next twenty years with verve and dedication, the perfectionist who is never satisfied with his accomplishments, driven to learn whatever was necessary to succeed at the highest level.

The Tippetts were assigned to a station and all of the responsibilities of the area governed from that station. This meant he had oversight over a "circuit" that included schools, churches and medical facilities. He had to deal with these ministries in a multicultural setting that involved seven or eight languages and considerable cultural diversity within the Fijian population, not to mention the sizeable Indian population. He says, "there was no escaping the fact that although Fiji through Church and Government was a religious and political unity, it was nevertheless a multicultural society" (ibid.:137). He had frequently to deal with the fact that, though he had learned the Bau language/dialect that had been chosen long before he came as the political and religious vehicle, during church meetings the people often lapsed into their own language/dialect and lost him until he got onto that language/dialect. This he did frequently, even learning to use these other vehicles in his preaching.

In 1942-43, the Second World War raged around them, interfering in various ways with the work. New Zealand and American troops were assigned to Fiji—70,000 of them along the side of the large island where the Tippetts lived. There were travel restrictions, mission and school buildings taken over, guns set up, trees cut down, mail delayed or lost and other inconveniences. The Tippetts did provide some hospitality for the troops and Alan occasionally served as chaplain for them.

Tippett calls 1942 "a debacle." In 1941 the churches had been vibrant with life, the war was far away and the Christians were full of enthusiasm. In 1942, however, thousands of New Zealand and American troops arrived, facing the Fiji Christians with a new view of Europeans. "Although church services were fine," he says, in reaction to this influx of nonChristian Westerners, "hundreds of Fijians stopped going to church." For there was a new type of Westernism confronting the Fijian. Westernism as he knew it was either commercial of the Company type; missionary of the paternal type, or government with an Oxford accent . . . Hitherto the Fijian had seen the European as a master race, and his ways as beyond his own grasp. . . . Suddenly the New Zealand soldiers came, and then the Americans, theirs was a new kind of Westernism nothing like the three forms he knew. Fiji was overloaded with white men doing the work of coolies, digging drains and trenches, making latrines, watching all night under army discipline for enemy ships. This was no white man's work. The Fijian took a new look at the white man (ibid.:148).

Morality declined precipitously, money and booze flowed. Even so, when the Tippetts returned to Australia in 1946, he concluded that Fiji had stood up to the wartime stresses better than Australia had (ibid.:149). Curiously, one result of the flood of soldiers from New Zealand and the USA was a new appreciation on the Tippetts' part for Americans.

Their second daughter, Joan, was born in 1944. The war was over in 1945. In spite of the disruptions, Alan was able to carry out an active ministry, much of it having to do with schools. During 1944-46, a new constitution was hammered out, largely at the initiative of the missionaries, moving the governance from Mission to Church.

Upon his return from furlough in 1947, the Church, now under Fijian governance, assigned Tippett, with another missionary, to start a Bible School. This Bible School played an important part in the Church's learning to function independently of missionary control. After four years, Alan and his missionary colleague were able to turn the Bible School over to the Fijian Church with a Fijian taking over as Principal. With his next assignment as a Divisional Superintendent, then, Alan got to face the problems of the transfer of authority to the Fijians at the local level. This experience was important to him later as he sought to teach missionaries what post-colonial mission is all about.

Tippett's next years involved a nine-month stint as Acting Chairman of the Mission, followed by a furlough (1952-53). He was then assigned by the Fiji Church to a challenging position as pastor of the church on Bau Island—the home of the most important traditional Chief of Fiji. This presented a challenge to Alan's concept of incarnational ministry in that he needed to learn and observe all of the niceties of Bauan custom, something that his predecessor never had done. That, of course, had been taken as high insult by the Chief and his people.

Tippett records, "From the middle of 1953, when we arrived in Bau, to the middle of 1955, the chiefly island was very much stirred up by ceremonial occasions," including the remodeling of the church building in traditional ways. "The spiritual life in Bau looked up considerably from this point" (ibid.:213). Tippett had determined to work within their customs. He did, however, suggest that the rundown church building was an embarrassment and that it might be appropriate to celebrate the hundredth anniversary of the conversion to Christ of their paramount chief. But the people of Bau took it from there, very elaborately. Tippett comments, "To minister in a Bauan world one is involved in Bauan custom." Tippett then wrote and published for the event a short history of Christianity in Fiji to 1867 plus a series of a dozen newspaper articles. The latter he duplicated and "bound them under the name 'Cakobau Papers' and ran off some 300 copies, which were in great demand among folk who attended the celebrations" (ibid.:213).

From early days, Tippett was a writer. He wrote continuously in English and Fijian. He often wrote for newspapers. Much of his writing deals with Biblical material, lessons and translations. Much deals with history and much with culture. In doing such writing and the research that led to it, he had produced extensive files that, through a series of "divine appointments" were viewed and used by Winburn Thomas, a World Council of Churches person "who had been assigned the task of writing a work on Christianity in Asia." Thomas, then, "tried to persuade [Tippett] to go to America and do a degree" (ibid.:236). Tippett laughed but, when papers came to be filled out toward a study program, he filled them out. That opportunity did not work out, so Alan decided to forget it.

However, he writes,

> suddenly out of the blue I got word from the World Mission body of the American Methodist Church that there was a Fellowship at a university in Washington, D.C. which would fit my most peculiar combination of requirements: History, Anthropology and Archives. Again in great haste I sent off such papers as they required and waited. . . . The Board release me and take care of Edna and the family, but again it seemed I would miss out somehow. Approvals came through unexpectedly [in September] and I had about a week to get

away. Before me lay a period of one calendar year to do what I
wanted to do. The family was keen for me to go. The Board
agreed to pay my fare, but beyond that I was on my own. I had
a $1500 fellowship, but little did I know what one could (or
could not) do with that (ibid.:236).

The year from September 1955 to September 1956 was both
incredibly difficult and incredibly valuable and influential for Tippett.
Though he calls it an "utterly fool-hardy venture," he profited greatly
in his study of anthropology, history and archives, coming away with
an M.A. in history that he was later able to build on for his Ph.D. He
was admitted to advanced classes in anthropology, bypassing the
introductory classes. Though this meant that he had to catch up on
the introductory stuff in his later degree work, what he learned was
invaluable. Apparently, Edna and the girls (by now three) spent the
time Alan was in America in Australia.

They all returned to Fiji, though, for one more term toward the
end of 1956. He was first assigned to Bau again but was soon
transferred to teach at the Theological College. Concerning his year
in America he says,

> I wish I could put down in black and white all the things I
> had obtained from that year of digging. But, really, the tragedy
> of it all is that most of it should have been available to me in my
> training, before I ever went to Fiji. I had lost 14/15 years of
> direction because of the shortcomings of our training program.
> At 45 years of age I was starting again where I should have been
> at 30. When I knew the time had come to check out of Fiji I
> knew also that somehow I had to communicate that truth to the
> home Church (ibid.:261).

This statement points up a major theme in Tippett's life—the
need for Boards to provide better training for their missionary
candidates. Another theme, of course, is that the Fiji Church, and
post-colonial Churches worldwide need to be free from missionary
domination. His transition from involvement in assisting the Fiji
Church to do its own theological education to becoming a trainer of
missionaries is well put in the following quotation:

> My five years in theological education in our educational
> centre at Davuilevu were drawing to a close. They had been
> possibly the most manifestly rewarding years of my missionary
> life. . . .

> . . . and I knew in my heart that there was nothing—nothing at all except colonial and paternal politics—which could stop Fiji becoming an independent Church.

> In that five-year term I had been sustained all the way by knowledge that I myself was better off in America. It had given me a definiteness in the pursuit of my goals, it had helped me direct our projects towards specific aspects of ministerial training, and it had assisted me in the elimination of obstacles. I knew that for the cause it had all been in the stream of His will. At the personal level it had improved my methodology at every point—my research, my communication, my evaluation, and my writing—not because I had a degree but because of the knowhow and the confidence it gave me (ibid.:260).

An Invitation From McGavran

By 1961, with the Fiji Church having quite fully entered into the new independence and self-government afforded by the new constitution, the Tippetts determined that they had accomplished what they were called to do in Fiji. So they resigned and returned to Australia, expecting that the Lord would open up a teaching position or, failing that, a pastorate for them. He writes of his conviction that he was in danger of staying too long in Fiji,

> I knew my men could carry on. I knew they could do it better then I could myself. I knew I had given them the tools. I knew they were creative in their own ways. I knew the time had come for them to go forth alone, and be themselves in the Fiji I now had to leave. Oh how it hurt to go, but I knew it had to be. I had no continuing city. I could only seek one to come. . . . There and then in the Synod of 1960 I broke my own heart, and announced that I had come to the end of the road (ibid.:262).

Having achieved what he called a "clear cut-off" from the training program, the vernacular publications and all else he was involved in, Alan felt that "it was appropriate for me to move out." However, to his chagrin, "Having returned to Australia I found myself lost in my own land" (ibid.:265). He says, "I expected to have the right to speak to the home Church and to be heard. When I got a poor hearing I was much disturbed. . . . Deputation was often a destructive and infuriating experience" (ibid.:267).

The family had settled in a town called Springvale, near Melbourne. Edna found a job "as a temporary teacher on a basis of her domestic arts record in Fiji school" and she soon gained a position

teaching in a girls' high school. Daughter Joan got a job, Lynette had
married in Fiji and third daughter Robyn was at school. The family
was settled. He goes on,

> In this way the Lord provided for Edna and the girls and I was
> able to look again at some writing or research project without
> too much strain, mark time, and reset my sights for whatever
> ministry might lie further ahead before me. I felt the Lord was
> in all this and that His way would shortly open (ibid.:272).

It was at this point that a letter came from McGavran inviting
Tippett to come to the ICG and offering him a scholarship and the
possibility of another M.A. degree, this time in missions. McGavran
had become interested in Tippett through reading an article by Tippett
published in the October 1960 *International Review of Missions* titled,
"Probing Missionary Inadequacies at the Popular Level." With the
hope of using the degree promised by McGavran, then, as a
steppingstone to possibly obtaining a teaching post in missions and
comparative religions at Queens University or some other institution
in Australia, he accepted the fellowship and embarked for America in
December of 1961. Tippett's plan was to spend the first nine months
of 1962 at ICG and to return to his family and whatever God led him
to do in Australia after that. Of this first contact with McGavran he
says,

> I had read some of McGavran's writing, including his
> *Bridges of God*. Indeed, I had summarized this book in six
> pages of foolscap for my students. When I read it I reflected
> and said to a friend in Fiji, "This is absolutely right but this man
> will never sell it to the mission Boards." So I was more than
> delighted when he wrote to me out of the blue. Our
> correspondence showed that we shared a great deal and had
> reacted to, and against, the same things in Christian mission . . .

> McGavran had realized that he needed an anthropologist's
> support at selling a number of his ideas. He knew that
> evangelical Christians in America at that time saw anthropology
> as anathema. He offered me a fellowship to do his courses and
> write a study of Christian mission in the islands, and maybe help
> a little with the teaching. This was a good concrete offer. It
> would give me a little time to go further with my mission study,
> to observe how he had structured his courses, and to draw from
> his experience, to meet other missionaries from other lands, and
> to do some writing. The idea was that it would lead to an M.A.
> in Missions if I so desired. Otherwise I could be satisfied with a
> Certificate in Church Growth. Once again the family wanted

me to take it up, and I felt that we ought to pause a little to consider whether we should seek another field of mission or await an opening in the teaching of mission somewhere, hopefully in Australia itself. Meantime the children needed to settle for a while in Australia we all felt, and Springvale was a good location for their purposes. So I went to join McGavran with a year or so in mind until the Lord should reveal where and how He wanted to use my ministry for the remainder of my years (ibid.:273).

So Alan headed again for America, arriving in Oregon in December of 1961 and starting classes in January 1962. But fairly sizeable changes of plans seemed to accompany his (and others') relationship with Dr. McGavran. For one thing, not many months into his studies at ICG, Tippett was enlisted to teach. His M.A. from American University was in history but with several advanced courses in anthropology as a part of that degree and his deep insight into the cultural dimensions of the Christian mission qualified him to add this dimension to the curriculum, especially since McGavran himself was weak in this area.

As Tippett mentions in the above quote, McGavran was aware of the fact that his program needed anthropological insight. He had depended on ICG students taking courses at the University of Oregon to supply this lack in the program. Indeed, McGavran had Tippett taking courses in anthropology at the University. Somewhere along the line, then, McGavran realized that Tippett had the ability to provide anthropological insight from a distinctly Christian perspective within the ICG program, reducing the need for ICG students to study anthropology from a secular perspective. So by the end of 1962 Tippett was taking courses at ICG from McGavran, taking courses from the faculty of anthropology at the University of Oregon and also teaching courses at ICG in anthropology, primal religions and a case study on Oceania. Tippett comments, "All my courses were learning experiences for me as well as teaching. I had to examine all my themes in relation to the basic motive of mission, which made them applied anthropology . . ." (ibid.:278). By Divine providence, then, the person under whom he studied at the U of Oregon and who eventually became his doctoral mentor, was Homer Barnett, one of the most respected applied anthropologists in the world.

The nature of ICG at this time was that of a kind of Church Growth "think tank," with Tippett and the other Research Fellows in constant interaction with each other and with McGavran concerning

the science of crosscultural mission. The three Research Fellows
who, in Tippett's estimation, contributed the most to him and to the
movement were Bill Read, a Presbyterian who worked in Brazil, Roy
Shearer, a Presbyterian who worked in Korea and James Sunda, a
Christian and Missionary Alliance missionary who worked in Irian
Jaya (Indonesia). Tippett writes,

> . . . the great historical convergence which I believe to have
> been in the purposes of God in 1962 and 1963 was not just my
> encounter with Donald McGavran, but also in the same meeting,
> with Bill Read, Roy Shearer and Jim Sunda.   I never did go to
> America for a degree. I went because I felt God was taking me
> there, and as I look back now I am certain that it was to bring us
> five together (ibid.:277).

Tippett feels that he learned much from each of those he studied
with (and taught) as well as from McGavran. In addition to the
pressure McGavran put on the Research Fellows to learn what he had
been learning, the presence of the four of them from such divergent
backgrounds and experiences put great pressure on McGavran
himself. Tippett says, "Each of us was researching, testing and
writing furiously, and Dr. Mac was working with each of us pushing
us relentlessly against the clock" (ibid.:278). As we have seen,
McGavran was a man on a mission and those who moved into his
orbit felt both the challenge and the pressure to work with him to
produce a new missiology.

An Unwanted Ph.D. Program

Another major change in Tippett's life that resulted from his
association with McGavran was his enrolling in a Ph.D. program at
the U of Oregon. As mentioned, Tippett had planned on a nine-month
stay in Eugene followed probably by advanced study in missions and
comparative religions in Australia. Toward the end of his nine-month
stay, when a disappointed Tippett discussed this plan with McGavran,
the latter's response was, "No! No! You have to do a Ph.D." Tippett
comments, "This annoyed me very much, and I could well have
packed up my bags and gone home there and then" (ibid.:279). But
Tippett stayed for another two years and earned the Ph.D. in what
might be viewed as a victory for Providence, though a lonely two
years for Alan in the U.S. and his family in Australia.

Tippett's comment was,

> Once I resigned to having been hoodwinked into a doctoral program, I determined to utilize the resources [of the superb library on the Pacific at the U of Oregon] to the utmost and to make the most of my course work; but I was resentful about having to do doctoral language exams, which were of no real value to me, and when the time came for a showdown I faced them with extreme depression and homesickness, my blood pressure went up, and I had to get medical advice and bring it down with medication (ibid.:279).

Tippett asks what it was that drew the five of these men together in such a creative way. Given the differences in their personalities and ministries, he finds that each was working in an area characterized by what came to be known as "people movements"— movements of large groups of people into Christianity at the same time. This fact, that such movements have happened in many places at many times down through history became a major theme of Church Growth missiology. McGavran had been alerted to this factor by Pickett's researches in India. It was characteristic of the approach that McGavran, Tippett and these other researches took to this and other such data that facts were recognized and theories developed from analysis of the facts. This approach contrasted with those approaches that advocate theories without the substance of historical fact to undergird them.

So, however reluctantly at first, Tippett worked on his Ph.D. at the University rather than returning to Australia and his family at the end of 1962 as he had planned. He next saw his family in June of 1964 and almost missed his second daughter's wedding. But we are ahead of our story.

Supporting McGavran

McGavran was a belligerent. Tippett was quite competitive as well and soon found himself a major apologist for McGavran's views, especially when those views related, as they often did, to cultural conditioning and dynamics. Tippett says,

> I found McGavran depending on me to sell many ideas to his audiences to bring the resources of anthropology into our orbit for seminars and classes. . . . His own constituency was reluctant to accept the ideas of anthropology (ibid.:282).

In the early sixties, antipathy toward anthropologists and the potential helpfulness of anthropological insight was endemic in evangelical circles, in spite of the fact that Wheaton College had been offering degrees in anthropology for two decades. Billy Graham got his degree in anthropology in 1943! Especially among those with theological training, however, anthropology was seen as incurably secular, relativistic and the enemy of Christian witness. Indeed, at the Church Growth Seminars and at other places as well, people would frequently comment to Tippett that this was the first time they had ever met a committed Christian who is also an anthropologist. With regard to his part in the quest for understanding and acceptance of the new missiology, he further comments,

> It encouraged me no end to think that I was helping Dr. Mac sell his ideas. I did not see then that we were creating a new missiology appropriate to the post-colonial era of mission. We did attract attention, however. Once, as conservative theologians we were establishing a scientific anthropological system, we began to emerge as a problem to the extreme liberal groups who had wiped us off as theologically unacceptable. We never came into debate with them because we never found a common base for discussion. Our biblical presuppositions were mutually exclusive.
>
> We were not disposed to battle with the extreme liberals who rejected biblical authority, or at the opposite pole with the extreme fundamentalists who were biblical literalists. But along the axis between these poles lay a large body of Christian people whom we wanted to win to a missiology appropriate for reaping the ripe harvests of the animist world which was manifestly breaking up and in an innovative mood (ibid.:282).

One exception to the indisposition to battle with extreme liberals was the already mentioned consultation called by the Department of World Mission and Evangelism of the World Council of Churches in 1963 at Iberville, Canada. The purpose was "to examine our viewpoint, discuss the problems it raised, and make a statement for the world Church" (ibid.:284). There were 20 or so participants with J.W. Pickett, D.A. McGavran and A.R. Tippett making presentations assigned by the sponsoring group. Tippett's appraisal of the consultation is as follows:

> The day before going on to Iberville, Pickett, McGavran and I met in New York and discussed all the critical issues we thought might arise, who, and how we would deal with them. We were ready for anything that might arise and I think we demonstrated that our ideas were data-based. . .

On the whole there was a good spirit and some good frank discussions. Those who were obviously opposed to church growth per se were unable to deal with our case. Some who did not accept all we said, were open and responded positively at certain points. Eventually we found that we ourselves were raising the critical points we felt ought to be discussed. . . .

One or two who had previously been extremely critical of McGavran's ideas were present, deliberately no doubt, but when confronted with specific cases they had very little to say. I think the very case we presented demonstrated the importance of research. . . .

. . . [Those who were negative came up with] pretty simplistic arguments for this level of consultation, coming by rationalization from people whose ideas had neither research nor biblical backing. I think they took it lightly, and took us as a bunch of non-academic bush theologians, and intended to "prick our bubble." It didn't work out that way. We produced a fairly good church growth statement (ibid.:285).

That statement, however, was "buried" by the World Council officials, signifying, apparently, that they did not want to lend their support to a Church Growth approach to mission. The statement was not published until years later (ca. 1968 in *IRM*) under pressure from McGavran.

The feeling that they had made their case among academically sophisticated liberals, however, buoyed up McGavran and Tippett. They became a team outside of the ICG as well as inside it. And they had an official statement that, though not used by the liberals who had sponsored the consultation, was very usable by McGavran, Tippett and other Church Growth advocates for their purposes. This whole Iberville experience demonstrated to Church Growth advocates that their arguments could stand up even against those of "establishment" missiologists. In fact, Tippett apparently made enough of an impression on Victor Hayward, the General Secretary of the World Council Department of World Mission and Evangelism, that he was asked by Hayward the following year (1964) to produce a book on Christianity in the Solomon Islands for the World Council of Churches series, World Studies of Churches in Mission. This book, *Solomon Islands Christianity* (1967) is considered by many to be Tippett's best published work.

With Tippett at his right hand, then, McGavran's perspectives were being forged in relation to both the liberal "left" and the evangelical "right." The Church Growth Seminars, the Church Growth Bulletin and the publication of ICG researches were winning over the evangelicals at a time when champions for the cause of traditional, conversion-based missionary endeavor were few. It was clear to those who read the researches and listened to the presentations that both McGavran and Tippett were biblically solid and totally committed to winning to Christ what McGavran liked to call *panta ta ethne* (all the peoples of the world). The claim that Church Growth Theory was biblical or that winning the world to Christ through conversion to Jesus was the only way, of course, angered the liberals. And many liberals simply wrote off the new doctrine, especially when they found they could not effectively defend their objections to it.

Overworked and Homesick

With all of this going on, though, Tippett had a Ph.D. to complete and a family to get back to. How he managed to get so much done in 1963 and 1964, we'll never know. But the fact is that, in addition to the consultations and seminars he participated in, he taught several courses for ICG, took several courses at the University of Oregon, prepared for his Solomon Islands research and wrote a Ph.D. dissertation (not to mention the studying for and taking of the language exams plus his blood pressure problem) that led to his graduation with a Ph.D. in June of 1964!

In addition to the impossible load Tippett was carrying, his path to the Ph.D. was anything but smooth. His previous academic work in Australia and at American University in Washington, D.C. provided a hodge podge of credits, including several in advanced anthropological study. But he lacked the basics. He had, as a part of his history degree at American University, 15 semester hours of graduate anthropology but "no general undergraduate anthropology prerequisites—no general or cultural anthropology, no physical anthropology, etc." He says, "I must have presented them with a major problem. My credits were all high-powered graduate courses . . . As a result of this, I was severely tested in a qualifying examination" (ibid.:287). He had great difficulty getting registered the first time but once admitted had what he calls "straight sailing with courses." The university must have made many allowances for him but did not make the academics easy for him. He was to be mentored by Homer Barnett, known as the most difficult professor in the department. He speaks of one course taught by Barnett that usually enrolled about 24 students, only seven of which would finish the course. That course was known by the students as the one that separated the men from the boys.

It was, however, providential that Tippett should be admitted to the Ph.D. program and that he would get to work with Barnett. Barnett's book on innovation, a classic in the field, Tippett says, came to be "the most influential book on my life, with the exception of the Bible" (ibid.:288). His other major professor, Theodore Stern, was equally demanding. So Tippett got a solid graduate program in spite of his lack of the expected prerequisites. In order to finish in 1964, however, he had to choose to do a study of Fiji material culture, utilizing material he already had at hand and that, in addition, was less likely to be rejected by a secular faculty, rather than doing something more missiological that would require more research and risk rejection.

A further miracle was the fact that during all of this demanding academic work, his mind was never at rest concerning his family and his future. Tippett was constantly aware of the fact that his private life was in a state of transition at best and experiencing a high degree of confusion in trying to figure out what the next stage of his life was to be. From his point of view, it was not clear that he should remain with McGavran, especially since his family was far away. And, in spite of the enthusiasm he felt in providing support for McGavran and the Church Growth movement, he felt used by McGavran and not fully appreciated for the contribution he was making. This feeling became a major theme of Tippett's life to the end of his days.

There were several rumors of positions he could apply for but nothing firm and everything taking time and energy to negotiate. His frustration comes through in the following statement from his autobiography:

> Although I found the courses in Anthropology heavy they were exciting. I cannot say the same about the degree, which I felt I had been tricked into doing. I thought I had probably got what I needed from the courses. Even after four months I was wondering where it would all end up. The post training missionaries in Sydney at All Saints was still open, but the General Secretary made no signs of committing himself. A year went by and there was still no end in sight and I was thoroughly homesick. Another possibility had been for a position at Queens. There was talk of a teaching post there in missions and

comparative religion, but my hope for that had been Colin
Williams who was my friend at court there. But he had moved
to America and told me that specialists were a problem in
Australia. The General Secretary advised me outright to accept
anything the W.C.C. might offer me (I think he had the
Solomons in mind) or any post in America. Either he did not
want me personally, or he did not want a missionary training
specialist. . . . McGavran and Griffeth were at me continually to
be a full time professor at N.C.C. and drove me to the Ph.D.
with this in mind. I had an offer from Asbury to join them as
Professor of Anthropology in the Department of Missions. I got
a nice letter from the Southern Presbyterians about my
presentations at Montreat. They appreciated my emphasis more
than the Church in Australia did (ibid.:289).

This last point developed as another major theme in Tippett's
life—the feeling, reinforced by several denials or expressions of lack
of interest in him, that Australia did not want him. He writes,

The rejection of my missionary vision in Australia annoyed and
depressed me. I knew how badly our trainees needed what I
could now offer. This did not help me mentally with my degree
program (ibid.:289).

He was offered a position in Washington as Dean of Foreign
Students at American University, with the offer attached of a church
and parsonage so he could bring his family. But each such offer
"made me sadder that Australia did not want me" (ibid.:289).
Meanwhile, McGavran continued to pressure him to take a permanent
position as his assistant at NCC. NCC had been very good to him,
giving him a job in a men's dorm to help his finances. In December
of 1963, however, the pressure had gotten so great that he informed
McGavran he was leaving for home. This move was countered by
NCC offering him a faculty position whether or not he had completed
his degree program at the U of Oregon. He says,

To the folk at home I felt bad for the long delays. For
abandoning N.C.C. after all their help I felt bad. For my
inability to finish off the degree I felt bad. I was utterly
miserable and my blood pressure would only stay down with
medication, and that too was depressing (ibid.:289).

The next paragraphs in his autobiography speak further of his
depression, some of it, he thought, caused by the blood pressure
medicine, much of it caused by his feelings of unwantedness by
Australia, on the one hand, and the ambivalence of his relationship
with McGavran on the other. But his major concern was for his

absence from his family, especially as the date for the wedding of his second daughter, Joan, approached. She had planned the wedding for early May of 1964. If he was to take part, then, he could not finish his program at the university. The family agreed to delay the wedding but only a few weeks. He says,

> Word had drifted through that my mother was losing patience with me. Joan was pressuring for her wedding. She wanted it in early May, which would certainly have ruled out the degree once and for all; and even at that late date I was disposed to throw in the sponge. I shared this with Dr. Mac. He said "These things happen. I missed one of my daughter's weddings also." The casual lack of sympathy hurt. I was alienating everybody I respected and loved most. Physically I was at the end of the tether. I packed my bags and tried to drown my unhappiness while the examiners were reading my dissertation, by typing a project for Fiji. But my heart was not in it. . . .

> I was awarded the degree, but I felt no elation whatever. I did not wait for the conferring, which would have meant missing Joan's wedding, and that I had no intention of doing. There were a few friends who wanted to celebrate, but it was no celebration. It was no achievement. It was one long, painful ordeal. I had never sought it. I had never wanted it. And I was utterly torn apart lest I had hurt those whom I loved more than life itself.

> The very next day [May 30, 1964] I was on a plane heading home to Australia. I had the degree, but something had gone out of my life. I wondered if I could ever get it back again (ibid.:290-91).

He continues in this vein for several paragraphs, noting the tastlessness of the food on the plane and the fact that he tried to console himself by labeling the degree "our degree"—that is, the possession of the family rather than simply his own degree. But he questioned whether he was any longer in God's will. He calls it "a long and almost tearful journey. There was no interest in anything I saw . . . just the depression of not knowing how I stood with those I loved and with my Lord" (ibid.:291). Back in the stream of things and the activity of the wedding, however, the depression began to lift and as he and Edna planned for the next few months together "and all possible degree programs now relegated to the past for ever, [he] felt a little better" (ibid.:291)

Solomon Islands, Family and Fuller

Tippett had been offered and accepted the research opportunity in the Solomons under the auspices of the World Council of Churches, but only on condition that Edna be built into the project as his secretary/assistant. He had proposed this to Edna in a letter and she had "responded positively and quickly." This led to them both spending the second half of 1964 in the Solomons after which they returned home to Springvale to write up the research during the first half of 1965.

This Tippett did, completing his research and writing what many consider his best book at the home Edna had kept waiting for him for two and a half years. He was able to submit what he considered a draft to Victor Hayward by the end of 1965. He was looking for comments toward a final revision. Hayward, however, had the draft published as it was! It was written so well in that draft form that only a perfectionist like Tippett could complain that it was not all that he intended it to be.

Meanwhile, McGavran was dickering with Fuller for the move of the ICG to Fuller. Though Tippett had been appointed to the faculty of Northwest Christian College, he had maintained that he would not make any decision beyond the Solomon Islands research without consulting his family. McGavran and Griffeth, however, expected him to return to NCC and Tippett knew he had a position awaiting him if he wanted it. His discussions with the family, then, included both this fact and the fact that he saw no immediate prospects in Australia. So he decided to take the NCC position and had begun the process of applying for a visa to come to the U.S. by the fall of 1965.

As usual, then, McGavran included Tippett in his plans without consulting him and made him a part of the Fuller discussions. It is not clear how much Tippett knew of the process or when he agreed to this latest of the changes in his life mandated by his association with McGavran. The impression Tippett left with me was that he knew virtually nothing about these arrangements until contacted by McGavran after the arrangements had already been made. Since the move to Fuller meant the rescue of the ICG, however, Tippett saw it as a positive thing.

Unforeseen, however, was the fact that visas for Aussies seeking to be employed in the U.S. were virtually impossible to obtain. The U.S. had a quota for Aussies seeking permanent residence in the States for the purpose of teaching at graduate level. And Tippett's application did not fit into that quota. So he was turned down with no hope of reconsideration for some time.

At Fuller, however, God was again at work on Tippett's behalf. Someone remembered that Billy Graham, an inactive Fuller Board member, had a relationship with U.S. President Lyndon Johnson. Contact was then made through Graham with Bill Moyers in the President's office and permission was granted. In Australia, then, Tippett was called to the American Embassy and greeted with words such as, "You must have contacts in a high place. We don't know how it happened but we have instructions to grant you a visa."

Immediately, then, Alan, Edna and their youngest daughter, Robyn, packed and headed across the Pacific, arriving on the very day SWM classes began in September of 1965. Tippett was, however, still on his way at the time his first class was to meet. So McGavran started the class of twelve students, turning it over to a rather travel-weary Tippett before the finish of that first session. It is likely, then, that Tippett had to "wing it" from there, since he had had no opportunity to get his feet on the ground before being thrust into the classroom.

Chapter 3

Meanwhile, at Fuller

Fuller Theological Seminary

Concurrent with at least the final chapters of the stories of McGavran and Tippett at ICG, another story was developing at Fuller Seminary. Fuller was established in the mid-forties by pioneer radio Evangelist Charles E. Fuller. His strong desire was to establish a school that would continue his legacy by training evangelists and missionaries. As mentioned in the Introduction, Fuller saw such a school as a logical extension of his own evangelistic commitment to winning the lost. He had a passion that lost men and women come to Christ, in particular those in out-of-the-way places—miners, lumberjacks, etc. He was impressed by the ability of radio to take the Gospel message to people wherever they found themselves, in the "boonies" or in the cities.

Charles E. was a layman who had graduated from Pomona College with a degree in chemistry and then worked until age 37 as an executive in the orange business. He then attended the Bible Institute of Los Angeles (now Biola University) where he was president of the graduating class of 1921. There he was considerably influenced by R. A. Torrey who had started the Bible school movement and founded both Moody Bible Institute and the Bible Institute of Los Angeles. This influence plus his six years as Chairman of the Board of Biola taught him invaluable lessons about schools and scholars.

Still he was primarily a man of action rather than an academician and an immensely influential radio voice. But his concern for the training of ministers and missionaries led him to speak frequently of wanting to see established a "Caltech" of evangelicalism. With this in mind, then, Fuller engaged in discussions with evangelical leaders such as missionary Samuel Zwemer and pastor Louis Evans, Sr. If such a school were to come into existence, though, its faculty would not only have to be evangelical but possess the highest academic credentials.

A friend of his, Harold John Ockenga, pastor of the prestigious Park Street Congregational Church of Boston was such a man. In the 1940s, he was one of the relatively few evangelicals with a Ph.D. He also shared Fuller's passion for evangelism and missions, regularly preaching "open air" to the people who happened to be collected on Boston Commons during the Second World War years. He also gave missions first priority at Park Street Church, following the example of Toronto's Oswald Smith in sponsoring a week-long missionary conference each year at which pledges were taken for missionary support and a sizable budget funded for that purpose.

So Fuller turned to Ockenga as the one who could provide the academic bridge between their shared zeal for evangelism and missions and the academic credibility that was needed for the training institute he envisioned. To be sure, Ockenga was also deeply concerned about the departure of many first line seminaries from orthodoxy. He had left Princeton with Machen and others who were concerned over the liberalism there. So he thought a seminary rather than a lower level school of evangelism and missions would be better suited to address the evangelical concern over the leftward drift of theological studies. He thought such a seminary could work on this most troubling matter and also strongly emphasize evangelism and missions.

The aim would be to create a seminary that would both train ministry practitioners and also maintain a high level of scholarship to prove to liberals that conservatives could do first-rate academic work. This became the vision of Fuller and Ockenga as they set out to attract a first-class faculty to bring it about. At first, then, the training of pastors, evangelists and missionaries—practitioners—was clearly in focus. In the early days, the seminary was strong in emphasizing these areas and could boast that for the first ten graduating classes a significant percentage of its students (as many as 35% from one class) went into missions. But a focus on evangelism and a focus on academics do not easily coexist. So the pressure of academics eventually relegated evangelistic passion to a secondary place. Dr. Daniel Fuller, son of Charles E., who returned in 1962 from study in Europe to assume the Deanship of the School of Theology says concerning this change:

When I returned from studies in Europe in '62 I noted that students now attending Fuller no longer had the zeal for missions that those in the graduating classes of the 50s had had. Social ethics was now in vogue. Civil rights was the big issue. The student body president, a graduate of West Point said to me the new Dean, "Why should we go and tell other countries how to be Christian, when we have treated blacks so badly?" Weyerhaeuser was then (1962) another factor that had changed things a lot during the 3 years I was in Switzerland. He was now on the Board and was talking a lot of his hopes of integrating Theology and Psychology (email: 12/15/04:3).

But I am ahead of my story.

The Seminary started classes in 1947, meeting initially at Lake Avenue Congregational Church before the first of the buildings on the present site were built. Ockenga was the first President, even though he had to commute from Boston, where he continued to serve his pastorate. They hired an outstanding faculty for academic purposes with men like George Ladd, William LaSor, Everett Harrison, Wilbur Smith, Edward Carnell, Carl Henry, Paul Jewett and Harold Lindsell gaining prominence for their scholarship both within and beyond the evangelical world. And there were in those early days several faculty, each outstanding in his/her field, whose emphasis was more practical, such as Lars Granberg in pastoral counseling, Clarence Roddy in preaching, Carlton Booth in evangelism and Rebecca Price in Christian education. There were enough Presbyterian faculty to attract evangelical Presbyterians and contribute to the reputation in some quarters that Fuller was a sort of "Princeton of the West."

Through the 50s, then, Fuller could justly claim a fair balance between the more intellectual and the more practical aspects of a seminary curriculum. But as Fuller moved into the 60s, several things seemed to change. As regularly happens with institutions of higher education, the more intellectual accomplishments came to take prominence over the more practical ones both at faculty and at student levels. With lots of help from the broader national situation, then, the zeal for ministry among the students suffered and commitment to missions, evangelism and pastoral ministry seemed to decrease.

By the early 60s, Fuller had achieved a good bit of its aim to become academically respectable. Administration and faculty were, however, in the throes of seeking a new President. Carnell, a brilliant scholar, had broken under the weight of administrative duties and needed to be replaced. Ockenga had taken over again, but a search was on for a new President. In 1963, then, after considerable internal wrangling, David Hubbard, a young Old Testament scholar who had been teaching at Westmont College and as an Adjunct at Fuller was appointed President. Among other things, he inherited a promise of a School of Psychology and an interest in paralleling that school with a School of Mission.

As mentioned, C. Davis Weyerhaeuser, a prominent member of the Board of Trustees, had been pressuring the administration to start a school of psychology. Charles E. Fuller, however, was, along with most evangelicals of that time, suspicious of psychology. Dan Fuller writes,

> One afternoon while I was serving as Dean in the fall of '63, my phone rang in my office and my father said, "They've started a psych school. Get busy and start an SWM to open its doors at the same time." My father, like most evangelicals in those days had little use for psychology, and he did not want it to push missions out of the picture (ibid..:3-4).

By 1964, Harold Lindsell, had left the faculty. He had been the one teaching missions, though he had had no missionary experience himself. He had also been Vice President of the Seminary and was bypassed in the search for a new President. To teach the missions course and, hopefully, upgrade it, then, Dr. Kenneth Strachan General Director of the Latin America Mission was invited for Spring Term of 1964. Works says,

> Strachan's presence on the campus, along with the concern of some faculty members that the newly established School of Psychology tended the Seminary too much in a "secular" direction, revived earlier interest in a School of Missions. As a result, the Fuller Seminary Board of Trustees indicated in their June, 1964, meeting that a School of World Mission should be the next major project of the Seminary (1974:309).

In addition, Charles E. Fuller was getting impatient to see his dream of at least part of his seminary devoted to evangelism. The percentage of Fuller graduates going out as missionaries, once averaging 35%, was decreasing and Charles Fuller's concern for the negative publicity likely to come with the start of the School of Psychology led him to put pressure on Hubbard and his colleagues. He also pledged $75,000 per year from Fuller Evangelistic Association funds for the new school. This grant continued for several years once the school was founded.

A Search Committee Set Up

So, a Missions School Committee was set up with Old Testament Professor William LaSor and Evangelism Professor Carlton Booth as co-chairmen. Each of these faculty members was strongly concerned with missions in general and anxious that Fuller move in this direction. LaSor considered this project so important that he dedicated a one-term sabbatical leave to it. Booth, for his part, had wide contacts among missionaries and mission sending agencies. The members of this Missions School Committee visited missionary training institutions and sought suggestions from those they considered knowledgeable in the field. A primary concern, of course, was to find the right person to head up the school.

In addition to Booth and LaSor, Preaching Professor Clarence Roddy was also appointed to the Committee, with Dean of Theology, Daniel Fuller involved as well.   Non-faculty on the Committee included Strachan and J. Christy Wilson, Jr., a missionary to Afghanistan.

Among those considered for the deanship of the school were three prominent field missionaries: Samuel Moffett from Korea, J. Christy Wilson, Jr. from Afghanistan and Warren Webster from Pakistan. The first two of these were Presbyterians and would, therefore, fit well into the primarily Reformed theology ethos of the Seminary. The third was a Conservative Baptist.

As the search committee made its contacts, however, one name kept being brought to their attention—Donald McGavran. To this point, McGavran's story had no connection or even a point of contact with Fuller Seminary. But whenever a member of the committee asked a knowledgeable missions person about the deanship, it was McGavran's name that was mentioned. For example, Dan Fuller found McGavran recommended by Arthur Glasser (who eventually succeeded McGavran as Dean) while at Fuller for a series of lectures and again by the mission leaders with whom he discussed the proposed school at the InterVarsity Urbana Missionary Conference at the end of 1964 (Middleton 1989:316). Yet McGavran was unknown at Fuller and Fuller was well outside of McGavran's Disciples of Christ background.

Concerning McGavran's first contact with Fuller, Middleton records,

In 1964 Fuller Theological Seminary was not a remote consideration as far as McGavran was concerned. After his visit to Eugene, President David Hubbard had described the ICG as "a uniquely creative venture." Hubbard and Griffeth developed a fraternal relationship throughout 1963-64, but the only contact between McGavran and Hubbard took place on a tour of the NCC campus in March of 1964. It was during that visit that Hubbard and C. Davis Weyerhaeuser sat in on McGavran's classes gathered around the Oak Table in the library stacks (1989:316).

With McGavran's name so frequently mentioned, and with the approval of many of the faculty and the search committee, Daniel Fuller wrote to him in January of 1965 informing him of Fuller's desire to establish a missions school and asking that he come to Fuller to share his insights with the Committee. "McGavran, delighted to be involved in plans for the training of missionaries, agreed to visit the Fuller campus in mid-February and meet with the Missions School planning committee" (Works 1974:308). In that letter, Dan Fuller showed how much the Fuller administration was on McGavran's wavelength, saying,

> Fuller Seminary is now working to found a School of World Evangelism. We are impressed by the great need for such a school as the Christian church faces a variety of complex tasks in attempting to carry out the Great Commission . . . We are also impressed by the fact that there is no evangelical program of study leading to a degree on a post graduate level which concentrates exclusively on matters directly related to world-wide evangelization. Furthermore, we recognize that there is a need for a school to serve as a center for grappling with the issues that confront Christians as they seek to establish churches throughout the world. Here research into these problems can be pursued and the results made available not only to the students but also to the Church at large (D. Fuller to McGavran in Middleton 1989:317).

Negotiations

With considerable interest on both sides but no formal commitment on either side, then, Dr. McGavran was invited to spend February 18-20, 1965 on the Fuller campus to "share his insights with the committee" and to give a lecture to the student body. While he was there, Hubbard asked him "to draft a plan for the Graduate School of World Missions." This he did gladly, providing a very evangelical statement that the purpose of such a school should be a focus on "proclaiming Jesus Christ and persuading men to become His disciples and responsible members of His Church" (ibid.:317).

Continuing his four-page writeup of "The Purpose, Objectives, Curriculum and Staff" of the proposed school, McGavran lays out an impressive plan that still characterizes the school. He says,

> Mission history will not be taught primarily as a record of what missions and missionaries have done, but as a record of what church multiplication has taken place, with ample attention to the reasons which operated for and against the growth of each specific Church . . .

> Theology of Mission will not be taught as some denominational system . . . which gives the only true answers whether churches in Africasia multiply or not; but will be taught as that Biblical system of truth which in Africasia God has blessed to the propagation of the Gospel.

> Mission methodology will be commended not on a priori but on pragmatic grounds. The best methods, if they do not work, will not be taught . . .

> Holding steadily to the essential purpose of Christian mission does not imply concentration on a narrowly conceived, stereotyped, North American evangelism . . . The establishment of growing Churches in every tribe and tongue and nation is a multi-sided operation.   Education, medicine, agriculture, development of national leadership, and the like are legitimate parts of mission, but the obvious present danger is that essential mission gets lost in these legitimate parts . . . The cure is to proportion training in mission so that the parts further the central purpose rather than frustrate it.   The phrase "church growth" is deliberately adopted as a term which while including . . . service and the like, steadily emphasizes the chief goal.

> Holding steadily to the essential purpose means (1) that this Graduate School will take its stand squarely on the assumption that the salvation of men through faith in Jesus Christ is the chief purpose of Christian mission.   (2) That the many good things done by mission today will not be permitted to obscure and hinder the supreme aim . . . (3) That conventional academic disciplines hallowed by use in older seminaries, will not be followed slavishly.   Indeed, they will be followed only to the extent that they provedly contribute to propagating the faith . . . in the world of today and tomorrow (McGavran to Hubbard, February 26, 1965 in Middleton 1989:317-318).

Naturally, the possibility of McGavran and ICG moving to Fuller had been discussed during McGavran's time in Pasadena. For, on March 5, 1965 President Hubbard wrote to McGavran that the Committee had gained faculty approval to "continue conversations with you about the possibility of moving the Institute of Church Growth to Fuller Seminary" (Hubbard to McGavran in Works 1974:310). Three events, then, strengthened Fuller's interest in McGavran. One was the death of Dr. Strachan in February, eliminating him from consideration as Dean. Another was a meeting between Hubbard and Norman Cummings at Strachan's memorial service where he enthusiastically recommended McGavran and the move of the ICG to Fuller.

The third event stemmed from the renewal of a relationship between George Martindale and Carlton Booth, the cochairman of the Search Committee. Martindale, a Conservative Baptist missionary to Japan and former student of Booth, had studied with McGavran during 1963-4 and was teaching at ICG while Tippett was away. In discussions with Booth and, at Booth's invitation, the Search Committee, the impression he gave of McGavran's program so impressed the Committee that one of the members remarked, "If McGavran can turn out a man who is as knowledgeable as [Martindale was], then he's the kind of man we want to head up the School of World Mission" (Works 1974:311). When Martindale returned to Eugene, then, McGavran plied him with questions about Fuller, leading, Martindale believes, to McGavran feeling more comfortable about the possibility of going to Fuller.

These events led to President Hubbard and Carlton Booth making their way north to Eugene, Oregon on April 5, 1965 to interview McGavran with a view toward inviting him to become the Dean of the new school. In the negotiations, McGavran insisted that the whole of the Institute of Church Growth be moved intact to Fuller. This meant that Fuller would hire Tippett as well as McGavran and that the ICG library and the Church Growth Bulletin would also move. The present students at ICG would be accepted at Fuller and the name Institute of Church Growth would be retained. This latter, however, required some further negotiation resulting in a dual name for the new school: School of World Mission and Institute of Church Growth.

Hubbard reported favorably to the Fuller faculty leading to a unanimous invitation for the move to be made, contingent on

McGavran passing the Theology Exam, a required interview with the faculty aimed at ascertaining the theological fit of any candidate for a faculty position. For this purpose, McGavran returned to Pasadena on May 18 and passed the exam.

McGavran, however, did not accept immediately. He was greatly concerned lest he and ICG simply be absorbed into a larger institution, serving the institution but not the Cause. On May 10 in a letter to both Hubbard and Griffeth he expressed his concern in an "impassioned appeal that the Institute of Church Growth must not be subordinated to other activities of a parent educational institution" (ibid.:313). In that letter, McGavran had quoted from a letter he had received from Tippett,

> Whatever you do, I hope you will retain the integrity of I.C.G. My fear at Fuller at this point is the possibility of becoming a small project within a missionary department of a seminary. I wonder if the School of Missions at Fuller is conceptually as significant and as big as I.C.G. My preference for Eugene is that I feel the entity of I.C.G. can emerge there better (granted abundant support), and in time may be I.C.G. *itself*, as it may never be at Fuller (Tippett to McGavran, quoted in McGavran to Hubbard and Griffeth, 5/10/65; Works 1974:313).

A second hesitation was the loyalty McGavran felt for NCC, the Churches of Christ and President Griffeth. For this reason, McGavran sought a guarantee from the NCC Trustees that the ICG would be continued and funded. He wrote to Hubbard on May 17, "If Dr. Griffeth and NCC can guarantee the future of ICG, Dr. Tippett, and me; can provide the housing, the classrooms, the scholarships, the $30,000 a year required as a minimum, we stay here. If they cannot do all this, I consider myself free to accept your call" (ibid.:314). NCC could not grant the request in full, and agreed to release the ICG to Fuller.

ICG Moves to Fuller

On May 30, after meeting with Hubbard and Griffeth on Fuller campus the day before to hammer out the final details, he met with the Fuller faculty and Trustees and formally accepted the Fuller invitation. McGavran had made a presentation to the Committee the day before that impressed them and he had come away from the meeting with the faculty and Trustees "more confident than ever that

the hand of God was in this" (Middleton 1989:320). Minutes of that
three-way meeting recorded eleven final issues, including,

> a budget to bring Tippett, the time table for the move was set for
> September 15 or before, moving budget for the Tippetts,
> confirmation of Lindsell as speaker for the fall church growth
> lecture series, details on publications, promotion and
> advertisement, details and policy on the functioning of the
> SWM student body on Fuller campus, assurance of potential
> funds for bringing David Barrett to Fuller as a special research
> fellow, and transfer of credit from the ICG for those students
> who studied in Eugene (ibid.:320).

With the cooperation and encouragement of Dr. Griffeth and the
NCC Trustees, then, the arrangements were completed for the move
of the Institute of Church Growth to Fuller Seminary to start classes
there in September 1965.

The move was formally announced at both Fuller and NCC on
June 9, 1965. The NCC bade farewell to the ICG with some relief on
the part of many but mixed emotions on the part of Ross Griffeth,
who had worked so hard to enable the Institute, often in spite of
McGavran's demands and the limited help NCC could offer. He must
have had many conflicts with his faculty and Trustees. But
McGavran's dreams were far greater than NCC could manage,
especially with a new President coming on who was unlikely to
support the Institute as fully as Griffeth had. Hubbard, sensitive to
what the move must have meant to Griffeth wrote him on June 2,
"Your willingness to see the move made as the best way to perpetuate
the Institute is a tribute to your stature as a Christian leader" (Works
1974:317)

Looking Ahead

In typical McGavran fashion, the May edition of the *Church
Growth Bulletin* carried an announcement of what he envisioned at
the new site. It is not clear from the documents whether this plan had
been negotiated or whether it was simply McGavran's dream. But it
shows what McGavran had in mind for the next few years,

> The School of World Mission at Fuller envisages ultimately
> a faculty of six and a student body made up of missionaries on
> furlough and missionary candidates under appointment.
> Graduate fellows from younger churches in Asia, Africa, and
> Latin America will strengthen the research arm of the School. It
> is expected that an International House will be affiliated with

the new School. Initially the School will offer the Master of Theology and Master of Arts Degrees to experienced missionaries (CGB May 1965:70).

In his dissertation, submitted in 1974, Works, who at the time was on the faculty of NCC, provides a summary of what the School of World Mission and Institute of Church Growth had become in its first eight years on the Fuller campus. He presents on pages 317-318 six developments he considers significant:

1. The curriculum established at NCC "became the basic elements of the new academic discipline, 'missiology,'" as practiced and taught at Fuller. The discipline became formalized during these early years "as the point at which theology, anthropology and history intersect."

2. The degrees mentioned in the above announcement were now offered at an accredited level, unlike at NCC where graduate, accredited degrees could not be offered.

3. The ICG grew during those early years to the predicted faculty of six, "including professors equipped in the basic areas of missiology," and a student body "six times the size of the largest class at N.C.C." The basic approach, with Church Growth at the center, had been retained, but now in a full-fledged school within a Seminary, not as a kind of appendage to an undergraduate Bible College. There were a much greater variety of courses and new office and classroom facilities that "have been outgrown almost before they were occupied."

4. Due to the enlargement of the program—more faculty, more students, a solid institutional footing—the research data on which Church Growth thinking and theorizing depends had been greatly expanded. Works speaks of "over 150 extended church growth studies" completed or in process, many published. These studies by students and faculty enable the next wave of students to probe further than their predecessors and to thus greatly expand the movement that can now be dubbed Church Growth Missiology.

5. Though Church Growth continued to be the major focus, ancillary areas of sub-specialization had either newly come into existence or grown in importance. Among them were Theological Education by Extension, Theology of Mission, Christianity in Culture and History of the Expansion of the Christian Movement.

6. The impact of the Church Growth Movement had increased considerably, especially in evangelical circles. As this influence increased, however, "so has the vigor of the opposition to the church growth school of thought. Nevertheless," Works adds, "the influence of church growth thinking on missionary strategy is much greater in 1974 than it was in 1965."

In conclusion, Works quotes McGavran saying, "Out of the struggle of one missionary, facing the complex challenges of his field, the church growth approach to missions emerged" (1974:318). Works then goes on to record part of a letter written to him by McGavran, ever single-focused, relative to the writing of his dissertation:

> Paint on a big canvas, Herb. What you are describing is much more than the work of any man, and certainly more than I have done. All I have done, really, is to walk through doors God has opened before me. My deepest consciousness is that of standing aside and watching while He has done some wonderful things. Some quite impossible things have been happening. Rolling back the waters of the Red Sea was a small miracle compared to them. Church Growth Thinking by 1965 extended to all six continents. Now, not only are we getting *more* evangelization and *more* churches, but the *meaning* of evangelization is being deepened and sharpened on dozens of fronts.

> As ever yours in battle, Donald McGavran (ibid.:318).

Transition

At Fuller Seminary in Pasadena, California, the four stories recorded in our Prehistory were about to converge to produce another story. We have featured the stories of McGavran, Tippett, the Institute of Church Growth at Eugene, Oregon and the search at Fuller for the personnel that would enable the founding of a School of Mission.

What the Search Committee found was a fully functioning Institute of Church Growth with two faculty members, several students, publication projects already in the works and big dreams. This would be expensive, though none of the documents I have seen mention any problem in this regard. On the other hand, the Institute could "hit the ground running" at Fuller. Fuller had just inherited a full-fledged School to add to the fledgling School of Psychology and the nearly two decades old School of Theology.

Now came the actual move, in itself a challenge in that classes were scheduled to start in Fall Term, late September 1965, and final negotiations hadn't been completed until May 30, the official announcement being made on June 9, 1965. This didn't allow much time.

A further complication was the fact that McGavran was scheduled to spend most of the summer doing research in Latin America, especially Brazil. Before he left, there were details to be worked out concerning the official announcement, speakers for the Church Growth Lectureships for 1965 and 1966, the transfer of a Lilly financial grant, the printing of letterheads and cards and even the final name of the School. There was also discussion over McGavran's concern that the *esprit de corps* of the Institute not be lost and his desire for a doctorate to soon be in place.

In addition, at the time of these negotiations, Alan Tippett was in Australia, writing up his findings on the Solomon Islands research he had just completed, following the completion of his Ph.D. program a year earlier, in June of 1964. Though he had an assured position awaiting him at NCC, and so knew he was destined to return to America, he was not in on all of the negotiations with Fuller. Getting him to America, however, turned out to be a challenge, as we have seen.

At this early date, then,

> Hubbard suggested that McGavran consider Ralph Winter as the next faculty addition. On McGavran's swing through Latin America in July and August 1965 he kept hearing positive comments about Winter and assessed him as "the kind of missionary who is able to excite good comment in his fellow missionaries, and I am interested in him." McGavran also perceived that the missionaries in Latin America would be more likely to be interested in SWM at Fuller than those heading for Asia or Africa; hence he determined that the next faculty member had to be "a top-flight man who is an expert and authority on Latin America and who talks their language and has met their problems and knows his way around" (Middleton 1989:321).

The move to Fuller ushered in a new phase of the Church Growth Movement. It increased the academic stature of the movement considerably. But becoming a part of a graduate academic institution brought with it the risk that the School of World Mission might become just another academic institution, long on theory but short on implementation. The next forty years would provide the temporal context in which the Church Growth *esprit de corps* would tangle with the tendencies toward an "ivory tower" mentality that were a part of Fuller Seminary.

The Missionary Training Context In 1965

It seems appropriate here to note that there was in 1965 a void in the area of missionary training both in the United States and worldwide. This void is pointed up so well by Wilbert Shenk in his article on Missiology in the *Encyclopedia of Protestantism* (2003) that it is worth a fairly long quote:

> In Europe and in North America long-standing mission study programs were in crisis in the 1960s. Both Roman Catholic missionary orders and Protestant mission agencies that had been at the forefront of the modern mission movement since early in the nineteenth century were experiencing a steady decline in the number of missionaries in service. They could no longer justify maintaining training programs and these were being curtailed or closed down. In North America, university and seminary administrations were even phasing out long-established programs in mission studies with endowed chairs. The prestigious Kennedy School of Missions of Hartford Seminary Foundation, founded in 1917 and a major training center, closed its doors in 1967. All of these programs had been based on the Anglo-American tradition of mission studies.
>
> This was also a period of change and reorientation for Roman Catholic seminaries and institutes. In the aftermath of reforms set in motion by Vatican Council II the number of vocations dropped precipitously. Catholic seminaries in the United States reorganized and consolidated their mission training at Catholic Theological Union in Chicago in 1969-1970.
>
> However, during this time a countermovement was taking shape. In 1965 Fuller Theological Sminary founded the School of World Mission and Institute of Church Growth. That same year Trinity Evangelical Divinity School organized its School of World Mission and Evangelism. Both schools were committed to offering programs in applied missiology and were at the forefront of a new phase of mission studies. These new schools of mission were enrolling far more students than had studied in the former mission studies programs.

The renewal in mission studies in North America can be linked to several facts. First, the Church Growth Movement, stimulated by the initiative and vision of Donald McGavran, provided a clear and fresh focus for missions. McGavran was not interested in mission studies in general. He insisted the study of the Christian mission concentrate on church growth. Although mainstream Protestant missions rejected Church Growth, evangelicals welcomed McGavran's views, especially his confidence that a challenging new stage in missions lay ahead. Rejecting talk of crisis he argued that this moment was "the sunrise of missions," not the sunset. Convinced that conventional missions had reached the end of their usefulness McGavran was especially interested in assisting mid-career missionaries to get retooled and reoriented for the next phase of minstry. It soon became evident, however, that leaders of the churches of Asia, Africa, and Latin America were eager for advanced training and by 1980 their numbers surpassed that of mid-career Western missionaries in the burgeoning schools of world mission in North America (Shenk 2003:6).

Thus, we can see that in 1965 the context was ripe for a new approach to missionary training. Though McGavran had started to meet this need at Eugene, he was now about to tackle the problem on a larger stage and with greater resources and greater respectability.

Now, on to the Fuller part of the story, a story that starts in September of 1965 with two faculty members, one of whom hadn't arrived in the U.S. yet, and twelve students. As mentioned, Tippett was still on his way from Australia at the time his first class was to meet. So McGavran started the class, with Tippett arriving to take over after about three-quarters of an hour.

Part II

The Six Eras

Chapter 4

The McGavran Era I: The Founders

1965-1967

By now McGavran was 67 going on 68 years old. He was, however, still a bundle of energy and vision, very perceptive and very committed to Christ and the Church. He had come from a liberal background but had moved into a very evangelical, almost fundamentalistic understanding of Christianity. He was still a very compelling speaker, a prolific writer of letters, articles and books and a master teacher and administrator. He had learned to communicate and to fight for his point of view through years of combating liberal mission practice and had learned administration through four and a half years of running the finances, the recruitment and just about every other aspect of the ICG not covered through the sponsorship of his good friend NCC President Ross Griffeth.

At this advanced age, however, he was "the new kid on the block" at Fuller, an institution committed to reflection and scholarship and often suspicious of passion and the kind of total commitment that McGavran personified. He was, therefore, a puzzle to many of his new colleagues who tended to consider him an academic lightweight because he believed that all theory had to be justified in practice. Though this spirited approach to Christian witness was what Charles E. Fuller had in mind for Fuller, the Seminary, in its quest to achieve academic respectability, was far from this. Whether by intent or not, the Seminary was in the business of producing scholars, not practitioners, though, to be fair to the Seminary, many graduates did become very good practitioners.

But McGavran, and especially Tippett, were not academic lightweights. They had paid their academic dues through developing theory but insisted that theory had to produce results. This might be called a "theory of practice" rather than theory for its own sake. From

McGavran's point of view, if a given theory didn't result in gains for the Kingdom, it was to be set aside, no matter how impressive it might be.   And he fiercely resisted the drag on ministry often accompanying the pursuit of academic theological sophistication. McGavran emphasized clear, rigorous thinking that faced the facts. He developed formal theory for this but called for "applied knowledge" rather than what might be called simply "academic" or "theoretical" insight.   Though he (and we) sought to do academic things, we always sought to have a practical output.   He (and we) would not, therefore, want to be identified merely as academics since, unlike many academics, we choose not to glory in theories — theological, anthropological or missiological—without much attention to whether the theories work out well in practice.   McGavran called this approach a "fierce pragmatism" and contended that academic theory and pragmatic practice are not necessarily mutually exclusive. The SWM was to be focused on a "theory of practice," not theory for its own sake.

As an administrator, McGavran "played his cards close to his chest."   He announced his decisions rather than discussing them.   And when he spoke, he simply assumed that he spoke for all of us.   There were no discussions of budget in those days, or of new programs or even of new hirings.   We learned of such things when McGavran announced them.   And we wrote articles or taught courses when he assigned us to.   He had been brought up and served in an old-time colonial mission in India, had clawed his way into a position of prominence in his own approach to missionary endeavor and was jolly-well going to run SWM in his own way.   This was his dream come true and he guarded it well.

McGavran's plan for the growth and focus of SWM was announced in the *Church Growth Bulletin* of June 9, 1965:

> The School of World Mission at Fuller envisages a faculty of six and a student body made up of missionaries on furlough and missionary candidates under appointment.   Graduate fellows from younger Churches in Asia, Africa and Latin America will strengthen the research arm of the School.   It is expected that an International House will be affiliated with the new School.   Initially the School will offer the Master of Theology and Master of Arts degrees to experienced missionaries (CGB I, 5: special news release).

Early Faculty

How much of this vision McGavran had discussed with the Fuller administration, I don't know. As mentioned in chapter 3, President Hubbard had encouraged McGavran to hire Ralph Winter. This suggests that Hubbard as well as McGavran anticipated an increase in the number of SWM faculty members. This fact would have helped assure McGavran that his fear of being simply absorbed into a seminary faculty was ill-founded. Apparently, Charles E. had designated funds deposited with the Fuller Evangelistic Association, to support SWM and enable some growth in faculty.

For a start, there were funds to enable him to invite a series of "adjuncts" to lecture and offer courses to enrich the program. A Fuller adjunct is a person who is not a regular faculty member but who teaches a given course once or several times. One of the earliest of those invited as an adjunct was Winter, a Presbyterian missionary to Guatemala who was part of a group who had initiated a program in Theological Education by Extension in Guatemala. McGavran had read about the TEE program and heard a lot about him in his travels in Latin America.

Since Winter regularly visited his parents in the Pasadena area, McGavran invited him to lecture and eventually to teach a course on TEE during his visits. During Winter's time at SWM in 1966, McGavran and Winter worked out an agreement that Ralph would teach at SWM for six months and work in Guatemala six months. Then McGavran got very sick and Winter was engaged to cover some of McGavran's mentoring and teaching. In the Fall Term of 1967 Ralph left his work in Guatemala to become the third member of the SWM faculty. Financing this was no problem since the Presbyterian (USA) Board actually assigned him to teach at SWM and continued to support Ralph for the next five years. President Hubbard, however, insisted on paying the Presbyterians back. By the grace of God, McGavran recovered from his illness and was back on track by 1968.

Other adjuncts in those early years included several who were prominent in mission theory and practice in the sixties. Among them were Harold Cook from Moody, Calvin Guy a Southern Baptist, Harold Lindsell former missions professor at Fuller, Stephen Neill and John V. Taylor from the Anglican Church Missionary Society, J.T. Seamands a Methodist, Jack Shepherd from the Christian and

Missionary Alliance, John Sinclair a Presbyterian (USA) and David Stowe from the Division of Foreign Missions of the National Council.

Among the students in the second year of the school's operation at Fuller (1966-67), was C. Peter Wagner, a missionary with Andes Evangelical Mission in Bolivia. Eddie Elliston, who later joined our faculty, was also a part of that class. Wagner "caught" the Church Growth perspective quickly and, in typical McGavran fashion, before the year was over was asked to teach a course on the growth of the church in Bolivia. The way Wagner imbibed the Church Growth perspective and taught that course led to Wagner becoming a permanent member of the faculty of SWM in 1971. But there were two more hires before Wagner joined us, making Wagner the sixth of the six faculty members McGavran had envisaged in 1965.

These two hires were Charles Kraft (1969) and Arthur Glasser (1970). We will get to them below.

Reverses

There were some reverses in these early days as McGavran was attempting to gather his six-man faculty. Edwin Orr, a specialist in revival attracted McGavran's attention and was invited to join the faculty in 1967. An institutional requirement of Fuller Seminary, however, was that a committee of the School of Theology was to conduct a "theological exam" of each candidate for faculty positions in each of the three schools that make up the Seminary. This interview nearly resulted in a negative vote on Ralph Winter who quite honestly described the Fuller statement of faith as "culturally particular" rather than crossculturally valid. His supporters, however, were able to buy time by getting him invited to appear a second time before the committee at which time he was passed. Orr, however, despite the fact that he had an Oxford D.Phil., was not considered sufficiently academic by that committee since he specialized in the study of revivals and so was not hirable as a full faculty member. It was allowed, however, that he be hired as an adjunct, teaching a regular course or two yearly but not to be appointed to a regular faculty position. Orr was with us, teaching one or two courses per year on revivals, until his death in 1987.

A similar thing happened when McGavran attempted to hire George W. Peters, a faculty member at Dallas Seminary. With Peters, the issue was not academics as it was with Orr. It was, I believe, the

Fuller theology faculty's strong aversion to Dallas Seminary, though his strong personality and the fact that he was then in his late sixties may have also entered into the decision. The theological positions of many Dallas professors and of the institution as a whole were not highly regarded by Fuller theology professors at that time. Peters was considered to be too fundamentalistic and too dispensational. So he, too, was rejected. These rejections left scars on McGavran, Tippett and Winter and contributed to the sour taste in our mouths over what came across as a lack of respect for SWM on the part of the School of Theology.

Plans for Expansion

An important part of McGavran's vision for the School of World Mission was to see Church Growth theory applied in every geographical region of the world. Thus, a major focus in the curriculum in Pasadena, as it had been in Eugene, was the regional courses. By 1968, there was coverage of India, the islands of the South Pacific and Guatemala, with Orr supplying insight into revivals worldwide. But McGavran saw the need for courses dealing with other parts of the world. Africa was one of the areas needing coverage.

This factor led to the joining of my own story with that of McGavran and the other SWM faculty members in the fall of 1969. More on this below.

I have mentioned that McGavran was considered lightweight as an academic, especially by the theological elite at Fuller and elsewhere, partly due to the fact that his Ph.D. was in education. In no area was this criticism greater than with regard to the theological grounding of Church Growth theory and practice. The fact that the Apostle Paul and most of the other New Testament authors were primarily activist missionaries and only secondarily and almost accidentally theologians, had long since been forgotten by theologians. So, the Fuller theological faculty, committed to gaining respectability among academic theologians, were playing by the rules of the academy and took a dim view of those who attempted to *act* like the Apostle Paul acted rather than simply *thinking* as Paul thought. McGavran was indeed committed to acting like Paul acted and teaching others to do the same and was, therefore, graded down by the academic establishment for the "pragmatism" of Church

Growth theory. The academic theologians critiqued a theology that, though now taught in an academic setting, gave prominence to bringing people to Christ and into church groupings rather than to what they considered "correct" thinking and reasoning concerning biblical doctrines.

Tippett responded to this challenge, applying his considerable intellectual gifting to the challenge of developing a "theology of Church Growth." His eleven part series, entitled "Biblical Basis of Church Growth" became a regular feature in the *Church Growth Bulletin* in 1965-67. In several other contributions to that journal, Tippett continued to show acute theological insight as well as to integrate anthropological perspectives into Church Growth thinking. In addition, McGavran sought for and published in the CGB contributions by others that were theologically oriented. Among the authors that caught his eye was Arthur Glasser.

Glasser was Home Director for U.S.A. and Canada of Overseas Missionary Fellowship (formerly China Inland Mission), having served in China as a missionary prior to the Communist takeover. As the 1960s came to an end, our faculty discussions often turned to the perceived need to make our theological thinking more visible and Glasser's name was frequently mentioned. He was well known to all of us, either personally or by reputation. In addition, McGavran was now in his seventies and ready to turn over the deanship to someone younger. So Glasser was approached and agreed to come, provided he would be allowed to complete the year of studies he had undertaken toward a Th.M. at Union Theological Seminary (1969-70) and then spend his first year at Fuller (1970-71) as a regular faculty member before taking over as Dean. This he did and became our second Dean in 1971.

McGavran, however, felt he needed an understudy—someone to apprentice to him in the area of Church Growth. His choice was C. Peter Wagner who, as mentioned above, had studied and taught at SWM in 1966-67 and then returned to Bolivia. After some negotiations as to when he would come, Wagner joined us in the fall of 1971.

Our regular faculty now numbered six, the number McGavran had envisioned in 1965 (plus Orr as a regular adjunct). We had students, a fairly stable position as one of the three schools of Fuller Seminary, a widely read periodical (the *Church Growth Bulletin*), multiple publications by students and faculty and had moved through the transition from McGavran to Glasser as Dean. In addition, we were disseminating the Church Growth doctrine through 2-3 regional Church Growth Seminars per year attended by missionaries and mission administrators. And the future was bright.

McGavran as Teacher and Scholar

For McGavran, the move to Fuller was a continuation and expansion of what he had already been doing at ICG, Eugene. He would teach the same courses, continue the same research, work with the same kind of missionary students but on a bigger stage with a more secure future.

As Tippett says, "McGavran is essentially a biblical missiologist" (1973:20) who, in addition to his considerable achievements in enthusiastically and sometimes even abrasively calling missionaries and mission societies back to making "the first thing the first thing," contributed three important concepts to missiology. These were 1) the concept of people movements, 2) the need to take advantage of "ripe fields" lest the opportunity be lost and 3) the differentiating between discipling and perfecting (ibid.:20).

McGavran was scriptural, and especially New Testament and Pauline in his missiology. The authority of Scripture is foundational to McGavran's approach and "the precedents of the early Church are his guidelines." Through the battles with liberals and his success with evangelicals in his pre-Fuller days, he became thoroughly evangelical, even sometimes theologically fundamentalistic by the time he came to Fuller. And his enthusiasm and optimism were contagious. His theology was not, however, of the academic kind. It was Pauline activism, theological convictions in action, that motivated him and infused all that he taught and wrote.

With respect to McGavran's emphasis on people movements, the early influence of Pickett and the fact that large-scale turnings to Christ had been happening in India has been noted. McGavran was fond of saying things like, "It was at J. Waskom Pickett's fire that I lit my candle." Some have remarked, however, that it was not a candle that he lit, but a skyrocket! (Works 1974:66) From this base, McGavran broadened his study of such movements to other geographical areas and back into history and Scripture. With Tippett's help, he also came to recognize the presence of sociocultural factors in the conversion process. Tippett helped with data also, since the conversion of the peoples of the South Sea Islands had largely happened in people movements. Though he did not teach whole courses in this area, one of my first assignments in joining the faculty in 1969 was to do a course entitled "Conversion With a Minimum of Social Dislocation" (his title). He had read Roland Allen whose "spontaneous expansion of the Church" could be seen as a precursor of McGavran's "Christward people movements" (Tippett 1973:22).

McGavran's *Understanding Church Growth* (1970) records the approach he took to his basic course at Fuller. He set himself to make sure that each of his students developed what he called, "Church Growth Eyes." This was the perspective that asked "hard, bold" questions and came up with "hard, bold" facts concerning what was really going on in any given missionary endeavor. One major ingredient of church growth thinking was the importance of looking for large-scale movements and the factors that contributed to them.

This characteristic was, however, perhaps the major part of McGavran's theories with which evangelicals had difficulty. Many felt that if people could come to Christ in large groupings (so-called "group conversion"), the evangelical doctrine that holds that each individual must make his/her own decision was being challenged. Those working from a theological mindset that works out doctrines purely on the basis of culture-bound theories arrived at through *reason* alone were not in a position to understand that McGavran was working out his theories from observation of what had actually happened.

McGavran had observed that large groups of people in India (and, he later found out, in many other places) had come to Christ at a single time and, as demonstrated by further research, had truly become and remained Christ-followers. From this *fact*, he developed the people movement theory, noting that the New Testament recorded such movements in passages such as Acts 10, where Cornelius' family and friends came at one time and Acts 16, where the Philippian jailer's whole household (probably including slaves) came at one time. McGavran moved from fact to theory, as behavioral scientists do, rather than from theory to a rejection of perspectives that don't fit the theory even if based on actual behavior, as philosophers and theologians tend to do. Western theological theories of conversion, based as they are on western individualistic understandings of human behavior cannot reasonably allow for people to make decisions in groups. So, McGavran and Church Growth

Missiology in general came in for strong criticism from many otherwise friendly quarters.

Such people, without understanding behavioral science methodology, also tended to pit such use of behavioral science methods against their theological assumption that the Holy Spirit works without reference to human understandings of culture, communication, receptivity, conversion and the like. Somehow it seemed more spiritual to assume that the Holy Spirit does what He wants to do regardless of what we do than to assume that He can use us better if we learn and use the insights of those who have studied human sociocultural behavior. "True," they would say, "people in nonwestern societies make 'group decisions.' But that's not the way the Holy Spirit works." Never mind that whole segments of the world's populations have come to Christ in people movements (e.g. South Pacific, India, Africa), these critics would still deny that this is the way it's supposed to be. They felt that McGavran's approach was too human. But, in his defense, Tippett writes,

> McGavran saw both the human and the divine side of "open doors," "Bridges of God" or "fields ripe unto harvest" whichever figure was being used. His methodology, however statistical, was never humanistic. The harvest field always reflected the will of God—ripeness meant God's time for harvesting. Harvesting represented man's responsibility. In the response to opportunity man had to know his resources and know how to use them. "The new methodology" he said "simply attempts to cooperate with God" (1973:31).

The second major contribution of McGavran was his concept of what has since been called "the opportune moment." He observed that people movements happened when certain sociological factors occurred. He surmised, then, that it might be possible for an informed observer (one with Church Growth Eyes) to discover when such factors would be likely to occur and, on that basis, to predict or even produce people movements. In his own Indian context, he was able in 1938 to point out to the missionary world the imminent movement of a large number of Hindus into something else. He saw a marvelous opportunity for Christians to win them to Christ. As it turned out, they converted to Buddhism and the opportunity was lost, from McGavran's point of view, due to missionary neglect. "McGavran was saying . . . ripe fields must be harvested and not all harvesters are Christian" (Tippett 1973:25).

So, McGavran was strong on the need for missionaries to observe the signs as well as the facts. And, though he had a realistic view of what missionaries would do, he maintained an optimistic view of what could happen if missionaries would capitalize on the opportunities uncovered through research. He sought, then, to influence as many as possible to seek and take advantage of those opportunities. His was a "Harvest Theology." He saw the world as "alive with opportunities. Theologically expressed—fields are ripe unto harvest, and harvesters should be sent into the harvest. This is God's hour. This urgency underlies much of his writing" (ibid.:26).

One of his best presentations, honed before he came to Fuller but delivered regularly to his Fuller students, was entitled "Sunset or Sunrise?" With a gleam in his eye, he would point out how difficult it is to tell the difference between a setting sun and a rising sun simply by looking at one or the other. Liberals, he said, had looked at the sun without doing research and decided that the day of missions was over. With a bit of research, however, one has to come to another conclusion— that the bright sun we are observing is really rising, not setting. If we would only look at what is really happening around the world, rather than what isn't happening in our home European and American countries, we could see a more positive picture and come to a more positive hope for the future. Furthermore, if we could get on board with what God is already doing around the world and deploy our resources to reap the white harvests, instead of simply doing "good" mission work, we could be involved in the greatest ingathering of souls for Christ that the world has ever seen.

He would cite an example from Congo in which a mission worked on both sides of a river without, apparently, noticing that the people on one side of the river were open and turning to Christ in great numbers while those on the other side were resistant. The mission, trying to be fair to both groups, had an equal number of missionaries and allocated an equal amount of resources to the work on each side of the river. What they should do, McGavran contended, was to recognize that the Holy Spirit was better able to work with the responding people and to allocate their personnel and resources so as to work with Him rather than simply to be fair to both cultural groups. They should keep a small number of their personnel on the resistant side in hopes and prayer that those people would turn receptive. But they should place priority on the opportunity presented by the receptivity of the group that was turning, lest that opportunity for reaping be gone.

Tippett aptly summarizes this part of McGavran's approach,

> McGavran's stress on opportunities and his distress at the Church's failure to do anything about them recurs in all kinds of settings. He weighs administrations, institutionalism, perfectionism, budgets, personnel distribution and many other things against opportunity for growth. He speaks of winnable people. In the last analysis his case for deployment of funds and personnel to winnable fields has an essentially biblical authority in the words of our Lord himself in Luke 10, a missionary passage.

> This is a theology of optimism, of hope, of promise, and a belief in man's stewardship under divine authority. Further back beyond this is a belief in the lostness of man without Christ. What more can be desired for the race of man, than that he should come to know Christ, and how can this be achieved, if those who know Him turn from the opportunities to share Him with those who are ready to listen? (ibid.:26-27)

The third of the features of McGavran's ministry and teaching as practiced in the Fuller years is the differentiation he made between discipling and perfecting. McGavran's passion was for reaching the lost. In advocating that this quest be foremost in missionary thought and practice, however, he had to find a place for the many other good things that missions and missionaries do. These he came to call "perfecting," observing that "there is a constitutional bias toward perfecting. The Churches gravitate toward caring for what they have. Their inbuilt nature prefers perfecting." (McGavran 1959:93) Missions likewise have come to give most of their attention to doing those things intended to produce growth in those already committed to Christ (e.g. schools, hospitals, agricultural and other self-help programs).

In making this distinction and contending that the primary goal of missions is the discipling (i.e. winning) of the nations, he stepped on the toes of missionaries and mission leaders. He contended that "missionary policy was extremely confused." He called such confusion "fog." And

> missiology owes much to him for sorting out the issues, classifying the various approaches, and forcing the missionary policy-makers to confront the precise choices before them. Many of them did not like it. Missionary vested interests were

threatened. But despite all the hard words, policy-makers have
learned much because of McGavran (Tippett 1973:28).

Perfecting, McGavran maintained, was a "good" thing to do.
But missionary effort had become unbalanced to the neglect of
winning the lost. And he wanted to call the missionary movement
back to its original intent with a balanced approach to discipling and
perfecting that produces churches that are as committed to reaching
the lost as they are to the social services they provide to their
members.

All of these issues, then, became the substance of what the
School of World Mission taught. These were also the main areas of
concern in the *Church Growth Bulletin*, the Church Growth Seminars
and the theses produced by SWM graduates. These concerns were
continually hammered home to missionaries, mission executives and
any others who would listen. McGavran has been accused of having
only "one string on his fiddle." He was not ashamed to be so accused,
rightly or wrongly, as long as what he did and taught contributed to
the winning of *panta ta ethne*, the peoples of the world.

McGavran was a visionary. He was frequently abrasive,
especially to those who, whether explicitly or implicitly, had other
goals than winning the lost to Christ. This was his single focus and
this is what he intended for the School of World Mission to stand for.

Tippett at Fuller

Tippett's move to Fuller at age 53 (he would be 54 in
November) was a welcome change from the hectic life of the past few
years. He was now in a stable position with most of the good things
he had experienced at NCC (minus, of course, the University of
Oregon library) without the financial insecurities. Furthermore, he
was now a part of a graduate institution, not of a stepchild of an
undergraduate program, dependent for its existence on a soon-to-
retire president. And best of all, Edna and Robyn were with him.
Lynette, their oldest daughter (they had no sons), was fairly well
situated in Fiji and Joan had just gotten married and so was on her
own. It would be good to be nearer to either or both of them but that
could not be if there was no satisfactory employment for Alan in
Australia or Fiji.

For the next twelve years, until his yearning to return to
Australia got the best of him, Fuller would be the context within

which he would function. He would teach the people he most wanted to teach—missionaries. He would do the kind of research he most wanted to do—missiological research. He would work with colleagues who loved and respected him. And Edna would be by his side as his secretary and driver as well as his wife.

A word about Edna would be in place here. She had coped marvelously with his long absences, teaching as well as parenting, keeping house and car in operation, in short, doing everything. I don't know when it started—perhaps back in Fiji, perhaps more recently during their stint in the Solomons—but Edna felt that her main calling in life was to enable Alan to be and do what he was meant by God to be and do. So, from her point of view, Alan was to devote his full attention to his academic work while she took care of everything else—children, house, car and all the rest. She even drove him wherever he wanted to go, since he had given up driving when he came to the States. And she served as his secretary during his years at Fuller. (Once Alan retired and was back in Australia, however, she refused to play secretary though she still functioned as driver.)

As can be seen by now, Alan was both brilliant and hard working. He was also a perfectionist. Whether for classes, for publications or for public presentations, he regularly over-prepared. This set him up for frustration in his classes because he could never cover much of the material he had prepared in Fuller's ten week terms. In addition, the students soon learned that he was much more interesting when telling stories than when lecturing. So they frequently got him off the topic. This added to his frustration over not being able to cover all of his material. Indeed, America in general frustrated him. In spite of his anthropological insight, he was continually in culture shock!

But the culture or language shock went both ways. His Australian accent regularly misled students. For example, he frequently referred to the American Anthropological Association, abbreviated AAA. But his Australian pronunciation of AAA was "ai, ai, ai," leading students to write I-I-I in their notes! On one occasion while I was about to start a class, he came into the classroom to post a notice on the bulletin board there. Finding no tacks, he queried, "All right, you blokes, who pinched the drawing pins?" In American English, of course, this meant "who stole the tacks?" We could take Tippett out of Australia but could not take Australia out of him!

I believe Tippett was the broadest and deepest missiologist of our generation. As I wrote in my article on him in the *Australian Dictionary of Evangelical Biography*, "He is considered by most missiologists one of the two or three best in our generation in terms of his ability to comprehend and articulate (especially in writing) the intricate relationships between biblical, cultural, personal and strategic aspects of the Christian mission" (1994:374).

But he suffered from a deep-seated inferiority complex. He writes in his autobiography of school and football experiences in which he felt he had to work harder than his classmates and teammates to prove himself. He never got over this attitude. Though his biblical insight was probably comparable to that of any of the Fuller Theology faculty, any confidence he might have gained by recognizing this was eroded by the fact that he felt inferior to those who had graduate degrees in theology, since he had none. He regularly complained that he only had an L.Th. rather than a graduate degree. And yet it was Tippett, rather than McGavran who did have a graduate degree in Theology, who came to the rescue over and over when the latter got into theological difficulty in seminars and print.

Playing second fiddle to McGavran, first in Eugene and then at Fuller, did not help his self-concept. If being "hoodwinked" into doing a doctorate by McGavran is what led to his high blood pressure, working side by side with him continued the problem. McGavran, as we have noted, was an old time colonialist in the way he ran his programs. This bugged Tippett no end. Though he saw himself as regularly defending and protecting McGavran in his intellectual battles, Tippett felt he never got the recognition and respect he deserved from "Mac" (his favorite name for McGavran when the latter was not within earshot). I used to discuss this problem with him, pointing out that McGavran showed little deference to any of his colleagues. That is, he treated us all as underlings, habitually "talking down" to us, probably not because he didn't respect us but more likely because that is just the way he was. As a matter of fact, McGavran had many good things to say to others about his colleagues, especially Tippett.

One of the things that grated on us most, and especially on Tippett, was the fact that McGavran regularly presented his views and opinions as if we had voted on them and elected him our mouthpiece. In point of fact, he did not always speak for all of us and never asked our opinions on many of the positions he attributed to us. To him, the movement he had generated was his and our positions were as supporting cast. But he didn't seem to notice or consider valid any different perspectives, continuing to use phrases like, "We at SWM feel/think/hold . . ." and linguistic barbarisms such as "Eurica" and "Africasia" or, worse, "Latfricasia," when editing our contributions to the *Church Growth Bulletin* (see Kraft 1971:159-161). Though this got us into difficulty from time to time and gave outsiders the impression that we were all in lockstep with McGavran, our commitment to the essentials of Church Growth Missiology kept us from bolting. It did not, however, keep us from discussing the matter when out of his hearing.

Tippett was especially capable as a researcher and writer. He was an inveterate collector of data on a large variety of subjects. Though I believe there were more, Dundon says he "wrote up 13 pieces during the Fiji period or shortly after. These did not include his M.A. thesis on the labour trade. . . . He wrote on the migration, the snake in Fijian culture and he explored war, special ceremonies, and language" (2001:3). He wrote for newspapers both before and during his time in Fiji. He wrote the history of the church in Fiji for the 100th anniversary ceremonies and several other studies of Fiji church history. Dundon writes about Tippett's transition from missionary to missiologist, in the process mentioning three of Tippett's unpublished volumes, done largely if not completely during the Fiji years: a biography of missionary John Hunt, entitled *Road to Bau, The Integrating Gospel* and *The Christian*,

> Twenty years of research, writing, teaching and pastoral work in Fiji convinced him that tribal peoples came to the Christian faith in cohesive groups; that churches needed to be indigenous from the start; that mission agencies would [wrongly] retain paternalistic control for as long as possible; that anthropology was a means of assisting with the communication of the Gospel; that anthropology would sharpen the critique of mission policies; and that anthropology would aid in the transition from mission to indigenous church. All these points emerge from his work on John Hunt, *The Integrating Gospel* and *The Christian*. This is why McGavran wanted him at Eugene, Oregon and why Tippett turned his attention to the study of church growth.
>
> It was at Eugene and FTS that Tippett developed more fully the intellectual basis for a post-colonial missiology (2001:6-7).

He continued his writing while at ICG and Fuller, including several years as editor of the journal *Missiology*. Many of his writings were published, many unpublished. My wife and I, with considerable student assistance, especially from (now Dr.) Larry Caldwell, took one of Tippett's unpublished volumes and got it published under the title, *Introduction to Missiology* (Wm Carey 1987). In retirement, he wrote several unpublished volumes, one an autobiography, another a biography of his father, yet another a biography of his father-in-law, still another a historical study of Fijian stamps. He also regularly collected his published and unpublished articles and bound them by topics and by years. I personally photocopied many of these volumes and deposited them in the Fuller library. Copies were also made for the Biola and Asbury missiological libraries.

During his time at ICG, he began to write on church growth topics, much of it as research papers both for ICG and for his courses at the University of Oregon. Though he had wanted to do his Ph.D. dissertation on culture change in Fiji, he settled for *Fijian Material Culture*, a brilliant piece based on some research materials he "just happened" to have on hand. His *Solomon Islands Christianity* (1967) is considered a classic, even though, as noted, Tippett himself felt that it needed another revision or two. His *Church Growth and the Word of God* (1970) and *Verdict Theology in Missionary Theory* (1973) were classic early statements of a theological basis for Church Growth.

Concerning *Church Growth and the Word of God*, Dundon writes:

> What the work provided was a skilful blending of the anthropological and the theological or biblical. It worked through the main themes of church growth such as diffusion, numbering, conversion, social structure, multi-individual group decisions, context, acceptance and rejection of the message, incorporation into a body or community and the different forms of growth such as qualitative, quantitative and organic. Tippett related these themes to diverse biblical materials in a conservative, but critical and historical way. In many ways he was using the Bible as a source of anthropological case studies in order to quell concerns of an important group. In this he was quite successful. . . . The book belonged to its time, answered questions for a specific group of people and was successful, at least for a number (2001:17).

As mentioned, both McGavran and Church Growth Theory needed Tippett. With all of his vision and insight, McGavran was quite limited in his understanding of cultural things. Tippett imported into CG Missiology the brilliant insights of Homer Barnett concerning how people change their cultures. For example, from his early days with Pickett, McGavran was very concerned with the process by which large groups turn to Christ. McGavran had changed his terminology from "Mass Movements" to "People Movements." Tippett, however, following Barnett, introduced a more precise term, "Multi-Individual, Mutually-Interdependent" choices as the way to label people movements that often involved thousands turning to Christ at one time.

He frequently saw himself as doing "damage control." McGavran's emphasis on numbering as a major, if not the only way, of gauging church growth, for example, challenged Tippett to write on quantitative versus qualitative church growth. His focus, however, was on "organic" church growth. When it came to the Church Growth challenge to traditional ways of doing mission, however, Tippett was right with McGavran in requiring research to determine exactly what the situation was. His concept of the kind of research needed was, however, much broader and deeper than McGavran's. Of his relationship to McGavran's approach, he writes,

> McGavran and I shared the theology of the Christ of Scripture as the only way to the Father, the basic paradigm of the Great Commission as our mandate for action, the belief that to bring people to conversion to Christ also involved incorporating them into fellowships for nurture in the Lord, and their own outreach in evangelism and service. To this common cause we were dedicated. Beyond that we were independent persons (quoted by Dundon 2001:20).

Tippett's courses were masterpieces of organization and theoretical sophistication. Unfortunately, the precision with which he organized and tried to teach were often at least partially lost on the students. Most of the students came with very little background in anthropological areas, so Tippett regularly spoke over their heads, answering potential questions they were not asking. Yet, he and his teaching were thoroughly admirable. Those students who had enough background and/or experience to catch onto what he was saying gained incredibly from him. And those who did not have such background usually got enough to really be of help in their ministries.

And when either group read his writings, they usually caught onto the fact that they were reading the marvelous insights of an incredible intellect with a heart as big as his intellect.

Tippett's main course was called "Animism." This was one of the five "core courses" required of every student in the early days at Fuller. This course established, among other things, that animism is the major faith of most of the peoples of the world, including the vast majority of those who consider themselves a part of one or another of the "world" religions. He also taught the introductory anthropology course until I came along in 1969. His focus was on understanding culture, culture change and their relationships to Christianity.

Barnett's concepts of innovation, advocates and innovators, recombination theory and the like relating to culture change were introduced into CG theory in these classes. So was Anthony Wallace's fertile concept of revitalization and the danger of introducing Western techniques in the wrong way chronicled in Lauriston Sharp's article "Steel Axes for Stone Age Australians." The concept of the "functional substitute," the process of introducing a new custom to serve the same function as was served by a custom that is done away with in the introduction of Christianity was another of his major contributions. So was the concept of "power encounter," the recognition that for most of the peoples of the world, any interest in converting is contingent on the demonstration that Christ has more spiritual power than their gods or spirits. One further focus was Tippett's revision of the concept of "indigenization" to get beyond the Western-oriented "three-self" formula. In these last two areas, Tippett foreshadowed two of the current SWM/SIS emphases, though we now use the term "contextualization" instead of indigenization. And in our dealing with power encounter we go much farther than Tippett did in his recognition that most people movements involved power encounters. His book, *People Movements in Southern Polynesia* (Moody 1971) documents this fact.

One of Tippett's major accomplishments while at SWM was to produce and edit a Festschrift in honor of McGavran, done quite secretly and presented to McGavran on his 75th birthday. It is entitled *God, Man and Church Growth* (1973) and consists of 29 chapters by colleagues and students covering a wide variety of topics relevant to the activities of God and humans in relation to God's activity in the human context. Through presenting a wide range of subjects, the book provides a state of the art representation of missiological thinking as of 1973.

He also taught courses on anthropological theory and ethnohistory, though the latter has not become as prominent in CG Missiology as he would have liked. For he saw ethnohistory, a methodology for doing research into history that focuses on the cultural dynamics of the history, as his own central concern.

In summary of Tippett's contributions to CG Theory and practice, Dundon helpfully points to 16 areas that were key in his thinking. Tippett was saying that Missiology has to:

1. come to terms with human diversity and the nature of culture,

2. take cognizance of the human group, its phenomenology, its structure and its place in the ministry of the Holy Spirit,

3. discover the significance of social structure . . .

4. abandon a static view of human society, and see the ongoing character of social change and the dynamics of its patterns and processes,

5. recognize the ramification of all kinds of animism in human society and study its bearing on social continuity and change,

6. explore the decision-making processes in society (including conversion) and identify the dynamic features of decision-making as a process, both for individuals and groups,

7. probe the whole problem of meaning, both for the Gospel advocate and the recipient, either acceptor or rejector,

8. probe the whole problem of motivation for acceptance or rejection,

9. illuminate the matter of process in ritual,

10. work at understanding the cultural voids many colonial evangelists left,

11. find ways of overcoming the cultural voids through the use of such ideas as functional substitutes,

12. explore the processes involved in syncretism especially in relation to functional substitutes and indigeneity,

13. study the events that preceded conversion,

14. develop processes of incorporation of new converts,

15. develop legitimate research methods,

16. [develop] a conceptualization of indigenous selfhood to overcome the inherited missionary paternalism and colonial ethnocentricity (2001:27).

Adjuncts and Students—1965-67

McGavran and Tippett were the founders of our school and the only full-time faculty for the first two years, starting those two years with twelve students. As was the custom in Eugene, however, McGavran was always on the lookout for teaching help from the experienced missionaries who came as students and from outsiders who might have something to contribute. Among those who were invited from outside either for one-term courses or for lectures during these first years, as mentioned above, were Stephen Neill, Calvin Guy, Jack Shepherd, John V. Taylor, J.T. Seamands, John Sinclair, David Stowe, Harold Cook and Harold Lindsell.

One who was invited to lecture, and then to teach, was Ralph D. Winter, missionary to Guatemala under the Presbyterian Church. Ralph would become the third faculty member. To him and the others that joined our faculty during the McGavran era we now turn.

Chapter 5

The McGavran Era II:
Completing the Six

1967-1971

When McGavran and the Institute moved to Fuller, he announced that they looked forward to a faculty of six. I was not able to locate any master plan as to who these six would be. But in retrospect, the Holy Spirit seems to have planned that there would be an understudy for each of the founders, plus a theologian-Dean and someone to deal with the history of the Christian movement in a new way—all to be in place before McGavran retired.

The first of these was Ralph D. Winter who attracted McGavran's attention first because of an article he wrote on church planting and then through his focus on Theological Education by Extension. He joined the faculty in 1967 to teach TEE but soon moved into a primary focus on a new missiological approach to history. During the year 1967-68, C. Peter Wagner, one of the students caught McGavran's attention and became his choice to take up the Church Growth mantle. But Peter didn't join us until 1971. In the meanwhile, I joined the faculty as Tippett's understudy in 1969 and Arthur F. Glasser came as theologian and Dean-elect in 1970. McGavran had had his eye on Glasser for some time to buttress the biblical and theological dimensions of Church Growth Missiology.

We turn now to each of the new faculty members in order.

Ralph D. Winter (1924—)
At Fuller: 1967-1976

Of the collection of players in the drama that is SWM, many would consider Ralph Winter the most interesting. Ken Mulholland, in his article on Winter in the *Evangelical Dictionary of World Missions* states the consensus of many of us, calling him "One of the

most innovative missiological thinkers of the twentieth century"
(2000:1019).

Winter's story starts in southern California. He was born into a
devout Presbyterian family of engineers in 1924 and brought up in
South Pasadena, about four miles from Fuller Seminary. His family
was, according to Winter himself, "strongly influenced by the global,
evangelical, mission-oriented Christian Endeavor movement, which
was not very conventional" (1995:56). It was at a CE event when
Ralph was about ten years old that he made a decision to follow
Christ. Interestingly, it was also a CE event that brought Tippett to
Christ. In high school Ralph was involved with the Navigators and
grew in his faith under their discipline and focus on Bible study and
memorization.

His family and the Charles E. Fuller family were close and he
and Dan Fuller, who later figured prominently in inviting McGavran
to Fuller Seminary, were boyhood friends. Later, when he and Dan
went off to Princeton Seminary together, they were expected by their
parents to keep each other from being influenced by the Princeton
professors to become theologically liberal.

Winter served in the Navy during World War II and, under the
GI Bill attended "eight schools beyond college" (Winter 1995:56).
His academic preparation included a degree in engineering from
California Institute of Technology, learning Greek at a Christian
college, a summer at Wycliffe Bible Translators' Summer Institute of
Linguistics, an M.A. at Columbia University in Teaching English as a
Second Language, a Ph.D. at Cornell in linguistics, anthropology and
statistics in 1953, finishing with three years at Princeton Seminary in
1956, followed by ordination into the Presbyterian Church (USA).
During his time at Princeton, one of his professors (Sam Moffett,
church historian and long term missionary to Korea) pointed him to a
need of the Presbyterian (USA) Board in Guatemala for an ordained
person with training in linguistics and anthropology whose wife was a
registered nurse. Though he had other tempting opportunities, he and
Roberta, who was a nurse, chose to go to Guatemala.

A defining part of their preparation was what Ralph calls

> a really marvelous six-months-long "graduate school of
> mission" designed by our denominational board . . . This was
> one of the most valuable experiences of my life. . . . [We] were
> exposed weekly to serious outside lecturers ranging from

Communists, Muslims, Hindus, and others to mission statesmen
like Kenneth Scott Latourette . . . (1995:56-57).

Not only was that experience to figure prominently in Winter's
future, but the contact with Latourette was to launch what later
became a major interest in and commitment to a unique approach to
the history of the Christian movement, looking at that history as a
missionary enterprise that is always expanding.

At the end of 1956, Ralph and Roberta, with their first two (of
four) daughters, headed for Guatemala under the Presbyterian Board
to work in one of that Board's "conservative" fields among the Mam
Indians. During the next ten years in Guatemala, Ralph was engaged
in equipping Guatemalan pastors of tribal churches to do their jobs
better. He noticed early, however, that throughout Latin America
pastors ordinarily were bivocational, supporting themselves through
some other occupation while pastoring part-time. Noting that
shamans were the people with the greatest prestige in the rural
villages, he came up with the idea of training pastors medically as
well as theologically. He comments,

> After my studies and all the decontextualizing influences
> through which we had gone, I'm sure we seemed radical to
> some of the missionaries. We precipitated a major rejection by
> some when, after a great deal of thought, we tried to promote
> the idea that pastoral leaders in our mountain tribal churches
> ought to be trained in both theology and medicine (in view of
> that same range of functions of the native shaman). We also
> wanted to give certain minimal modern-day medical skills to
> local shamans as a means of protecting the people in general
> from careless medicine as well as to become friends with them
> (1995:57).

With such creative ideas, Ralph quickly got into difficulty with
his colleagues who were loathe to "color outside the lines" that had
been drawn by generations of their missionary predecessors.
Recognizing this, Ralph goes on to say,

> Such ideas encountered hopeless opposition [from the
> missionaries]. But we did train our future pastors in various
> kinds of business activities that enabled them to be itinerant or
> at least not to be tied to the soil (1995:57).

Winter's creativity was, however, not always the issue. What
often disturbed his colleagues (both in Guatemala and later at SWM)
was the fact that embracing his ideas often required more effort than
his colleagues were willing to expend. He was (and is) a master at

generating genuinely better approaches to things. But, given limited resources and personnel, colleagues would often opt to continue or adopt a lesser approach rather than to implement Ralph's better idea. For implementation of the better idea sometimes called for large expenditures, radical restructuring and/or discarding of other programs. Ralph's innovativeness thus sometimes led to considerable frustration both on his part and on the part of his colleagues.

But one idea that did catch on for some and become a worldwide movement was Theological Education by Extension. For those who were willing to go to the trouble of reworking their approach to educating church leaders, TEE became a very valuable tool. As Ralph and his colleagues, James Emery and Ross Kinsler, attempted to train Guatemalan pastors, they began to realize that "residential seminary training, so prized by our ... Presbyterian tradition back home, was clearly a mixed blessing in rural areas, where full-time professional ministry did not readily fit" (ibid.:57). Though it took work and the surmounting of the opposition of the traditionalists to bring it about, they were able to convert a seminary from a residential school to an extension center. The ability to study by extension, then, "suddenly made ordination available to the Mayas and rural poor" church leaders who could not afford to move to the seminary. This experiment in Guatemala eventually attracted the attention of both conciliar and evangelical mission agencies and became a worldwide phenomenon.

Winter's Contribution to SWM

Winter fascinated McGavran. He was (and is) an enthusiast, a visionary, one strongly committed to winning unreached people to Christ, especially those he has come to call "frontier peoples." Through reading and personal contact, he had become a strong supporter of McGavran. Ralph was very good with statistics, in the days before calculators, he always had a sliderule with him and he was ready at the drop of a hat to figure out things on the sliderule like the "decadal growth" of a church.

But he was always overbooked. On one occasion, after I had bailed Ralph out of a double booking and the result was positive both for Ralph and for SWM, McGavran's comment was, "That Ralph. We don't even think he's in the ballpark but there he is hitting a home run!" Ralph was always doing something unorthodox. Usually his ideas were good ones. Implementing them, however, often resulted in more work for the rest of us.

As a teacher, Winter was (and is) a spellbinder, especially when dealing with areas of his interest. His lectures would regularly "lift you to the skies," reported one student to me. He regularly turned nearly every class into an exciting discourse on whatever he happened to be thinking about that day. In self-recognition of this tendency, Ralph once half-seriously suggested to our faculty that our courses should not be titled by subject (e.g., History, Church Growth, Anthropology, etc.) but by simply using our names: "Winter 1," "Winter 2," "Winter 3," "McGavran 1," "McGavran 2," "McGavran 3," "Tippett 1," "Tippett 2," "Tippett 3," etc.

In addition to his teaching, Ralph, like McGavran, did a lot of "business" for the cause. He was constantly traveling, making presentations, making contacts, advocating church growth thinking, pushing for articles and books to be written supporting the cause of church growth. But his outside activities and especially the correspondence that accompanied them got out of control. Perhaps the most famous story from Winter's days at SWM is that of the bathtub full of unanswered mail. At that time we were housed in the old house across Oakland Avenue that is now the "meeting and eating spot" called "the Catalyst" and Winter's office had a bathroom attached with an unused bathtub in it. Over the weeks and months as mail came in that he didn't have time to deal with, Ralph threw it into that tub. Eventually the tub got fairly full and continued to fill until he first hired Doris Wagner, then Linda Holland, the wife of one of our students, to be his secretary. They organized Ralph and emptied the tub!

Highpoints of Winter's career at SWM included a textbook entitled *Theological Education by Extension* (1969). Once one of Winter's best students, Fred Holland, was ready, though, we hired him as an Adjunct and Winter turned the teaching of TEE over to him. Before he came to us, Fred had worked extensively with TEE in Zambia. Another highpoint, frequently pointed to by evangelical missiologists, was his presentation at Lausanne 1 (1974) entitled "The Task of Highest Priority: Cross-Cultural Missions" published in Douglas (1975). In this presentation Ralph introduced his concept of labeling cultural distance in terms of E1 (evangelizing the people of one's own culture), E2 (evangelizing those of the same language but a different subculture) and E3 (evangelizing those of a different language and culture).

What fascinated Winter to the end of his days at SWM, was his pioneering approach to Christian history that combined traditional church history with the history of missions into a single course he called the Historical Development of the Christian Movement. If McGavran lit his candle at the fire of Pickett, Winter lit his history candle at the fire of Kenneth Scott Latourette, a Yale historian who had been a missionary to China. He effectively brought Latourette's *A History of the Expansion of Christianity* into Church Growth Missiology. Winter also wrote an important supplement to Latourette's magnum opus called *The Twenty-Five Unbelievable Years* (1970), dealing with developments since Latourette completed his seven-volume history. With reference to that book, Tippett, who had a sparkling, though complex sense of humor, once introduced Ralph as the author of the book, "*The Twenty-Five Years*, by the unbelievable Ralph Winter!"

Additional significant publications by Winter include, Warp and Woof: *Organizing for Christian Mission* (ed. 1970), "Planting of Younger Missions" in Wagner 1973, "The Decade Past and the Decade to Come: Seeing the Task Graphically" (1974) and *Frontiers in Mission* (2005).

Ralph also had a lot to do with the development of our first doctoral degree, the Doctor of Missiology (D.Miss.). Though Ralph worked on developing the degree, he did so reluctantly, since it was not a Ph.D. We had applied to the Fuller administration to be allowed to offer a Ph.D. in about 1974 or '75 but were turned down and told that we did not have enough faculty strength to operate at that level, this despite the fact that before agreeing to come to Fuller, McGavran and Tippett had been promised they could offer a Ph.D. With six full-time faculty members, four with Ph.D.s, two without (Wagner and Glasser) but with Glasser having fully the equivalent of a Ph.D., we strenuously objected but could do nothing to get the decision reversed. So we felt that, for the sake of our students, we needed to develop an applicational degree we called Doctor of Missiology. I had researched various Ed.D. degree programs with a view to creating the D.Miss. at that level. We then put "meat on the bones," and had a doctoral degree that was less than we had wanted but did give us a doctorate to offer to our students.

We were later allowed to develop a Ph.D. degree offered jointly by SWM and the School of Theology. The concerns of the two schools differed to such an extent, however, that neither the students who opted for the degree nor we SWM faculty who tried to make it work were ever happy with that arrangement. Eventually, though, we were able to work out our own Ph.D. and dropped the joint degree.

Winter's Contribution to Missiology

As we have noted, one of McGavran's passions as he advocated church growth thinking was to get as much as possible into print. He was able to arrange for the first of the ICG church growth studies to be published in India and was later able to get Eerdmans to publish several studies. It was, however, the genius and willingness to risk of Ralph Winter that led to the formation of what amounted to a Church Growth publisher. In 1969, Winter, with our encouragement, founded a publishing company he called William Carey Library with the aim of getting significant books out fast and inexpensively. Though pundits predicted the company would never sell more than $500 per year, WCL continues in operation 35 years after its establishment, having published over 400 of its own books and handled more than 300 titles of other publishers over the years.

It is probably impossible to estimate the influence that these books have had on the missionary world. In the early days, many of them were technically little more than the author's typescript, reduced in size from 8 and 1/2 by 11 inches to book size and bound. But they were inexpensive and found their ways into the minds and hearts of thousands, many of whom received each new publication of WCL or significant publications of other publishers through the Church Growth Book Club. As computers came along and with them the ability to format with greater technical excellence, the quality of the printing increased. So has the variety of offerings. WCL is now a part of the U.S. Center for World Mission.

A point that Fuller President David Hubbard made in those early days was that for an academic discipline to be taken seriously, it needed to be supported by an academic organization and a journal. Recognizing this, Winter and Gerald Anderson, a Methodist missiologist who became the Director of the Overseas Missionary Studies Center in Ventnor, New Jersey (now in New Haven, Connecticut) got their heads together in the early seventies and called a meeting in 1972 that resulted in the founding of the American Society of Missiology, designed to "bring together 'Catholic, Conciliar, and Conservative' streams of mission scholarship" (Winter 1995:58). Anderson was elected President and Winter Secretary "and de facto Business Manager."

Recognizing the need for an academic organization to have a journal, at the same meeting they inaugurated *Missiology: An International Review*, electing Alan Tippett to be the first editor (Glasser became the second editor in 1976). Hearing that the important missiological journal *Practical Anthropology* was about to cease publication after 19 years, Winter and Anderson were authorized to negotiate the incorporation of *PA* into *Missiology*. This was accomplished, enabling *Missiology* to begin publication in 1973 with an initial subscriber list of about three thousand.

This was an important coup for the new journal and the society that sponsored it. *Practical Anthropology* had been quite influential in the lives and ministries of many of us by helping us to develop a perspective that was both theologically and anthropologically sound. As I point out below, that journal was very influential in my own life. But the American Bible Society Translations Department under Eugene Nida had supported *PA* for most of its years, using it to showcase the brilliant cultural and biblical insights of William Smalley (editor from 1955 to 1969), William Reyburn, Jacob Loewen, Nida himself and many others. And they and Charles Taber of Emmanuel School of Religion, who had taken over the editorship in 1969, felt it appropriate to feed it into the new journal. With Tippett as editor, then, it was assured that the anthropological emphases would be well taken care of.

A further extremely significant contribution to missiology that Winter has made is the inauguration in 1974 of the widely used *Perspectives* program. This is a program designed to introduce lay people to up-to-date missiological thinking through meeting once a week for 15 weeks to hear prominent mission speakers leading discussions on a variety of relevant topics arranged under four categories: Biblical, Historical, Cultural and Strategic. These topics relate to writings in a large compilation of readings (782 pages, 124 chapters by various authors) edited by Winter and Steve Hawthorne, entitled *Perspectives on the World Christian Movement* (3rd edition 1999). As of this writing, there are over 180 Perspectives courses offered in North America yearly, mostly in local churches, attended by more than 7,000 people and coordinated by some 900 locals who have taken a special training course. By 2005, about 60,000 have taken the Perspectives course, many for academic credit through Trinity International University or other schools that recognize the course as credit-worthy. Of all the influential things Winter has done over the years, the Perspectives program may be the greatest.

J. Edwin Orr (1912-1987)
At Fuller: 1968-1987

Jacobus Edwinus Orr was born on the 15th of January 1912 in Belfast, Ireland the third child of a father whose parents had migrated to the U.S. and were, therefore, American citizens. When Edwin's father wanted to marry, however, he returned to Ireland and married an Irish lass. This gave Edwin dual citizenship, a valuable thing to have when he grew up and began traveling widely as an evangelist.

Orr's parents were fervent Christians, greatly influenced by an evangelical awakening in Ireland. His mother led him to the Lord at the age of 9 and had a strong influence on his early life. His father died when he was 10 and his older siblings within the next few years, so at age 15 Edwin became the breadwinner of the family, forcing him to drop out of formal schooling. During these early years, he was greatly stirred by stories of revival and gathered regularly with other schoolboys to study and pray about revival.

Though Orr started his undergraduate studies 10 years later than would have been normal, he made up for it and ended up with 6 graduate degrees in History and related subjects from universities in the U.S. (Northwestern, Northern Baptist and UCLA), India (Serampore), England (Oxford) and South Africa (University of South Africa).

Orr was an evangelist and recorder of revivals. He traveled widely across the world, preaching the Gospel in great campaigns in 140 countries on all six continents. He had by the mid-sixties written a score of books, detailing revivals in many parts of the world. These eventually attained a circulation of over a million with translations into a dozen languages. His historical books are, however, more collections of stories than scholarly history and thus looked down on by academics. This fact probably played an important part in his being denied a full-time position by the Fuller theological faculty.

Orr's collections of stories of revivals are published in books with titles like *The Second Evangelical Awakening in America* (1964), *The Light of the Nations: Evangelical Renewal and Advance in the Nineteenth Century* (1965), *Evangelical Awakenings in the South Seas* (1976), *Evangelical Awakenings in Latin America* (1978) and *Evangelical Awakenings in Southern Asia* (1978). He also did collections like these latter three for India (1970), Africa (1975) and Eastern Asia (1975).

McGavran was intrigued with the possibility that revival in Christian churches might lead to increased evangelistic outreach and, therefore, to ingatherings of new believers. Somewhere along the line, Orr had caught McGavran's eye and was invited by the latter to come teach at SWM. As mentioned, McGavran was not able to get Orr a permanent position on our faculty but he was able to engage him as a regular Adjunct to teach one or two courses yearly dealing with revivals.

There was, however, a significant theoretical difference between McGavran and Orr, though McGavran tried not to undercut Orr in his teaching and writing. Orr strongly contended that revival produced church growth. McGavran saw no such conclusion warranted by the data. Instead, McGavran contended that revival primarily affected believers, not unbelievers who needed to be converted. McGavran saw large-scale conversions (i.e. people movements) as possibly one of the byproducts of revival but an exception rather than the rule. He defends his point very well in a chapter in *Understanding Church Growth* (McGavran & Wagner 1990) while making it look as though they agree.

In any event, Orr taught his point of view without interference from McGavran and added an important spiritual dimension to SWM. Though both McGavran and Orr worked with only one string on their fiddles, they appreciated each other and the contribution each made to the whole.

Orr continued as a regular Adjunct until his untimely death of a heart attack while on a speaking trip in 1987.

Charles H. Kraft (1932—)
At Fuller: 1969—

I was born in 1932 and brought up in Wolcott (near Waterbury), Connecticut, the son of a factory worker and stay-at-home mother who was converted rather dramatically through a letter from her cousin who had attended Wheaton College and gone to Sudan as a missionary. Thus, in my early years I heard of Africa, missions and Wheaton College as significant in my mother's life. When, then, I came to Christ at age 12, it soon became a goal of mine to serve Jesus in Africa. So, when I reached college age, it was to Wheaton I went to prepare for Africa, find a wife and prove to my father that I could succeed in athletics. All three happened by the time I graduated in 1953. Meg and I married that same year.

At Wheaton I majored in anthropology and took the equivalent of the basic Wycliffe Bible Translators training in linguistics. We learned to deal with culture anthropologically and Biblically, to be positive toward people's cultures, working toward bringing people to Christ *within* their cultures rather than by extracting them from their cultures. I thus was learning to deal with culture and crosscultural ministry in a way that put me at odds with the majority of mission programs in Africa, as well as in most of the rest of the world.

We then sought in vain to find a mission board working in Africa that agreed with the approach we had learned, so I applied and was accepted to begin studies at Fuller Seminary in the fall of 1953. However, my pastor father-in-law was a member of the Missionary Board of the Brethren Church (Ashland, Ohio) who had just begun to work in cooperation with the Church of the Brethren Mission in northeastern Nigeria. So he tried hard to recruit us, promising that we would be able to apply anthropological and linguistic insight in a newly-opened area where CBM was pioneering. We felt led, then, to accept the invitation to move into what seemed like an ideal situation for us. So, in 1953 I joined the Brethren Church, withdrew my application to Fuller Seminary and enrolled in the Brethren seminary at Ashland, Ohio. I was ordained into the Brethren ministry in 1955.

During my seminary years at Ashland, I heard of the program of missionary training at Hartford (Connecticut) Seminary Foundation's Kennedy School of Missions. This was a program started soon after the great Edinburgh Missionary Conference in 1910 and was the closest thing available in those days to SWM. Our mission board agreed to support us for a year of pre-field training at KSM, so we moved to Hartford for the academic year 1955-56. At KSM I took courses in anthropology, linguistics, African studies, ethnomusicology and Islamics (under Kenneth Cragg). For the two Islamics courses I did long term papers on Islam in Nigeria that I designed to become the core of my B.D. thesis at Ashland. During that year I also became a Ph.D. candidate. We returned, then, to Ashland for the fall semester of 1956-57 to finish my B.D. This was finished by April or May of 1957, but they wouldn't let me graduate in absentia. So my degree wasn't granted until we returned from Nigeria in 1960.

During that year at Hartford, I came strongly under the influence of Eugene Nida, Bill Reyburn and Bill Smalley of the American Bible Society, especially through their writings in the journal *Practical Anthropology* and the Bible Society *Confidential Papers* that were made available to a few of us. *PA* had been started in 1953 by one of my Wheaton teachers, Robert Taylor, and in 1955 was taken over by Nida and the Bible Society. The value of this journal and of the perspectives of Nida, Reyburn, Smalley, Loewen and the others who wrote for *PA* is inestimable in the lives and ministries of those of us trying in those days to present Christianity in a culture-affirming way. Anthropological and biblical perspectives were brought together into what I later dubbed "ethnotheology," a crosscultural approach to biblical and theological interpretation. If McGavran was Wagner's "guru," Nida was mine.

So, what I took to Nigeria was Wheaton anthropology and linguistics and Ashland theology, honed into incarnational missiology at Hartford and in reading *PA*. Into the mix, then, came a copy of McGavran's *Bridges of God* that I read in Nigeria. McGavran's approach came to me as presenting a perspective that I had long since imbibed and even gone beyond in my own thinking.

Nigeria

In spring of 1957, Meg and I, with our two small children (twins, nearly 2 years old), headed for Nigeria. We learned the trade language of the area—Hausa—and moved to a tribal area to learn the language of the Kamwe (then called Higi) people. Our assignment was to supervise a dispensary, half a dozen very small churches, several schools, and to learn and reduce the language to writing. As I got acquainted with the church leaders, it became obvious that they needed instruction and guidance. So I gave myself to helping them and, at least partly because we were affirming Kamwe culture, the people became very receptive and the Church began to grow rapidly. So, I turned away from learning the Kamwe language in order to focus on the extension of the Church throughout the Kamwe area. The result was what we learned later to call a "people movement" to Christ, based on a culture-affirming approach to conversion and Christian behavior. We sought to develop a Christianity that functioned *within* the culture, not *against* it, in spite of the fact that the mission's approach was largely the latter.

The rapid growth of the Church among the Kamwe, then, became a problem for the mission leaders. In spite of the fact that converts were required to go through a six-month training period before they could be baptized and accepted into the churches, there came a time when I was baptizing 100 to 150 converts monthly, all of whom had been examined by the local church leaders, not by me. With less than 100 church members when we came to Kamweland, then, there were nearly 1,000 when we left and the number has steadily increased to more than 40,000 today.

But, since we expressed criticism of certain mission policies, policies that the local Nigerian leaders also questioned, the leaders of our mission didn't trust us. For in comparing Nigerian customs with Scripture, we saw no support for several mission policies, including refusal to baptize believing polygamists, the prohibition of dancing and drums in worship and the mission's approach to disciplining those caught breaking mission rules. Furthermore, I had become (from the mission leaders' point of view) disturbingly popular among the Nigerians. So, after we had spent but three years on the field, the field leaders of the mission refused to allow us to return to Nigeria after our furlough.

On the Shelf

So we returned to Hartford in 1960, completing Ph.D. coursework in 1961 and my dissertation (on Hausa syntax) in 1963. Meg graduated with an M.A. at the same time with our four children looking on. Wanting to return to Nigeria, we joined Wycliffe Bible Translators but found that they would not send us back to Nigeria. So, with great curiosity over what God was doing in our lives, we felt we should accept the offer of Michigan State University to join their African Studies faculty to teach Hausa, African linguistics and related subjects. This we did for four of the next five years (1963-68) with one year (1966-67) spent under the auspices of MSU in northern

Nigeria, collecting language data and reconciling with the leaders of our former mission.

Our five years at Michigan State were followed by an invitation to teach African languages and linguistics in the prestigious African Studies program at UCLA. We went there in the summer of 1968, assuming that my future lay in dealing with African languages and working unofficially with missionaries from a university position. But then came a "divine appointment" that would change our professional path and the rest of our lives as well. We decided to renew our acquaintance with Ralph and Roberta Winter.

SWM

In early 1969, we invited Ralph and Roberta to come share a Sunday noon meal with us at the home we were renting in West Los Angeles. Meg and I learned quite a lot about SWM that afternoon but were rather startled near the end of our time together to hear Ralph ask, "Would you ever consider teaching at the School of World Mission?" Though surprised by the question, I remember saying something like, "Well, we've never felt that God has rescinded our call to be missionaries, so we'd consider it." That discussion issued in a meeting with the SWM faculty (McGavran, Tippett and Winter), followed by a lecture to the SWM students. McGavran had read and been impressed with an article of mine published in *Practical Anthropology* in 1963, entitled "Conversion: Cultural or Christian?" So, my name was known to him. But we had had no other contact prior to this time and I only knew McGavran from having read *Bridges of God.* I did not know Tippett at all, even by reputation.

The meetings and the lecture all went well and were followed by an offer to join the SWM faculty, contingent, of course, on passing the "theology exam" required by the Fuller administration. I passed the exam.

Since UCLA wanted me to stay, I arranged to continue teaching there full-time with my classes on Mondays and Wednesdays while scheduling my Fuller teaching on Tuesdays and Thursdays. I was to be paid half-time at Fuller, but McGavran assigned me a full-time teaching load! So for the next four years (1969-73), I taught a full-time load at both places!

The SWM faculty were interested in what I could contribute in the anthropological area and also in dealing with Africa. With Tippett's help, I worked out an introductory course and one on culture change. Tippett then moved to more advanced topics. I was also assigned a course McGavran titled, "Conversion With a Minimum of Social Dislocation" and an Africa Area course.

The anthropology courses eventually led to the publication of one of my major works, *Anthropology for Christian Witness* (Orbis 1996). In this book I attempt to show what an anthropological approach based on Christian presuppositions can look like and can contribute to the cause. I also introduced communication theory into Church Growth Missiology, both in my classes on intercultural communication and in another of my books, *Communication Theory for Christian Witness* (Nelson 1983, revised edition Orbis 1991).

But neither of these would be considered my *magnum opus*. That would be *Christianity in Culture* (Orbis 1979, revised edition 2005) in which I attempt to develop what I have called "Ethnotheology," a crosscultural approach to theological interpretation. In this book I presented an early evangelical approach to contextualization based on my own attempts to integrate what I had learned of theology and anthropology with what I had learned of how to deal with biblical data in a nonwestern context. In some ways it is an angry book, developed out of the frustration of working in a mission approach I called "extractionist" in contrast with Jesus' approach that I called "identificational" or "incarnational."

In addition to *Christianity in Culture,* my approach to contextualization is developed in articles such as "Conversion: Cultural or Christian?" (1963) and "The Contextualization of Theology" (1978) and especially in the book *Appropriate Christianity* (2005) that I edited and to which I contributed eleven chapters. I have published a collection of my articles over the years and a fairly complete bibliography in *Culture, Communication and Christianity* (2001).

Since 1982, I have added a focus on spiritual power to my approach to missiology, in recognition of the fact that most of the peoples of the world are more concerned with spiritual power than with the kind of intellectualized Christianity we often bring. From my point of view, an incarnational approach to contextualization demands that we do as Jesus did—healing, delivering people from demons and conducting missions as spiritual warfare—as well as teaching what Jesus taught. I have listed two of my publications in this area in the Bibliography (1989, 2002).

I will deal with the events that led Wagner and myself to emphasize spiritual power in our lives, ministries and missiological theorizing in Chapter 7, the Pierson Era I.

Arthur F. Glasser (1914—)
At Fuller: 1970-1999

Arthur Glasser was born in 1914, the second son of a medical doctor practicing in upstate New York. His childhood was spent in Paterson, N.J. where he attended elementary and high school. He says of himself, "I was extremely nominal as a church person until that wonderful summer just prior to going to Cornell University" (1990:112). That summer at a Keswick Bible Conference he met Christ and that decision, he goes on to say, "brought an entirely new orientation to all realities." He went on to attend Cornell University, growing in his faith and graduating in 1937 with a degree in engineering. From there he took a position in Pittsburg with an engineering firm, enjoying his work and giving the church all his spare time.

During that time, however, Glasser developed a strong commitment to taking the Gospel to the lost. So he turned aside from what he had assumed would be his life's work and, in 1939, entered Faith Seminary (B.D. 1942) with the goal of becoming a missionary. There he was radicalized. He says, "I was determined to put all heart and conscience to telling forth the Gospel—on the streets, if need be" (ibid.:112). This he literally did, spending weekends and summers witnessing and preaching on the streets to Jews as a volunteer with the New York Bible Society during the years Hitler was tormenting the Jews in Germany. This last fact contributed to Glasser's growing concern that Christians live out their faith in the context of needy people.

His plan now was to give his life for Jewish evangelism but, it seemed, the Lord wouldn't allow this. Instead, within a week after his graduation he began a stint that would take him to the South Pacific for two years as a Marine chaplain. While in the States preparing to go abroad, however, he married Alice in 1942. Glasser writes, "God gave me Alice, the blessing above blessings—a wonderful wife committed to Christ and to missions, gracious and attractive, and clear in her head" (1990:113). Three weeks after their wedding, however, Glasser was off to the South Pacific.

Glasser's experience in the South Pacific, where he served in areas of heavy combat and had the privilege of leading a number of Marines to faith in Christ, confirmed his call to missionary service. Seeing so many so close to eternity without Christ left an indelible impression on him. So he and Alice offered themselves for service in China under China Inland Mission, landing there at the end of 1946. They were sent to southwest China, eventually being assigned to a tribal group, many of whom had come to Christ through a large people movement. Though they would have gladly stayed there for the rest of their lives, the Communist takeover of China eventually forced them to leave in 1951.

Both the Marine experience and their time in China with a mission made up of missionaries from quite a variety of church and theological traditions had a broadening influence on Art. His later concern that evangelicals be serious about such things as what he called "the cultural mandate" as well as about the "evangelistic mandate" had its roots here. Such a concern took him a long way from the extremely rigid perspective he was taught at Faith Seminary. He approached this broader concept of Christian mission, however, with the same passion he had shown in doing street evangelism in New York City. Glasser was given to asking difficult questions concerning the impact of Christianity on societies such as Communist China and Hitler's Germany. Though he was serious about church growth, his greater concern, as he developed it theologically, was for the growth of the Kingdom. This was the core of what he brought to Fuller.

After China, he taught for four years at Columbia Bible College and then was appointed Candidate Secretary for the US and Canada for China Inland Mission (now renamed Overseas Missionary Fellowship). For the next 15 years he lived in Philadelphia working for CIM/OMF and teaching missions at Westminster Seminary. In addition, he was a favorite speaker at the triennial InterVarsity Urbana Missionary Conferences. There and elsewhere, he spoke and wrote effectively on topics related to the biblical basis for missionary involvement. One of his books, co-authored with Eric Fife was *The*

Crisis in Missions (1960). This was a fine interpretation of the "new day" in missions and was widely read.

Paul Pierson writes concerning these post-China years,

> These were years of reflection. . . . Arthur went far beyond most evangelicals in raising key issues for Christian missions. Writing in a spirit of humility, wanting to hear God speak to the church through its apparent defeat in China, he said that missionaries should reject any lingering paternalism and strongly encourage national leadership. Secondly, while he affirmed the necessity of communicating the center of the gospel, criticizing liberals for their one-sided social gospel, he also scolded evangelicals for failing to teach the "whole counsel of God contained in Scripture," for erecting a false antithesis between the material and the spiritual worlds, and for failing to transmit the deeply rooted social concerns of both the Old and New Testaments. Anticipating a number of emphases that would receive attention in subsequent decades, he called for a greater focus on the unreached, more concern for the urban centers, emphasis on non-Caucasian missionaries, a more positive approach to Chinese culture, and greater recognition of the Pentecostal movement. Missionaries had been far too naïve about Western imperialism, he said, but he still expressed his confidence in the sovereignty of God, working in China and the church here (1993:5).

Moving to SWM

As mentioned, our faculty was looking for a theologian and a Dean to succeed McGavran. McGavran had become aware of Glasser from his writings and lectures and was impressed with both his commitment and his skill in using the whole Bible, not simply a few verses, to support the missionary enterprise. Keenly aware of the criticism of the Church Growth Movement for its lack of theological sophistication, McGavran set his sights on attracting Glasser as the theologically and Biblically-oriented thinker he wanted to join us. I suspect there was extensive correspondence going on during this time between McGavran and Glasser concerning the possibility of Glasser's coming.

Glasser had already decided to do something different and had resigned his position with OMF. Opting for further study, then, he enrolled in a Th.M. program at Union Seminary in New York City, studying with a liberal Dutch theologian of mission, Hans Hoekendijk. He also studied Chinese culture at Columbia University and put in some time at the Jewish Seminary. So he spent the year 1969-70 studying and beefing up his credentials for whatever he was to do next.

He says,

> I was rescued from great uncertainty touching my future by a call to join the faculty of the School of World Mission at Fuller Theological Seminary. At once, I found myself among like-minded colleagues and began struggling with them. Overnight I was caught up in the growing ferment of church growth and the need to make sure that researching local situations must precede all strategizing. Furthermore, I found it folly to expect all churches everywhere to seek the same agenda. This led to new insight into the evangelical obligation to make laboring for church renewal a top priority, equal in importance to the task of planting new churches. . . . All churches, new and old, need to be brought to the place where the renewing of the Holy Spirit is both sought and cherished (1990:114).

Glasser added to our curriculum courses such as Biblical Foundations of Mission, The Church in Hostile Environments, Theology of Religious Encounter and Ecumenics and Mission. Though he lacked a theological doctorate, Glasser read voraciously and was able to hold his own with the best scholars in dealing with current theological issues, including Roman Catholic and Eastern Orthodox theology. He was a spellbinding teacher, especially adept at using various colored pens on the overhead to illustrate his points! His ability to find the mission of God in every part of Scripture, from Genesis to Revelation was phenomenal. He made Scripture live with missionary motivation and activity.

His constant theme was the Kingdom of God, relating the Church to the Kingdom as God's means to the Kingdom end. He thus broadened Church Growth theory from a focus on the Church to a focus on the Kingdom. In this way, he sought to avoid the dichotomy between evangelism and social action by combining within a Kingdom emphasis "the evangelistic mandate" with "the cultural mandate." Though his passion to win the lost was no less than McGavran's, Art was a bridge builder rather than the kind of enthusiast who alienates people. He was strong on the need to relate to both evangelicals and ecumenists, though in private he could be very critical of the latter. As mentioned, he also sought to bridge between an emphasis on evangelism and a commitment to social action.

He was, of course, committed to Chinese evangelism and, after his retirement from the deanship, was active in getting a Chinese study program started in SWM. But in his later years before retirement, it was still Jewish evangelism that was his greatest passion. Indeed, he was so prone to turn any discussion to God's concern for the Jews that we used to joke about just how many seconds it would take him whenever he began to talk to mention the Jews! But he was also concerned about Muslims, and sponsored in 1978 what we called "the year of the Muslim," a year devoted to a special emphasis on Muslim evangelism at SWM. That year he was a prime mover in establishing the Samuel Zwemer Institute, headed by Don McCurry, with Art's daughter Carol as administrative assistant.

In a brilliant summary of Glasser's life and contributions, Pierson, Glasser's colleague and successor as Dean, writes,

> His conversion took place in a warmly pietistic context which focused on the importance of personal faith in Jesus Christ as the only way to personal salvation, coupled with a high view of Scripture. These concepts have continued to be central in his thought, even as his understanding has grown that the gospel must be seen as good news for the poor and the oppressed in this life as well. . . .

> He wished that his mission—and others—had shown greater love for Chinese culture and traditions, had moved more aggressively to build up the Chinese Church and its leadership, and been more holistic in its approach. Thus he longed to see missionaries better prepared. This would become an important aspect of his ministry at Fuller.

> His broadening understanding of the church has been remarkable. Graduating from a seminary on the extreme edge of the separatist movement, he has discovered and affirmed Christians in a variety of traditions without compromising his own deeply held evangelical convictions. . . .

> Glasser's pilgrimage eventually led to what he would term a "Copernican revolution" in his theology, the rediscovery of the biblical motif of the Kingdom of God. Secularized by the social gospel movement, pushed safely into the future by fundamentalist dispensationalism, and ignored by most others, the Kingdom of God provided a unifying framework for the understanding of conversion and the Christian life, of mission, and the church. Glasser also believed it could provide a common meeting ground for evangelical/ ecumenical discussions. . . .

How to characterize such a unique individual? Central to his life's pilgrimage has been the desire to be a thoroughly biblical Christian, and such a person never fits into neat categories. His focus on the incarnation, the cross, the resurrection, and the lordship of Christ are central to his faith and life. That is accompanied by a strong conviction regarding the authority of Scripture and his desire to study, reflect, understand, and live out its mandates. With this goes a passionate concern that men and women everywhere, of every race, language, and culture, have the opportunity to know Christ and become His disciples. . . .

Strong and secure at the center, he has not been afraid to relate to those with whom he differed theologically, nor has he feared to examine any number of issues in the light of the gospel. In his eagerness to continue to learn and discover new aspects of the truth, and in his refreshing humility and contagious enthusiasm, Arthur Glasser has been a constant stimulus and friend to his faculty colleagues. We will forever be in his debt (1993:8-9).

Glasser was a prolific writer of articles but only did a few books. A complete bibliography up to 1993 is contained in Van Engen, et al *The Good News of the Kingdom* (1993). His articles show some of the breadth of his interests. Among them are "Church Growth and Theology" (1973), "What is 'Mission' Today?" (1974), *Contemporary Theologies of Mission* (with McGavran 1983), "The Evolution of Evangelical Mission Theology Since World War II" (1985), "Old Testament Contextualization" (1989) and "Evangelical Objections to Jewish Evangelism" (1991-2). His magnum opus, then, is *Announcing the Kingdom* (2003), published with help from some of his Fuller colleagues.

C. Peter Wagner (1930—)
At Fuller: 1971-1999

Peter Wagner was born in 1930 in New York City. His father struggled for work during the depression, ending up in the retail business. This entailed frequent moves from department store to department store so that Peter, through his 12 years of schooling, had attended 13 schools in four states. Desiring to plant his roots in a hometown of some kind, he adopted his father's birthplace, St. Johnsville, NY, where he spent every summer from age 5 working on farms. He was bicultural, both urban and rural, but he chose the rural culture as primary and enrolled in the College of Agriculture at

Rutgers University, expecting to go into a career in dairy farming (email: 4/22/04).

At Rutgers he distinguished himself for his ability to hold large amounts of liquor! He also was noted for the amount of profanity he regularly used. He calls himself "a committed heathen, dedicated to fulfilling the desires of my flesh in as respectable a way as possible" (2001:164). He says,

> I cannot recall ever hearing about the Gospel or even knowing a Christian friend before I went to Rutgers. I soon fell into the lifestyle of a fraternity party boy, with alcohol the drug of choice in those days. Then things changed. During the summer between my sophomore and junior years, I was milking a cow on the farm where I was working when into the barn walked an old friend of mine with a farm girl his age named Doris, also from St. Johnsville although we had never met. I was immediately attracted to her, and I playfully squirted a stream of milk on her bare toe. When I saw how well she took it, I decided to marry her.

> Not much time passed before I asked Doris to marry me. She said, "I can't." I said, "Why not?" She replied, "Because I'm a born again Christian and I promised God that I would only marry a Christian." So I said, "Well, what does it take to be a Christian? Can you help me?" She said, "Yes, but there is one more thing. I promised God that I would be a missionary." I said, "Missionary? What's that?" So she explained what a missionary was, assuring me that there were cows on the mission field. I said, "That sounds good to me. I think I'll be a missionary also." So we got down on our knees in that farmhouse and I accepted Christ and dedicated my life to be a missionary the same night! (email: 4/22/04).

In order to prepare for missionary service, Peter and Doris trekked from New Jersey to the west coast, he to attend Fuller Seminary, she to go to Biola. Wagner graduated from Fuller in 1955 with an M.Div, having absorbed all of the meager missionary training offered at that time in the School of Theology. In 1956, he and Doris then went to Bolivia in response to a call from South American Indian Mission for someone trained in agriculture. Their involvement in agricultural work was, however, short-lived. Peter records, "even before I had mastered Spanish, I was assigned to be the director of a new Bible institute for training pastors. No one else on the field had graduated from a seminary, and I was considered the most qualified" (ibid.:164). So he began to teach what he had learned at Fuller, noting, however, that what was taught did not produce effective Bolivian pastors. He was also involved in planting a church that, to Peter's surprise is still "doing well for a church in a rural community."

In their second term they "transferred" to the Bolivian Indian Mission (later renamed Andes Evangelical Mission, now a part of SIM International) and Wagner taught in a seminary. Again, though, he taught with an essentially North American approach. He eventually became field director of that mission but with an uneasiness about the relevance of what the mission was doing.

This uneasiness led to the Wagners spending their 1966-67 furlough back at Fuller, but this time to study under McGavran in the newly established SWM. Peter had read *Bridges of God* in Bolivia and been impressed with McGavran's insights. So he decided to return to his *alma mater* to learn what McGavran had to offer. As was McGavran's custom with students he was especially impressed with, he engaged Peter to teach as an adjunct in 1968. This experience led to McGavran inviting Peter to join the faculty, an offer Wagner resisted at first but finally accepted.

Peter is a very enthusiastic person. When he returned to the field after his year at Fuller, he was zealous about implementing what he had learned. One of the ideas he had learned was Theological Education by Extension. Upon his return to Bolivia, he sponsored a major conference for all the missions. Winter was one of the presenters with 140 attendees. The conference was very efficiently organized and had a considerable impact on those who attended. A major part of Wagner's reticence to accept McGavran's invitation to come to SWM was the fact that he now had a much better understanding of mission and the opportunity to put the new ideas into operation.

Wagner's explanation of why he resisted coming to Fuller provides another insight into how God leads. In an email to me dated April 5, 2004, Peter says,

> It is true that I resisted the invitation to teach, but later accepted. The reason behind the resistance was that, when I was there 1966-67, I was alarmed at the liberal directions I saw the School of Theology taking. I knew that McGavran couldn't lead SWM very much longer, keeping the strong emphasis on biblical evangelism and fulfilling the Great Commission that he had maintained so far. But my hesitation came in not knowing

whether his successor would be seduced into a more liberal, social-action School of Theology stream. Virtually the day after I heard that Glasser would be McGavran's successor, I had all the confidence in the world that SWM was in good hands, and I began to pack my bags (email: 4/5/04).

He joined us for the academic year 1971-72 to teach Latin American subjects and to understudy McGavran in the Church Growth area. Thus by 1971, the six faculty McGavran had envisaged were all on board.

Wagner's Contribution to SWM

Wagner came on as McGavran's understudy, a second person in Church Growth. McGavran was nearing the end of his teaching days, though he did some teaching through the remainder of the 70s and retained his office until shortly before his death in 1990. So Peter soon began to teach the Church Growth courses and to put his own stamp on them, moving more and more over the years into a primary focus on American church growth since, as Wagner says, his ministry and research context had now become the USA rather than Bolivia.

Though Wagner, like Glasser, had come from a very conservative background, one that was quite suspicious even of Fuller, under McGavran's influence he had begun to broaden. McGavran taught him to study growing churches to try to discover what it was that was making (or allowing) them to grow. Since Peter worked in Latin America, this meant studying Pentecostal churches, since they were the most rapidly growing churches. This posed a problem for Wagner who was personally anti-Pentecostal and, as he admits, "I had become a chief adversary of the Pentecostal leaders in Bolivia" (2001:166). Indeed, his mission required that he be at least non- if not anti-Pentecostal. However, when he returned to Bolivia after a year with McGavran, he began to study Latin American Pentecostalism. He says of this challenge,

> So, my work was cut out for me. First, I had to make friends with my Pentecostal adversaries. Then, I had to research those churches earnestly, which I did. I was surprised at the quality of the believers and the leaders that I found there. I thought I would have plenty of theology to teach them, but instead I found myself learning new theology that turned out to be more biblical than some of mine. I soon realized I was getting in touch with the cutting edge of the kingdom of God at

the time, and I recorded my findings in a book, *Look Out! The Pentecostals Are Coming!* (2001:166).

Wagner was faithful to his mentor, opening himself up to research and study into the reasons for valid church growth, no matter what the denomination. For the first few years of Wagner's time with us, he stuck pretty close to McGavran's approach, doing theory and case studies pretty much as McGavran had patterned things. He delineates the issues that became important to him and that he contributed to SWM as follows:

> McGavran's missiological pragmatism pointed the future direction of my pilgrimage in mission. If God wants the lost sheep found, let's do what it takes to find them and bring them into the fold. If this task involves stimulating people movements or using numbers or gauging resistance and receptivity or identifying unreached people groups or dismissing unproductive missionaries or incorporating anthropological insights or redefining evangelism and mission or rejecting universalist theology or advocating the homogeneous unit principle or scorning biological and transfer growth or drawing a line between discipling and perfecting—so be it! If increased numbers of lost souls were saved and brought into life-giving churches, I was ready for all of the above and more (2001:166).

Wagner was a true disciple of McGavran. He applied church growth principles in Latin America when he was living there. The context in which he was living when he moved to SWM was, however, America. So, in the mid-70s his crosscultural instincts led him to ask, "I wonder if church growth principles apply to American churches?" To test the possibility, he arranged to teach a modified version of his basic church growth course to a group of practicing American pastors at Lake Avenue Congregational Church. Reluctantly, McGavran agreed to team-teach with him. The course was a resounding success.

When Wagner moved to Pasadena from Bolivia, he was asked to head up the Fuller Evangelistic Association in return for which two-thirds of his Fuller salary was paid by FEA. This was an organization started by Charles E. Fuller to distribute endowment funds to organizations involved in world evangelization. Charles E., when he died, left FEA in his son Daniel's hands. However, Dan, who at this time was Dean of the School of Theology, had no taste for administering FEA and so was happy to have Peter take it over. So Peter was to teach at SWM full-time but also to administer FEA.

This position at FEA allowed Peter to travel extensively over the next several years, distributing FEA funds for world evangelization. As the available funds diminished in the mid-seventies, though, he looked for a new vision for FEA. By that time Wagner was deeply involved in American church growth and teaching church growth in the Doctor of Ministry program under the School of Theology, largely to American pastors. In one of these courses, he met a Quaker pastor named John Wimber. Peter and John bonded and Wagner invited John to join him in birthing a sub-unit of FEA designed to focus on strengthening churches across America with church growth principles. This sub-unit would be called the Charles E. Fuller Institute of Evangelism and Church Growth (CEFI). For the next several years, Peter and John went around the country planting church growth seeds widely.

Though McGavran also gave some of his attention to church growth in America, he was disappointed that Wagner no longer gave his major attention to church growth in nonwestern contexts. Perhaps partially for this reason and partially for other reasons, the stream of nonwestern church growth studies published while McGavran was at Eugene and in the early years at Fuller began to taper off—though studies of American church growth began to proliferate. This enthusiastic reception and application of Church Growth theory by American pastors and churches has provided an energy on the American church scene probably not experienced since the Awakenings of the seventeenth and eighteenth centuries. It looks, therefore, as though God has been in the American Church Growth Movement and in Wagner's influence on it.

One important factor in the application of church growth thinking to American churches was the fact that Wagner began to teach in the Fuller Doctor of Ministry program. This program is for experienced pastors and the emphasis on church growth soon began to attract the attention of this group as they sought to attain doctorates. Peter's classes became the most popular classes in the D.Min. curriculum and the number of theses dealing with church growth issues often outnumbered all the rest of the topics combined.

In 1974, Wagner enrolled in a Ph.D. program at the University of Southern California. He and Glasser—two of the six of us—had joined us without Ph.D.s. This put limits on us as we began to offer doctorates. So Peter felt it necessary to upgrade his academic credentials. The area he chose to work in was Social Ethics. He completed his work quickly and was awarded the Ph.D. in 1977 with a dissertation entitled *The Ethical Dimensions of the Homogeneous Unit Principle of Church Growth*, later published under the title *Our Kind of People* (Knox 1979). This study broadened our base by giving us competency to supervise research in another area.

A major area of Wagner's contribution to SWM lies in his movement into researching and practicing the spiritual dimensions of Christianity and Church Growth. Wagner now calls the approach he took to church growth study and teaching during the '70s "technical church growth" (ibid.:166) "because around 1980 it had become clear to me that there must have been a concomitant spiritual dimension to church growth that Donald McGavran had not particularly emphasized in his teaching and writing" (ibid.:166). He discussed this with McGavran, however, and found that if he was to pursue the spiritual factor in church growth, he would have to go it alone. This he has been doing, especially since 1982.

I discuss the events of 1982 and beyond below under the Pierson Era. Suffice it to say here that it was Wagner who brought John Wimber onto the scene. And it has been Wagner who, through his books and teaching, has been the main articulator of the incorporation of spiritual power into evangelicalism. It is Wagner that we can thank for the fact that Fuller, a major evangelical seminary with roots in Reformed Theology has for over 20 years now become a center for the teaching and practice of the power dimension of the Great Commission—a dimension that for generations has been ignored by Evangelicals.

Few would argue that this power dimension is not of great importance for missiology. Most of the peoples of the world are power-oriented. The fact that Evangelicals, in spite of Jesus' example, have usually presented the Gospel philosophically (theologically) rather than with spiritual power, means that we have not been "speaking the language" of most of the peoples of the world. We believe and teach contextualization. Presenting the Gospel as Jesus did with healing, deliverance and other power demonstrations is perhaps the major missing facet of a truly incarnational, contextualized approach to biblical Christianity. Wagner stands for this and we are ever grateful to him for pioneering in this area. I have partnered with him, but could never have done the job as well as he has.

Among Peter's contributions is the fact that he has published more than all the rest of us combined. At this writing, he has published (written and edited) a total of 66 (!) books, mostly dealing with Church Growth and spiritual power. The five he rates most significant are *Your Church Can Grow: Seven Vital Signs of a Healthy Church* (1976, 1984), *Your Spiritual Gifts Can Help Your Church Grow* (1979, 1994, 2005), *Confronting the Powers* (1996), *Churchquake! How the New Apostolic Reformation is Shaking up the Church as We Know It* (1999) and *Acts of the Holy Spirit: A Modern Commentary on the Book of Acts* (2000).

Peter left SWM in 1999 to pursue power ministry more freely than was possible at Fuller. We miss him.

Summary of the McGavran Era

By 1971, the original configuration of SWM was complete—six faculty members, a student body of 67 career missionaries, a core curriculum of Church Growth, Missiological Theology, Anthropology, History and Animism, a set of offices in a newly constructed part of Payton Hall, regular Church Growth Seminars in the Midwest and the West coast and widespread acceptance within the missionary community of the Church Growth point of view. We were able to offer a masters degree built on an M.Div.—the equivalent of a Th.M., though at this time we called it an M.A. and proudly guided students in their research and thesis writing on Church Growth topics. We chafed a bit over various aspects of our need to accommodate our commitment to the cause of missions to the restrictions of an academic institution. Among the things that bothered us most was the fact that we were not allowed to offer a Ph.D. But, in general, we were feeling pretty good.

McGavran was ready to hand over the deanship to Glasser. He did not, however, relax his advocacy of Church Growth Missiology nor his abrasiveness in relating to those who opposed him. He still worked hard at recruiting, writing and teaching, slacking off only slightly as he approached 90 years of age. And he still made pronouncements for us all, usually without checking to find out whether or not we were really with him. Tippett, for his part, was actively engaged in teaching, writing and supervising research. He was frequently assigned by McGavran to lecture or write on some topic in support of Church Growth, or prompted to write or lecture by a feeling that McGavran was vulnerable at some point and needed his help (e.g. his book *The Biblical Basis of Church Growth*). He frequently complained about the fact that he had to do things for "Mac" rather than doing his own things. But he carried out these responsibilities well and probably, in his perfectionism, would not have written so much without such a push from our leader.

Winter was rapidly developing his approach to history and extending his influence both in Theological Education by Extension and in History nationally and internationally. Whereas McGavran was a tireless letter-writer, Winter regularly ran up incredible phone bills. He was also getting William Carey Library going, providing the kind of outlet for Church Growth books that we felt we needed. Orr was doing his courses on revivals and the discussion between him and McGavran over whether revival came before or after church growth was a fairly frequent topic when we got together. I was getting into the picture as the "first stop" for students in dealing with the relationships between Christianity and culture—delighted to be doing something that really counts, rather than the African linguistics I was doing at UCLA. Though I was doing the core courses on anthropology and culture change, I was becoming more and more concerned with what we now call contextualization in courses on conversion, indigeneity and Christianity and culture.

Glasser was settling in as a teacher and learning to be Dean. His approach to the theology of mission with the Kingdom of God rather than the Church as the primary context was refreshing for the students and broadening for Church Growth Missiology. McGavran's approach was to use the term Church, as if the Church, often interpreted as local congregations, is to be the final goal of Christian activity, as indeed it is in his Campbellite church tradition. He meant more than this, of course, and used Church as a near synonym of Kingdom. Glasser made the Kingdom emphasis explicit and I think we would have done well to develop Church Growth theory to take greater recognition of the fact that, Biblically, the Church is to serve the Kingdom. We might well have changed our emphasis from Church Growth to Kingdom Growth. Whether or not this would have helped the movement to deal with some of our critics we'll never know.

Wagner was just joining us at this time and was pretty much learning the ropes and walking in McGavran's tracks. In a couple of years, though, he emerged from under McGavran's shadow and established himself first as a stout defender of the "homogeneous unit principle" (HUP) and then with regard to American church growth. The HUP was a term McGavran used to focus attention on the fact that people group together with people of like mind, usually with others of their same ethnic and linguistic group. Peter studied this principle as his Ph.D. project and, when he got into American church growth, broadened it to deal with sociological groupings other than strictly ethnic groups within the American scene.

The story of this period would not be complete without mentioning Mary McGavran's considerable role in making people feel comfortable. In contrast to Dr. McGavran's drivenness, Mary was gifted at hospitality and encouragement, especially for the women. Many is the student who came from afar who can attest to the fact that it was one or more overnights enjoying Mary's hospitality that made all the difference at the start of their time as SWM. And many is the woman whose loneliness caused by her husband's study program who can point to Mary's ministry to the women as the major factor in keeping her sane. So, during this era we praise God for both Donald McGavran and his singleminded commitment to the cause of mission and for Mary McGavran for her warmth and ministry to the women of SWM.

Another feature of this time period was the Friday evening get-togethers during which students would take turns in presenting analyses of their mission work. These were fellowship times involving meaningful semi-formal interactions with both students and faculty participating to critique the various missionary situations represented in our student body. Those studying with us in those days often found as much profit emerging from these Friday evening sessions as they did from the classes.

We turn now to SWM after the McGavran Era.

Chapter 6

The Glasser Era

1971-1980

By the fall of 1971, the foundations had been laid, the six faculty members originally envisioned were in place, students were coming, we were being noticed, Glasser, designated to be our next Dean was here, we even had new offices. Our spirits were good and we forged optimistically into the next era.

What students found as we spent several days together during orientation week was a confident, enthusiastic McGavran, his dream being realized, a solid, scholarly Tippett who, though not always intelligible, was always impressive and an attractive supporting cast of Winter, Kraft, Glasser and newly arrived Wagner.

In those days, we spent fully four days together with the incoming students and their wives at the beginning of each fall term, with some sessions for the returnees as well. Each of us faculty members made one or more presentations demonstrating our contributions to the overall perspective. Though we were known for McGavran's concept of Church Growth, we had broadened considerably as we looked into cultural, historical and theological ramifications of how people come to Christ and how, therefore, we should be presenting the Gospel. I feel we've lost something now in not having the kind of orientation program we had in those early days.

I think the death knell for these orientation programs was sounded, however, when some of us got too technical for the beginning students. I remember one presentation by Tippett on "models" that was so far beyond where these incoming students were that no one (including most of us faculty members) could understand very much of what he was saying. I think the year of that lecture was the year these programs were terminated. Rightly or wrongly it was decided not to take the risk of another such lecture with the possibility that it might scare students off!

At the start of SWM/ICG's existence at Fuller, the Dean (McGavran) was given a small office near to that of the Dean of Theology (Dan Fuller), with the offices of Tippett and Winter in other places on campus. By the time I joined the faculty in the fall of 1969, we had moved to the old house across Oakland Avenue that now houses the student meeting and eating place called "the Catalyst." In many ways, this was an ideal setting with our offices in the various rooms on the first floor each opening into the central room that once served as the living room of the house. Whenever we stepped out of our offices, then, we would often run into each other in that central room. This setting contributed greatly to our *esprit de corps*. We lost something when, in 1971, they built a kind of bridge between the library and the main part of Payton Hall with offices on it that they turned over to us. From then on (to the present) our offices were/are lined up in a line rather than in a circle, requiring more intentionality to meet each other.

This office arrangement was intended to be temporary—just until a new building could be built for us on the corner of Union and Oakland, now the south entrance to the Fuller campus. That building was expected to be mostly funded by the Presbyterian Board of Missions who would sell a Pasadena property called "Hope House" that they maintained for furloughing missionaries and put that money into the new building. The new building, then, would house the SWM offices on the lower floors with two upper floors devoted to housing units for international students. This project never got past the dream stage, however, reportedly because the New York office of the Presbyterian Church felt we were too evangelical to warrant their support.

Glasser as Dean

Glasser joined a fairly focused group. We each were committed to the vision of churches that were both biblical and well-related to the peoples they served. We worked with a core curriculum that provided instruction in Church Growth (McGavran and Wagner), Theology of Mission (Glasser), Anthropology (Kraft), History (Winter) and Animism (Tippett). Our student body was made up largely of career missionaries looking to be retrained in order to be more effective in ministries they were already engaged in. The ship was sailing smoothly.

Oh, we had some differences. But we gladly submerged them for the sake of the cause. We all chafed under the restrictions imposed upon us by virtue of the fact that we were a part of a seminary. Rightly or wrongly, we saw ourselves as unappreciated by most of the rest of the seminary and frequently discussed what it might be like to be independent. But we had agreeable colleagues, hungry students, an important Cause to serve and a stable administration over us. So we really had little of substance to complain about.

Glasser, then, moved into an enviable situation as Dean. In addition, he had had a year with us before he took over to get used to that situation. So the transition was smooth and the ship continued to sail with little to bother it, at least for the first half of the decade.

During the latter half of this period, the entrepreneurial tendencies of several of us began to manifest themselves. McGavran, of course, was an entrepreneur of the first water and was given to volunteering us for various tasks related to our Cause. Winter, then, was exercising his creativity in a number of directions (see below). Glasser, too, had items on his agenda such as a Chinese program and a Jewish program. I was anxious to see us develop a Bible translation program and Wagner began his movement into American Church Growth.

We remained quite stable, however, in spite of the loss of Winter and Tippett and the changes required by the gain of the Brewsters, Hiebert and Gilliland. By 1980, then, we had two of us in Theology (Glasser and Gilliland), two in Anthropology (Kraft and Hiebert), two in Church Growth (McGavran and Wagner) and a Language Acquisition team (the Brewsters) but no Historian. With adjuncts, though, we also had Theological Education by Extension (Holland) and Islamics (McCurry) plus the "In Service Program" that sent our courses out on tape to missionaries overseas. More on these aspects of the Glasser Era below.

Glenn Schwartz

Within a year or so after Glasser took over, it became apparent that the administrative load was more than Art could handle alone. We recommended, then, that he find someone to assist him. In our student body, just finishing up his M.A., was a missionary named Glenn Schwartz who had worked in Zambia with the Brethren in Christ Mission.   Glenn was hired as Glasser's Administrative Assistant and International Student Advisor in 1973. The smoothness of our ride, then, was in no small part due to the partnership in administration between Glasser and Schwartz. Glenn had a lot to do with our successes during this period until he left that position in 1979.

Glasser was more scholar than administrator and depended on Glenn for most of the routine administrative matters. Glenn was good at what he did and a great help to Glasser, allowing him to devote more of his attention to academic things and less to administration. He carried most of the administrative load during the Glasser era and also served well as student advisor.   Many students (especially international students) during this time were helped greatly by Schwartz's advocacy both at entrance and when difficulties arose relating to their studies or living arrangements.   The advising load soon became greater than he could handle, however, so we hired Laura Raab who ably handled the students' concerns.

As Glasser's tenure as Dean was coming to an end, however, it was decided that the time had come for Glenn to move on also. He has since developed a very important ministry focused on assisting African churches to become self-supporting. The story of this era would not be complete, however, without noting the truly significant contribution Schwartz made to the continuance and growth of SWM.

Initiatives

As mentioned in our discussion of Ralph Winter's contributions to missiology, the American Society of Missiology was started in 1973, largely through the efforts of Winter and Gerald Anderson. The purpose of this society and its journal is to assure that the discipline of Missiology is represented, like other academic disciplines, by a society and a journal. The Society by design is made up of three distinguishable groups: Evangelical Protestants, Conciliar Protestants and Roman Catholics. It conducts annual meetings every June.

The first officers of the Society were Gerald Anderson, President and Ralph Winter, Secretary/Business Manager, with Alan Tippett the first editor of the journal *Missiology*.   They were originally appointed for three year terms, though now the President is elected annually. As mentioned above, the Society and its journal *Missiology* received a major assist when Winter was able to arrange for the 19 year old journal *Practical Anthropology* with its 3,000 subscribers to be absorbed into the new venture. The fact that Tippett was to be the editor assured the readers of *PA* that the important emphases of that journal would be continued in the new publication. When Tippett retired after three years, Glasser became the editor.

Our belief in education by extension plus a concern for the fact that missionaries in distant lands wanted to take our courses before coming to Pasadena led in 1974 to the inauguration of a Distance Learning Program (before that name came into vogue). We called our effort the "In Service Program." One of our students,

Martin, who had been a seminary president, was especially enthusiastic about supplying overseas missionaries with our courses, so we made him Director of the program. We were not very sophisticated at first. We simply recorded classroom sessions on audio tape (noise and all), packaged the tapes with whatever printed materials were used in the on-campus classes and sent them out. We were initially limited to granting credit for only the five core courses but this stricture was relaxed later.

Though the materials were often not well suited to distance education and the tapes were often of poor quality, student feedback indicated that lives and ministries were being changed through these courses. Our present Individualized Distance Learning (IDL) program is a great deal better technologically than the original program and continues to be a vehicle of God to change lives and ministries.

Fred Holland, a Brethren in Christ missionary in Zimbabwe and Zambia, came to us to teach TEE with Winter early in 1974 for five weeks. As a result of that teaching, Glasser invited him to return in the fall of 1974 to become a teaching fellow to team-teach Training the Ministry (the basic TEE course) with Winter and to study Church Growth. Fred had been much involved in the TEE ministry in Africa. He did workshops on TEE and programmed instruction throughout Africa and was involved in the translation and publication of programmed texts (now numbering over 40 books in over 170 languages). By 1976, when Winter left, we asked Fred to take over the teaching of TEE. This he did until 1981, expanding our course offerings by adding courses in writing programmed texts, administration of theological schools, research in theological education and church growth and the design of curriculum for TEE.

McGavran started the Institute of Church Growth to serve as a research and training center for career missionaries. The School of World Mission at Fuller was conceived of as continuing that emphasis. With this in mind, a minimum of three years of crosscultural experience was required as prerequisite to admission. Though we did admit a few who had not had field experience, there was no program for pre-field students. We had many faculty discussions concerning the problems we noticed in trying to meet the needs of pre-field people in classes primarily aimed at dealing with the concerns of experienced missionaries. One subject of discussion was the fact that we were receiving a certain amount of pressure from the administration to initiate a non-thesis degree, the reasoning being that such would bring in more money with less faculty effort. So, in the fall of 1975 we initiated what we called the Cross-Cultural Studies Program (CCSP) for pre-field people.

Our original idea was to provide separate classes for experienced crosscultural workers and for those without crosscultural experience. Though this increased the load for us as faculty, it worked well for the students. We could not, however, provide two completely separate streams, so in some of our courses we had both levels of students in the same classes. This changed the teaching and learning dynamics from what we were used to from the early days when our students were all experienced missionaries.

A further initiative was undertaken when, aware of the awesome challenge of the Muslim world, we designated 1978 "The Year of the Muslim." Don McCurry, a long-term Presbyterian missionary to Pakistan, was in our student body. Glasser in 1974 had promised Don that "if you come to study at SWM on your furlough, we will inaugurate 'The Year of the Muslim,' and will not look back" (McCurry email: 3/17/05). In addition, we invited Ken Bailey, a long-term missionary to Muslims and resident of Israel to come teach us about reaching Muslims. Gilliland was on our faculty and did his part also. This proved to be an enlightening year and resulted in our hiring of McCurry to teach on Muslim evangelism. The emphasis of that year also fed into a conference, jointly sponsored with World Vision, held at Glen Eyrie, Colorado on reaching Muslims with papers collected in the book *The Gospel and Islam* (1979), edited by McCurry. It also stimulated the founding of The Samuel Zwemer

Institute with McCurry as Executive Director and Glasser, Chairman of the Board. These events, then, prepared the way for the coming of Woodberry, first as an adjunct, then permanently in 1985, and the development of our present significant Islamics program.

The Broader Scene

A major event during this period was the Billy Graham sponsored meeting called the International Congress on World Evangelization in Lausanne, Switzerland in the summer of 1974. All of us were invited, though I had to choose between going to Lausanne and going to Nigeria to help my wife with her field research toward her D.Miss. degree. I chose to be with her back in a Kamwe village not far from where we had lived for two and a half years. I did the right thing and had a good summer renewing old acquaintances and helping Meg, but missed the major missiological event of the seventies.

Everyone who was anyone in evangelical missiology was at the Lausanne meeting and quite a few of the issues that were important to us were raised to the attention of the missionary world. In these meetings, the prominence of SWM in missiological thinking became obvious to many. As mentioned, one of the presentations that has received the most attention was that by Ralph Winter, entitled "The Highest Priority, Cross-Cultural Evangelism" that focused missiological attention on people groups rather than geographical regions. Others of note were McGavran's, "The Dimensions of World Evangelization," Tippett's workshop on "Evangelization Among Animists" and Wagner's on "Church Growth Principles."

The Lausanne meeting spawned the Lausanne Committee for World Evangelization that, with its various subcommittees became the major evangelical agency sponsoring missiological thinking and activity for the next fifteen years. Peter Wagner was named to the LCWE Central Committee of 48 individuals, and represented SWM in that body until 1989. Wagner became the founding chairman of the LCWE Strategy Working Group that connected with Ed Dayton of World Vision and pioneered the research on unreached peoples.

Leighton Ford provided leadership for LCWE which sponsored six more consultations and a large number of publications and other initiatives over these years. Among the consultations were Pasadena 1977 (Homogeneous Unit Principle), Willowbank 1978 (Gospel and

Culture), Glen Eyrie 1978 (Muslim Evangelism), Pattaya 1980 (Consultation on World Evangelization), Grand Rapids 1982 (Evangelism and Social Responsibility), Wheaton 1983 (The Church in Response to Human Need) and Manila 1989 (Lausanne II). The findings of each of these consultations were summarized in one or more Lausanne Committee publications. The Pasadena, Willowbank, Glen Eyrie and Pattaya meetings fall into this period and involved major SWM participation. The Willowbank meeting is mentioned below, since it dealt with contextualization.

By the time of Lausanne II (1989) in Manila, Thomas Wang, Director of LCWE, cast a new vision in a pivotal article entitled, "By the Year 2000: Is God Trying to Tell Us Something?" He partnered with Luis Bush to launch the AD2000 and Beyond Movement that in many ways replaced LCWE as the central catalytic agency for world evangelization during the decade of the 90s. AD2000 was built around ten semi-autonomous tracks, one of which was the United Prayer Track. Bush invited Peter Wagner to coordinate the prayer track, and that became one of Wagner's principal focuses of ministry during the 90s. This involvement moved him to begin wrestling seriously with the spiritual dimensions of church growth and world evangelization. This led to the establishing of Global Harvest Ministries which continues to constitute the base for Peter and his wife Doris' ministry at the time of this writing.

Contextualization

During this period a new word was birthed—contextualization. It was coined apparently by Shoki Coe of The World Council of Churches in 1972 and quickly embraced by conciliar missiologists. As Evangelicals, we were still wed to the term "indigenization," however, and were loathe to accept the new term lest we be aligned in people's minds with the extreme conciliar understandings of the aim of mission. We at SWM were, of course, committed to an incarnational approach to mission, but, in line with other Evangelicals, we continued to call it indigenization for a while.

For nearly a century, the guiding principle of the most culturally sensitive mission agencies was the so-called "Three Self Principle": self-support, self-government and self-propagation. As far back as 1958, however, William Smalley in a seminal article in *Practical Anthropology* entitled "Cultural Implications of an Indigenous

Church" had questioned the way the three selfs were ordinarily applied. He pointed out that if any or all three of these ideals were after western models, there is no way the church could be called indigenous. He noted that in many (probably most) cases, what the three selfs meant was self-support after western models, self-government after western models and self-propagation after western models. I taught a course on Indigeneity but by the early to mid-70s the word had become pretty heavily encumbered with assumptions of staticness and a "primitive" tribal mentality and was in need of a replacement that, hopefully, could be invested with more dynamic, receptor-oriented meanings.

So along came the concept of churches that are appropriate to their contexts, hence contextualized. We at SWM were in the forefront of thinking in these terms. Tippett wrote on the subject (see Tippett 1969, rev. 1973), I wrote on the subject (see Kraft 1979), Hiebert wrote on it in various places (e.g. 1984, 1985) and we appointed a professor (Gilliland) to make contextualization his major focus.

Among the major events signaling the acceptance by Evangelical missiologists of this new term and the dynamic concept with which it was invested were the Willowbank Consultation, sponsored by the Lausanne committee and an issue of *Evangelical Missions Quarterly*, both in January 1978. In the Willowbank Consultation, held at Willowbank, Bermuda, for the first time in contemporary missiological experience, anthropologists and theologians met together to hammer out some of the issues related to the contextualization of Christianity. The papers from the consultation were edited by John R.W. Stott and Robert T. Coote and published in 1979 under the title *Gospel and Culture*. The Foreword states,

> In January 1978 a group of 33 theologians, anthropologists, linguists, missionaries and pastors representing six continents met to study issues related to the question of "Gospel and Culture." The meeting, sponsored by the Theology and Education Group and the Strategy Working Group of the Lausanne Committee for World Evangelization, was an outgrowth of the Lausanne Congress on World Evangelization held in 1974 (1979:vii).

Participants included theologians and biblical scholars James Packer, I. Howard Marshall, Stephen Neill, Rene Padilla, Orlando

Costas, Bruce Nichols, S. Ananda Kumar and Harvie Conn, anthropologists Alan Tippett, Jacob Loewen, Charles Taber, Donald Jacobs, Alfred Krass and myself plus Kenneth Cragg, I. Wayan Mastra and Gottfried Osei-Mensah with John Stott leading the discussions and writing up the report. For the first time we anthropologists felt we were being taken seriously.

The contextualization issue of *Evangelical Missions Quarterly* (January 1978), then, further strengthened the case for a new round of thinking on the relationships between the Gospel and the cultures of the peoples of the world. In that issue, several of us "younger generation" missiologists (e.g. Conn, Buswell, Kraft) wrote key articles relating to the concept of contextualization and why we were abandoning the older term "indigenization."

Two further developments were the beginning of a new periodical edited by Charles Taber named *Gospel in Context*. The first issue was April 1978. Though very promising, the journal only lasted a couple of years and then went out of business due to a lack of financial support. The second development was the publication of my *Christianity in Culture* (Orbis 1979), hailed by some as groundbreaking, by others as heretical because they didn't like the way I was using an anthropological (rather than a philosophical) approach to theologizing that I called "Christian ethnotheology." I was contending that looking at theological topics from a cross-cultural perspective is both instructive and more helpful in assisting the communication of the Gospel in nonwestern societies.

Tom & Elizabeth (Betty Sue) Brewster
Tom (1939-1985) Betty Sue (1943—)
At Fuller: 1975—

Then, in the fall of 1975 we added Tom and Betty Sue Brewster to our faculty. Meg and I had invited Tom and Betty Sue to share Thanksgiving dinner with us in November of 1974. We had met them first in the early 70s in Nairobi where they were working with Daystar Communications on a translation project sponsored by Living Bibles International. We met again, a few years later, at Arrowhead Springs where they were helping Campus Crusade with translation and adaptation of the Four Spiritual Laws into various languages. So I naturally associated them with translation.

During our time together that day, it became clear to me that they were quite on their own financially, volunteering their services to Crusade rather than employed by them. Tom had disability compensation and they were in the habit of offering their services at minimal charge to their sponsors. And it occurred to me that Fuller might be as good a base for them as Crusade headquarters at Arrowhead Springs, California. So, late that evening I asked a question similar to the one Ralph Winter had asked me in 1969.

I asked, "Would you be interested in making Fuller your base?" I had been looking for someone to join our faculty, hopefully at little or no cost to us, to initiate and run a Bible translation program. And, since they were presently involved in translation it seemed to me that they might be able to run a program for us. "Of course, we have no salary to offer," I said, "And I have no official permission to offer you a job. But perhaps Fuller would be just as good a base for you as any other place."

After a bit of discussion, they seemed open to the possibility of making Fuller their base. So I presented this possibility to Dean Glasser and our faculty and received a favorable response. Glasser did the legwork and by fall of 1975 they joined us on a part-time basis. They wanted to be free to travel the rest of their time.

Tom was born in 1939 and brought up in Colorado. His father was a college student at the time and became a high school teacher and a very committed Christian. Tom was his first son. Betty Sue was born in 1943 and brought up in Venezuela, the daughter of missionary parents. They had met at a Spanish language school in Guadalajara, Mexico, worked together there, fell in love and married. Tom, however, had had an accident on a water slide in 1958 at age 18 and was quadriplegic, confined to a wheelchair. In spite of Tom's disability, they both had worked hard to complete their Ph.D.s, Tom's from the University of Arizona (1971) and Betty Sue's from the University of Texas (later in 1971).

In addition to the translation programs with Daystar and Crusade, they had been involved with several ministries and missionary training programs focusing on language acquisition. They put in several years at the Guadalajara language school and several in the Toronto Institute of Linguistics, a missionary language program that ran for many summers in Toronto, and together became arguably the best teachers or, as they would prefer, "coaches" of language acquisition in Christian circles.

The Brewsters' Contribution to SWM/SIS

As soon as the Brewsters came aboard, it was language acquisition (their primary concern) rather than translation (my plan for them) that they began to emphasize. Since they were involved in translation with Crusade, I had assumed they would want to continue in that area of linguistics with us. I guessed wrong, but that was okay. What we got was spectacular. So, thankful for what they brought to us, I happily continued my quest to find someone to start a Bible translation program. And that happened later.

Language learning, then, became a very important component of the pre-field training program, making their presence very important to the CCSP. They offered classes in language acquisition that, among other things, forced their students to get out among the people they wanted to relate to. The Brewsters contend that "language learning is a social, not an academic activity." Therefore, they get people out into the community practicing speaking. This is in line with their dictum, "learn a little, use it a lot," even if all you can say is "hello, I'm trying to learn your language, that's all I can say, goodbye."

The textbook the Brewsters wrote is called LAMP (*Language Acquisition Made Practical* (1976). The so-called "LAMP method" has now come into use around the world through the Brewsters' seminars, sales of the book and the classes they have taught at Fuller. In addition, they have published *Bonding and the Missionary Task* (1981), an important article that they've also put into pamphlet form entitled, "Language Learning is Communication—is Ministry" (1982) and an edited volume entitled, *Community is My Language Classroom* (1986). Betty Sue has added to their joint publications "Preparing Life-Long Learners," a chapter in *Helping the Missionary Language Learner Succeed*, edited by Lonna Dickerson (1995).

The Brewsters are also strong, like all of us at SWM, on incarnational ministry. There's a difference, though. We all talk about such ministry as something to do when people get to their fields of service. The Brewsters, however, make their students get out and do ministry as a part of their (now just Betty Sue's) courses. For, to them, ministry also is a social activity and the process of learning the language and culture is itself a form of ministry.

Tom was an amazing person by any standard. Betty Sue, an amazing person in her own right, had to work hard to keep up with him. They published their own materials even before computers made it easy for us. They were, however, one of the first, if not the first of our faculty to begin using a computer. I learned how to use a computer in their apartment. They took pride in the fact that Tom's was possibly the most traveled wheelchair in the world. They estimated 90 countries. And Tom continually shocked us by saying that his accident was the best thing that ever happened to him and that he was sure glad he was paralyzed from the neck down rather than from the neck up! His brother Dan has written a brilliant biography of Tom entitled *Only Paralyzed From the Neck Down* (1997).

Tom was a runner before his accident. He had taken part in several runs up Pike's Peak. The accident, of course, took away his ability to run physically but couldn't keep his mind inactive and when he died we lost a lot. But he left us with Betty Sue who continues to teach their courses and to conduct seminars all over the world, influencing missionary language learning and missionary practice wherever she goes. We'll never know this side of heaven how many souls will be there because Tom and Betty Sue, now just Betty Sue, committed themselves to enable missionaries to communicate more effectively—and became very good at it. Tom also left us with their son Jed. He's now grown up, graduated from college and married with two children of their own. But we older faculty members remember Jed best as a baby in a carrier, then as a child, riding on his father's lap as Tom wheeled his wheelchair to faculty meetings, or as the youngster who read and colored as he quietly sat through those weekly meetings. We literally watched him grow up, for he seldom missed a meeting.

I personally lost a dear brother when Tom died, a brother whom I picture now with healthy legs running all over heaven! As I have written in the Foreword to Dan's biography,

> Though "challenged" (to use today's politically correct term) by a body that did not permit the normal support for his very creative mind, he (with lots of very capable help from Betty Sue) set a pace that few of us could keep up with. Our eyes told us he was disabled from the neck down. But his mental alertness, his brilliance, his creativity, his wisdom, and above all his commitment to Jesus Christ and to enabling Christian witnesses to communicate Jesus' love effectively—these characteristics of Tom kept us continually aware of the fact that what God had given him from the neck up was functioning well and made him a valued member of our team.

Only Paralyzed from the Neck Down is the story of a life lived all out for God in spite of the challenge of quadriplegia. No one would have faulted Tom if he had attempted no more than his body allowed. But that was not Tom. He who, when his body was at full strength, regularly challenged Pike's Peak, was not about to let the limitations imposed on his body cripple him. He went to school to prepare for a future the doctors refused to predict for him. He married. He eventually earned a Ph.D. So did Betty Sue. They traveled and traveled and traveled. They have a son. They taught effectively. They wrote books. And they have inspired many and changed many lives (1997:viii-ix).

Transitions

A frequent topic in SWM faculty meetings was the difficulty of coordinating our commitment to the cause of missions with our involvement in the academic program of Fuller Seminary. All of us felt the tension of attracting international students who might be major players in their home countries or missionaries who might be very effective in their mission contexts but who could not be admitted because their previous academic work did not measure up to graduate school standards or who did not do well academically once they had been admitted. We wanted to encourage such students and to help them to do their ministries more effectively. But our major means of encouragement lay in the granting of degrees. And some of those who were best in ministry did not measure up when it came to meeting the academic requirements. However, especially the internationals would be shamed if they returned to their home countries without the degree they promised their people they would attain.

This problem and others led to frequent discussions of the tensions we felt between our commitment to "the Cause" and our involvement in an academic program. All of us felt greater allegiance to the Cause than to the institution. But the reality was that we were involved in both. We all were quite impatient with the "academic drag" produced by the institutional rules and structures of the Seminary and the ways they seem to interfere with the carrying out of the Great Commission. So we talked often of setting up another organization that would not be hampered by academic rules and regulations. It would be lean, mobile, flexible and adaptable to carry out the "activist" ideas we generated that didn't fit into our academic programs.

We even had more or less formal discussions over a two-year period involving both outsiders and Fuller insiders. In these meetings our "ideas began to converge into the concept of a major 'annex' to SWM that would implement new strategies and functions essential to the things we were talking about in class" (Winter email: 7/5/04:2). With a publishing component added, then, we foresaw a three-part structure involving the Fuller academic part, the mobile "annex" part that would not be administratively under Fuller and a publishing house. This idea was presented to the Fuller administration and received a negative response.

Ralph, then, more than the rest of us began thinking more concretely, looking at possible buildings to house such an entity and conceptualizing what it might look like. He came to envision a center where various mission boards would headquarter, enabling them to work cooperatively to get the job done. It then came to Ralph's attention that the former campus of the Pasadena Nazarene College was for sale. He then gave himself to the possibility of taking over that campus and creating the U.S. Center for World Mission with the aim of implementing the focus of his 1974 Lausanne presentation.

So in the fall of 1976 Ralph resigned from SWM to give his full attention to acquiring the "Pas Naz" campus and surrounding houses (for nearly $15 million) and setting it up as the home of the U.S. Center. Though we as faculty members had discussed the need for such an organization and the tensions we experienced in the Fuller setting, and McGavran was one of his strongest supporters, none of the rest of us joined Ralph in his new organization. I believe this was a big disappointment to Ralph. Though some interpreted our hesitation as a lack of faith in God, it was more likely (as it was for me) a feeling that what was planned was much larger and more diverse than we had envisioned, necessitating leaving Fuller rather than serving as an adjunct to our work at Fuller.

Having lost Winter in 1976, it was not good news for us that Alan Tippett planned to retire in 1977, when he reached the age of 65. His strongly held desire was that he be able to devote his final years to his beloved Australia. As the time approached, Tippett could hardly wait. He began packing his books soon after the year began, catching me off guard in my attempt to copy for our library the yearly bound volumes he had made of his published and unpublished writings. He had these volumes already packed before I realized it and I had to copy them later in Australia. They are in the Fuller, Biola and Asbury missiological libraries now.

So Tippett searched around Australia for a place to house his library and give him a base. The most logical places would have been Sydney or Melbourne but none of the possibilities in these areas seemed to be what he wanted. St. Marks, a small Anglican ministerial training center in Canberra, however, offered him a very nice physical setup—a state of the art library room with shelves on tracks, allowing for his extensive book collection to be completely shelved in stacks that slide together or apart on the tracks.

So he had a great place to study and to write. Unfortunately, his physical location was in Canberra, off the beaten track for those in missions who might have valued his services. And, in addition, neither St. Marks' faculty or students had more than a passing interest in missions or missiology. They had little awareness of the value of what had landed among them, nor did the rest of Australian academia or missions, and Tippett again felt devalued. In a chat I had with him about a month before he died in 1988 (due to what appeared to be medical mismanagement), Alan said sadly, "I think I retired too soon." I agreed.

Paul G. Hiebert (1932—)
At Fuller: 1977-1990

Tippett's leaving meant that we needed to find another anthropologist to take his place. We thought of Jake Loewen but, in a visit to SWM, he unfortunately made a negative impression on McGavran and Wagner. Wagner suggested Paul Hiebert whom he had met and been impressed with as he was teaching a summer course on anthropology at Daystar Communications in Nairobi, Kenya. The rest of us had heard good things about Hiebert also and Winter gave a glowing report of his teaching in the classes called "Understanding World Evangelization" that later developed into the Perspectives program. So we decided to go after him. He was a tenured Associate Professor of Anthropology at the University of Washington who had been brought up in India and returned there as a missionary with the Mennonite Brethren, serving from 1960 to 1967.

Paul likes to introduce himself in terms of what he calls his "Three Ms." He is an M.K. (missionary kid), an M.B. (Mennonite

Brethren) and an M.A. (missionary anthropologist). He was born (1932) and raised in India, attending high school at Kodaikanal, a missionary children's school in India. He then attended Tabor College in Hillsboro, Kansas (B.A. 1954), Mennonite Brethren Biblical Seminary in Fresno, California (M.A. 1957) and the University of Minnesota (M.A. 1959 and Ph.D. 1967 in Anthropology).

He is genuinely bicultural, just as at home in either India or America. He also considers himself "bi-theological." Though his roots are firmly in the Mennonite/Anabaptist tradition, he has been strongly influenced by pietist/evangelical Christianity as well. He says, "this means I see theologies as our understandings of Scripture and not to be equated with Scripture and that the Church is the hermeneutical community, informed by but not controlled by experts" (email: 12/14/04).

He also sees himself as bivocational: a missionary and an anthropologist. He went into anthropology to become a better missionary. This he did for the seven years as a missionary in India. But his wife Fran's health problems dictated that he take employment in America. So he taught Anthropology for six years at Kansas State University, followed by five years at the University of Washington.

Having heard good reports of him both within and outside of our faculty, we took the next step and invited him to come for a visit and to do a lecture. He liked us and we liked him. So he joined us in the fall of 1977, giving up his tenured position at Washington to become a major part of what might be regarded as a "second wave" of SWM faculty.

Hiebert was a sterling addition to our faculty. He is a quiet, even shy, humble and gentle person with a fine sense of humor and a combination of scholarly brilliance and practical commitment to Jesus Christ. He is also a fine artist when given the opportunity (usually in faculty meetings) to decorate styrofoam cups!

His ability to see and present deep insight in creative ways soon made him a favorite of both students and faculty. Who of us will ever forget his way of presenting a variety of epistemological understandings in terms of how a baseball umpire interprets his judgments? As he puts it, some umpires see themselves as simply reporting what the pitch is ("I calls 'em the way they is"), or as making the pitch what it becomes ("When I calls 'em, I makes 'em a

ball or a strike"), or as simply doing the best they can ("I calls 'em as
I sees 'em").   The latter is his humorous way of helping us to
understand the "Critical Realist" approach to interpreting reality that
is so crucial to life and missionary endeavor, since it allows for
cultural and individual differences in interpretation.   The critical
realist does his/her best to interpret correctly but allows for the
possible validity of the interpretations of others who are trying to do
their best also but come from different sociocultural backgrounds.

Another humorous way of stating an important insight is the
way he characterizes the plight of missionary kids who never quite
know where they belong. He says, they are only at home on the
airplane (on their way to what they hope will be a better place to
stay). Another insight that has now become a part of Fuller's self-
image is his characterization of Fuller as made up of three "tribes"—
Theology, Psychology and Mission.

In reflection on his time here, Paul writes,

> Of the things that come to mind, one is the long sessions we
> spent in setting up the Ph.D.in Intercultural Studies, even though
> we had little support from the administration to add faculty and
> to set aside doctoral level classes. So we ended up with tutorials
> which we carved out of our own hides because we taught full
> loads in addition to the flow of tutorials that flooded in.

> I think one of our unique contributions was to raise new sets
> of questions that had not been asked before, particularly in the
> study of humans. Most of us were trained in Scripture but had
> little clue on how to study the people we served. Consequently,
> much of what we did in missions did not get through or was
> seen as foreign and colonial. Adding the study of humans
> forced us also to realize critical questions of contextualization,
> of partnership and of a global perspective on missions. Now, of
> course, all these impacts are well documented in our
> publications and in the responses to our writings which were
> often quite diverse (email: 4/13/05).

And, I might add, many of the ideas that we hammered out in
those discussions now seem to be taken for granted by today's
students and colleagues. It was exciting to have Hiebert's input in our
discussions. We all learned a lot in our interactions with him.

Hiebert's Contribution to SWM

Hiebert's coming kept up our tradition of providing first-class
anthropological insight into the cause of Christian mission. He

brought to us a depth in dealing with culture similar to Tippett's and a wealth of illustrative material, largely from India. He moved right into the teaching of Animism, one of Tippett's specialties and alternated with me in teaching Introductory Anthropology and Worldview.

His teaching and writing have enhanced our reputation and endeared Paul to the generations of students who studied under him here (and also at Trinity). He soon became the most admired of our faculty by the members of the other two schools at Fuller and was often chosen to represent us in meetings with Trustees and outsiders on whom the Fuller administration sought to make an impression. We lost a lot when he moved to Trinity but consider ourselves blessed to have had him here as long as he stayed.

Hiebert's perceptiveness comes across well in his writings. Beyond his quality anthropology text (*Cultural Anthropology* 1976/1983) and his helpful articles collected in *Anthropological Insights for Missionaries* (1985), his insights into epistemology, now collected in *Anthropological Reflections on Missiological Issues* (1994) have been seminal. His "Flaw of the Excluded Middle" (1982) has served to make many aware of the spiritual power issues in mission and his "Critical Contextualization" article (1984/1987) has proved a touchstone for those looking for a balanced view of this important subject. With his wife Frances, Paul published *Case Studies in Missions* in 1987, a very useful case study approach to dealing with missiological problems. Beyond his time with us, he has teamed with Dan Shaw and Tite Tienou to provide a basic text for the Animism class (*Understanding Folk Religion* 1999) and, with his daughter Eloise Meneses (*Incarnational Ministry* 1995), wrote a very useful text dealing with the issues of contextualization in the various types of the world's societies.

Dean S. Gilliland (1928—)
At Fuller: 1977—

Dean Gilliland was our next faculty acquisition. He was born in Akron, Ohio, brought up in the Evangelical Church that merged in 1948 with the United Brethren in Christ to become the Evangelical United Brethren Church. The E.U.B. then united with the Methodist Church in 1968. Born in 1928, Dean had much positive contact with preachers and missionaries in his growing up days and he decided in third grade that he would be a preacher. He changed that to missionary as the years went by, with a special commitment to becoming a missionary in his junior year at Houghton College (B.A. 1952) in response to messages by Norman Grubb. The same evening he went forward to give his life to missions, the daughter of a Sudan Interior Mission medical missionary to Nigeria named Lois Harris also went forward. They got together, then, and married in 1950.

From Houghton, Dean went to Evangelical Theological Seminary in Naperville, Illinois, graduating with a B.D. in 1954 but, he says, "often impatient because so much of the B.D. curriculum and professors did not touch on my plans for the mission field" (2001:119). He was, however, mentored by a former missionary on that faculty, Wilbur Harr, who had served in Nigeria and studied under R. Pierce Beaver and Kenneth Scott Latourette.

Dean and Lois applied to the EUB Board of Missions in 1954 and were commissioned in that year. Even though Dean had served three years as pastor in Clinton, Iowa during his seminary days, the Board required him to serve another year in the ministry before going to Africa. He did this in Akron, Ohio as minister of music and youth until June 1955. Then, on their way to Nigeria they were required to spend three months in England learning "to be comfortable with British culture and understand the British philosophy of rule and education" (2001:120).

They landed in northern Nigeria in January 1956, and were sent to serve among tribal peoples, expecting to do evangelistic work. However, after six months of language study, Gilliland was "immediately handed responsibility for a training school for lay evangelists and catechists and was the only teacher for all subjects." He had to teach in Hausa, the trade language of that part of Nigeria (ibid.:120). During the next few years, he says he learned how to teach (rather than preach) and how to see the Gospel "from the interior of another culture." He says, further, I gained "a much broader definition of mission than I was prepared for" and "that I could embrace other denominations and work comfortably in an intermission context" (ibid.:120).

But they ended their first term greatly discouraged with questions about fellow missionaries and the African church. Their idealism had taken a heavy hit. With questions about their future, then, Dean enrolled in a Th.M. program at Princeton Seminary. He says about this year,

This step proved to be a lifesaver. Not many mission courses were offered at Princeton in 1960. So I studied Paul to understand the contextual diversity of his churches, his frustrations, and his creativity in nurturing first-generation believers. I became bonded to Paul and have been turning to him as a model for contextualization ever since. My book *Pauline Theology and the Mission Church* (Baker, 1983) came out of this Princeton study (ibid.:120).

The Gillilands returned to Nigeria to serve as principal of a vernacular pastors' school and supervise the EUB Nigeria work until invited to teach at the Theological College of Northern Nigeria in 1966. I met him at about this time while I was doing linguistic research in Nigeria. We discussed my recently completed Ph.D. program at Hartford Seminary Foundation and he decided to go there, completing his Ph.D. at Hartford in 1971 with a dissertation on the interaction between Islam and traditional religion in Northern Nigeria.

In 1962, Dean met Willem Bijlefeld who had come to Nigeria to initiate a program "for the study of Islam and the training of pastors in witnessing to Muslims" called the "Islam in Africa Project." He says of the influence of Bijlefeld in his life and ministry,

> Bijlefeld's careful scholarship . . . and his sensitivity to phenomenology was a new approach to methodology that for me was a deepening and integrative experience. My early years as a missionary were so given to unreflective activism that I had failed to see people in their search for God. In my efforts to communicate the message of the Gospel, I had made little use of the rituals, symbols, and stories of human persons created in God's image. Bijlefeld helped me see Muslim people as they are in God's sight rather than as stereotypical adversaries of Christians and the church. Through his depth in phenomenology I saw both African traditional practice and Islam in a much more positive, even exciting way. Bijlefeld left Africa to become dean of Hartford Seminary and editor of the journal *Muslim World*. I followed him to Hartford in 1968, where he mentored me through my Ph.D. studies in African Islam.
>
> After sixteen years in Africa I could now see religion and theology as a much more integrated whole, enriching my appreciation for both and bringing me to a new hermeneutic of the biblical text. With Nigerian people from over thirty ethnic groups as the everyday human reference and my widened understanding of ecumenism in mission, I was gratified by the

new word "contextualization" that was coming into use around
1972 (ibid.:122).

To Fuller

During the 1976-77 school year, a Nigerian student mentioned
to me that the Gillilands had been forced to leave Nigeria due to a
family problem.   Upon hearing that, I found out Dean's phone
number and called him.   As we discussed his future, I asked if he
would be interested in teaching at Fuller.   I was thinking, as when I
asked the Brewsters this question, that it might be possible for him to
come supported financially by his mission board.   The idea of coming
here sounded good to him, but he saw no possibility that his United
Methodist Board would pay his salary to teach at a non-Methodist
institution. I passed on his name and situation to Dean Glasser and he
to President Hubbard.   With little hope, then, Dean inquired about the
possibility of United Methodist salary support with Tracy Jones, the
General Secretary of the Board of Global Ministries.   Jones called
George (Chuck) Hunter, a faculty member at Perkins who was taking
a sabbatical at Fuller.   With Hunter's confirmation that Fuller wanted
Dean, Jones began the support process with the Board and worked out
an unprecedented plan with Hubbard for the United Methodist Board
to pay Gilliland's salary full time for one year and half time for the
next year after which Fuller picked up his full salary.

With Gilliland coming on, we had to decide what niche he
would fill and what his title would be.   We Evangelicals were just
beginning to get comfortable with the term "contextualization" as a
replacement for terms such as "indigenization."   As mentioned, this
term had been invented and used by the Conciliar Movement and, for
that reason, was problematic to the more conservative wing of the
church.   But it was definitely the term of the future.   I suggested,
therefore, both that this be the area of Gilliland's focus and that his
title be Assistant Professor of the Contextualization of Theology.   We
were disappointed that the institution, judging him by his lack of
publication rather than his years of service, would not start him at
Associate Professor level but were forced to live with it.   Dean,
however, moved steadily through the promotional steps and made it
to full professor by 1990.

We were, however, pleased to have him aboard as the first (and,
I believe, to date, the only) person in an academic institution with

"contextualization" in his title and the assignment to develop this area in classes and writing. He says,

> At Fuller I could now organize and systematize the African years and the graduate work done at both Princeton and Hartford. The disciplines of biblical theology and the study I had done in phenomenology, combined with our continuing love for Africa and a specialized interest in Islam, served me well for this new position (ibid.:122).

At Fuller, Dean's world was "much enlarged." He was now able to work from his understandings of Paul and the cultural issues he had been reflecting on both with relation to Africa and to Islam to "bring these insights into mission theology, African studies, and especially contextualization" (ibid.:122). These were the main areas in which he taught for us, providing for him "a fitting way to bring all those earlier years closer to maturity."

Contribution to SWM

Gilliland has provided for us a focal point of what should probably be seen as the central focus of SWM/SIS in the 21st century: Incarnational Witness commonly called Contextualization. Though all of us deal with this important topic, Dean's involvement has been more overt. His course entitled Doing Theology in Context has been a highlight for many of our students, providing a theoretical basis for a number of doctoral dissertations. His edited collection of SWM approaches to contextualization in *The Word Among Us* (1989) was an up-to-date statement on the subject as of 1989. In addition, Dean took over my Africa area courses and did much more with them than I had been doing, continuing McGavran's emphasis on area studies. His course on African Independent Churches contributed greatly to the students' understandings of independency and its relationships to contextualization. He also taught sections of Glasser's Theology of Mission courses.

His Pauline Theology of Mission course, along with his book, *Pauline Theology and Mission Practice* (1983) was a paradigm shifting course for many. And his expertise in Islam in Africa contributed to the development of Islamic studies after 1978. In this area, he published *African Religion Meets Islam* (1985) based on his doctoral dissertation. His continuing focus on the Incarnation and Paul as models for contextualization are highlighted in "First Conversion and Second Conversion in Nigeria" (1991), "Modeling the Incarnation for Muslim Peoples" (2000) and "For Missionaries and Leaders: Paul's Farewell to the Ephesian Elders" (2004). Then he breaks new ground in his contribution to the new contextualization volume *Appropriate Christianity* (Kraft ed. 2005) with his chapter, "The Incarnation as Matrix for Appropriate Theologies." To honor Dean, we dedicated that volume to him.

In addition, we tapped Gilliland several times for his considerable skill as an administrator. Soon after he joined us, he was asked to run the Cross-Cultural Studies Program (CCSP) for pre-field students. He helped us in a major way by setting that program on solid footing. We had started the program a year or two before Dean joined us and had it run by two students, Phil Elkins and Robert Douglas. The Fuller administration, however, was alarmed by what they called "creeping appointments" of persons at sub-faculty level (e.g. Martin for ISP, Holland for TEE, McCurry for Islamics, Schwartz as Dean's Assistant and Elkins and Douglas for CCSP) who exhausted our financial resources and kept us from hiring faculty-level persons. So when Gilliland came on, we began to rectify this situation by asking him to take over the CCSP and dropping two of our sub-faculty level people. The CCSP continues to this day as the M.A. in Intercultural Studies.

In 1982, then, we experimented with a summer program that we called the Summer Institute of Missiology with Dean administering it. 199 students attended that first year. We eventually discontinued the Institute but continue to offer many summer courses on a regular basis. So, among Gilliland's contributions to SWM we need to list the administrative role he played in these programs.

Accomplishments during the Glasser Era

During the Glasser period, we began to experience a large influx of international students. To this point our student population had been largely mid-career missionaries. Now, both the number of students and the number of internationals were increasing. Our student body as a whole increased from 67 in 1971 to 162 in 1980. Our faculty increased from the original six to eight plus Orr with the Brewsters, Hiebert and Gilliland coming on while losing Winter and Tippett.

Probably the most important thing we did, however, was not in the classroom or with students. We decided that we as a faculty needed to meet weekly for sharing, prayer and stimulus through keeping up with each other's ideas. So, we set aside two hours on Wednesdays to meet together, spending approximately half of the time sharing and praying with and for each other with the other half devoted to sharing ideas, sometimes in the form of a paper, sometimes simply a discussion of some relevant topic. All of us traveled a lot and regularly came up with new ideas, so this was a way of keeping track of each other physically and thought-wise. We also got to enter into each other's personal life through praying for each other.

We still get together weekly, though we now meet on Tuesdays. People often have wondered about the *esprit de corps* of the SWM faculty. These weekly meetings are the reason. We don't always agree with each other, but we learn during these times to respect and trust each other. We also often invite guests to these meetings. Several have expressed the blessing they have received simply by watching us in action. When Pierson came on as Dean and began to attend these meetings, he exclaimed one day, "You people really like each other, don't you!" Such camaraderie is rare among faculty in academic institutions—even Christian ones. I have been a part of two secular university faculties and never experienced in those institutions anything like the warmth of the relationships fostered in these weekly get-togethers. Of all the decisions we have made over the years, I believe the best and most important one was to set aside time for these weekly meetings.

As mentioned above, we experimented with a distance learning program (the In Service Program--ISP) that started with high marks for the learning the students received but low marks for the technology. It did the job, however, and we now have upgraded it significantly both in technology and in content. We also experimented with a summer program but now simply offer a full range of summer courses.

To accommodate the increasing numbers of pre-field students, we started the Cross-Cultural Studies Program (CCSP) in about 1975. The Brewsters, when they came on in 1975, soon became important contributers to that program with their emphasis on language acquisition and incarnational ministry. Initially, we had a couple of advanced students running the program but, as mentioned, when Gilliland joined us, we turned it over to him. Our focus on training people pre-field has increased over the years and the foundational organization worked out by Gilliland has given this program staying power.

We started a four page newsletter under Glasser's deanship as well. It was called *Forwarding the Missionary Task* and was sent out to alumni. It has served a good purpose in keeping alumni somewhat informed on what is going on at SWM. Unfortunately, budgetary considerations forced us to discontinue it in 1999.

During this decade, the appeal of Church Growth thinking to American pastors increased enormously. This led to Wagner teaching in the Fuller Doctor of Ministries program and, for a time, the CG courses and the theses they spawned became the major focus of that program.

Over the years, we have been involved in several overseas training programs. The first of these was a joint program in Korea in cooperation with ACTS (Asian Center for Theology and Mission). This involved several of us teaching courses at ACTS to strengthen their missions offerings.

The fact that the journal *Missiology* was edited at SWM for the first six years of its existence is significant. This fact led to the spread of our points of view either in articles by our faculty members or through editorials by Tippett and Glasser. Both of these men were given to insightful and ground-breaking editorials.

Another important contribution of Fuller faculty is the previously mentioned *Perspectives* program that by 2005 had burgeoned into a major, nationwide and even global program. This was/is an introductory missiology course taught off campus. It started as an expansion and adaptation of a course Wagner was asked to write in 1972 for the Moody Bible Institute Extension Department. That course was first aided by a book of readings called *Crucial Dimensions in World Evangelization*, a book mainly edited by Roberta Winter behind the scenes. The course drew on the four major spheres of emphasis at the School of World Mission: Bible, Mission History, Cultural Anthropology, and Mission Strategy. Later, the same approach was adapted as a follow-through for Urbana students showing interest in mission careers. By 2005 it was being taught annually in 150 places in the USA alone and in other languages around the world. More than 600,000 copies of the reader, *Perspectives on the World Christian Movement* were in print.

Several academic programs were initiated during the Glasser era. Before this period all we could offer was an M.A. and a Doctor of Missiology. By the middle of this period, then, we had a Ph.D. in Missiology (in cooperation with the School of Theology) and by the end, our own Ph.D. in Intercultural Studies. Our two doctorates (D.Miss. and Ph.D.) are distinguishable by the fact that the D.Miss. is patterned after the Ed.D., with a focus on the application of missiological insight. The Ph.D. is a more theoretical degree, focused on developing missiological theory, though we encourage our students to show at the end of their dissertations how their theories can be applied to the work of mission.

At the master's level, we experimented a bit. We started with a single M.A. Missiology for field people that required an M.Div. or equivalent (e.g. B.D.) as a prerequisite and was, therefore, at the level of the Th.M. We then added an M.A. Missions for pre-field people. This got confusing, so we decided to rename the M.A. Missiology, a Th.M. and to call the pre-field M.A. an M.A. CCSP (Cross-Cultural Studies Program), later an M.A. in Intercultural Studies. We then developed an M.Div. CCSP offered jointly between SWM and the School of Theology.

It is likely that most academic programs suffer from a lack of secretarial assistance. Certainly ours did. During this period, we were blessed through a Mennonite program that recruited volunteers to provide missionary organizations with secretaries. Glen Schwartz arranged that we got four secretaries through this program for two years—supported by the Mennonite Board but assigned to help us. I personally benefited by having one of these young women assigned to help me with the time-consuming tasks of typing and duplicating materials (by mimeograph and spirit duplication) in that day before computers and photocopying. The one who helped us most, however, was Jean Barker who was assigned to assist Glen Schwartz in helping Glasser. She played an important part at the end of this period and on into the Pierson Era by staying on after the others had left. Eventually, then, she took Schwartz's place as Dean's Assistant.

Though Glasser was every bit as knowledgeable as anyone with a Ph.D., he always felt a bit inferior academically to the rest of us because he didn't have that paper credential. It came to his attention, though, that he could be accepted into a Ph.D. program at the University of South Africa. So, in the spring of 1979, with the strong encouragement of our faculty and the Fuller administration, Art headed for a well-earned spring and summer sabbatical in South Africa to work toward a Ph.D. under David Bosch. Unfortunately, he never got it finished. But the experience of most of a year with Bosch, probably South Africa's greatest missiologist, before his untimely death, was of inestimable value to Glasser.

Meanwhile, back at SWM, with our Dean gone, we were governed by a committee of senior faculty members—Hiebert, Wagner and myself. But the main administrative work continued to be done by Glen Schwartz. This meant that the three of us met regularly with the Provost, Glen Barker, and things went quite well in spite of Glasser's absence. It did mean, however, that we uncovered some things that needed to be fixed.

The End of This Era

Glasser was now turning 65 and running into the Fuller rule that when an administrator gets to 65, he or she needs to step aside. So a committee was set up to find a new Dean for SWM. The story of how Paul Pierson was chosen by that committee is told in the next chapter.

Our enrollment was now 162 (in 1980), our faculty numbers six full-time, with Hiebert and Gilliland replacing Winter and Tippett, plus Orr, Holland and McCurry regular part-time and the Brewsters half time. In addition, Alvin Martin was administrating the In Service Program on a part-time basis. As Pierson came on, McGavran retired from teaching at age 83 but kept his office, continuing to write and correspond until his death in 1990 at age 93.

Chapter 7

The Pierson Era I

1980-1984

The Pierson Era was a time of unprecedented growth. During these 12 years we added eleven new faculty members and our student body grew from 162 in 1980 to 358 in 1992. Some of the faculty additions were planned, some God just sort of "dropped them into our laps." But all had a unique contribution to make to the whole.

As 1980 approached, Glasser was about to turn age 65 and, according to seminary policy, to step down as Dean. So a Dean's Search Committee was set up to find his replacement. It was a large committee of perhaps 25 persons, and we went through a large number of documents related to a number of potential candidates. After several meetings, we had reduced the number to two and were about to choose which of the two to invite for a formal interview. Both of these men were outstanding missiologists and, either would have done a fine job leading us. But one of them had signaled that he was unlikely to accept our invitation if it fell in his direction. And, though the other one was a strong scholar, we had doubts concerning his interest in administration.

Nevertheless, we were about to vote when Don McCurry, an alumnus and Adjunct in the area of Islamics, raised his hand. Provost Barker, who was chairing the committee, recognized Don and his question changed the course of SWM history. He asked, "Have we ever considered Paul Pierson?" Most of us, including Provost Barker, thought, "Paul who?" But Barker, knowing that many of us were uneasy about the choice we were considering, wisely opened up the nominating process again.

Paul Pierson, after serving for 14 years in Brazil and then 2 years in Portugal under the Presbyterian (USA) Board of Foreign Mission, was now pastoring First Presbyterian Church in Fresno,

California. The close proximity of Fresno to Pasadena, plus the fact that Fuller had friends (including a board member) in that church made it fairly easy to obtain information concerning him. All that we got was extremely positive. He was well liked by all, was doing well administering a large church and had a Ph.D. from Princeton Seminary in History, with a dissertation on Presbyterianism in Brazil. All of these were plusses. We needed a historian to replace Winter and we needed an administrator to pick up the pieces that were scattered when Glenn Schwartz left.

As for Paul, he was stunned at our invitation! He had come to admire Fuller, especially SWM, and had brought Glasser to speak on Fuller's behalf in his church. He also had had contact with President Hubbard and others from Fuller. He had taught a Fuller course in Fresno and encouraged one of his key elders to accept President Hubbard's invitation to become a Fuller trustee. But none of these who knew him best were on the Search Committee. He was an unknown entity to most of us.

Things moved rather quickly from that point. Information was gathered, people were interviewed, Dr. Barker met with Pierson and he visited us. And we soon decided to invite him to become our Dean—voting unanimously for him in preference to the other two we had been considering. But then he went fishing! It was his custom to spend a couple of weeks of vacation each summer fishing. It was nearly time for that vacation and he and Rosemary decided they would use it to get away to a cabin in the mountains near Fresno and pray about this new possibility, with the promise that he would let us know his decision when he returned from vacation. But for us who waited to hear what his decision would be, this became a very long few weeks.

But finally they returned from their vacation and we received word that he would accept our invitation to become Dean. I remember clearly the sense of relief I felt when I heard the good news! Pierson says in an email,

> When we returned, I phoned Barker and told him of our acceptance. He flew up a couple of days later to talk further. He said they wanted someone with five characteristics: mainline denomination, solid Ph.D. in church history, Latin American experience, leadership skills, and administrative skills. The last two are subjective so I won't comment on them. But there did seem to be a strong convergence and I have never doubted that

this was a call from God. But it was very hard to leave the church in Fresno, where we were very happy and I think had an effective ministry in helping the church to look more toward the whole world (email: March 23, 2004).

For Pierson this meant taking a cut in salary while moving to an area with much higher living costs.

One reason we were so anxious for Paul to come was that Schwartz's departure had left us with a big administrative hole that someone would have to dig us out of if we were to survive. I had predicted that things would be a bit tough for awhile as a new leader attempted to get acquainted with our situation and to rectify it. This was a prediction I was glad to see not come true, due largely to the presence of Jean Barker (no relation to Glen Barker).

Jean Barker had worked for us for several years in the administration of SWM, largely as Glenn Schwartz's assistant. She had come to us as a member of the group of Mennonite volunteer workers. That program had been phased out by 1980, but Jean had stayed on. The fact that she "knew the ropes" of SWM administration made it possible for her to step right into Schwartz's position as Administrative Assistant to the Dean where most of the administration was centered at the time. In that position, she was able to orient and serve the new Dean quite effectively. She was an able person and played a major role in orienting Pierson to his new job, enabling Paul to "hit the ground running" and to keep us from most of the problems that could have accompanied this transition.

Pierson, for his part, turned out to be just the capable administrator we were looking for. He soon got onto the complexities of operating a school within a school. We got along well with him from the start and rejoiced over the firmness with which he handled things. He, however, seemed to suffer a bit from awe of his faculty, feeling (wrongly) that he was not in the same class as a scholar and missiologist. We never felt that way and respected Paul all the more for setting aside his opportunity to build his reputation as a scholar for the sake of building (and repairing) SWM administratively. He was helped greatly to feel he had made the right choice by the love and acceptance we all had/have for each other and that we gladly extended to him. Our Tuesday faculty get-togethers helped a lot to set this tone. As mentioned, not long after he came on board, he said to me in amazement, "You guys really like each other, don't you!" Indeed, we do. And we liked him from the start.

Paul E. Pierson the Person (1927—)
At Fuller: 1980-1992

Paul E. Pierson was born in 1927, the third son of an industrial worker in Torrance, California. He was brought up in Southern California and attended a very conservative American Baptist church in which his father was a pillar. In that church he came to Christ at age six. Upon graduation as valedictorian from high school in 1944, Paul headed for Berkeley to attend the University of California where he did one year before enlisting in the Navy. He spent the next year and a half in the Navy then completed his studies in chemical engineering at Berkeley. During the first year and a half, Pierson attended a Baptist church in Berkeley but kept hearing about a Presbyterian pastor named Robert Boyd Munger. So, one Sunday in early 1948, he went to hear Munger and, as he says, he "never looked back." He got involved in First Presbyterian Church, Berkeley and became a Presbyterian.

Munger, who in his later years served with Paul on the Fuller faculty, had a profound influence on the young Pierson, challenging him to go beyond the salvation message to recognizing the Lordship of Christ and the call to mission. According to Paul "I struggled over that for nine months before telling Him (Jesus), quietly in an evening service, that He could do what He wanted to with my life" (email 3/30/04). Pierson graduated from Berkeley in 1949, expecting to make engineering his career and took a job with Colgate, Palmolive, Peet. He met Rosemary, his wife, at Munger's church during his senior year and they married in 1950. "Then one Sunday night," he says, "ten weeks after our wedding, we sat in our car and talked after church, not even going into our little apartment, and we suddenly knew God was calling us to ministry. For me that meant mission, and Rosemary was open and willing to go that direction. We have always been grateful that the call came to us together" (email, 3-30-04).

Pierson went on to Princeton Seminary, graduating in 1954. He pastored for a year and then (1955-56) became part of a Presbyterian missionary training program, part of which was conducted at the Kennedy School of Missions, Hartford, Connecticut where I was studying at the time. I don't remember having met him there, however. From there he proceeded to Brazil. He returned to Princeton to complete his Ph.D. in 1971. Pierson then served in Portugal before going to Fresno.

Each of us has his/her story of how we conducted and eventually ended the field missionary part of our lives. Pierson's first four years in Brazil were spent planting churches on the Bolivian border (just across the border from where Peter Wagner was working), then ten years teaching in Presbyterian Seminary of the North, Recife, and, as a visiting professor, in a Baptist seminary, also in Recife. He was president of the Presbyterian seminary from 1962-65 and started new programs for lay training. Pierson never met Wagner on the field. Nor did he ever meet McGavran while in Brazil, though he had started a group to study McGavran's *Bridges of God*. This led to the group inviting McGavran to come to Brazil to teach them. McGavran did this in the summer of 1965 while Mary McGavran moved them from Eugene, Oregon to Pasadena! Unfortunately, Pierson was at Princeton finishing up his Ph.D. at the time and never met McGavran till years later.

With his lay training concerns, then, Pierson was sent to Portugal by his Board to start a Theological Education by Extension program for three Portuguese denominations (Presbyterian, Methodist and Anglican), the sponsors of the small seminary where he taught in Lisbon. He says,

> When I got there I discovered they did not want such a program, all three churches were very ingrown and we had about as many faculty as students in the seminary. So after two years we felt it best to leave since apparently the only reason the church wanted a missionary was to continue support from New York and Nashville. We returned to the States in June, 73, with four kids, one in college and three more coming up, no money, no house, no job (email, 3-23-04).

He was, however, soon contacted by the search committee seeking a pastor for First Presbyterian Church, Fresno, and spent the next seven years there. But he never lost his passion for better training for church leaders. When, then, he got to Fuller, this was one of his first concerns.

Pierson as Scholar

Besides being a really fine person, a statesman, wise, competent and thoroughly admirable, Pierson is a solid scholar. We are disappointed that he has not put more into print. His dissertation on Presbyterianism in Brazil is a fine work published by Trinity University Press and the Presbyterian Historical Society. He chose that topic, at least in part, to study the leadership training offered by the Presbyterian mission and became even more convinced during this research that traditional missionary methods of selecting and training leadership were too elitist and inflexible. He suggested, in quite a non-Presbyterian way, that we need to learn from the Pentecostals and early Methodists. This concern for better training of leaders added another qualification to all that we had been learning about Paul that lined him up with the needs and desires of our faculty.

He took over the History course a few years after Winter left us and continued Winter's broad view of the expansion of the Christian movement. Although not as flamboyant as Winter, the solidness of Pierson's insights has been every bit as appealing as Winter's best. He also taught Latin American Theologies and History and Theology of Evangelical Awakenings.

In the latter, Pierson brought back into our curriculum an emphasis on renewal that we lost when Orr died. He has a strong interest and insight into the processes by which Christian groups who have grown cold can be revitalized. His 19 factors present in renewal movements, gleaned from his study of past renewals are highly valued by students. My summary of several of these would be:

> Movements usually start at the periphery of the establishment with a transforming experience in the life of a leader resulting in a new vision, a new hunger for the Word, new spiritual dynamics, new models of leadership, rediscovery of the activity of the Holy Spirit and the giftedness of every believer. This decreases the distance between social classes, clergy and laity, races, denominations, men and women and becomes, therefore, countercultural, raising opposition from the establishment. There is spiritual warfare and supernatural manifestations such as healings, visions and dreams. The structures are flexible. There is growing compassion for the marginalized, concern for mission and renewal of the broader church. Lastly, there will be those in the movement who fall into fanaticism.

We are grateful that the above insights and others are to be published in 2005 under the title, *Transformation from the Periphery: Emerging Streams of Church and Mission.*

Though administration rather than publication has been his strong suit, Pierson has published three books, chapters in about 15 other books and several articles and contributions to dictionaries. In addition to his study of Presbyterianism in Brazil, he has done a popular commentary on the Book of Acts, *Themes From Acts* (1982), a brilliant portrait of Arthur Glasser entitled "Arthur F. Glasser: Citizen of the Kingdom" (1993) and a chapter in our latest SWM/SIS statement on contextualization, *Appropriate Christianity,* entitled "Renewal, Revival and Contextualization."

But Pierson's main contribution has been as an administrator and fund raiser. After the difficulties that emerged during the previous era, we were in need of a firm hand at the wheel. Pierson supplied it.

Administrative Assistants

As mentioned, this era started with Pierson being ably assisted by Jean Barker who had worked for several years in various capacities under Glenn Schwartz. Though Jean was very able and a great help to Pierson, she struggled in her relationships with some of the other staff due in part, as we found out later, to the effects of a life-threatening physical problem that was later corrected through very risky surgery. After a year and a half, she decided to leave.

Late in 1981 Pierson chose, against Provost Barker's advice, to hire a faculty wife, Marilyn Clinton, to be his right hand person. Marilyn soon endeared herself to everyone, both because of her ability to handle whatever came her way and because of the loving way she related to people. Marilyn soon came to know almost everyone in the Seminary and knew how to get things done. She became everyone's "Mom," combining efficiency with caring and was loved by all. She served under both Pierson and Woodberry for nearly 20 years, from 1981 to 2000.

Doris Wagner, Peter's wife, also ably carried administrative responsibilities. She started by serving Peter's expanding responsibilities but soon added to her responsibilities such areas as publicity and alumni matters. She and Peter put out our newsletter, *Forwarding the Missionary Task,* mailed to all SWM alumni and maintained the alumni mailing list. She knew almost everyone who had been at the school and knew where to go to get anything at Fuller. Arguably, the office has never been run as well as under the duo of Marilyn Clinton and Doris Wagner.

Fran Hiebert was another faculty wife who began her Fuller career working in the SWM with Dean Gilliland, assisting in the Cross-Cultural Studies Program. She later went on to an important role helping coordinate the Office of Women's Concerns for the whole FTS campus.

In 1982, Betty Ann Klebe returned. As mentioned, she had worked for Dr. McGavran in Eugene. She and her family then went to Kenya to work with Daystar Communications in Nairobi. But now her husband. John, an early disciple of McGavran, took a stateside position with Daystar and came to live in South Pasadena next door to us. In her familiar position, first as McGavran's secretary, then as SWM Receptionist, she continued her very valuable service as the one to go to for any information concerning SWM past or present. She served McGavran until shortly before his death in 1990. She continued working under Dean Woodberry until she remarried after her husband, John, died. Her passion for healthy eating kept everyone in the office on their toes concerning what they ate and drank. This made things especially difficult for Woodberry who often had to sneak around to get his second and third cups of coffee when Betty Ann, whose station was just outside the Dean's door, wasn't looking!

Nancy McRae also served faithfully for several years as Receptionist.

Partners and Leadership

One of the concerns we on the faculty had was the need to have more financial support than the tuition paid by students. We noted that other institutions often developed a group of lay supporters who met from time to time to learn what was happening in their institution and who supplied financial assistance for programs and provided hospitality for students. We encouraged Pierson to start such a program. Though negotiating the institutional waters proved to be a challenge, Pierson was soon able to start what we called "SWM Partners." The Fuller administration was rightly concerned lest this new attempt to raise funds compete with other fund-raising activities. So they had to be assured that we would be going after new supporters rather than attempting to tap those already supporting the institution.

Pierson soon proved himself to be a master fund-raiser. He started with his contacts in Fresno and soon was raising enough to support the starting of some new programs. One of Paul's favorite things to do was to sponsor a dinner or to arrange for a preaching opportunity in which he interviewed international students and, sometimes, American students and faculty members. In these interviews he would prompt the students to speak of their reasons for coming to SWM and the things they were learning with us. This kind of program got many people quite excited about our programs and the opportunities to influence the work of Christ around the world. Membership in the Partners group and funding soon followed these events. The Partners groups in the Pasadena and Fresno areas have been especially active and have provided funds for student scholarships and several innovations in our programs.

Perhaps the major innovation supported initially by the Partners groups was the Leadership program. A Leadership program was at the top of Pierson's agenda. In addition, we on the faculty had from time to time discussed the fact that we were training leaders, but we recognized that none of us was a specialist in leadership training. We all treated the subject from the perspective of our own disciplines, but there was no one who attempted to pull all of the insights together in a focused way. Hiebert and I would frequently point to anthropological insights into leadership problems. Wagner would do the same from a Church Growth perspective and, while Winter was with us, he would do the same from a historical perspective.

So, though we knew of no other programs specifically focused on Leadership, we encouraged Pierson to make the development of such a program a major part of his administration. In discussing who should be the one to develop the program, then, we soon fixed on one of our own students. We felt that a person who had heard each of us faculty members deal with leadership issues would be best suited to bring our perspectives together to develop the new field. That person was "Bobby" Clinton.

J. Robert ("Bobby") Clinton (1936—)
At Fuller: 1981—

"Bobby" Clinton was born in 1936 in the Chicago area, the oldest of four children. His parents had moved north to find work in the 30s but moved back south soon after Bobby's birth and he grew up in Jackson, Mississippi where he attended high school and played baseball and track, graduating in 1954. He attended Southern Baptist churches, coming to Christ at age 10 and dedicated his life for service in a Billy Graham campaign in 1953. Following high school, he studied electrical engineering at Auburn University. He met Marilyn at Auburn and they married in 1957. Upon graduation, Bobby went into the Marines, serving three years active duty and six years in the reserves, retiring as a Captain. During this time he was strongly influenced by the Navigators.

In the midst of an electrical engineering career with Bell Telephone Laboratories, in Columbus, Ohio, Bobby and Marilyn responded to a challenge to become missionaries. They enrolled in Columbia Bible College, moving there with their four children to study for the next three years, graduating with an M.A. in 1970. They then went under the West Indies Mission to teach and be Principal of the Jamaica Bible College. Marilyn served as Registrar. They served there for three years, then were assigned to the home office in Miami where he was involved in training mission leadership and Marilyn directed the Learning Resource Center.

While in that position Bobby, influenced by Harold Dollar (later a Biola professor), began to take courses from SWM's In Service Program. "These courses were so helpful and challenging," says Bobby, that he and Marilyn "decided to come to Pasadena and pursue a doctorate of missiology" (email: 4/19/04).

Clinton came to us as a student in 1979. Between 1979 and 1981, Bobby impressed us as a student and served as a Teaching Assistant for both Wagner and myself. As a TA, he was well-organized and innovative. He not only learned what we had been teaching, he took opportunities in his work as a TA to organize our materials in creative ways that were often very helpful to the students. He did his Doctor of Missiology under my direction with a focus on Ethnotheology, graduating in 1981.

As mentioned, Dr. Pierson had Leadership at the top of his agenda and so did we on the faculty. In discussions about the need for a Leadership concentration, we all agreed that Clinton would be a good choice, since he had studied under all of us and had worked in his mission on leadership training. So we hired him, starting in the fall of 1981, with Leadership as his field. Funds contributed by the Partners would make this possible at first with the expectation that increased enrolment would enable us to make the position permanent before long.

As it turned out, Leadership soon became one of our most popular concentrations so that by 1985 Bobby's position had become a solid tenure-track position and we found it advisable to hire a second person (Elliston) to teach in the Leadership area. In addition, Bobby decided to do a Ph.D. under Hiebert, focusing on Leadership Emergence Theory. He finished this in 1989.

Clinton's Contributions to SWM

Bobby's first contribution was to develop a brand new field within missiology. He began to develop new courses on leadership selection and training and a new vocabulary to go along with it. He began to study biblical leaders and extra-biblical leaders to attempt to discover how God develops leaders over a lifetime. One disturbing finding was that most Christian leaders both within and outside the Bible do not finish well. He developed courses on change dynamics, leadership training, leadership development, organizational development and biblical leadership.

During his 24 years with us, he has done breakthrough research into leadership emergence theory—how leaders develop and how they succeed or fail over a lifetime. He has studied and taught on mentoring and put into practice the mentoring of numerous students over the years. In addition, he has written a large number of books and articles and done several CDs on leadership, including a series of biblical commentaries with leadership in focus. Among his major books are *The Making of a Leader* (1988), *Connecting—The Mentoring Relationships You Need to Succeed in Life* (1992), *Focused Lives—Inspirational Life Changing Lessons From Eight Effective Christian Leaders Who Finished Well* (1995), *Strategic Concepts—That Clarify a Focused Life* (1998) and *Clinton's Biblical Leadership Commentary, vol. II* (2004)—a CD with 14 leadership commentaries on it.

There were good reasons for the fact that Leadership soon became the concentration that attracted the largest number of students. For one, the students we attract either are or expect they may be called on to be leaders. So, the topic is relevant. Another reason is that the research and presentations of the findings are fresh and innovative. Though Bobby's propensity for new labels for various entities can be a bit of a burden, the value of the insights outweigh considerations of vocabulary! A third reason is Bobby himself. He gives himself to his students. He not only teaches how to mentor, he demonstrates it, and a number of his mentorees are making themselves significant in the lives of their mentorees.

Viggo Sogaard (1939—)
At Fuller: 1981—

We also hired Viggo Sogaard at this time (1981). Viggo was and is a world-class communication specialist from Denmark who had done an M.A. in Communication at Wheaton under Dr. James Engel and was advised by Engel to continue his studies with us. With this in mind, I arranged for Dr. Pierson to meet with Sogaard at the Lausanne Committee conference in Pattaya, Thailand in late 1980. He had impressed the whole conference at Pattaya with what were perhaps the best presentations made to that group of 1,000 or so mission leaders.

Sogaard was born into a large Danish family in 1939, just before World War II broke out. His family turned to farming to survive the war. He got into a church scouting program in his early teens and came to Christ at age 14 at a scouting summer camp. Unlike the other children in his family, he had the privilege of attending high school. He then applied to the Danish Navy Radio College, interested in the job but also interested in the access it gave him to a free education. He says,

> It was during that time I started to read missionary stories and I began feeling the call to give my life to mission. Our church had work in Thailand, and this was the country that was most in my mind. . . . [O]ne morning I told God in my prayer that if He wanted me to be a missionary, then I would do it, but I wanted to be absolutely sure. If He would let me know in such a way that there was no doubt, then it would be the rest of my life. Just a couple of hours later the postman arrived, and he gave me the youth magazine of our church. I looked first at the back page which was blank apart from a quote in the middle of the page. The quote was from Is. 6:8, "The Lord said, who shall I send, who will go for us? Then I said, here I am, send me." This came as a real jolt, and I said to God: Okay, this will be the rest of my life. Within a month I applied to our church to go into missionary training when my contract with the navy was finished (email: 4/20/04).

He went to Glasgow Bible College and there earned a University of London Dip.Th. degree, doing the four year course in three years. He got engaged to Ketty after his first year at GBC and she joined him as a student there for the next two years. They married after graduation in 1963, leaving for Thailand three months later. They spent the next 13 years in Thailand. In his second year

Viggo started the communication ministry called the Voice of Peace. This has been a significant ministry to the present. He also started what was probably the first Bible teaching program on cassette tapes. Between their second and third terms Sogaard was able to study communication at the Wheaton Graduate School, earning an M.A. in 1973 with a thesis on cassette ministry that was later published as *Everything You Need to Know for a Cassette Ministry* (1974).

With Thai personnel running Voice of Peace, his children needing to be in Danish schools and his own international ministry developing, they moved back to Denmark in 1976. He has been involved in the Lausanne Movement from the beginning, figuring significantly both on the Lausanne Committee and the Lausanne Strategy Group and making important presentations at Lausanne 1974 (workshops) and Pattaya 1980 (2 plenary sessions).

At Pattaya, Pierson invited Viggo to come as a student and part-time instructor in communication. This Viggo did, arriving in the fall of 1981, completing his Ph.D. under my supervision in 1985 and enhancing our focus on communication considerably from that time till the present. He has continued to reside in Denmark, holding a regular half-time position with us commuting to Fuller three times a year from Denmark or, often, from some other part of the world where he's been teaching or consulting.

When not with us, Sogaard is constantly "on the go." For several years, he was Senior Consultant for Ministry Communication for World Vision International, traveling constantly to World Vision outposts with the aim of integrating effective strategies with development projects. Later, he became Media Consultant for the United Bible Societies, pioneering creative ways to communicate the Bible to non-literates and training Bible Society personnel to do the same. This has involved numerous projects around the world and constant travel, teaching and production of handbooks.

In addition to his worldwide work with World Vision and the Bible Society, Viggo started and runs The Asian Institute of Christian Communication, held for a month every second or third year in Chiang Mai, Thailand. The Institute in 2005 was the twelfth. This is a training program in communication in which he and I from Fuller participate to assist Asians, some of whom are from organizations such as World Vision and the United Bible Societies, others from radio ministries. It is an important non-formal learning opportunity.

Sogaard's Contribution to SWM

It is impossible to estimate Sogaard's publicity value in advertising SWM around the world. Wherever he has gone, SWM/SIS has been advertised and honored. Beyond this considerable contribution, he added to our curriculum courses in such areas as Communication Strategy, Survey Research, Understanding Media and Communicating to Non-Literates.

Sogaard is also very effective in supervising doctoral research, often meeting with his students in places other than Pasadena where they live and he visits. Viggo is an activist and very personable. He not only helps students, he disciples them. He is one of our best researchers and supervisors of research. In addition, he has published a number of valuable books, starting with his M.A. thesis, *Everything You Need to Know for a Cassette Ministry* (1975), still a classic on that subject. For the United Bible Societies he published *Audio Scriptures Handbook* (1991) and *Communicating Scriptures* (2002). In addition, he has produced two books that encapsulate what he has been teaching in some of his courses at SWM/SIS—*Media in Church and Mission* (1993) and *Research in Church and Mission* (1996).

In line with his traveling, Sogaard works hard to enable missionaries and internationals to learn in their home contexts. The AICC in Thailand mentioned above is one example. More recently, Sogaard has been involved in setting up a Ph.D. program in cooperation with SIS in India to train seminary and Bible school level teachers of missiology. He also was able to work out a program with the University of Copenhagen, enabling several of our professors to teach our courses within the Faculty of Theology there. This program ran for several years but is presently on hold.

R. Daniel Shaw (1943—)
At Fuller: 1982—

Since I had trained as a Bible translator, one of my dreams was to see SWM training Bible translators. In the summer of 1974, my wife and I lived in a Kamwe (Nigeria) compound with Roger Mohrlang, the person Wycliffe Bible Translators had assigned to work on a Kamwe New Testament translation. During our time together, I had literally talked Roger out of attending Gordon-Conwell Seminary, where he was already accepted and planning to start M.Div. studies in the fall. I offered him a position as my Teaching

Assistant for the purpose of teaching a course on Bible translation. He taught the translation course and TAed for me, then, for 2 years while he completed an M.A. in New Testament, leading to a doctorate at Oxford and a career teaching New Testament at Whitworth College in Spokane, WA. Roger did a good job, but my dream was for a whole program that would offer degrees specifically in Bible translation. Wycliffe training at that time was in linguistics with translation training being largely relegated to on-the-field workshops.

So when Roger left, I taught the course but was still on the lookout for someone to do a program. I have already mentioned my hopes that the Brewsters would take up this challenge. But that didn't work out. In 1979, then, I was in Papua New Guinea teaching on contextualization at the Wycliffe base at Ukarumpa. While there I discussed a variety of things with the Wycliffe Director of Technical Studies, Ken McElhanon. These discussions led to his making Dan Shaw available to come to Fuller while on furlough in 1980 with three purposes: to check us out as a possible place for Wycliffe missionaries to do advanced study, to teach the Bible translation course and also to discuss the development of an SWM extension program in PNG.

Dan, the son of missionary parents, was born in 1943 in Seattle. He spent his early life in India and the Philippines. He and his wife Karen spent 12 years among the Samo people of PNG. In addition to his language and translation work among the Samo, Shaw had earned a Ph.D. in Anthropology from the University of Papua New Guinea (1976) and had extensive experience both in translation and in anthropological research.

We arranged for Dan to come for fall term in 1980 as an Adjunct. Concerning a chat I had with him one day during that term, Shaw writes,

> I was in Chuck's office one day when he asked me what a translation curriculum would look like. I replied that I had no idea—I was an anthropologist who did translation, not a translation theoretician. Chuck's response was to give me two large folders overflowing with materials he had collected over a decade. He challenged me to look them over and develop a curriculum for a translation program at Fuller. Over the next month I was busy going through the SWM curriculum in order to lay out a program of courses most beneficial to SIL people in PNG. At the same time Chuck kept asking if I had looked at his stuff. So, finally to get him off my back, I went through the

materials and began to think this could be fun. I got a hold of folks in Dallas and they sent me what they had, and it went from there. When I showed the material to Chuck he was delighted, and the next thing I knew, Paul Pierson was touting the possibility of a new Translation program at SWM, with Dan Shaw as the director (email, March 2004).

Several times over the years, I had mentioned to our faculty that I'd like to see a Bible translation program in SWM but that I felt it to be a low priority unless we could get outside funding. On one occasion when I had mentioned my dream in a faculty meeting, Paul Hiebert exclaimed something like, "Why should such a program need outside funding? I think this is important enough that we should make it a priority and find funding from within our budget!" I felt supported.

Meanwhile, Dan went back to PNG in January 1981 and Pierson and Hiebert visited the Wycliffe officials in Dallas seeking to arrange a joint program with Shaw seconded to us to direct it. With a generally positive response to this plan, Pierson arranged to go to PNG in April to discuss the translation program and proposed extension program with Shaw. As the two of them drove from institution to institution looking for a site for the extension program, Pierson attempted to convince a reluctant Shaw that SWM needed him more than the Samo needed him to complete their New Testament translation. Dan says, Pierson "tried to convince me this was a strategic time in the school's history and their need of my coming to serve both in anthropology and Bible translation. I kept saying I was happy, the Samo needed the rest of the NT and I had no plans to leave" (email, March 2004). But it took an amazing interaction with God Himself to finally bring Shaw to us. He says,

> On our next visit to the village, immediately after this trip, I was sitting on the floor of the community center watching a literacy class led by one of our promising Samo instructors . . . As I watched, I suddenly heard a voice (over my left shoulder) asking, "Whose church is this?" I recognized this was not your usual conversation as I looked around and saw no one. The question was repeated, and I realized I was face to face with the Lord—and the rest of my life. . . . So I said,
>
> "It's yours Lord."
>
> "So then, I can take care of it."
>
> "Yes, but . . . they need Scripture to survive, lots more than they have now."

"You don't think I can take care of that?"

"Yes, but, we know what we're doing and are ready to do it."

"I have another job for you. You have filled your role here, I will take care of the Samo. I want you to make a broader impact on Bible translation. Go to Fuller and develop the program you have worked out with Kraft and Pierson. You will have a broader impact on many more people from all over the world."

"But Lord . . ." The conversation was over—God won! (email March 2004).

As a footnote, Dan adds that soon after they left the Samo a people movement started, leading to over half of the Samo becoming Christians. But, to the disappointment of the Shaws, little new translation has been done. There have, however, been missionaries continuing to assist the growth of Christianity among the Samo and now, at long last, Samo are being trained to be involved in Bible translation.

Shaw's Contribution to SWM

After adjuncting with us in Fall 1980 and Fall 1981, Shaw joined our faculty officially in July of 1982, having worked out the details of the joint program and funding with SIL (Summer Institute of Linguistics—the academic wing of Wycliffe Bible Translators). SIL courses were incorporated into the SWM degree programs and certain SIL personnel would teach for us over the years. Over the next 10 years, that program yielded over 100 graduates with masters and doctorate degrees, many of them nationals who returned to make a strategic impact on Bible translation in their home countries.

Shaw's coming to SWM added the Translation Program to our offerings. And he had a direct impact on our extension programs. He initiated the PNG program in which several of us taught between 1982 and 1994. We taught many missionaries but, disappointingly, few PNG nationals. Many of our students learned incarnational ministry through these courses. And many eventually came to SWM campus, including our present Dean, Doug McConnell who started his M.A. program in PNG. Dan has continued to function in our various extension programs and now chairs the SIS International Cooperative Programs Committee.

In addition to these things, Shaw has added several anthropology courses to our curriculum and kept up relationships with other Christian anthropologists. Over the last several years he has become a major player in the developing and tightening of our Ph.D. program, especially in the Research Design course that is prerequisite to entrance into the Ph.D. program. He is also one of our best in supervising Ph.D. dissertations.

Along the way, Dan has published several books and articles. Among them are *Transculturation: The Cultural Factor in Translation* (1988) and *Communicating God's Word in a Complex World* (2002, with Chuck Van Engen) dealing with communication, *Kandila: Samo Ceremonialism and Interpersonal Relationships* (1990) and *From Longhouse to Village: Samo Social Change* (1996) dealing with his experience as a missionary-anthropologist among the Samo of Papua New Guinea and *Understanding Folk Religion* (1999 with Paul Hiebert and Tite Tienou) dealing with animism.

Che Bin Tan (1937—)
At Fuller: 1982-1991

For some time, Glasser had been anxious for us to do something on China. Finally, in 1982, Che Bin Tan (Ph.D. 1973), a theology professor from the faculty of China Graduate School of Theology in Hong Kong became available to start a Chinese Studies Program.

This program ran from 1982 to 1991 and though it never attracted a large number of students, it did turn out some outstanding leaders. It also became a catalyst in helping Chinese Americans to mobilize for mission, leading to a number of mission conferences among them.

Tan was born in Kobe, Japan in 1937 into a family that had fled China for political reasons. Soon after he was born, however, they returned to China and Che Bin did his primary school there. Through a series of circumstances, including his father's death in the Philippines during the Second World War, with his mother and a brother he ended up in Hong Kong in 1949. There, he says, "I was able to grow up . . . in an environment which was free from political turmoil. But most important of all, I became a Christian in Hong Kong" (email February 2005).

Influenced by his mother, Tan attended evangelistic meetings and quietly committed himself to Christ. He then participated in what he calls "a flourishing student work [that] contributed to a fundamental change in the make-up of the Chinese Church in Hong Kong" (ibid). He was touched by God especially through church summer camps and "became convinced of God's calling me to engage in full-time ministry." So, upon graduating from high school in 1955, he enrolled in Bethel Bible Seminary, Hong Kong, to prepare himself for a ministry of evangelism and church planting. He discovered, however, that his primary gifting was in teaching.

Accordingly, he enrolled in Westminster Theological Seminary in Philadelphia to pursue advanced degrees toward a teaching career. He was there from 1963-68, during which time he met fellow student, Esther Yang, who he married in 1968. At Westminster he solidified his faith and emerged in 1968 "much more committed to Jesus Christ and His gospel" but convinced that graduate theological education needed to be done differently if it was to meet the spiritual needs of Chinese. Whereas in America, seminaries assume that the spiritual needs of students will be met through their church involvement, he felt this is not an adequate approach for Chinese students. So, during his seminary days, he and three others dreamed up what in 1975 became China Graduate School of Theology, headed by one of the four, Jonathan Chao. A major aim of CGST, in reaction against the perceived neglect in America of the students' spiritual growth, has been to incorporate the spiritual dimension more effectively in the lives of students.

Before joining the CGST faculty in 1977, however, Che Bin took what he calls "a few detours." He says,

> Before I taught full-time in China Graduate School in 1977, Esther and I joined Overseas Missionary Fellowship as Associate Members, to serve on the faculty of Discipleship Training Center and Singapore Bible College in 1968-70. Then we taught for one year in China Evangelical Seminary, Taipei, Taiwan, when they got started in 1970, and returned to serve as their Dean of Academic Studies again, in 1974-77. In between, I fulfilled my residency requirement for my graduate work in New Testament in the University of Manchester under Prof. F.F. Bruce in 1971-73. It was in this period that I found out that, politically I was a "stateless" person in the eyes of many governments of this world, and therefore, for the purpose of ministry, I got U.S. citizenship . . . So, in effect, I did teaching ministry as an American missionary (ibid).

In addition to the Hong Kong Board, CGST established an American Board to support the school. Winter was on their first Board and in the early 80s, Arthur Glasser served as Chairperson. Out of concern for the need for training for Chinese pastors in America, Glasser and other Board members began to discuss the possibility of Fuller and CGST cooperating on such training. The result was the establishment in 1982 of a joint program on Chinese Studies and Evangelism with Che Bin seconded by CGST to SWM to initiate and direct the program.

For the next nine years, Tan ran what he considers "the most viable training program in the United States" for Chinese and Chinese Americans. Though Che Bin and Glasser did most of the teaching, they also involved China specialists such as Ralph Covell, Wing Hung Lam, Jonathan Chao and several local Chinese pastors. Dr. Gail Law, a CGST professor and SWM doctoral student, was of great assistance in the early years of the program as were Che Bin's wife, Esther Tan, and a student Rudy Mak. Esther, especially, worked tirelessly behind the scenes to make the program go. Gail Law also worked with Tan to set up a research program with the Chinese Coordination Center of World Evangelization in Hong Kong to enable Chinese students to do research on church growth and contextualization. This program resulted in several of the CCCWE publications during this period.

To solicit the support of the North American Chinese community, a team of leading Chinese pastors in North America was set up. One of the members of this team was Hoover Wong, who later (1988) joined the faculty of SWM.

Tan says of his time here,

> Personally, the time at SWM was a time for me to wrestle with the problem of contextualization of the gospel in the Chinese context. I found the SWM environment very favorable to such effort, because this was in line with the purpose of the School and the faculty was very supportive. In all the different courses I offered while teaching in the School, the integrating center is the cross-cultural perspective. I examined, in particular, the New Testament from this perspective. My purpose is to build a Biblical foundation for a Chinese contextual theology and to address the core values of the Chinese culture from New Testament Biblical Theology (ibid).

Signs and Wonders

A major event in the history of SWM/SIS was the addition to our curriculum of an emphasis on working in the realm of the healing power of Jesus. Sometime in the spring of 1981 Peter Wagner came to a faculty meeting saying something like the following, "My friend John Wimber says he could teach a course on healing. Are we interested?" Several (not all) of us were interested in such a course. After some discussion, then, we decided the topic was important enough to our students that we should sponsor it.

We had come to know Wimber during the mid-seventies as a Church Growth strategist working with Wagner under the Fuller Evangelistic Association, doing research and teaching concerning the growth of churches in the US. He had been associate pastor of a large Friends church in Yorba Linda, CA after his conversion in the midst of a life in the popular music industry. He left the church position to work with Wagner full-time.

We knew John as a very intelligent strategist and a very likable person. In the mid-seventies, however, he was not into healing. He had attended a dispensational Bible school where he had been taught that God was not doing miraculous things anymore.

However, in the late 70s, John and his wife Carol were leading a Bible class, the members of which were starting to believe in miracles. This class soon grew into a church that by 1981 was attracting over 2000 worshipers every Sunday morning and again in the evening. And John, contrary to his Bible school teaching that miracles had ceased, had become convinced that he and his followers were to pray for healing. So his church affiliated with Calvary Chapel but soon joined the Vineyard movement (a spinoff from Calvary Chapel), and became a healing church, believing in and practicing healing under the power of the Holy Spirit. John was an attractive preacher, gifted in healing himself and had a team of others working with him who were also gifted in healing.

At SWM, some of us were feeling the need for more understanding of the part played by the Holy Spirit in mission. I, for one, while working as a missionary in Nigeria, had been asked by the church leaders what to do about evil spirits. But I had no answer for them. I didn't know. I had never been taught on that subject in Christian college or seminary. Nor had I ever been a part of churches that dealt with demons or that practiced faith healing. Wagner had a similar story from his days in Bolivia. Both of us had operated in non- or even anti-Pentecostal circles. So Peter and I especially were anxious to learn more and to have our students learn more concerning the power of God for healing and deliverance.

For us, John Wimber was a "credible witness" to the readiness of God to heal in our day. We would not have responded positively to a highly emotional approach to healing that characterizes many Pentecostal and charismatic leaders. But John seemed balanced and credible, not easily stereotyped as weird. So Wagner and I to a greater extent and others of our SWM faculty to a lesser extent, opened ourselves up to Wimber's teaching and the demonstrations provided in class concerning the healing power of the Holy Spirit.

The class, named "Signs, Wonders and Church Growth," (MC510) was initiated in January of 1982 with about 85 students plus Peter and Doris Wagner and my wife Meg and myself. Wagner was what we call "the Professor of Record," the faculty person ultimately in charge of the course, with Wimber as an Adjunct teaching most of the sessions. We met every Monday evening from 7 to 10 or later. John typically taught for two to two and a half hours and then would close his notebook and say, "Now let's do the stuff!" That meant it was ministry time—a time that usually would start with John inviting the Holy Spirit to come and take charge. He would then wait until someone, either himself, one of his team members or one of the students, would volunteer a "word of knowledge" concerning a physical problem someone in the class was feeling. Following this "word" from the Lord, John would usually simply say, "Who is it?" And a person would identify him/herself as the one with the stated problem. The fact that the Holy Spirit had identified a person by pointing out that person's problem was taken to mean that that was a person God wanted to heal. So one of the team members would pray for that person and healing would usually follow.

Seeing the Holy Spirit make His presence manifest right in our classroom by healing people was breathtaking for me. Often there were 8-10 or more people healed each evening. However, I found the "words of knowledge" even more impressive, since these represented information revealed directly to people in the class. And they were often so specific to a person's condition that we easily dismissed the possibility that they came by chance. It was clear both from the words of knowledge and from the healings that followed that God was doing something quite new, and right in a seminary classroom!

For many of the students as well as for the Wagners and Krafts, the experience was nothing less than transforming. We watched. We went through a paradigm shift in our thinking. And then, with prompting and guidance by Wimber, we went through what I have called a "practice shift." We began "doing the stuff" ourselves both in class and outside of it.

Without wanting it, however, we found that this course generated controversy within Fuller. For one thing, it attracted a large number of students, within the next few years (1982-85) becoming the largest class in the history of the school. At its height, over 250 students were enrolled and we had to meet in the basement gymnasium of the Congregational Church just off campus. Though many received healing and the presence of the Lord was regularly felt in class, the size of the class, its charismatic nature (in a hitherto non-charismatic seminary), the fact that the class attracted media attention and a lack of trust in Wimber on the part of many of the faculty in the School of Theology conspired to generate criticism within the seminary.

The critics contended such things as that the nature of the course did not fit into the traditional Reformed Theology of Fuller (true), that it raised unwarranted expectations among students (perhaps true for some) and that it is not proper for an Adjunct to be attracting so many students since the institution has no real control over a non-faculty member. Unfortunately, this last criticism was not entirely unwarranted. For Wimber himself was not careful in public statements to define the nature of his position at Fuller. He allowed himself on several public occasions to be introduced as "a faculty member of Fuller Seminary," rather than simply as an Adjunct. This gave a wrong impression of him and of Fuller and forced faculty members who were not in favor of the course or of charismatic theology into the embarrassing position of having to explain how a course like this got into the Fuller curriculum. Though those of us in favor of the course could sympathize with this criticism and were upset that Wimber did not define his position accurately, we feel that the reaction to the situation was not handled well.

The upshot was that the Provost made it known to us that he planned to cancel the course. To save him the trouble, our faculty, led by Dean Pierson, took the initiative and officially canceled the course after the Winter Term 1985. The FTS Administration, for their part appointed a faculty committee to do a study of the situation and to produce a report. That report was published in 1987 under the title *Ministry and the Miraculous.* To those of us in favor of the course, the study and the publication were very disappointing.

A group of students, however, appealed to the Provost to be allowed to offer a substitute course as a student activity, for no credit, in the Spring Term of 1986. The Provost gave permission and even contributed to the fund they were raising to provide honoraria for speakers. That noncredit course was offered and attracted about 135 students, with several prominent people (plus Wagner and myself) invited to lecture.

Wagner and I did not give up, however. We decided we could develop a substitute course, if allowed to. It would not be the same as Wimber's course, and not likely to be as good as we felt his was, but a course nevertheless. As full professors with tenure we knew we could not be dismissed as Wimber had been. Wagner and I were determined that our students would not go to their fields of service as ignorant as we had been concerning how to work in the power of God. So we went to the Provost with the proposal that we teach a different course on healing. He agreed to allow this for an experimental three years on condition that we structure it as a discussion of both the pros and the cons of a healing ministry. We would, therefore, have to agree to invite speakers who were not on our side of the issues. This we did, numbering the course MC550, in hopes that people would not view it as simply a continuation of the prior course. For the designation MC510 had gotten to be a buzzword for the healing emphasis at Fuller.

We started this course, then, in January of 1987, with good enrolment, and ran it this way for two years. During these years the controversy calmed down somewhat. And the students were involved in a more typical seminary course. In the process at least two of the Theology faculty who lectured for us seemed to develop a more positive attitude toward the course.

Since by this time I was getting more and more involved in inner healing, Peter and I decided I should develop a course on Inner Healing. He would continue with the present course, restructured to focus on physical healing and following a Wimber approach rather than the discussion of pros and cons approach that the Provost had mandated. So I worked out a plan for my course and we presented our intent to the Provost. He agreed to allow the Physical Healing course but to our surprise disallowed the course on Inner Healing. To our greater surprise, however, he suggested I develop a course on Power Encounter. So, in 1989 we went back to a single course on Physical Healing, taught by Wagner. And by 1990 I, at the invitation of the Provost, began to teach the Power Encounter course.

Since 1990, then, we have been teaching several courses on healing and spiritual warfare, each with a focus on *doing* such ministry (just as Wimber taught us), not simply *thinking about* healing, deliverance and spiritual warfare.

Chapter 8

The Pierson Era II

1984-1992

So much happened during the Pierson era that we devote a second chapter to it.

Edmund (Eddie) Gibbs (1938—)
At Fuller: 1984-1988, 1996—

With the retirement of McGavran, Wagner especially felt we needed a second Church Growth person. In addition, it was rumored that McGavran had made it a condition of his funding of the Chair of Church Growth that Wagner occupied, that there be a second CG person. Wagner had taught and been impressed by a British fellow named Eddie Gibbs in his D.Min. courses and thought of him first. Gibbs was at the time working with the British and Foreign Bible Society in London. So he was approached, accepted and joined us in 1984.

Gibbs was born in Nottingham, England in 1938 and gave his life to Christ in 1954 at St. Paul's Anglican Church, Nottingham. After secondary school, he did a stint in the Royal Air Force and then enrolled at Oak Hill Theological College and spent the next five years (1958-63) preparing for ministry in the Church of England. During that time he was also a visiting student at London Bible College where he prepared for the London University B.D. (granted 1962) as an external student.

After ordination he served in the South London parish of Wandsworth (1963-66) and then responded with Renee his wife to the call to become missionaries under the South American Missionary Society. Eddie writes,

> [We] worked in Chile for the next four years, pastoring the Anglican Center in Santiago and church planting in Quilpue. Eddie was also asked to work on the restructuring of the

Anglican Diocese, which at that time covered the three
Republics of Chile, Bolivia and Peru! They returned to the
United Kingdom in 1970 for Eddie to take up the position of
Home and Education Secretary of the SMS (email 4/11/04).

From 1977 until he came to SWM in 1984, Eddie was with the
British and Foreign Bible Society managing their area representatives
and leading their team that was publishing Bible study materials. He
entered Fuller's Doctor of Ministry program in 1979 and then began
leading church growth seminars for church leaders throughout the UK
based on what he was learning in that program. From 1982-84 he was
on loan to the Billy Graham Mission England evangelistic project as
National Training Director. In this position he creatively prepared
small groups to receive the new converts from the six Graham
regional missions.

He first taught at SWM as an Adjunct in 1983, then joined our
faculty full-time in 1984, partly funded by the Anaheim Vineyard
Church, pastored by John Wimber. In 1988, though, he left SWM to
serve as the first occupant of the Robert Boyd Munger Chair of
Evangelism in the Fuller School of Theology from 1988-91. He then
took a church position as Associate Rector of All Saints' Episcopal
Church in Beverly Hills, CA until 1996 when he came back to SWM
as the Donald A. McGavran Professor of Church Growth.

Gibbs' Contributions to SWM

Gibbs has had great concern to learn why churches decline,
even though they might have started out strong. He used to make
statements like, "Wagner teaches about how churches grow, I teach
about why they die!" He studies the causes of nominality and what to
do about situations where church members are brought in but not
discipled.

One of his greatest contributions to evangelism and discipleship
theory was to recognize that new converts need new churches. In
working on the Billy Graham missions in 1982-84, he helped
Graham's advance people to recognize that new Christians seldom
survive in old churches. An important part of the advance work
should, therefore, be to provide new bodies of believers for the
converts to fit into. For two years before the preaching started, then,
small, home fellowships were started made up of people whose
primary concern was to disciple new Christians in ways relevant to
them and most likely quite different from the established churches.

More recently he has concerned himself with researching and documenting new forms of church that are reaching the never churched and the disaffected former churched, especially among the under 35s in the UK. He finds many younger Britishers who have not given up on Jesus but are not comfortable in the established churches. They are, therefore, creating radically new church forms and influencing many who have no Christian background.

Eddie is a prolific writer. Among his most important publications are *I Believe in Church Growth* (1981, 1985, 1990), *The God Who Communicates* (1985), *Followed or Pushed?* (1987), *In Name Only—Tackling the Problem of Nominal Christianity* (1994) and *Church Next* (2000). Coming out in 2005 are *Leadership Next* and (with Ryan Bolger) *Emerging Churches: Creating Christian Community in Postmodern Cultures*.

He is currently working on ways to assist the next generations of Christian leaders. He is seeking to identify passionate leaders and to equip them to use their gifting to extend Christianity both locally and globally.

From Extension to Partnership

During the early 80s, especially with our interest in Dan Shaw, the possibility of helping in the training of missionaries and national leaders in Papua New Guinea began to form in our minds. We had long talked of the fact that it was/is very expensive in time and money for national leaders to come to Pasadena for training and that it would be much better for us to go to them.

And we had had sort of an extension program in Korea where, starting in the 70s several of us took turns in teaching courses at the Asian Center for Theological Study and Mission (ACTS). One of our graduates, Marlin Nelson was teaching mission courses there and experiencing a good bit of friction with certain of the theologians. Whether for this reason or simply to enrich their program, he invited us to teach courses for ACTS credit.

With Dan Shaw taking the lead, we ran an extension program in Papua New Guinea from 1982-94 that was successful in training people and in attracting quality people (including future SIS Dean, Doug McConnell) to come to Pasadena to continue their studies. But the program struggled financially.

During the late 80s and early 90s, we initiated an extension program in Nigeria in response to a request by a number of Nigerian church leaders who had contacted Dean Pierson on a trip he, Dr. Gilliland and some SWM partners took in 1987. It was to be for a five-year period and was largely funded by First Fruits Foundation. Though it did not support itself financially and so was not renewed after the five years were up, a number of significant leaders were trained, some of whom came to Pasadena to complete masters and doctoral degrees, while others transferred the credits to programs in Nigerian schools.

Though many of us on the SWM faculty had contacts in various parts of the world that led us to suggest extension or partnership programs, our administrators became skittish over the strain on our limited finances. Among the places suggested for extension programs were Israel, Brazil, the Philippines and South Africa. But the fact that the PNG and Nigeria programs did not pay for themselves kept us from launching anything more. Though a program we wanted to launch in South Africa might have paid for itself, certain Fuller Trustees shot it down lest we be seen as endorsing Apartheid.

One bright spot has been an arrangement with Fuller to grant credit to certain students who attend Sogaard's Asian Institute of Christian Communication, mentioned in the last chapter.

During the mid-80s and early 90s, Sogaard was appointed to the Extension Committee and began to suggest to the faculty a different approach to what we had always visualized as extension. His idea was that we ought to enter into cooperative programs or partnerships with overseas institutions in which we would help those institutions or programs to achieve goals that they themselves set. These would not be extensions of our programs but cooperative ventures with these other institutions. In 1996, Sogaard and Elliston wrote a paper outlining this approach (published in Van Engen 1996). This led to a change of the name of the Extension Committee to the Committee for International Cooperative Programs and led to cooperative programs in Denmark (University of Copenhagen), Indonesia and India.

Perhaps the best example of our involvement in cooperative programs is the relationship Sogaard worked out with the Faculty of Theology at the University of Copenhagen. Viggo got to know a fairly conservative member of the otherwise very liberal faculty named Hans Raun Iversen. He was then asked to give some guest lectures and to teach a course. Sogaard writes,

The relationship developed, and a program called Theological Communication was established. A local committee coordinated the program, and [I] represented [SWM] on the committee. Eventually four different courses were taught each year, and several Fuller SWM professors were involved . . . The courses were well accepted and drew quite large groups of students. . . . Unfortunately, some internal conflicts at the faculty in 2002 caused the program to be reduced significantly, and presently only a few courses are taught (email: October 2004).

The program in India is of quite a different sort. The aim is to train Indian missiologists who are already in faculty positions up to Ph.D,. level without requiring them to leave India. The program, now in its third year, is the result of a plan developed during a three-day consultation by Indian Christian leaders and mission educators, attended by Sogaard and Shaw in March 1999. "The participants strongly felt that the primary need was for a doctoral level program in mission studies" (ibid.). So, by 2001, they had formed the Consortium for Indian Missiological Education with four Indian institutions cooperating with Fuller. The program was officially inaugurated in June of 2002. So far, four SWM/SIS faculty members have taught courses in India plus several Indians, including some of our graduates. "The program is run in a modular form with seminars taking place at member institutions around India" (ibid.).

With all of the good things stemming from both extension and partnership programs and with all the good will that SWM/SIS has toward assisting with training programs that do not necessitate students coming to America, there are still major issues with regard to funding. We don't seem to be able to work things out so these programs pay for themselves. With funding for our home base in Pasadena also a major problem, the future of partnerships is bleak unless major grants can be attracted. The India program, for example, is only possible because of funding from First Fruits Foundation who provided a challenge grant, with Fuller raising the matching funds to meet the $120,000 budget. Approximately half of those funds have been spent but the prospects for new funding are uncertain. Thus, the future of this program and others is uncertain.

J. Dudley Woodberry (1934—)
At Fuller: 1985—

In the early 80s, Don McCurry invited Dudley Woodberry (Ph.D. Harvard), the premier American evangelical Islamicist, to join him in the Zwemer Institute. The Institute was based in Pasadena, at the U.S. Center. Woodberry was teaching at Reformed Bible College (1979-83) in Grand Rapids, Michigan but moved to Pasadena in 1983 to become Director of Academic Affairs at Zwemer. He then taught in joint programs between SWM and Zwemer and thus became an adjunct with us. His time at Zwemer lasted two years, during which time I and probably others let Dudley know that if the Zwemer Institute situation did not work out, we would do whatever we could to find him a place on our faculty. When it did not work out for him to continue at Zwemer, we were able to arrange for him to join us at SWM in 1985. The fact that this delightful man with such scholarly credentials just kind of landed in our lap can be seen as another of God's pleasant surprises. We had wanted an Islamicist, a desire intensified by the focus we gave to Islam in 1978. McCurry taught a course for us but we felt we would like to be able to offer a specialty in the area.

John Dudley Woodberry was born in 1934 in the Chinese province of Shandung of missionary parents and grandparents. He spent his early years in China but it was during a furlough at age three that he committed his life to Christ. Back in China, an experience of falling through the ice, contracting pneumonia and nearly dying "led to a sense that [he] had been saved for a purpose" (2002:24). He says,

> My early awareness of the need for mission developed as I heard Chinese wailing at gravesides and saw them going into the Buddhist temple near our home to burn incense before a Buddha. I sensed my parents' response as I rode the crossbar of my father's bike in Panglai, where he was an evangelist at a Presbyterian mission school (ibid.:24).

While in a China Inland Mission boarding school, World War II broke out and the children became prisoners when the Japanese strung barbed wire around their school. The children's parents were elsewhere and Dudley and the others did not hear from them for a full year. Then a Christian Japanese officer was able to arrange an exchange of prisoners to free them and reunite them with their parents. Alas, they missed their train but that was providential. They saw later that guerrillas had derailed the earlier train! Reunited with his parents, they returned to the States where his parents studied agriculture at Cornell University. Then his Father returned to China and

> Mother, one sister, and I moved to Nyack on the Hudson River, where Mother ultimately taught missions at the Missionary Training Institute (now Nyack College). Here we listened to a stream of missionaries and each year attended the Congress of Bands in Carnegie Hall, New York, to hear missionary reports from around the world. But it was through Samuel Zwemer's challenge to go to the most needy and difficult lands that God called me to the Muslim world. This call was nurtured by biographies such as *Borden of Yale* (ibid.:24).

Dudley attended Stony Brook boarding school where the headmaster, Frank Gaebelein apparently saw such promise in him that he prayed for him every day. Woodberry says of this, "Whatever it was that made him see the need, my vision became more focused" (ibid.:24). After high school, he enrolled in Union College, Schenectady, New York (B.A. 1955) and was strongly influenced by the pastor of a large Presbyterian church plus missionaries such as Christy and Betty Wilson who had gone from that church to Afghanistan. God then used the triennial InterVarsity Urbana conferences, a trip to Latin America and a stint in Lebanon with the American Friends Service Committee to build a goat barn to confirm Woodberry's call to missions and especially to the Muslim world.

He next attended Fuller Seminary where he was deeply influenced by Charles E. Fuller and Edward John Carnell. During his second year at Fuller Dudley felt the need to go to the Muslim world as a student to get better acquainted with Islam in its heartland. So he enrolled in the American University of Beirut (1957-59), receiving his M.A. subsequently in 1963. This allowed him to start formal Islamic studies under scholars such as Kenneth Cragg and Daud Rahbar. He also met Roberta Smith there, whom he married after she finished her studies at Beirut College for Women and he finished at Fuller (M.Div. 1960).

They established their first home in Cambridge, Massachusetts, where Dudley studied for his doctorate at Harvard University under Sir Hamilton Gibb (Ph.D. 1968). They also served part-time in Park Street Church in Boston under Harold John Ockenga, ministering to international students. At Harvard he specialized in Islamic fundamentalism, a topic not much valued at the time but crucial today.

The Woodberrys applied to the Commission on Ecumenical Mission and Relations of the Presbyterian Church USA (now the World Wide Ministries Division) and were assigned to the Christian Studies Centre in Rawalpindi, Pakistan. Having studied "book Islam" at Harvard, he says,

> The first thing I noticed was the contrast between the formal Islam of the textbook and the folk Islam of the street, where people were far more interested in a savior from fear (of evil forces and spirits) than a savior from sin. That began for me a lifelong study of what Muslims actually believe and do rather than just what they are supposed to believe and do and how the Gospel meets these needs. Ours was a task of dialoguing with Muslims and equipping church leaders so their witness was relevant to the Muslims around them (2002:26).

Woodberry then served as a pastor in Kabul, Afghanistan and Riyadh, Saudi Arabia. In the latter place, in the very heartland of Islam, they were able to build the church in three years to 700 worshipers before the government shut them down. Even then, however, a network of house churches continued and, due to Woodberry's distribution of copies of letters attributed to Muhammad allowing Christian worship, the house churches were officially permitted.

In 1979, the Woodberrys had to return to the States "when there was no more local schooling for [their] oldest son, and when Roberta's allergies became too severe" (op cit:26). Dudley took a position on the faculty of Reformed Bible College in Grand Rapids, Michigan, teaching general missiological subjects there until their two oldest boys finished high school (1979-1983). With a desire to return to a focus on the Muslim world, Dudley responded positively to an invitation to join the Samuel Zwemer Institute of Muslim Studies (1983), based in Pasadena. This involvement enabled him to also teach Islamics at SWM on an adjunct basis and eventually to move to Fuller full-time in 1985.

We were able to bring Dudley on largely due to the financial support of Dr. Mary Varker whose son had been Dudley's roommate at Stony Brook. She supported him for his first three years and later gave a million dollars to fund a chair in Woodberry's honor.

Woodberry's Contribution to SWM

As concern for Christian witness to Muslims has grown over the last few decades, it became more and more apparent that any school of mission that was going to do its job properly needed a program in Islamics. In recognition of this fact, as mentioned in Chapter 6, we dubbed 1978 "The Year of the Muslim" and did various things to heighten our involvement in Muslim evangelism. We invited Ken Bailey to teach an adjunct course. And those of us who had worked in Muslim areas and done some research and publication dealing with Islam (e.g. Gilliland, myself) made it a point to emphasize Muslim evangelism in our classes. We also hired Don McCurry as an Adjunct to teach on reaching Muslims.

But we didn't consider ourselves really on the map in this area until Woodberry came along. His becoming available and our ability to hire him are among the many miracles embedded in the story of SWM. Woodberry is the premier Evangelical Islamicist. His coming put us in an enviable position with regard to dealing with the Muslim world. Since Dudley joined us, we have had a steady stream of students who work or plan to work in the Muslim world. It is unfortunate that since Hiebert left we do not have a similar degree of expertise in Hinduism. Nor do we have a specialist in Buddhism.

One of Woodberry's strengths is to deal with folk Islam. As noted above, in the early stages of his getting acquainted with Muslims, he began to realize that what he had learned in his studies about formal Islam was not sufficient for dealing with ordinary Muslims. What he discovered was that animism is a major ingredient of Islamic belief and practice at the grassroots level. Though he can handle Islam at either level, it is crucial that those who work in Muslim lands learn to approach people where they are rather than as if they were academics. Woodberry's emphasis on folk Islam fits well with my teaching that spiritual power is a major concern of the peoples of the world, as it was for Jesus.

Among Woodberry's publications are his important edited volumes *Muslims and Christians on the Emmaus Road* (1989), *Where Muslims and Christians Meet* (1989) and *Reaching the Resistant: Barriers and Bridges for Mission* (1999). He has also written *Dimensions of Witness Among Muslims* (1997) and jointly edited with Charles Van Engen and Edgar Elliston *Missiological Education for the 21st Century: The Book, The Circle and the Sandals* (1996) and with Osman Zumrut and Mustafa Koylu *Muslim and Christian Reflections on Peace—Divine and Human Dimensions* (2005).

I will leave Woodberry's contribution as Dean for the next chapter. From the excitement of focusing on Woodberry and Islamics, then, we must turn to one of the more difficult moments in our history.

Tom Brewster Dies

December 12, 1985 was a memorable day for us—that's the day our colleague and friend Tom Brewster went to be with the Lord. He had been having difficulties with his bladder and had been getting medical advice from various doctors, including Provost Larry DenBesten, who had been a medical doctor on the staff of UCLA Medical School before accepting the post as Provost of Fuller Seminary. After much thought and prayer, it was decided that it would be best for Tom to undergo an operation to repair the bladder. The operation began well, but in the process Tom's heart stopped and he never regained consciousness.

The funeral was a celebration of a life well-lived. The old sanctuary at Lake Avenue Congregational Church was filled and no one who was there will forget six-year-old Jed's recitation from memory of Psalm 100. Tom was buried in a plain pine box, according to his request—though getting the sellers of coffins to find and sell them a simple coffin was a considerable challenge. The picture many of us had, though, was not of Tom's body in that box but of him running again all over heaven with even stronger legs than those that challenged Pike's Peak when Tom was young.

An interesting side note concerning Tom is an event that happened about two months before his death. Tom could sometimes be demanding and abrasive in his interactions with other people. One day two of the young ladies who worked for Tom came into my office to complain about the way he was treating them. As we talked, it became obvious that I was the person Tom would most likely listen to if their concerns were to be raised. I did not want the job but had to agree with them that I was the best one to try to get Tom to treat them more gently. So, I asked Tom if he would come to my office on a particular day and I practiced my speech so that I would raise the issues as tactfully as possible. The last thing I wanted to do was to hurt my friend.

At the appointed time, Tom wheeled into my office. We exchanged pleasantries, then out of my mouth came the words, "Tom, treat people better." After having practiced a tactful approach, I was devastated to hear those tactless words come out of my mouth first thing! But Tom was gracious saying, "Have people been talking?" I said, "Yes," and we had a really good discussion of the problem. This discussion, then, led Tom to begin to think of people he felt he had mistreated and any he had issues with and started him apologizing to them. Those he could meet in person, he apologized to in person. Others he wrote letters of apology to. It was as if he knew his time might be short.

Edgar J. (Eddie) Elliston (1943—)
At Fuller: 1985-1998

We had great expectations when we started the Leadership program but it grew even beyond our expectations. So in 1984 we set up a search committee to look for a second professor to work with Clinton in this area. Since we had only one woman on our faculty, we looked for a woman and did in fact have one on our short list of four. But she turned us down. So we went for the person at the top of our list, Eddie Elliston.

Eddie had studied at SWM in 1966-68 by a special dispensation from McGavran, since he had no field experience and three years in a field situation with the ability to use the field language were required at that time. But Eddie was a candidate with the Christian Missionary Fellowship of the Christian Churches (an evangelical wing of the "Restorationist Movement" related to McGavran's denomination, the largely liberal Disciples of Christ). He was thus favored by McGavran and, though pre-field, allowed to enter the student body with the agreement that he would receive no degree until he had been on the field for three years and spoke the language.

Elliston is the first child of a farming family, born in Hays, Kansas in 1943 while his father was in military service in Germany. He never knew his father until he was about three years old! He grew up in a church supported and attended by three generations of his mother's family. Following their footsteps, he became active in the church, among other things, playing the piano and organ regularly. He attended a school where his grandmother and mother had taught.

His family was involved with missionaries in Chile, Belgian Congo and the state of Washington. By the time Eddie was in fourth grade, then, he had determined that he would be a missionary. Church camps and the opportunity provided by his pastor to lead church services further confirmed his commitment. After high school he attended Manhattan Christian College from 1961-66 and also became a student pastor. He met Donna at a church camp in Colorado when he was only 15 years old. They courted at long distance and after five and a half years, married in 1964. Soon they volunteered for missionary service and by 1966 they were on their way to California and SWM. Though he was attracted by the reputation of Dr. McGavran, at SWM Eddie did most of his work under Dr. Tippett and some with Dr. Orr. He also served as a Teaching Assistant for Dr. Winter.

Following his time at SWM, he and Donna spent a summer at Wycliffe's Summer Institute of Linguistics at the University of Oklahoma. This helped them in learning Amharic and, later, Oromo and Maasai. They studied literacy on their first furlough. They were, thus, about as well prepared as any missionary could be for the multiplicity of tasks they were involved in during their 14 years in Ethiopia and Kenya.

By the time we were considering Elliston for a faculty position, then, he had worked in Ethiopia 8 years and Kenya 6, and also completed a Ph.D. in cross-cultural education under Ted Ward at Michigan State (1982). He had been involved in church planting, literacy work, leadership development, relief and development and translation work. I was asked to interview him while in Kenya in 1984 and returned with a very positive report. So we offered him the position and he joined us in 1985. Eddie characterizes his situation in Kenya at the time we contacted him as a time of transition. He writes,

> I had completed work on the Maasai Bible translation; one child had graduated from high school and the second was a senior; the leadership training program for the Maasai was at a point where much of the work was being transferred to Maasai leadership; my work as a researcher for placement and planning with CMF had been completed; and, my research in the Sudan, Uganda, and Tanzania had been completed for the Mission. I was considering a position with United Bible Society for Africa, a position with Food for the Hungry in Geneva and a position with HEART program with Warner Southern College. When

the invitation to come to SWM arrived, I could not believe it (email 4-12-04).

Contribution to SWM

Eddie is a solid scholar with much to communicate at both theoretical and practical levels and is meticulous in his handling of research and writing. His reputation for being able to zero in on any sloppiness in theses and dissertations struck fear into the hearts of those he supervised (and those supervised by others who had chosen him to be on their doctoral committees). He is one of the best we've ever had at supervising theses and dissertations.

In the classroom, he was not known as a spellbinder in his teaching style but had a reputation for providing solid information and expecting a lot from his students. He taught in the area of training and educational program design and worked with the doctoral committee to improve our own program design. He also taught leadership development and how to produce curricula for contextualizing education and leadership development. Eddie focused on the administrative part of leadership, complementing Bobby Clinton's more personal and biblical focus. He also taught some of the first courses we offered in development. As I point out in the following chapter, Elliston was made Associate Dean under Woodberry with primary responsibility for the academic programs.

While with us, Eddie was able to publish two books and get another two ready that were published after he left. Two are important contributions to the literature on Leadership. They are *Home Grown Leaders* (1993) and *Developing Leaders for Urban Ministry* (with J. Timothy Kauffman) (2000). In the Development area he has written *Christian Relief and Development: Developing Workers for Effective Ministry* (1989).

Unfortunately, Elliston was lured away from us in 1998 to become Provost of Hope International University, a school of his denomination the Christian Church/Church of Christ. His decision to leave was a hard one for him and Donna and left the rest of us in shock. But the opportunity for him to take a university to new heights was both personally challenging and within the scope of his training and ability. He has, however, now moved on to Jessup University in Northern California.

Charles ("Chuck") Van Engen (1948—)
At Fuller: 1988—

By the early 1980s we had begun to look for a person first to teach alongside Glasser and then to succeed him in dealing with Theology of Mission. Glasser was soon to move into semi-retired status as a "Senior Professor"—still active but teaching on a course-by-course basis rather than with a full-time load (and salary). Though all of us, and especially Glasser, wanted Chuck Van Engen to fill this position, we conducted a search to see if there would be anyone "better" out there. That search turned out negative, so we contacted Van Engen, a missionary to Mexico who in 1985 had taken a position on the faculty of Western Seminary in Holland, Michigan, the seminary of his denomination, Reformed Church in America. There he taught a broad range of missiological subjects but his grasp of Theology of Mission was what impressed us the most.

We knew Chuck from his days at Fuller in the early 70s (M.Div. 1973) and from various contacts since then. We had followed his career as he returned to Mexico (Chiapas) where he had grown up, the son of RCA missionaries. He had worked there in various capacities until he moved to Michigan in 1985. During that time he also completed a the Doctorandus Degree in 1978 and the Ph.D. in 1981 at the Free University of Amsterdam, having submitted an impressive dissertation entitled *The Growth of the True Church*.

So we began "courting" him in 1984 when he was invited to teach an intensive course as an Adjunct professor. We invited him back to teach another intensive course in 1987 and at that time he was formally invited to join our faculty. He agreed to come, starting in the fall of 1988.

Van Engen was born in 1948 and, as mentioned, grew up in Mexico. His parents served there as missionaries from 1943 to 1978. Chuck and his three siblings were home-schooled by his mother, a professional teacher, for their elementary education. He was then sent to Ben Lippen School in Asheville, North Carolina for high school, graduating in 1966, and from there attended Hope College in Holland, Michigan, graduating in 1970 with a Philosophy major and marrying Jean Taylor a week after their graduation. Two months later they drove an older car and a small trailer across the country to Pasadena, arriving in front of Payton Hall late in August, 1970 with $56.00 to their name. Chuck then began his M.Div. studies in the School of

Theology (1970-73) but with plenty of contact with folks in SWM. Chuck writes,

> Long before there was a cross-cultural missions track in the M.Div. program at Fuller, I found a way to take all my elective courses in SWM. So I was able to take courses from Ralph Winter (Mission History), Peter Wagner (Church Growth), J. Edwin Orr (History of Revivals and Apologetics), James Emery (Theological Education by Extension), and Arthur Glasser. At the time, Glasser taught the course in missions that was required of all M. Div. students. The major assignment was to do a Church Growth study of a local church. So I walked across Oakland Avenue to the house where all the SWM offices were located. There I met Donald McGavran and asked him how to do a Church Growth study. Without answering, McGavran went to a shelf and pulled off a small tri-fold pamphlet and gave it to me. The title was, "How to do a Church Growth Study." I did that research on the Pasadena Christian and Missionary Alliance Church where Jean and I had been attending and where I had served as the janitor and the Youth Pastor. I still keep that little pamphlet safely in my files somewhere (email: January 2005).

In Mexico, Van Engen developed and served as Dean and Administrator of a Presbyterian Seminary using an adapted form of Theological Education by Extension that he had learned at Fuller. The seminary's curriculum was focused on training lay evangelists, church planters and growth-oriented pastors. Van Engen wrote several programmed texts and study guides for that program. One of the foundational courses was Principles of Church Growth that made use of the Spanish programmed text in church growth by Wayne Weld and McGavran.

In addition, Chuck administered a small coffee ranch, supervised the building of a conference center and was involved in evangelism in rural and city contexts and also, through camping, among university students. With Jean he was involved in helping the women of the church to establish a women's Bible school, directing refugee relief efforts and functioning as a consultant to pastors of the Presbyterian churches in southern Mexico. With all of this and more going on in his life and ministry, Chuck began a life of writing and publication that has continued and intensified to the present. He writes (in the third person) in his March 2000 vitae,

> Chuck served as creator, consultant and guide for the project of writing the history of the beginnings and early development of the Presbyterian churches in Chiapas, written by

Rev. Hugo Esponda and published in 1986 as *Historia de la Iglesia Presbiteriana de Chiapas: Inicio y Desarrollo*, Mexico City: Publicaciones El Faro.

Chuck served as representative of the Reformed Church in America in the creation of a new partnership structure for mission with the National Presbyterian Church of Mexico. He also worked with the National Presbyterian Church of Mexico as consultant and assistant in relief work in the aftermath of the volcano eruption in Chiapas (1981). He was the creator of and consultant to "Plan Hebron," a program to aid approximately 80,000 Mayan refugees who fled to Chiapas from the violence in Guatemala, 1982-85 (vitae, March 2000).

During these years, his life and ministry kept interweaving with what was going on at SWM. The *Church Growth Bulletin* and SWM's newsletter, *Forwarding the Missionary Task* were his stimulus to read our publications. He says, I "devoured most of the writings of Alan Tippett, Chuck Kraft and Ralph Winter, along with all the writings of Donald McGavran, Art Glasser, and Peter Wagner" (email: January 2005). When, then, in 1977, Van Engen enrolled in the Free University of Amsterdam, he decided to make our approach to missiology the focus of his research and writing.

In the fall of 1981, with his newly achieved degree from the Free University in hand, Chuck tells of a telephone call received in Michigan as he and his family were preparing to return to Mexico. It was a very friendly call from Art Glasser, during which Art stunned him with the comment that he would like Chuck to be his successor at Fuller. Van Engen didn't know how to respond and, in fact, did not take the comment very seriously. So they went back to Mexico. From about that date, we at SWM just assumed that Chuck would someday take Glasser's place among us.

In addition to his academic duties with us, Chuck has served in a number of capacities in missiological and denominational circles. In this part of his life, his greatest honor to date was his election (in 1997) as President of the General Synod of the Reformed Church in America, his denomination.

Much of Chuck's energy now is directed toward establishing and operating a Ph.D. program in missiology for Latin Americans.

Contribution to SWM

Chuck is both brilliant and enthusiastic with a loud, hearty laugh that brightens any conversation or class with him. He is also extremely perceptive and quick to get to the core issues when working with faculty or students in attempting to conceptualize programs and dissertations. Working with him in dissertation proposal defenses is a delight for us faculty members. Students may not at first feel that way, though, since his participation will usually mean a thorough reconstruction of the proposal, much to the improvement of the project. They thank him afterward! In the classroom, students love his combination of sincere enthusiasm for the cause of Christ with his brilliance in analyzing the theological issues supporting that cause. They also enjoy the singing that he usually starts his classes with.

Academically, Chuck has continued and enriched Glasser's focus on Kingdom Theology in his courses and in his writing. He has also assisted greatly in the improvements that have been made in our doctoral programs in recent years. Among his important books are *The Growth of the True Church* (1981), *Hijos del Pacto: Conversion y Mision en el Bautismo* (1985), *God's Missionary People* (1991), *You Are My Witnesses* (1992) and *Mission on the Way* (1996). A recent major contribution that he, Gilliland and a doctoral student, Shawn Redford, have made is to get into print Glasser's magnum opus *Announcing the Kingdom: The Story of God's Mission in the Bible* (Baker, 2003). This is an editing of the material Glasser taught over the years in his major course, The Theology of Mission. Glasser was such a perfectionist that he had difficulty bringing this book to completion. We are greatly indebted to Van Engen, Gilliland and Redford for getting this book into print.

Hoover Wong (1928—)
At Fuller: 1988—

As mentioned, we had long been interested in establishing a Chinese Studies program at SWM. This was one of Glasser's dreams and something that Tan, Che Bin worked hard at without much success. In 1988, Dean Pierson appointed Hoover Wong to assist in developing the program, especially with respect to attracting "ABCs" (American Born Chinese) and raising money from Chinese churches to support the program.

Hoover is an ABC, born in 1928 and brought up in Plymouth and Cape Cod, Massachusetts, the seventh child (of 12) of the head of a Chinese *tong* (= mafia). He joined the Navy after high school, came to Christ "on my own" and after a time, received a letter from a stranger, Jim Elliot, of Wheaton College, who told Hoover he had been praying for him. Upon discharge, Hoover enrolled at Wheaton. There, he and I played three years together on the Wheaton football team. Graduating from Wheaton in 1952, Wong worked for eight years (full and part time) as an organic chemist, during which time he also studied at Faith Seminary and Covenant Seminary (B.D. 1958). Later, while pastoring, he earned a D. Min. at Fuller (1975).

Wong served Chinese and multicultural Presbyterian (USA) churches for 35 years in Los Angeles, Chicago and Hawaii. While pastoring in Hawaii, he came to SWM 2-3 times a year to teach with Tan in the Chinese Studies program. Then in 1988 Hoover joined us full time, directing the Chinese program for five years after Tan left.

Tan says of Hoover,

Hoover's joining the team is an important factor for our launching a Th.M. program in the School of Theology for training pastors for the Chinese-American churches. . . . It is our conviction that pastors for North American Chinese churches need a good theological training with cross-cultural perspective. As a second-generation Chinese American, Hoover brought with him years of pastoral experience in the Chinese-American churches, and was a recognized leader. I am happy to see that he continued to make significant contributions to the School as a whole after I left to pastor a Chinese-American church in 1991 (Tan email: February 2005).

Hoover worked hard to attract students and money for the Chinese program. But he, like Tan, was frustrated by the fact that the American Chinese community just would not trust Fuller. So the program was dropped in 1993, though a trickle of Chinese students continue to come for our other programs. Even though the program eventually had to be phased out, Wong's knowledge of the Chinese community was a gift to us, as was his pleasant personality. His great strength was his solid pastoral experience.

He has published two useful books, *Coming Together or Coming Apart* (1998) and *How to do Church* (2003) and been in demand as a lecturer and preacher.

Losses and Other Changes of Personnel

Though we rejoiced in the growth of SWM, there were several changes during this period that did not bring joy to our hearts. Had we not been so close, the changes that resulted in losses would not have been so hard to take. But the family bond has been strong and the losses hit us hard.

The first of these, as mentioned, was the death of Tom Brewster at the end of 1985. We felt this deeply. He was a special part of our team and, though we rejoiced that Betty Sue remained with us, we missed and still miss the peripatetic Tom and his wheelchair.

The next death happened at a distance. It was Edwin Orr on a speaking trip in 1987. He went off on one of his many speaking assignments, the telephone rang here and we were told he would not come back. We miss his expertise in dealing with revival and renewal movements. We also miss the bright humor he brought regularly to our Tuesday noon faculty get-togethers.

Next, came the death of my good friend and mentor, Alan Tippett, in September of 1988. Meg and I had been with him in Canberra during our summer (Aussie winter) of that year and I had had the privilege of interviewing him on audio tape for the Australian National Library Archives. Though he suffered from •multiple myeloma, he was doing alright until a doctor, ignoring the fact that he had a head cold, gave him a treatment that canceled out his immune system and resulted in his death.

In 1990, then, at age 93, Dr. McGavran went to be with the Lord. In spite of the ups and downs of his health—he carried nitroglycerin tablets with him at all times lest he have a heart attack—he made it to 93! And, up to the last six months before his death, he came regularly to his office at SWM, usually to spend at least half a day working at his desk.

Less traumatic was the loss of Eddie Gibbs in 1988. Fuller's School of Theology, after extensive searching, could find no one to occupy a Chair of Evangelism. So they asked Dean Pierson for permission to consider Eddie for the position. If appointed, he would switch from SWM to the School of Theology to teach evangelism for them. Reluctantly, he and we agreed. So we lost him, but not permanently. He came back later!

More permanent was our loss of Paul Hiebert in 1990 when he decided to move to Trinity Evangelical Divinity School in the

Chicago area. Paul is a giant of a person and represented the best we could offer as a scholar and we felt his loss keenly as a scholar. But, more than that, he was part of our family and his leaving left us with a deep sense of loss. He and Fran, his wife, of course, had their reasons for leaving but none of them made sense to us. And we still miss him, though we rejoice that he has been able to continue to benefit the cause from his base at Trinity.

Then in 1991 Che Bin Tan decided to leave to take up a pastorate. Though the call of the pastorate was strong on Che Bin, I believe discouragement with the lack of interest on the part of the Chinese also figured into his decision to leave.

Jude Tiersma Watson (1953—)
At Fuller: 1992—

With the world becoming increasingly urban, we were constantly being asked how our approaches applied to urban areas. Most of us on the faculty had served primarily in rural areas, leaving us with a gap in this important area. So in 1992 we again found one of our students, Jude Tiersma (the Watson came later) to develop courses in an area not previously covered. Jude was both concerned with urban ministry and had chosen herself to live in a poor, immigrant area of Los Angeles to do such ministry. She had completed a masters program with little desire to go on for a Ph.D. But she eventually got over that hurdle and received her Ph.D. from SWM in 1999.

Jude was born Jitske Grietje Tiersma, the second child of a farmer in Friesland the Netherlands in 1953. Her first language was Friesan, with Dutch also spoken in the home. Both her parents and all her grandparents were raised on dairy farms, as was she. And all were raised in the Christian Reformed Church (Gerefermeerede Kerken). Her parents lived through the German occupation during World War II.

Her parents with their three children immigrated to the United States in 1958, before she started school. Her father found employment as a "milker" for other farmers and they moved frequently during Jude's early years, living in little frame farm worker homes in the San Joaquin Valley. By the time she entered high school, though, the family had settled in the Central Valley of California and had their own dairy.

Elementary school was a major challenge for little Jude since when she entered kindergarten she did not yet speak English. She says she went through that whole year without speaking a single word in school! In first grade, then, she attracted a lot of attention from her classmates when she whispered her first English word, "Holland" in response to the question, "Where were you born?" Lack of English, shyness, living in an area where there were few immigrants plus the frequent moves combined to scar her early school years and it wasn't until seventh grade that she found herself academically.

She attended College of the Sequoias for two years, then transferred to Westmont. While at Westmont she did a semester in their San Francisco urban program. This had a great impact on her. She majored in Sociology and then stayed an extra year to get a teaching credential with the aim of working with disadvantaged children. She then taught fifth grade for three years followed by a trip to Europe with the aim of getting to know her grandparents. While there, she worked in a Christian youth hostel. She then joined YWAM, working under their auspices for a year and a half in Amsterdam, followed by two years in Nepal.

Jude arrived at SWM in the summer of 1985, planning to check us out and then go back to teaching elementary school. Influenced by conversations with Art Glasser and Dan Shaw, however, she entered an M.A. program in January of 1986, completing it debt-free in 1988. During her M.A. years, she made such an impression on the Fuller faculty that she was hired as Teaching Assistant for four professors and became student advisor for the missiology program. These activities paid her way and also gained her a very positive reputation among the faculty. She was especially helped academically and personally by Paul Hiebert and by the constant affirmation by the faculty of her giftedness as a woman. But she chose to do a non-thesis M.A. since she never planned to go beyond that level.

But God has a way of changing one's plans. She writes,

> After graduation, I thought I would return to Asia, to work in one of the great cities there. But God, in the ways that God speaks to us, told me I was to move to LA, one of the "nevers" of my life. I resisted for a time, but then moved into a Latino immigrant barrio just west of downtown LA. That was summer 1988, and I have been there ever since. And living here has been a source of great joy to me. It didn't take me long to realize that this face of LA in Westlake Pico-Union had more in

common with Central America than the LA we all know through Hollywood movies (email June 2004:2).

At SWM, we had hired Fletcher Tink, one of our students who had special competence in urban ministry, as an Adjunct to teach the Urban Ministry course. Jude was then engaged as his Teaching Assistant. Fletcher, however, moved to Washington, D.C., so Jude was asked to teach the course as an adjunct in her own right, starting in 1990. Then came the most dramatic change in a life full of challenging changes. Jude writes,

> [In 1991], the search committee (then still under Paul Pierson, mainly Chuck Van Engen and Dan Shaw) approached me to see if I would consider returning to Fuller half-time as an instructor in Urban Mission, and also enter the Ph.D. program. The time didn't seem right to me—so I said no, or not yet. (Marilyn Clinton laughed when I told her—she said that many people would give their right arm to teach at Fuller, and I turned them down! But this was not how I had seen my life. I saw so many people go to Fuller and then not go back into mission, and that wasn't going to be me. And I had never seen myself writing a dissertation or teaching at a seminary) (ibid.:2)

So, "kicking and screaming," Jude has become a part of our faculty and now is a seminary professor who has written a Ph.D. dissertation, and a good one. "In my early years teaching at Fuller," she writes, "I saw teaching there as taking me away from my real passion here in LA. But over the years, I have truly come to enjoy teaching and see it also as my vocation" (personal note, January 2005). She has become a "scholar practitioner." Not only did that part of her picture of herself get changed, she met John Watson, a man whose commitment to urban ministry matched hers and they were married in 1995.

Jude's Contribution to SWM/SIS

Urban ministry was an obvious gap in our offerings. Though each of us faculty members would make comments from our own perspectives, ministry in urban areas was not a part of the experience of most of us. So it was a great addition to our programs to be able to engage someone as perceptive as Jude who also has committed herself to doing urban ministry. She has been able to take whatever she has learned from our faculty and mix it with her own creative insights and experience to develop a fine and practical urban ministry concentration. She also does a course on spirituality in mission and another entitled Self-Care in Mission. In 1994, she and Chuck Van Engen published an important book entitled, *God So Loves the City*, a text widely used in urban ministry classes.

Jude has only allowed herself to serve us half-time so that she and John can continue to devote themselves in a primary way to ministry in the inner city. To do this, they continue to live where they minister in the inner city. On campus, then, she represents SIS on the Fuller three-school Center for Youth and Family Ministry. "This pulls together [her] interest in integration with the other schools at Fuller as well as [her] passion for urban youth and kids at risk in cities around the world" (ibid.:3).

Summary of the Pierson Era

As mentioned, this era was a time of unprecedented growth—growth in faculty, growth in offerings and growth in the number of students, especially those coming from nonwestern nations.

As noted, the Leadership program soon became the one that attracted more students than any other. Whereas Church Growth had been our major focus through the McGavran and Glasser eras, Leadership had come to be the facet of our emphases that was now drawing most people's attention. Students still were required to take basic courses in Theology of Mission, Anthropology and Church Growth but more and more students were opting to make Leadership their primary area of concern.

Meanwhile, Communication was coming more into focus. The addition of Viggo Sogaard, first as an Adjunct and then as a half-time faculty member meant the addition of his courses to the two that I had been teaching in this area.

The largest classes, however, were in the area we have come to call Spiritual Dynamics. Starting with the Signs and Wonders course in January of 1982 that attracted 85 students right away, the attendance grew to over 250, as students coming from Evangelical backgrounds with little or no experience of the power of God, flocked to Wimber's class and in every class session observed God healing people. And, though after Wagner and I took over the class, the attendance never reached 250 again, to this day the spiritual dynamics classes that Wagner used to teach and that I still teach are consistently among the largest classes in SWM/SIS. So, the interest continues and we now have 3-5 courses in this area offered annually in place of the one we started with.

Another area that attracts a lot of students is Islamics. Since Woodberry came on in 1985, our Islamics program has become easily the best Evangelical program in the world. By 2005, then, we have had to bring in 2-3 other adjunct instructors to handle the classes.

The Bible Translation program never attracted large numbers of students but the level at which the students have worked is consistently high and several of the 100 or so who have gone out from the program have made major contributions in their fields of service. This is an innovative program, the first of its kind and, to date, the only one we know of. Shaw has done a good job in setting it up and running it.

The ability to add an Urban Ministry component to our offerings filled a badly needed void. Though we probably still need to do more in this area, what Jude Tiersma-Watson has brought us is of great value, and far better than what we didn't have before.

The China Studies Program began and ended during this era.

We also initiated a Jewish Studies Program and had a considerable number of Jews for Jesus students work through our various emphases with the evangelization of Jews as their focus. From the start our aim was to enable Messianic Jews to launch their own program. Art Glasser devoted much of his energy during his final years at SWM to promoting Jewish Studies and Jewish Evangelism. A number of adjuncts also taught in the program.

By the end of this period, students could focus their studies in several areas in which we grouped our courses into Concentrations. A Concentration consists of at least six courses in a given area. Those available in 1992 were Anthropology, Bible Translation, Communication, Contextualization, Church Growth, Chinese Studies, Development, History, Leadership, Islamic Studies, Theology, and Urban Studies.

During this period our student body grew from 162 in 1980-81 to 324 in 1985-86, to a high of 428 in 1987-88, then dropped to 320 in the fall of the 1991-92 academic year.

Chapter 9

The Woodberry Era

1992-1999

It was again time to search for a Dean. Pierson was to leave the deanship at the end of the 1991-92 school year. So a committee was appointed to search for someone to fill Pierson's shoes. We looked at quite a number of candidates but found none that we were happy with until one day during a Search Committee meeting Dudley Woodberry let us know that he would be willing to serve, at least for five years, if we thought that to be a good idea.

This sounded good to us from an administrative perspective but we had misgivings concerning his ability to handle both the deanship and the growing Islamics program plus the writing we felt he owed the world. He assured us, however, that he would lean on his faculty more than previous deans had and that he would in that way be able to handle things. In spite of our misgivings, then, we decided to go with him and to call off our search.

I don't recall whether, in our discussions prior to his appointment, Woodberry let us in on the basic change he planned to make or not. What he did immediately, though, was to appoint Eddie Elliston Associate Dean in charge of academic matters. Elliston, then, would be "Mr. Inside," looking after most of what we did internally, while Woodberry would be "Mr. Outside," relating us to the seminary as a whole and the world at large, as well as having overall responsibility for SWM.

I had felt for some time that we were large and diverse enough to need an Associate Dean. I had on several occasions urged Pierson to appoint someone to take part of the load off his back. Had he done that, he might have done more writing. But Pierson didn't think an Associate was necessary. Dudley did and it worked well.

Elliston, as I have mentioned, is very capable of handling academic things and took this opportunity to organize our operation academically better than it had been previously. In this position, he revised our degree programs at both Masters (M.A. and Th.M.) and Doctoral (D.Min., D.Miss, and Ph.D.) levels. For D.Miss. and Ph.D. degrees he developed a course we call Research Design and made it a prerequisite for anyone seeking to enter those degree programs. As Associate Dean, Elliston also carried responsibility for developing and maintaining some of our international programs (e.g. Nigerian Extension Program).

We were sorry to see Elliston leave in 1998, responding to the opportunity to become Provost of Hope International University, a school of his denomination, the Churches of Christ.

Woodberry came to a program that had been administered well. So there were few bumps, so far as we were concerned. And Pierson was on the scene to help when needed. In fact, Pierson had been appointed acting Provost for that year and so became Dudley's boss.

Under Woodberry, we experienced a period of consolidation as well as further growth. Eight faculty members were added, counting the return of Eddie Gibbs, several new programs and, perhaps most important of all, four new Chairs established. This latter, of course, added significantly to the financial soundness of SWM.

Young Lee Hertig (1954—)
At Fuller: 1992-1995

The large number of Korean students we were attracting mandated that we increase the Korean presence on our faculty. In our student body was Young Lee Hertig (Ph.D. SWM 1991), a Korean woman who was married to another of our Ph.D. students, Paul Hertig. She was appointed half-time in SWM and half-time in the School of Theology. For SWM she taught in the areas of class, gender and ethnicity from 1992-95 and then as an Adjunct from 1996-98 until she and Paul left to take positions at United Theological Seminary, Dayton, Ohio in 1998.

Young Lee was born in 1954 and raised in Seoul, Korea, the second daughter of four. Her mother had become a devout Christian in response to an incredible experience of divine comfort after the death of her first child. Her father, though "deeply embedded in Confucian ethics . . . [was] unlike a typical Korean father [in that] when it came to his daughters he made sure that [they would] pursue [their] dream" (email: 12/14/04). She struggled with her "inherited faith" for a time but was solidly impacted by God through the Billy Graham crusade in 1973 and Campus Crusade's Explo '74. Though she later struggled spiritually again, especially during political turbulence in Seoul, she got involved in World Evangelization Crusade's event in 1980 and from there headed to America to study at Bethel Seminary in St. Paul, Minnesota.

At Bethel, she took courses from Fuller Alumnus, Dr. Herb Klem and was exposed to the approach and writings of SWM faculty. She also met a missionary to Korea named Paul Hertig in the fall of 1981, to whom she was married at the end of 1983. After the wedding in Minneapolis, she followed Paul to Korea where he completed the last year of his mission term. They then came to Fuller where both of them enrolled in Ph.D. programs. Young Lee worked under Paul Hiebert and, when he left, Paul Pierson, completing a dissertation entitled, *The Role of Power in the Korean Immigrant Family and Church* (1991). This was published in 2001 with the title *Cultural Tug of War: The Korean Immigrant Family and Church in Transition.* In it Young documents and analyzes the loss of power felt by second-generation Korean immigrants and suggests what to do about it. While with us she co-authored with Hiebert "Asian Immigrants in American Cities" (1993) and wrote, "Asian-American Women in the Workplace and the Church" (1996) and "The Asian-American Alternative to Feminism: A *Yinist* Paradigm" (1998).

Young Lee was just starting her teaching at Fuller when the LA riots broke out. She writes,

> Another theological/spiritual breakthrough emerged in April 29, 1992. The City of Angels was burning and Koreatown was heavily damaged. That was the context when I began my teaching career at Fuller. The firsthand experience of the LA riots deeply impacted me and consequently I was deeply committed to multiculturalism and racial justice. A teaching experience at Fuller cannot be compared to any other seminary. The diversity of the student body and the combination of the three schools . . . brought an amazingly enriching experience in the classroom. Furthermore, the depth and width of mid-level career missionaries made diversity a reality in the classroom (email 12/14/04:6).

After leaving Fuller in 1998, both Young Lee and Paul taught missiology for the next four years at United Theological Seminary,

Dayton, Ohio. These were what she calls "challenging years." In 2002, then, they happily moved to Azusa Pacific University where they serve as of this writing.

Wilbert R. Shenk (1935—)
At Fuller: 1995—

With Pierson phasing out, Woodberry felt that we should look for another historian. He had known Wilbert Shenk from American Society of Missiology (Secretary-Treasurer, 1979-88; President, 1994-95) meetings and decided to give him a call in May of 1994, asking if he would be willing to discuss the possibility of joining our faculty. Shenk was cautious, since he had authored several articles and edited two books critical of the Church Growth Movement (Shenk 1973, 1983). But Woodberry was encouraging and by the end of 1994, he and Juanita, his wife, had decided to come to SWM, starting in the fall of 1995. Shenk was by that time an established historian of mission, teaching at the Associated Mennonite Biblical Seminary in Elkhart, Indiana (1990-95).

Shenk was born in 1935 and brought up in Oregon though, as a good Mennonite, he attended college in Goshen, Indiana (B.A. 1955). He then applied to the Mennonite Central Committee for overseas work and was assigned to Indonesia, serving there from 1955-59 mostly as a secondary-school teacher involved in helping the Mennonite churches reestablish educational and medical service programs as they were recovering from the Indonesian war of independence from the Dutch. He was then tapped for administration, first by the Mennonite Central Committee (1963-65), then by the Mennonite Board of Missions as administrator of international programs from1965 to 1990. Along the way, he completed an M.A. at the University of Oregon (1964) and a Ph.D. under Andrew Walls at the University of Aberdeen (1978) with a focus on history and a dissertation on Henry Venn, a major missions leader of the nineteenth century.

Shenk is a solid scholar and has added significantly to our academic excellence in history. His writing (see below) is exceptional both in content and in readability. And his teaching wins admiration from all serious students who easily recognize the much greater value of competence and content over charisma. Whatever the question, Shenk can usually come up with the answer or find it quickly in his files. Both within SWM/SIS and outside Shenk commands respect. In a 2005 tribute to Wilbert, Darrell Whiteman writes what all of us feel:

> The common theme woven through the tapestry of Shenk's life has been his commitment to God's mission in the world as an expression of the Reign of God. His irenic and ecumenical spirit has enabled him to be equally at home among evangelicals, ecumenicals, and Roman Catholics. He has an eye toward the practical application of missiological insights as evidenced by his missionary experience in Indonesia, and later as the mission administrator for the Mennonite Board of Mission. However, his teaching and writing as exemplified in his work as a missiology professor . . . have done much to advance the scholarly development of the field of missiology (Whiteman 2005).

Shenk's Contribution to SWM/SIS

When Shenk came to SWM, he brought with him a seven-year funded research program called "A Missiology of Western Culture." His interest in this area led Woodberry to ask him to develop a concentration in "mission to contemporary culture." He has added this emphasis to our curriculum in addition to handling history courses. He is very concerned that we heighten awareness within Missiology of the need to work at evangelization of "post-Christendom" societies.

In 1994, he became involved in another funded project, the "North Atlantic Missiology Project" (NAMP), and served as coordinator of the consultations carried out in North America as a part of this six-year initiative. In 1998, he coordinated an international consultation sponsored by Fuller, entitled "Toward a Global Christian Historiography," that brought together forty-five scholars from all continents to rethink the field of Christian history in light of the changing demographics of world Christianity. From the proceedings of this consultation an edited volume was published entitled, *Enlarging the Story: Perspectives on Writing World Christian History* (2002). Other books he has done include *Changing Frontiers of Mission* (1999) and *By Faith They Went Out: Mennonite Missions, 1850-1999* (2000). In addition, Shenk has edited *North American Foreign Missions, 1810-1914: Theology, Theory and Policy* (2004) and contributed numerous articles to edited volumes, including, "Recasting Theology of Mission: Impulses from the Non-Western

World" in *International Bulletin of Missionary Research* (2001) and four major articles in *The Encyclopedia of Protestantism* (2004).

An important contribution to Missiology has been Wilbert's involvement in the American Society of Missiology (ASM). From its start in 1972, the only annual meetings he missed were in 1974 and 1975, while he was completing his Ph.D.studies in Aberdeen. He served as Secretary-Treasurer from 1979 to 1988 and President from 1994-5. His presidential address that year was an expression of his great concern over the lack of mission theory in contemporary discussions of mission and was published in *Missiology* under the title of "The Role of Theory in Mission Studies" (1996). He also has written a history of ASM up to 1987 in *The American Society of Missiology, 1972-1987* (1987) followed, in cooperation with George Hunsberger by *The American Society of Missiology: The First Quarter Century* (1997). His expertise in nineteenth century missiology is exhibited in his 1983 volume, *Henry Venn: Missionary Statesman.*

Robert (Bob) Freeman (1949—)
At Fuller: 1995—

The Fuller off-campus programs had been growing over the years to the point that many considered the extension programs to be the fourth school in Fuller. To the extent that this is true, the Associate Provost in charge of what is now called the Horner Center for Lifelong Learning functions as a fourth Dean. This department handles the extension programs in Seattle, the Bay Area, Orange County and Sacramento, California, Phoenix, Colorado and several smaller programs. They also handle the Doctor of Ministry programs (English), what is now called Distance Learning, Continuing Education and on-line courses. In 1993 the position of director of this important part of Fuller became vacant and the administration engaged in an extended search to come up with a person who could assume this major responsibility. They found Bob Freeman at Gordon-Conwell and waited until he could join us in January of 1995.

At Gordon-Conwell, Freeman had been Director of Continuing and Distance Education Programs from 1985-95. He thus had responsibility for a full range of programs that grew to 2800 registrations, including seminars and conferences for pastors, extension and Saturday classes for laypeople, and distance education courses.

In the Fuller system each faculty person appointed as both teacher and administrator is required to be a part of one of the three schools. Freeman and his wife Kerry had planned to become missionaries with a special interest in Theological Education by Extension. This didn't happen but Bob had lived and worked briefly in Guadalcanal and been involved in a TEE program in New England for Gordon-Conwell and a Globalization of Theological Education project. These interests led him to choose to join the SWM faculty (rather than the School of Theology) if we would accept him. We did.

Bob was born in Massachusetts in 1949 and brought up in New Hampshire, the firstborn of parents who were nominal Christians, active in a Congregational church that Bob attended regularly. His family life was challenging as his father slowly died of a brain disease and his mother was forced to take on the role of provider and single parent. At least partly to escape his home situation, he jumped at the chance to attend the Air Force Academy, graduating with a B.S. in Economics in 1971. This was followed by an M.A. in Economics from the University of Hawaii in 1973 and four years, first as a management analyst, then as a financial analyst in the Air Force (1973-76) at Langley Air Force Base in Virginia. From there, Freeman went into business but, he says,

> During these years, through various individuals, I became aware of a personal Jesus. One of these people was my future wife who lured me downtown [in Colorado Springs] to a church where people talked about their personal relationship with Jesus. However, both of us were more interested in seeing each other than in seeing Jesus.
>
> After marriage and a few years of euphoria of pursuing young married life and our careers, in 1976, our youthful habits of church and Sunday School attendance brought us back to a church in Virginia where the right combination of the Holy Spirit's conviction and Biblical teaching led us to understand who Jesus was and what He offered us. A few weeks later during a stressful time of changing careers we each quietly and uneventfully confessed that we were sinners in God's eyes and asked Him to come into our lives and take control (email 4/12/04).

After several years in business, Freeman entered Gordon-Conwell Seminary in 1983 "out of a desire to develop my gift of teaching and to 'work full time for the Lord'" (email 4/12/04), not in pastoring but perhaps in missions, due in part to a lecture by Ralph Winter. As mentioned, he was especially attracted to overseas work in Theological Education by Extension, an interest that predicts his future involvement in extension education. At Gordon-Conwell, he soon found himself working part time to start a TEE program in New England. After a couple of years, then, they offered him a full-time position that he held until his move to Fuller in 1995. He had already begun a doctoral program in Adult Education with a concentration in Distance Education at Nova Southeastern University. He completed his Ed.D. in 1996.

As for his move to Fuller, Bob says,

> After several years at Gordon-Conwell, my wife and I were feeling restless and ready to move on, we thought, to the mission field. During a lunch conversation with Ralph Winter, he challenged us to consider that we could have a bigger influence on changing the leadership development paradigm of the church by transforming the way North America views it, rather than going to the mission field. His view was that the rest of the world mimics North America.

> At the same time I was in the process of a paradigm shift in terms of my views on the Holy Spirit, largely influenced by Peter Wagner. I invited him, Eddie Gibbs and John Wimber to speak at Gordon-Conwell (which made a lot of people nervous).

> In the winter of 1993, Eddie Elliston called me to ask if I would be interested in a job at Fuller as Associate Provost for Continuing and Extended Education. The chance to visit a warm climate in winter was very enticing, so my wife and I came to Pasadena for an interview without much intention of moving. My experience during the visit convinced us that this was a continuation of the Lord's promise to open doors. I was offered the job, but after counting the cost on my 4 teenage daughters, we turned it down. Fuller then agreed to wait one year for my oldest to graduate high school and we again realized that this was a call from the Lord (email 4/12/04).

Freeman's Contribution to SWM

Though Freeman only teaches one or two courses for us, he has done our program a great service in improving and expanding our distance learning program, called Individualized Distance Learning (IDL). His aim is to set the pace in the development and use of in-ministry training for missionaries and international church leaders. He combines the latest adult education theories with the new information technologies to offer some of the radical new ways in which this paradigm can be applied. He says,

> My calling at Fuller is to show that this paradigm works by implementing it at Fuller as an example for the rest of the world. We have done this by renaming our division the Center for Lifelong Learning to signal the different paradigm and by expanding Fuller's programs for people who are in ministry such as the new online degree, Master of Arts in Global Leadership (email 4/12/04).

This online degree program (M.A. in Global Leadership) involves the teaching of our courses interactively via email. This is a big step up from IDL and is attracting quite a number of students who want the benefits of classroom interaction but cannot come to campus. His distance learning courses have attracted Course of the Year awards in 1991, 1992, 1993 and 1994 from ACCESS and Christianity Today. He also was awarded a prize for the Online Course of the Year in 1999 for his course *Leadership Selection and Training in the Info-tech Age*.

Pablo Deiros (1945—)
At Fuller: 1995—

Pablo Deiros was a pastor of Central Baptist Church in downtown Buenos Aires, a 5,000 member church with a significant reputation for a sane charismatic approach to ministry. He also has a Ph.D. (1985) in History from Southwestern Baptist Theological Seminary. Peter Wagner had gotten to know him in Argentina and recommended to Dean Woodberry that we consider him. Woodberry, then, sent a fax to Pablo inviting him to teach as an Adjunct, starting in 1994. He did well in these classes and we needed a Latin America specialist, so in 1995 we took him on half-time to teach, both in SWM and in the School of Theology Hispanic Studies Program. In SWM he was expected to do Latin American Studies and some Theological courses as well as History.

Deiros was born in Asuncion, Paraguay in 1945, the son of Argentine medical missionaries. He grew up, however, in Rosario, Argentina attending elementary and secondary schools there. He came to the Lord at age 11 and felt the call to ministry soon after. At age 17, he went to Buenos Aires to study at the International Baptist Theological Seminary, graduating five years later with a Th.M. and marrying Norma. During these years he was involved in youth ministry and in planting three churches in various locations in Argentina. From there, they went to Bahia Blanca to serve a small Baptist church. They were there for five years and, in addition to the church work, Pablo completed two degrees in history (M.A. and Licenciatura) and Norma got her M.A. in English.

In 1973, they moved to Buenos Aires, where they served another Baptist church for the next seven years. Deiros also served as Professor of Church History at the International Baptist Theological Seminary. He says, by 1979 "I was involved in more commitments than anybody can hold" (email: February 2005). He continues,

> During those years I was serving as pastor of a local church; professor, director of publications and director of post-graduate studies at the Seminary; executive secretary of the Association of Seminaries and Theological Schools in Latin America (ASIT); adjunct professor of methodology of historical research in the Department of History at the Universidad de Moron (a private university), several denominational commitments at a regional, national and international level; lecturing, writing, translating, publishing, teaching, etc. (ibid).

From 1983-85 he and his family (three boys) lived in Fort Worth, Texas while he attended Southwestern Baptist Theological Seminary and served as the First National Guest Professor. He completed his Ph.D. in History, then, in July 1985, a degree he had started at the Instituto Superior Evangelico de Estudios Teologicos under Jose Miguez-Bonino. Returning to Buenos Aires in 1986, he took up his responsibilities at the Baptist Seminary and began his service as senior pastor at Central Baptist Church. When he arrived, Deiros writes, "the church had some 350 members; today we are more than 5,000, with close to 50 satellite congregations in Buenos Aires, some of the provinces and overseas." He continues, "The church has gone through impressive seasons of renewal and revival, and has developed an amazing ministry to the community . . . and enjoys an enormous prestige both within the government and the Christian family" (ibid.)

About his coming to Fuller, Pablo writes,

My coming to Fuller was something totally out of anything that I had planned for my life. One day in 1994, a fax arrived in my church office in Buenos Aires, with an invitation to join the Faculty of SWM. This invitation came out of the blue and took me by surprise. With Norma, we began to pray and ask the Lord for directions since the challenge represented a major change in the course of our ministries and the life of our family. Before we realized it, I was committed to a half-time faculty position with SWM. I began to teach two courses on Dynamics of Church Growth and Leading Large Churches, mostly based on my experience as a pastor in a large and growing Baptist church in Buenos Aires (email: February 2005).

Deiros elected to come for Winter Term each year, and sometimes for additional shorter teaching stints. To do so, he has had to do a major job of juggling his church and teaching responsibilities in Buenos Aires. In the year 2000, however, in a public meeting "a group of about 50 pastors representing more than 10 different evangelical denominations" laid hands on him as "[his] local church dedicated [him] to an apostolic ministry," a ministry he's developing "through teaching, leadership formation, ministration to pastors and leaders, impartations, mentoring of key national leaders in several countries" including his teaching at Fuller (ibid.).

Deiros' Contribution to SWM/SIS

As a pastor, Pablo has been involved in a healing ministry. He, therefore, teaches courses on healing at SIS, as well as History and Latin American Studies. His teaching and ministry to Hispanic students both in SIS and in the School of Theology fills an important gap. Pablo founded a School of Mission at Central Baptist that now has 20 branches in Argentina and overseas. He is also involved with Chuck Van Engen in the Latin American Doctoral Program. He is an important part of the future of SIS. He says,

My involvement with Fuller has given me a unique opportunity to come into contact with hundreds of students and to be instrumental in bringing vision, encouragement and spiritual renewal to their lives and ministries. As I try my best to comply with my teaching responsibilities as a half-time faculty to SIS, I multiply my efforts to use the other half of my time (and energy) to serve the Lord as an apostle of his catholic church (ibid.).

As to his academic work, he has published 36 books and many articles on a variety of subjects, most of them in Spanish. Relating to

Latin America, he has written on Evangelicals and Political Power (1986), on Protestant Fundamentalism in Latin America (1991) and Histories of Latin American Christianity (1992), Latin American Protestantism (1997) and Hispanic Pentecostalism in the Americas (2001). In addition, he has done a book documenting the action of the Holy Spirit in history (1998).

Timothy Kiho Park (1948—)
At Fuller: 1996—

With the growth in the number of Korean students in our programs, we decided to offer degrees in Korean. So in 1996 we hired Tim Park to join our teaching faculty as Associate Professor of Asian Mission and to run a program in Korean. Tim was a missionary in the Philippines, who had done his Ph.D. in our program in 1991.

Park was born in 1948, the third of seven children of a religiously eclectic Korean farm family. There was no church in their village but Tim's family allowed a church from another village to hold evangelistic meetings on their property. This early influence probably planted seeds that bore fruit when Tim accepted Christ at age 16 through the landlady of the boarding home where he lived during high school days.

Park became ardent in his Christian Faith, entering Chongshin University, majoring in Christian Philosophy and studying several languages in preparation for graduate theological studies. He devoted himself to prayer, Bible-reading and evangelism. In his first year at college he felt called to missionary work. He then studied in Chongshin's Graduate School of Theology, receiving the equivalent of an M.Div. degree in 1976. While studying in the graduate school Tim felt he needed some practical missionary training so began work with the Korean Navigators mission organization. He participated in a discipleship training program and did campus ministry at two universities. Following this, he served for three years as a chaplain in the Korean army.

Remembering his call to missionary work, he resigned from the army and enrolled in the Asian Center for Theological Studies and Mission (ACTS), studying missiology. He graduated with a Th.M. in 1982. While at ACTS, Park was invited to serve in the Philippines by the Global Mission Society of the Presbyterian Church of Korea. He and his family headed for the Philippines in 1981.

Park served as a church planter and seminary teacher for two terms before coming to Fuller to study. He founded the Presbyterian Theological Seminary in the Philippines and worked as professor and president. He was also Field Director of his mission and president of the Association of Korean Missionaries in the Philippines. At Fuller, he completed an M.A. in 1988 and Ph.D. (Intercultural Studies) in 1991 mentored by Paul Pierson. He says of his Fuller training:

> What I learned from Fuller Theological Seminary School of Intercultural Studies during my furlough years produced a great change in my life and ministry as a missionary. My ministry changed from an activity-centered ministry to a prayer-centered ministry, and from a grass-roots ministry to a leadership development and partnership ministry (email 10/2004:2).

Along with these changes Tim had developed a strong desire to see his colleagues receive the same kind of training at Fuller that he had received. However, he knew that not all of them could afford a year or more in the States, nor could all of them handle English well enough to do such a program. So he campaigned for Fuller to offer courses in the Philippines and, hopefully, a full degree program in Korean. The Fuller administration agreed to offer courses there and as of 1994 Tim became responsible for a Philippine extension site. By 1996, it was decided to invite Park to come to Pasadena to teach and to develop a Korean-language training program here. Of this invitation, Tim says,

> Because of my desire to continue the work of educating ministry candidates from the Philippines, Asia, and Africa [in the Philippines], I did not seriously consider coming to Fuller. However, considering the active participation of the Korean Church in world mission and the need for mission education in the Korean/Asian Church, I felt that there was no other place like Fuller as an effective place of ministry. I was convinced that as a professor at the School of Intercultural Studies it would be meaningful to develop the leadership of various Korean denominations and mission agencies, to mobilize the mission movement of Korean-American churches, and to work for the missiological development of the Asian Church. Thus I accepted the invitation and came to Fuller in July 1996 to serve as an Associate Professor of Asian Mission (ibid.:2).

SWM/SIS is now offering masters degrees, a Doctor of Ministry in Global Ministries and plans to offer a Doctor of

Missiology degree in Korean from the fall of 2005 under Park's guidance. He says further,

> Although my main ministry at Fuller is in teaching courses and providing guidance for dissertations, every year I visit Korean missionaries around the world to provide mission education and consultation, lead seminars for the indigenous church leaders they are working with, lead seminars and offer consultation for churches and mission organizations, etc. I am also currently serving as a facilitator to encourage Korean church leaders and Christian businessmen to support the development of Fuller through their prayers and financial contributions (ibid.:2).

Park's Contribution to SWM/SIS

In addition to his work on campus, Tim serves in several important capacities in Asian and Korean mission and missionary sending organizations. He travels frequently conducting seminars and providing consultation for Korean missionaries. He is also a good fund raiser, largely responsible, among other things, for attracting the funds supporting the Sun Hee Kwak chair that I occupy. Such activity has prevented him from publishing a lot. He has, however, produced two books on Korean missionary work: *Missionary Movement of the Korean Church* (1999) and the forthcoming *Mission History of the Presbyterian Church in Korea During Japanese Colonial Rule*. Among his articles and chapters in books are "Missionary Orientation" (1983), "Trends of World Mission Toward A.D. 2,000 and the Mission of the Korean Church" (1992) and "Mission Cooperation of Korean Missionaries in the Philippines" (1996).

Under Dr. Park the Korean program at SIS has grown greatly. More than one third of our present students are Korean. Further, our ability to serve the large and growing Korean missionary movement has increased.

One Eddie Returns, the Other Leaves

In 1996, Gibbs who had been pastoring in an Episcopal church in Beverly Hills decided to leave that position. When we found out about that, we asked him to rejoin our faculty and he agreed.

As already noted, then, we lost Eddie Elliston in 1998 to Hope International University in Fullerton, California.

Roberta R. King (1949—)
At Fuller: 2000—

Roberta King was born in 1949, the firstborn of her parents who were living in San Luis Obispo, California at the time. Her parents are musical and both before and after her birth she accompanied her mother to choir rehearsals! She writes:

> Music surrounded me so much that it was natural that I would want to take it up. I began piano lessons at the age of 6. I'm told that I would get up early in the morning to practice before I left for school. In the third grade . . . [I] was encouraged to take up the French Horn . . .

> It was a song that triggered my . . . receiving the Lord Jesus Christ at the age of six. I had grown up singing *Heavenly Sunshine* and *I'm a Child of the King*. With the last name of King and having always attended church since an infant, I had come to assume that the name King automatically meant Christian. . . . It distressed me when I learned that I was not spontaneously born into the family of Christ. Thus, it was around the kitchen table as I dialogued with my parents that I came to understand that I needed to make an intentional decision to invite Jesus Christ into my life. There was no hesitancy at all; I wanted to belong to Him! (email 5/29/2004:1-2).

As she grew up in Concord, California, music was her whole life. She played the organ in an American Baptist church while still in junior high and played in a Baptist General Conference church throughout her senior high years. In high school she "was also actively involved in playing French horn in the school orchestra and marching band, was a songleader/cheerleader, took weekly piano lessons, and served as an officer in student leadership" (ibid.:2). She attracted a Regent scholarship to the University of California at Santa Barbara to study music. She wanted to major in organ but ended up in piano and was indirectly introduced to ethnomusicology through a focus on Hungarian folk music. She then was able to spend her junior year abroad, in Goettingen, Germany, studying musicology and piano and playing the French horn with the university orchestra. She says, "This is where I discovered my love for learning languages and interacting with peoples of different societies" (ibid.:2). She also was able to attend theological lectures there. She graduated with an M.A. in Piano Performance from UCSB in 1972.

Roberta then did a second masters degree at the University of Oregon in music education and began teaching. During her university years she twice attended the InterVarsity missionary conference in Urbana, Illinois and made a commitment to go into missions. This resulted eventually in her applying to go to Daystar Communications in Nairobi, Kenya. She arrived at Daystar in 1978 and took a course on Intercultural Communication that my wife and I were teaching there during the summer of 1978. Discussions with her at that time concerning the need for effective use of music in the African context resulted in her coming to Fuller in 1981, after her first term of service at Daystar. Though she had been thoroughly prepared for a career in western music, she had felt called to missionary work.

Of the course we taught, Roberta says,

> Throughout the course I repeatedly realized the potential and reality of music communicating at deep levels beyond that recognized within western musicology and the western church. It began to become apparent that each society defined music differently, according to its own set of normative rules . . . Chuck Kraft noticed my interest and challenged me to come study at the School of World Mission. To my amazement he suggested that I do a Ph.D. in Communication and Ethnomusicology. I was not sure that I wanted a Ph.D. . . . Yet . . . I longed to immerse myself in academia, the scripture, and theology books, especially if they could help me to be more effective in making Jesus Christ known and understood among the nations (ibid.:4).

In the same year, 1978, God brought a South African missionary, Joyce Scott, into her life who had just been appointed by Africa Inland Church "to lead in the development of indigenous songs for worship, evangelism, and discipleship for the burgeoning church in Kenya" (ibid.:4). She and Joyce began to do mobile schools of music throughout Kenya. These were "eye-opening" for Roberta and led to "a paradigm shift in [her] understanding the differences of perceptions as linked to cultural assumptions and expectations about music" (ibid.:4). In addition, Roberta came in contact with an ethnomusicologist named Dr. Mary Oyer who became a mentor to her in the area of ethnomusicology. Dr. Oyer had studied African music with the foremost African ethnomusicologist, J. H. K. Nketia, and mentored Roberta as they "worked through Nketia's ground-breaking 1975 book, *The Music of Africa*" (ibid.:4). She was, thus, well on her way to a career in ethnomusicology when she came to us in 1981.

In 1982 she completed her M.A. in Intercultural Studies and also joined the Conservative Baptist Foreign Mission Society (now CB International). She was then appointed to the previously unknown position of ethnomusicologist with that society and seconded to Daystar University College (successor to Daystar Communications) with an agreement that she would teach for six months each year at the University and spend the other six months working with CBFMS missionaries and churches across Africa.

> Since CBFMS's work was mostly in French-speaking Africa, [she] studied French in Paris for 13 months, ultimately earning the Sorbonne's Superior Certificate in the French Language and Civilization. Acquiring the French language led to [her] doing Ph.D. field research among the Senufo peoples of northern Cote d'Ivoire (ibid.:5).

After her French study, Roberta worked under this six-months-in-Nairobi, six-months-in-the-field arrangement for the next four years and then came back to Fuller to finish her Ph.D. The assistance she was able to give to the churches in music communication, especially among the Senufo, proved both transforming for these churches and extremely valuable for Roberta's education. In addition, she was able to gather materials for her Ph.D. dissertation which she did under my supervision with a great deal of input from Nketia who was teaching at UCLA at the time and served on her committee. She completed the degree in 1989.

Ultimately, over the course of her 22 years as a missionary, she has become one of the foremost Africanist ethnomusicologists. She worked in eleven African nations under this half and half arrangement, "helping to set Scripture to song in over 80 different African languages" (ibid.:5). She also directed the choir at Nairobi Baptist Church where she was able to introduce African music into this urban upper-class westernized church. In addition, she participated in the founding of a department of Christian music communication in Daystar University's Institute of Christian Ministries and Training. This institute was committed to taking ministerial training (including music training) "on the road" all over Kenya and held intensive, in-service training courses for missionaries, pastors and church leaders from more than twenty-six African nations.

King's Contribution to SWM/SIS

King brings to us a unique blending of communication, music, worship and spirituality. Though her position as Associate Professor of Communication and Ethnomusicology sounds quite academic, she gets well beyond the academic aspects of these subjects into the lives of her students. And as she does this, she models for them the kind of field ministry that can be truly transforming in a people's relationship with Jesus. It is clear that she is competent academically, but it is Roberta, the caring person, who will be remembered by students when her pioneering efforts toward establishing an academically respectable Christian ethnomusicology has faded in their minds.

She teaches courses in intercultural communication, ethnomusicology, worship, qualitative research and spirituality. At the heart of her concern is to rectify what has been a major omission in missions—"the development of culturally appropriate music, sometimes referred to as heart music, for the purposes of the *missio dei*, as it relates to worship, evangelism, spiritual formation, and leadership training" (ibid.:6). She is involved on campus in the development of the Brehm Center for Worship, Theology and the Arts. Off campus she is a member of the newly organized International Council of Ethnodoxologists. Through this organization and other contacts she seeks to apply "ethnomusicology to mission, redeeming a people's music for the sake of the Kingdom" in renewal and in worship (ibid.:6). She also seeks to lay a theological foundation for the development of an academic discipline of Christian ethnomusicology. She says,

> My driving passion is to see God glorified through the drawing of all nations to come before Him in worship, bringing honor to Him (Ps. 89:9). At Fuller Seminary, I long to see the working out of "preparing men and women for the manifold ministries of God" to become one that mutually respects, recognizes, and integrates with discernment both the learning about God (theology) and spiritual growth (trusting/clinging to God) in the lives of all members of the seminary and the churches we serve as two sides of the same coin. In other words, not only must we know the deeper things about God, but we must also know God deeply: to trust, wait upon, listen to, and recognize God at work in our personal lives, in our ministries, and throughout the world. I long to see the fulfillment of Paul's words break through the constraints of academic boundaries so that we all "reflect the glory of the Lord

with uncovered faces; and that same glory, coming from the Lord, who is the Spirit, transforms us into his likeness in an ever greater degree of glory" (II Cor. 3:18 TEV) (ibid.:6).

Roberta is just starting to publish academically. She has done some very helpful practical writing published in Kenya, though, including "The Role of Music in Theological Education" (1990). Her 1999 manual *A Time to Sing: A Manual for the African Church* breaks new ground in her attempt to guide the African Church to produce its own music. Her dissertation, *Pathways in Christian Music Communication: The Case of the Senufo of Cote d'Ivoire* (1989) provides a solid case study of the usefulness of culturally appropriate music in evangelism and church growth. And her "Variations on a Theme of Contextualization: Music Lessons from Africa," (2005) in our new contextualization text *Appropriate Christianity* makes a solid contribution to the important place of music in contextualization. On the more theoretical side she has written "Towards a Discipline of Christian Ethnomusicology" (2004).

Administrative Assistant

When Marilyn and Bobby Clinton went on sabbatical in 1993, Dean Woodberry needed someone to replace Marilyn. Denise Shubert was the person. She had worked for Ted Engstrom at World Vision and then for David Hubbard until he retired in 1993. Then she came to us and stayed in the position until Lingenfelter came on. She then worked under Lingenfelter for a year, sharing responsibilities with Wendy, who came with him from Biola. Then, due to physical problems, she retired from SWM in 2000.

New Academic Chairs

The Woodberry era was marked by the acquisition of four academic chairs, each of which involved Dean Woodberry in sometimes lengthy negotiations with one or more donors. An academic chair is a faculty position supported by an endowment. The interest from that investment, then, provides the salary of the faculty member that "occupies" the chair. We already had a McGavran Chair of Church Growth.

Dr. Mary Varker, an admirer of Dudley Woodberry funded a Chair of Islamic Studies, provided that Woodberry himself occupy it and that the chair not be named after her. The establishment of this chair assures that we will have an Islamicist on our faculty for as long as the school exists.

The Glasser Chair of Biblical Theology of Mission was established by the seminary Trustees to honor Dr. Glasser and to permanentize that subject within our curriculum. Chuck Van Engen was "installed" in that chair and has been a worthy successor to Glasser.

A third chair was partly funded during this period, though the final funds to complete the endowment did not come until 2004. This is the Paul E. Pierson Chair of Mission History and Contemporary Culture. This chair was set up, of course, to honor Pierson and to assure that mission history continues to be a part of our curriculum. A friend of Pierson and one of his sons were major donors. Wilbert Shenk is the worthy incumbent in this chair.

The fourth chair that was set up during this period came from a Korean donor who is a part of the congregation of one of our early Korean doctoral graduates, Sun Hee Kwak. Our Korean faculty member, Timothy Park, played an important part in interesting Dr. Kwak to show his gratefulness to SWM for teaching him the church growth and cultural principles that enabled him to plant and grow a church of more than 40,000 members. The chair was named the Chair of Global Mission and should eventually be occupied by an Asian, since its funding has come from Korea.   But the administration judged that we do not yet have a senior Asian scholar ready to occupy it. Since I was on Dr. Kwak's doctoral committee and am the only faculty member still here who was teaching when Kwak was studying at SWM, they assigned me to the chair.

Statistics

By 1994, 30 years into our history, we could count approximately 4,500 students who have spent at least one quarter with us, with 827 theses and dissertations written and 1,627 degrees granted by SWM. In the academic year 1993-94, there were approximately 800 enrolled in our various programs (359 on campus in the fall), counting each enrollee in residence during the four terms of the year, 200 more in the distance learning program, 44 students in three extension centers and all active doctoral candidates (several off campus).

Our Pasadena student body included students from 65 countries with no less than 135 languages spoken by students, faculty and staff. At the 30 year mark, we had come a long way from the twelve students that greeted McGavran and Tippett in the fall of 1965.

In addition, our faculty were making an important mark in the academy and in ground-breaking research. During this time, three of our faculty—Gilliland, Shenk and Woodberry—were elected Presidents of the American Society of Missiology, while Brewster was elected to the Presidency of the Association of Professors of Mission. And Sogaard and Woodberry continued to provide leadership for the Lausanne movement. As for research, we attracted two six-figure grants from Pew Charitable Trusts for studies of witness and church planting among Muslims in Asia and Africa. And Shenk brought with him when he joined us his research and publication program concerning mission to Western cultures.

So this was a time of considerable activity in the area of scholarship as well as in our regular training program.

Chapter 10

The Lingenfelter Era

1999-2003

It was time to seek a new Dean. Woodberry had reached the end of the time he had promised and was anxious to get back to his calling as a teacher and scholar. So, a Search Committee was appointed and we began to work through information on several possibilities. One of the issues we discussed was whether we should seek an insider, one already on our faculty, or an outsider. After considerable discussion, there were two finalists, one an insider and the other an outsider.

The outsider was Sherwood Lingenfelter, the Provost of Biola University. Provost Spittler, in seeking a quality outsider, had talked Lingenfelter into applying and Sherwood had been given the green light to apply by his boss, President of Biola, Clyde Cook. The insider finalist was Chuck Van Engen. The Committee members were very impressed with the qualifications and potential of both candidates and discussed thoroughly the reasons for and against insider or outsider. It was a very tough decision that none of us wanted to make but, weighing everything we could think of, it seemed as though it would be better to choose the insider to give us continuity. So we voted for Van Engen.

The appointment of deans is, however, the prerogative of the President. The Committee's function is purely advisory and our feeling that an insider would be best was not convincing to President Mouw or Provost Spittler. So they chose Lingenfelter.

At the time we felt disappointed that our recommendation was not followed. But God was in it. And the nature of our relationships within SWM is such that we refused to hold a grudge and determined to give Lingenfelter every opportunity to prove that he was indeed God's choice for the job. And prove it he did. And we soon came to appreciate the wisdom of their decision. We, of course, have no idea how things would have gone if Van Engen had been chosen. Probably he would have done a great job. But we do know that Sherwood turned out to be a superb leader from the start.

It was obvious from the beginning of Lingenfelter's deanship that we were in good hands. Sherwood knows how to administer, how to consult, how to keep his faculty satisfied and engaged. He, however, considers his most important contribution the appointment of three new faculty members, Hanciles, Glanville and Smith (see below).

Sherwood G. Lingenfelter (1941—)
At Fuller: 1999—

Lingenfelter is an extremely competent person in everything he does and especially gifted in administration. He is an anthropologist who in his years at Biola had developed a strong desire to move into Missiology. He had joined the Biola School of Intercultural Studies in 1983 after teaching from 1969-1983 in the State University of New York (SUNY) at Brockport. He then was appointed Provost at Biola in 1988 and learned that job well.

He was born in 1941 in Holidaysburg, Pennsylvania, and grew up in Virginia and Ohio, the oldest son of a Grace Brethren pastor. Feeling a call to missions, he attended Wheaton College where he was influenced by Dave Winter, Ralph's brother, who was teaching anthropology there at the time. Graduating in 1963, he enrolled in a Ph.D. program in anthropology at the University of Pittsburgh. There he found his faith severely tested and, while doing fieldwork for his dissertation on the island of Yap he rejected his Christian commitment. After completing his work at Pitt, he accepted the position at SUNY Brockport where by 1982, the year before he moved to Biola, he had risen to the position of full Professor.

In 1975, while at SUNY and in his backslidden state, a woman enrolled in one of Lingenfelter's classes who attracted his attention because she was such an outstanding student. This led to a conversation with her in which he discovered that she was a missionary with Wycliffe Bible Translators. As Sherwood has written,

> In the course of our conversation she asked if I would consider coming to Peru to provide these lectures for the

Wycliffe teams in Peru. I told her that I didn't think they would be interested in a secular anthropologist like me. She then assured me that Wycliffe was very open to secular anthropologists and quite willing to have people from secular universities participate in their training. By this time she had captured my interest. The commitment that I had made as a teenager to serve in missions and then my motivation to enter anthropology to serve a Christian mission community had always been a part of my identity and thinking. In my walking away from the Lord I had assumed that I would never participate in such an exercise and I developed a very negative attitude toward missionaries during my field research in Yap (unpublished memo 5/18/04:3).

This conversation led to the decision for Sherwood and Judy to attend Wycliffe's Summer Institute of Linguistics at the University of Oklahoma in the summer of 1975. At the Summer Institute they met people committed to Christ and also to scholarship. Largely through the influence of Marvin Mayers, Lingenfelter "decided to give Christianity a second look" (ibid.:4). So he returned to SUNY open to helping Wycliffe if asked and committed once again to Christ and His church.

The invitation to be a Wycliffe consultant came and Sherwood took part of a sabbatical to go to Brazil in 1977 for four months while Judy began graduate study in Intercultural Education at Pittsburgh. He spent two and half months living in a jungle village with a Wycliffe missionary doing ethnographic research and "came away from Brazil with the deep understanding that being an anthropologist for the kingdom of God was far more rewarding than being an anthropologist for my own professional goals" (ibid.:6)

The next few years, while still at SUNY, involved some more stints with Wycliffe plus another year of research in Yap, during which his wife, Judy, did fieldwork for her Ph.D. Then, in 1983, at the invitation of Dean Marvin Mayers, he moved to Biola University as Professor of Anthropology. Mayers had taken the position of Dean of the School of Intercultural Studies at Biola and wanted Sherwood (and soon Judy) to join him there. This they did, with Sherwood teaching anthropology from 1983-88, then moving to the Provost position in 1988 though still teaching part time. During this time, Sherwood and Mayers developed a useful little book entitled *Ministering Cross-Culturally: An Incarnational Model for Personal Relationships* (1986).

Eleven years as Provost at Biola became a proving ground for the next stage of his life. In addition to learning how to run the university, during this time Lingenfelter was able to develop insight into the status of Christianity in Japan and Korea plus a strong interest in church and mission leadership to add to his competence in dealing with political leadership and change that he had researched in Yap. He also became concerned to provide tools for missionaries to aid them in doing anthropological research. This concern led eventually to the publication of *Transforming Culture* (1992, 1998) and *Agents of Transformation* (1996). More recently he has partnered with his wife, Judy, to publish *Teaching Cross-Culturally: An Incarnational Model of Learning and Teaching* (2003).

The invitation to come to Fuller precipitated a crisis for Sherwood. For the Biola Trustees had given him a vote of confidence plus a significant raise in salary to keep him. But his desire to re-engage in missions tipped the scales in our direction. After "much prayer and reflection" (ibid.:10), he accepted the SWM deanship.

In addition to his work as Dean, Sherwood has maintained his relationships with Wycliffe, doing two-week workshops in Cameroon, Kenya and Mozambique on crosscultural partnerships. From these workshops he has gained considerable insight into the changes going on in twenty-first century mission. These insights have led to changes in the way he goes about teaching his courses on crosscultural leadership. He also served on the SIL/Wycliffe International Board as well as on the board of Grace Brethren International Missions.

Lingenfelter's Contribution to SWM/SIS

With the addition of Lingenfelter as a faculty member we gained a superb teacher, researcher and supervisor of research. Because of his administrative duties he is only able to teach a limited number of courses, but they are rated by the students as among the most helpful offered.

Administratively, Sherwood proved himself an able and inspiring leader during the short time he was our Dean. And the appointments of Hanciles, Glanville, Smith and especially of McConnell define his legacy as of high quality in his appointments and as very important in the upgrading of our degree programs. Further discussion of Lingenfelter's contribution to SWM/SIS follows in the biographical sketches of these faculty additions below and in the final section of this chapter. Though we miss him as Dean, his outstanding contribution to the Seminary as a whole and indirectly to SIS continues to prove that he is the right person for the job of Provost.

Wendy Walker

When Sherwood came on as Dean in 1999, it wasn't long before he convinced his Biola Administrative Assistant Wendy Walker to join him here. This she did, even though for the first few years she continued to live nearer to Biola than to Fuller. Wendy says of her move and her demanding job,

> I thought my position would be similar to what it had been at Biola, but due to restructuring of staff positions, Sherwood gave me the title of Director of Operations, a position held for twenty years by the much loved Marilyn Clinton, who had just retired. Betty Ann Klebe had also just retired after serving the School of World Mission as receptionist for almost twenty years. . . .

> My first year in the School of World Mission was a challenge and a huge learning experience. Not only did I need to learn the "culture" of SWM, and the unique nuances and the challenging organizational structure of the wider Fuller community, but I also had to jump right in and start taking care of business. My responsibilities included the oversight of the school's budget, hiring and supervising staff, communicating with faculty and staff, encouraging faculty and staff morale and building a sense of community within the school (including students), managing the SWM Dean's Office and handling Sherwood's correspondence, course work, and travel schedule.

> At the end of my first year, Denise Shubert left SWM due to health related issues and Jeff Borowiecki left as his one-year special appointment position had ended. With their departures, I assumed many of their responsibilities, including faculty meeting schedules and agendas, faculty committee assignments, new faculty contact and orientation, maintaining faculty bio/vitas, facilities care and management, and the planning and organizing of all SWM events. At this time, we made some budget changes and hired Deb Hannaford as our full-time receptionist, and Jen Bloch continued as part-time office support in the Dean's office (email May 2005).

Wendy soon demonstrated why Lingenfelter wanted her here. She brought a competence to the office that we quickly came to appreciate very much. Her expertise had a lot to do with the fact that Sherwood could handle both the Dean's job and that of Provost for two years until McConnell was able to take over as Dean. Of that two years, she says, "Sherwood spent most of his time in the Provost's office and gave the daily oversight of the school to me to handle, with specific oversight of the academic programs to several faculty members" (ibid).

Once McConnell had arrived in April 2003, Wendy played a major role in orienting him to his new responsibilities. In June 2003, then, she accepted Lingenfelter's invitation to move to the Provost's office to assist him there. Deciding to move was one of the more difficult decisions she has ever had to make. It was very difficult for us to face as well, for she had teamed up with Deb Hannaford, our Receptionist, to make the SWM Dean's office one of the most pleasant places on campus. However, she also trained Debbie so that she could move into the Dean's Administrative Assistant position when Wendy left. Of her time with us, Wendy says,

> I thoroughly enjoyed my four years in the School of World Mission. It was a time of learning and growing for me personally, but also a real sense of being in the right place at the right time. I had the opportunity to work with many wonderful people, all unique and gifted, and have been blessed by their presence in my life. It was a difficult decision to leave SWM and move to the Provost's Office with Sherwood, but I believe I made the right decision. I also believe that SWM has an exciting future and am thankful that I had a part in its history (ibid).

C. Douglas McConnell (1951—)
At Fuller: 1999—

Ever since McConnell graduated with his Ph.D. from SWM (1992) many of us had been watching his career with interest. He had attracted our attention as a student in our Papua New Guinea extension program and impressed us when he came to campus to complete his Ph.D. We continued to watch as he took a faculty position at Wheaton College (1992-98) becoming head of their intercultural studies program and distinguishing himself as a teacher there.

In 1998, he was appointed to a five-year term as the first International Director of Pioneers, an international church planting movement formed from the merger of Asia Pacific Christian Mission and South Seas Evangelical Mission. A year into his five-year term with Pioneers, Dean Woodberry approached McConnell about teaching part-time at SWM. He joined us then part-time in 1999 as Associate Professor of Leadership, to teach intensive courses on a regular basis.

During the next four years, while Doug was fulfilling his commitment to Pioneers, it became clear to several of us on the faculty that he would be a strong candidate for Dean if that need arose. The need did indeed arise when Lingenfelter was appointed Provost of the whole Seminary, so we invited McConnell to become Dean, starting in the spring of 2003.

Doug McConnell was born in 1951, the firstborn son of Charles and June McConnell. He grew up in New Mexico, attending elementary school in Albuquerque and high school at New Mexico Military School. College years found him attending California State University, San Bernardino, where he majored in history and education. Between high school and college, Doug had visited California, where he was introduced to the daughter of a business partner of his dad, Janna.

Janna was a dedicated young Christian and led him to Christ in 1969. She had felt called to missions as a child and her calling became Doug's calling when they married in 1970. Though they knew of Fuller at that time, two of Janna's uncles having graduated from Fuller, they never expected to have Fuller become a part of their lives.

To fulfill this missionary calling, the first step in 1974 was employment with the Queensland Department of Education in Australia. Soon after arriving, they requested to be transferred from the coast to a school with a high percentage of Aboriginal children. It was there that they had their first taste of crosscultural missionary service. They also began supporting a missionary couple serving with Asia Pacific Christian Mission (APCM) in Papua New Guinea.

In 1976, the McConnells were confronted with the need to move into full-time missionary service. After praying and discussing their calling, they approached APCM about taking up the duties of the headmaster of the international school in Port Moresby. As

McConnell says, "I can't believe the conservative Aussie leadership accepted a couple of young hippie types, but they did!" In the years that followed (1976-1991) the McConnells served as teachers, church planters, urban missionaries among the squatters in Port Moresby and finally in mission leadership. A good Aussie friend would often comment that taking a risk on these Yanks was a good decision.

In 1981, the national president of the indigenous church they were serving asked Doug if he would consider attending the SWM extension program in PNG that was to start in 1982 as a delegate from the Evangelical Church of PNG. After praying through the invitation and the impact on their family of five, they decided to accept. Acceptance of that invitation, meant that they were also committing themselves to a life of service to the Church. While at the time they didn't realize it, they were also committing themselves to SWM as a vital part of their lives.

By June of 1985, Doug had completed all the extension courses we offered in PNG, completed his M.A. on the Pasadena campus and gained entrance into our Ph.D. program. Upon their return to PNG, McConnell was asked to become General Director of APCM, a position he accepted in 1986. It was extremely unusual for an American to be asked to head up an Australian mission, but for the next five years he carried out this responsibility admirably. This position also gave him a great opportunity to test what he had learned from SWM.

He returned to Fuller to complete his Ph.D. in 1990 and, upon completing his doctorate, was offered a teaching position at Wheaton. He served there with distinction from January1992 to June 1998, being appointed head of the missions program in September 1992 and chosen as Junior Teacher of the Year for 1996-97.

In the late nineties, then, the Asia Pacific Christian Mission that he had directed from 1986 to 1991, merged with South Seas Evangelical Mission to form Pioneers of Australia and Pioneers of New Zealand. McConnell was asked to head up the new venture as International Director. This he did for the next five years while also teaching half-time at SWM for four of them.

When we contacted Doug about the possibility of becoming our Dean, he had completed four years of his five-year appointment with Pioneers. This meant he could not come immediately. So

Lingenfelter carried both the deanship and the position as Provost for that year, with McConnell joining us in March of 2003.

Contribution to SWM/SIS

Apart from the deanship, McConnell greatly strengthens our Leadership program. In addition, he brings a great concern for one of the major problems on the world scene—the widespread plight of an estimated 1.5 billion children living in poverty, often without parents who have died of AIDS, and often exploited by unscrupulous adults. He has been able to add to our curriculum course offerings and a Chair dealing with what we call Children at Risk.

Among his research interests, other than the plight of children at risk, are teamwork and leadership within crosscultural environments and the role of financing in missions. He has published numerous articles, in the *Evangelical Dictionary of World Mission* (2000), *Evangelical Missions Quarterly*, and *Missiology*, edited the book *The Holy Spirit and Mission Dynamics* (1997), co-authored the book *The Changing Face of World Missions* (2005). He is currently working on a project with the Viva Network to edit a volume on a biblical basis for understanding God's heart for children at risk.

Jehu J. Hanciles (1964—)
At Fuller: 2000—

From 1998-2000, we had the privilege of getting to know Jehu while he held a post-doctoral fellowship with the Global Research Institute, an institute that awards grants to non-Western scholars to come to Fuller to work on research and writing projects. He came regularly to our Tuesday noon informal faculty get-togethers. We got to know him as a person and to respect him as a young historian with a strong recommendation from his mentor, Andrew Walls, arguably the premier British historian of mission.

As the time of his fellowship was coming to an end, Dean Lingenfelter felt that we should consider the possibility of adding him to our faculty to add both a competent historian and an African to our faculty. As a faculty, we agreed with Sherwood and Jehu was appointed to a full-time position beginning in September of 2000.

Jehu was born in 1964 in Freetown, Sierra Leone and grew up in what he calls a "fairly strict" Anglican home. Though this, plus the influence of Scripture Union, gave him a good background in Biblical teaching and Christian nurture, he became quite rebellious with an intense dislike of church and the Christian life that he faked. He writes,

> This period of conscious rebellion and unresolved spiritual tensions eventually culminated in a major crisis about the time I got "confirmed" in the Anglican Church. Among other things, the preparatory Confirmation classes were led by a youthful evangelical pastor whose teaching of Scripture made great impact. The decisive moment came in December 1980 when I read *Hunger for Reality* by George Verwer . . . Overwhelmed by its radical message, I made a decisive commitment to Christ and my life went through a profound transformation that was characterized by extreme zealousness for Christian service (email: December 2004).

This transformation led to a full church scholarship to study for the ordained ministry at Fourah Bay College, Sierra Leone's premier institution of higher learning. At FBC he earned a License in Divinity (L.Div.) and a B.A. in history and sociology. He also discovered "a fondness for teaching and scholarship." He discovered that he had "a natural love of knowledge" leading him to a great enjoyment of "finding out things (research) as well as presenting ideas" (ibid). He became fascinated by history but afraid that his new interest and the fact that it could turn him from pastoral ministry to teaching might be perceived as ingratitude toward those who had expended huge sums of money to train him for ordained ministry.

On the verge of ordination, Jehu's "inner crisis" became unbearable, so he mustered up courage to discuss his problem with the Bishop. To his surprise, this turned out well. "To my great relief and gratitude," he says, "the bishop quickly grasped the nature of my dilemma (probably because he was a seasoned academic himself) and appointed me lecturer at the Sierra Leone Theological Hall and Church Training Centre" (ibid). This was an institution funded by several denominations with some students preparing for ordination and others merely seeking theological training perhaps leading to greater involvement in the church. There he taught a variety of subjects in addition to history and also was involved in the college's Theological Education by Extension program.

While in this position, Jehu enrolled in a masters in theology program at Fourah Bay where he began what would be a life-long interest in developing "a fresh understanding of the Western missionary and colonial encounter" (ibid). Initially, this study was devoted to the experience in Sierra Leone. Soon he was being seen as "a resident 'expert' on Sierra Leone Christianity." His work then attracted the attention of Andrew Walls and he was offered a scholarship to study with him at his Centre for the Study of Christianity in the Non-Western World at the University of Edinburgh. He went there in September of 1990 and during the next five years completed M.Th. and Ph.D. degrees. Jehu states, "studying with Andrew Walls profoundly transformed my intellectual life and shaped my scholarship. I have not had a more influential mentor in my academic pilgrimage" (ibid).

In contrast to the very exciting academic experience at Edinburgh, Hanciles experienced what he calls a "spiritual wilderness" in the Scottish churches. He also came face to face with racism and the "diminished self-esteem that comes from being an alien" in a secular culture (ibid.). He continues,

> This cross-cultural experience tested key paradigms of my African evangelicalism and presented unique challenges for growth and service. I will never forget the experience of turning up in Glasgow (some 50 miles away) to preach at a church, only to be told just before the service that my 'sermon' should be no longer than 7 minutes! Years of faithful Christian commitment stood me in good stead, though, I quickly learned to shop on Sundays and fellowship with Christians who frequented Scotland's ubiquitous pubs (ibid).

The good news is, in 1991 he married Biffoh, whom he had met three years earlier in Sierra Leone. With this added responsibility, however, he took on the task of becoming a part-time "Christian Education Worker" at a sizable Presbyterian church where he and Biffoh faced "the formidable task of attracting and ministering to the conspicuously absent youth" as the only non-Whites in the church, daily wrestling "with cross-cultural issues, adapting African-inspired approaches to ministry" (ibid).

Desiring to serve Africa with his Ph.D., and unable to return to Sierra Leone because of the civil war there, Hanciles accepted a post teaching Church History in Africa University, a newly established United Methodist institution in Zimbabwe. This was for him a delightful experience, teaching enthusiastic students from 20 African countries. He was, however, "struck for the first time by the extent to which Eurocentric perspectives and assumptions dominated the books and theological curriculum." He found this problem even in missiology. He worked hard, then, "to adapt or apply precepts and concepts to the African experience" and found the students' responses very rewarding (ibid). Their church experience in Zimbabwe, as part of a Pentecostal fellowship, turned out to be very rewarding as well.

From Zimbabwe, having fulfilled his three-year contract, he came to Fuller in 1998 for his post-doctoral fellowship. This resulted in a book entitled *Euthanasia of a Mission: African Church Autonomy in a Colonial Context* (2002) as well as his employment on our faculty. Jehu writes about this next stage in his career,

> Academically, Fuller has been a stimulating and enabling environment, even though being the "first African" faculty member imposes some isolation. Privileging non-Western experiences and voices in my teaching and writing has also been both fulfilling and challenging. But the top level faculty and diversity of the student body makes for enriched scholarly engagement and dynamic classroom interaction; and being able to teach about the issues I deeply care about—issues related to mission history, African Christianity, and globalization—is a great blessing. My journey, both academic and spiritual, continues (ibid).

It is encouraging to hear that he and his family have found a church that they are happy in even though again, as in Edinburgh, they feel like they need to function as missionaries to the West.

Hanciles' Contribution to SWM/SIS

Jehu is a sterling representative of the best of the intellectual abilities of his country and his continent. In addition, as one of our younger faculty, he is an important part of what will be the future of SIS. We are fortunate to have him on our team. Though we are probably at least as challenged by him and his perspectives as he is by us and our perspectives, we highly applaud his commitment to a cause that we western missiologists have given some attention to—that of "de-Westernizing" missiology. He has the academic ability required for such a task plus the experiential qualifications that we Westerners can never attain to go much farther in this area than we have been able to. He and we western missiologists, however, share the same challenge to evaluate the past efforts of missionaries and learn from their mistakes without being too judgmental toward them.

In addition to the valuable perspectives on history that Hanciles brings us, he has a deep interest in and concern over the influence of globalization on Christian activity. The information age has brought such instant awareness of what is going on worldwide that we can no longer assume that we can do anything in isolation from world currents. This has important ramifications for the tasks of Christian witness.

Jehu is just at the beginning of his publishing career, having recently published his first book, *Euthanasia of a Mission: African Church Autonomy in a Colonial Context* (2002). He has, however, published several useful articles dealing mostly with Christianity in Africa and its implications for missiological understanding. Among them are "Anatomy of an Experiment: The Sierra Leone Native Pastorate," (2001), "Mission and Migration: Some Implications for the Twenty-First Century Church" (2003), "Conversion and Social Change: A Review of the Unfinished Task in West Africa" (2004), "Missionaries and Revolutionaries: Elements of Transformation in the Emergence of Modern African Christianity," (2004) and "Back to Africa: White Abolitionists and Black Missionaries" (2005).

Elizabeth (Betsy) Glanville (1943—)
At Fuller: 2000—

One of Lingenfelter's aims as he assumed the deanship was to put the degree programs on solid footing. Our faculty, especially Shaw and Van Engen, had been solidifying the doctoral program. Betsy Glanville, who completed her Ph.D. in Leadership under Clinton in 2000 was already teaching Leadership courses as an Adjunct and also serving as Research Librarian (the one who gives final approval to dissertations and theses). In this capacity she began working with the Doctoral Committee to set up a doctoral studies office which, in 2001, she was hired to direct. In 2002 we added her to our faculty full-time as Assistant Professor of Leadership and Director of Doctoral Programs.

Betsy was born in 1943, the oldest of four children, to a Navy Lieutenant Commander. When her father left the Navy, the family moved to Wellesley, Massachusetts and then to Toledo, Ohio where Betsy did most of her elementary and all of her secondary schooling. She spent summers on Cape Cod with grandparents, swimming and sailing. As a teenager, she raced small boats and taught sailing. The family moved from the Episcopal church in Wellesley to the Congregational church in Toledo and Betsy was very active in church and Sunday School. But, she says, "I really had never heard anything about what it meant to believe in Jesus, to make Him Lord and Savior of my life" (email 4/27/04). As a college freshman, however, she attended an IVCF conference at which Kenneth Pike spoke and she committed herself to the Lord.

Betsy attended Wellesley College from 1961-65, receiving a BA in Chemistry, cum laude. She belonged to Park Street Congregational Church in Boston during these years and met her husband, Lew, either at Park Street Church in 1962 (his story) or at an InterVarsity conference in 1963 (her story). They were married in 1965 and she taught high school chemistry while he went to Gordon Divinity School (now Gordon-Conwell). After Lew's graduation, they worked in inner city Chicago and developed "a ministry of exposing the problems and issues of the inner city to suburban churches through multimedia shows" (email: 4/27/04). In 1972, they moved to Los Angeles to work with the InterVarsity multimedia team and from there connected with Fuller, completing an M.A. in Marriage and Family Counseling in the School of Theology in 1975. Betsy and Lew have been involved in charismatic renewal since the 70s, planting a church in the 80s and working with the Vineyard for several years from 1985 on, including directing the Vineyard Bible Institute correspondence program from 1994-98.

Betsy first came to SWM in 1991 to audit Clinton's course on Lifelong Development. "During that class," she says, "God began to talk to me about being called as a leader myself, not just as the wife of a leader" (email: 4/27/04). She completed an M.A. in Leadership in 1993, confirmed in her desire to teach young leaders the things she wished she had known in her earlier years. Clinton, then, talked her into doing a doctorate, contending that if she really wanted to teach, she would need a Ph.D.

Contribution to SWM/SIS

Betsy's major contribution so far has been to reorganize and oversee the doctoral programs. Previously, the doctoral advising and the masters advising were combined. As the number of doctoral students increased, however, it seemed best to separate the functions. Betsy has improved things considerably as Director of Doctoral Studies.

She also teaches various leadership courses and mentors women leaders. Among her innovations is the expansion of Clinton's Leadership Emergence course to include leadership development for women. She also co-taught with Bobby a course on Leadership Development for Women in Ministry. Her dissertation was on this subject: *Leadership Development for Women in Christian Ministry* (2000). Betsy is rated very highly by the students both as teacher and as mentor. And for the doctoral students (and the program in general), she is invaluable.

Stephanie Smith (1973—)
At Fuller: 2002—

When Lingenfelter came on, he determined to raise the status of our degree programs by appointing faculty-level directors for both the doctoral and the masters programs. Having done this for the doctoral programs by appointing Betsy Glanville, he now looked for someone to head up the masters programs. Several people were considered, but the application of Stephanie Smith particularly attracted him. She was a doctoral student at St. Andrews University in Scotland who applied after finding the position advertised on-line.

Stephanie was born in 1973 in Virginia and raised in South Carolina in a solid Christian home, the daughter of Joe and Jan Smith. She was attracted to missions early in life through reading a series of novels. Her first overseas trip was to the Philippines at age 16 where, with a canon of the Episcopal church, they visited and encouraged those doing church and development work. She says of this experience, "The plight of the poor in the Philippines had a shocking effect on me, which continues to reverberate through my work, inspiring my interests in economic and social issues of justice" (email: January 2005:1).

She attended Wheaton College, graduating in Business and Economics in 1996. During her college years, however, she took two years out to work with Youth With a Mission, returning to YWAM after graduation to serve in Malaysia (1996-97) and Montana (1998-99) as a lecturer with their School of Biblical Studies. She so enjoyed this teaching experience that she enrolled in Regent College in Vancouver, Canada to work on a Masters of Christian Studies, concentrating on Spiritual Theology under James Houston. Completing that program in 2000, she moved to St. Andrews

University in Scotland to pursue a Ph.D. in Theology under Alan Torrance. In her doctoral work she was able to focus on the theological anthropology of Karl Barth and John Paul II in a study that combined her interests in systematic theology and social ethics. She completed her doctoral dissertation during her first year at Fuller, successfully defending it in the summer of 2003.

Smith's Contribution to SIS

As an administrator, Stephanie has helped to strengthen the organization of the masters programs and to "implement, define, and market a new degree for pre-field students, the Masters of Crosscultural Studies." She has also worked with our faculty to revamp the Th.M. program. During this transitional time, with enrollment decreasing at the Masters level, Stephanie is attempting to bring new vision into the masters programs in order to adjust to the new realities and challenges of mission.

Stephanie was hired, however, not just to administer. One of the things that attracted our attention to her was her teaching ability and the fact that she would bring a new and important area into our curriculum—the emphasis on spirituality and mission. In her teaching, she is able to "blend her interests in theology, spirituality, and social concern by teaching courses in these areas" (ibid).

In 2005, a new possibility has opened up for Stephanie. She is turning over her administrative position to another and moving into a research position that puts her in collaboration with representatives from the University of Southern California and the Fuller Schools of Psychology and Theology "to research the best practices that empower churches and communities affected by HIV/AIDS in Southern Africa." Her research will focus on "the relationship between theology and the practices of Christian communities who are grappling with the AIDS tragedy" (ibid).

Summary of the Lingenfelter Era

This is the shortest of the "Eras." It ended when Sherwood, under pressure from the Trustees, felt he had found an adequate replacement (McConnell) and agreed to be appointed Provost. In the short time Sherwood served as our Dean, however, there were some important happenings. Lingenfelter is (justifiably) proud of the fact that he brought onto our faculty two more women and an African.

For years we had discussed the importance of having more women and non-Westerners on our faculty. But in our searches for faculty additions we found few in these categories who came up to our standards. We did have Betty Sue Brewster, Jude Tiersma-Watson and Roberta King. But only King was full-time.

With the appointments of Glanville and Smith, however, not only did we gain two fine women faculty but both our doctoral and our masters degree programs were strengthened, since each of them were assigned administrative as well as teaching responsibilities. Betsy Glanville has continued the shoring up of our doctoral programs and Stephanie Smith has reorganized our masters programs.

Lingenfelter says of these appointments:

> The addition of these two women on the faculty was very important for two reasons. First, they both had significant administrative gifts and added significant strength to the administrative team. By reorganizing our committee structure to develop a team for doctoral programs and a team for masters programs this created an organizational structure that required significant administrative leadership from a faculty perspective. Dr. Glanville's appointment was the first and she did an outstanding job of providing administrative leadership for the doctoral team. Because her qualifications as a faculty member were exemplary, within a year we appointed her to a . . . faculty position [as well] (ibid.:12).

Jehu Hanciles is the first African scholar appointed to our faculty. He came with the strong recommendation of his doctoral mentor British scholar Andrew Walls who regards him as one of the best African students he has ever mentored. He has been an important addition because of both his scholarship and his African perspective.

Three other initiatives made while Lingenfelter was Dean should also be mentioned. The first was the development of an M.A. program for Koreans in the Korean language. Since 1990, Korea has sent out more than 16,000 missionaries to 151 countries, most of whom have little or no missiological training. We had already begun offering a Doctor of Ministry degree in Korean in the Philippines and in Korea itself. This program is growing and will hopefully make a difference in the quality of Korean missionary endeavor.

A second initiative was to work out dual degree programs with Hope International and Biola Universities. "This initiative was an attempt to provide opportunities for our masters-level students to get preparation in technical fields of TESOL and international development," areas that we do not have faculty for (ibid.:13). Under this program, students could work on degrees at both Fuller and one or the other of these other institutions at the same time.

The third initiative was to attract Dr. Doug McConnell to be the next Dean of SWM/SIS. With the retirement of Russ Spittler as Provost, the Fuller Trustees asked Sherwood to become Acting Provost in addition to the deanship of SWM. He did so well that both Trustees and President Mouw put heavy pressure on him to move from the SWM deanship to the Provost position. Though very reluctant, Sherwood made the statement that if someone better could be found to be the Dean of SWM, he would move.

As mentioned, McConnell had been teaching part-time for us in the Leadership program since 1999, in addition to his full-time position as International Director of Pioneers Mission. We were impressed with him and in casual discussions some of us sometimes mentioned that he would make a good Dean for us when Sherwood had had enough of the job. Though I'm not sure Sherwood was aware of these discussions, he invited Doug to stay with him one weekend and decided he had found someone who would be "better" than himself as our Dean. Discussions with our faculty and the Fuller administration, then, resulted in McConnell's appointment in March 2002 to take effect in March 2003 when his commitment to Pioneers was to end.

Chapter 11

The McConnell Era

2003—

When McConnell took over as Dean, he was immediately faced with one of the bigger challenges in our 40 year history—that of changing our name. We could have wished for a smoother entry into his new position. But that was not to be.

The Name Change

For years our faculty discussions often included mention of the problem the word "mission" in our name caused for some of our graduates. We got reports from some of our graduates working in Muslim contexts, for example, that they could not get visas or be appointed to positions that required government approval as soon as it was known that they had degrees from a school of mission.

As the years went by, we received more and more of such reports both from the Muslim world and from several other places dominated by Hindus, Buddhists or repressive secular governments. Many of our international students were especially affected by our "name problem" when they attempted to get teaching positions in their home countries.

We tinkered with things during the 70s by naming our Ph.D. a Doctorate in Intercultural Studies rather than in Missiology, though the compelling reason for not calling our Ph.D. a degree in Missiology was the fact that we had in existence at that time the joint Ph.D. doctoral program with the School of Theology that used that name. We were happy for the help the more neutral name gave those who were working in limited access countries.

As we discussed the name problem seriously over about a two-year stretch, several problems emerged. For one thing, we anticipated a difficult time with our constituency if we adopted a secular name.

237

We deemed it unlikely that the more conservative of our supporters would really understand the seriousness of the plight of certain of our students and how sympathetic we were with their problem. Indeed, we suspected that they would feel that a change of name, especially if the new name sounded "secular," betokened a move on our part toward liberalism and a loss of missionary zeal.

A second problem that emerged has not yet been tackled. That is the fact that even though our school now has a secular name, the whole institution is still "Fuller Seminary." And the degrees are given by the Seminary, not by the individual schools. As we discussed our problem, we frequently found ourselves wishing that the whole institution would change its name to something like "Fuller University" or "Fuller Graduate Schools." But, though this isn't happening, students do now have the option of having "Fuller Graduate Schools" rather than "Fuller Seminary" on their diplomas. A similar unsolved problem lies with our Doctor of Missiology degree. Since it is patterned after the Doctor of Education (Ed.D.) degree, we sometimes talked of changing the name to Ed.D. We found, however, that our accrediting agencies would require us to teach some education courses in order to offer an Ed.D. and so dropped that idea.

A third problem was that we could not agree on what name to choose. It seemed that each of us had his/her pet name to suggest and we developed factions on our faculty, each faction lining up behind their preferred alternative. Since we are quite close in our relationship with one another, however, none of us felt comfortable advocating strongly lest we hurt one another's feelings. Nor was our Dean going to impose a name on us. Thus it went on for several weeks even after we had definitely determined that we were going to risk the change.

In the end, it came down to either choosing a name that would be unique to our school or choosing the name that is already in use at Biola and other schools as a secular-sounding label for missiology instruction. We eventually chose the latter. Thus in 2003, the School of World Mission officially became the School of Intercultural Studies.

With the change, though, McConnell's early days as Dean were challenging. He spent months in meetings and correspondence attempting to explain the reasons for the change in such a way that people would join with us in our concern and agree that the change was a good idea. And in the conversations with concerned people he won most of them over. McConnell says of the challenge:

> I found that the ratio of positive to negative exceeded 10 to 1. In the end, there were really only about 6 major concerns raised by individuals compared to an avalanche of requests for changes to individual diplomas [to change the name from SWM to SIS] and congratulatory comments from alums and supporters. (email: June 2005)

In addition, there was a real positive aspect to the change. The discussions gave our new Dean a golden opportunity to interact with alums and supporters, getting to know them and to be known by them. So, in spite of the pressure put on McConnell by the change, in retrospect, the results have been far more positive than negative.

McConnell as Dean

We had anticipated that Doug had all the makings of becoming an outstanding Dean. Though it is too early for any meaningful evaluation, I think the faculty would join me in saying, so far we have not been disappointed. He demonstrates the maturity needed for such a position and a willingness to tackle whatever comes his way, motivated to do whatever it takes to bring about the good of all concerned. He is a team player deeply concerned that all of us know what is going on and have opportunity for input. I predict that he will become just as outstanding as any of the leaders we have had over these 40 years.

An unenviable challenge faces him, however, with the imminent retirement or moving to half-time of several of us. As mentioned, Fuller has a semi-retirement status called "Senior Professor" that we use to label those who have gone off salary but are usually asked to return to teach one or more times each year and are paid course by course. Pierson, Gilliland, Sogaard and Wong are already Senior Professors. Shenk will move into that category at the end of the 2004-2005 academic year, with myself and Clinton probably the following year. Meanwhile, Gibbs and Woodberry are scaling back to half-time in the next two years.

So, McConnell comes at a crucial time in our history. With his solid background both in academics and in mission administration, he seems admirably prepared for the tasks before him. Stephanie Smith, who works closely with Doug on masters programs writes concerning him,

I would say that his primary gift has been bringing a fresh vision for the direction of SIS in the new century. He has been able to recognize new trends and create new responses because of his extensive experience on the mission field and as the Director of Pioneers. Doug has brought a great vision to SIS to push the school forward in continuing to break new ground in responding to vital issues of the mission field, including (1) the training of pre-field missionaries through courses that deliberately address their needs . . . (2) raising academic standards, (3) revamping the D.Miss. program, (4) rebuilding ties with [the School of Theology] and working with SOT for the benefit of our students, (5) creating a strong administrative team that runs the day-to-day operations, (6) launching the children at risk curriculum which immediately became one of our top concentrations, (7) working to establish the HIV/AIDS research project, (8) he's very talented at discerning where people will fit best, putting them there, and providing resources for their growth (email: January 2005).

Debbie Hannaford and Christine Cervantes

When Wendy Walker made her difficult decision to leave SIS to work with Lingenfelter in the Provost's office, it looked as though it was going to be very difficult to find a replacement. However, recognizing that the job of Director of Operations had grown too big for one person Dean McConnell split the job into two parts. Debbie Hannaford, who as receptionist was underutilized and had been able to assist Wendy with many tasks that would not ordinarily fall into the receptionist's job description, was tapped to manage the Dean's office with the title "Administrative Assistant."

For the other function (Executive Assistant for Academic and Financial Affairs), Christine Cervantes (Marilyn and Bobby's daughter) was promoted. She had been handling the scheduling of classes plus dealing with faculty loads and adjunct faculty. To these duties were added the budgeting and handling of SIS financial affairs.

We could hardly have a more competent and affable senior staff than these two. Debbie and our Receptionist, Joan Krayer, continue to make the Dean's office one of the pleasantest and most efficient places on campus. Christine, for her part, in quiet competence, carries well the heavy load of scheduling and dealing with finances. SIS is in good shape administratively.

Ryan Bolger (1963—)
At Fuller: 2002—

Ryan Bolger came to Fuller as a student after a business venture failed that was dedicated to assisting the poor to start businesses for themselves. The soul-searching that followed that failure forced Ryan to reassess his life and to return to a calling he had received from God years earlier to employ his gifts in Christian service. The concern he had developed for crosscultural ministry while serving with Youth With a Mission in Belize (1980) led to his enrolling in SWM/SIS in 1996. Following the completion of two M.A.s—one in Theology the other in Cross-Cultural Studies—he enrolled in our Ph.D. program, completing it in 2003.

Bolger is a native of Southern California, born in 1963 and raised in Southern California, with the exception of three years in middle school in Minnesota. He came to Christ during these years in Minnesota. Then, back in California and at the University of California, Davis, he "had encounters with Christ and his church that transformed him even further. Beyond any sort of cognitive understanding of faith, he knew he had met God, and he would never be the same again" (email, 10/13/04:1).

While at college, he was very active in Christian ministry. After college, then, and after marrying fellow student, Julie, he served on two church planting teams with the Vineyard and worked as a systems analyst/programmer for several manufacturing firms in Irvine, California.

At Fuller he received several awards and impressed us all with his abilities and commitment. This led, upon completion of his Ph.D., to his appointment as the Academic Director of a new program at SIS—the M.A. in Global Leadership. This is a distance learning degree that has attracted strong interest (which means students) from missionaries and other Christian leaders who cannot come to campus for residence study. He was also appointed as Assistant Professor of Church in Contemporary Culture. His primary area of academic interest and expertise, and the subject of his dissertation *Jesus for and Against Modernity* (2003), is the relationships between postmodernity and emerging churches. He has even in his brief time with us been able to do a considerable amount of research in the US and UK "looking at congregations and interviewing leaders in which

postmodern culture thrives in the life of their respective communities"
(ibid.:1).

Ryan is just getting started with publications. He has, however,
coauthored with Eddie Gibbs an important book called *Emerging
Churches: Creating Christian Community in Postmodern Cultures*
(2005). He also did with Gibbs an article "Tracking the Emerging
Church" (2004). Earlier he published "Dwelling, Distinctiveness, and
Dialogue: The Missiological Triad of John Howard Yoder" (1998).

It is important that SIS continue the development, started by
Wilbert Shenk, of a specialization in reaching those whose cultural
context is postmodernism. We are pleased to have someone with
Ryan's interest and competence on our faculty.

Evelyne Reisacher (1955—)
At Fuller: 2002—

With the growth of Islamic studies in SIS, it has become
important to add to our faculty in this area. As a student with a
considerable background in ministry to Muslims in Europe, Evelyne
Reisacher impressed us in her M.A. studies and was encouraged to go
on for a Ph.D. Then, after teaching a couple of courses as an Adjunct,
she was invited to join our faculty in 2002.

Reisacher was born in 1955 in a small French town named
Selestat in Alsace Loraine. Since this area has over the course of
history sometimes been French, sometimes German, she grew up
bilingual with a concern for intercultural communication and conflict
resolution. She attended a Lutheran church that was full of reminders
of Martin Bucer, a prominent reformer who was born in that town.
She says,

> I loved sitting in the first row during meetings because I did
> not want to miss a word from the Bible teaching. My mother
> was a model of compassion and prayer-filled life, and my father,
> a lawyer, taught me to help the needy and seek justice. . . .

> At the age of thirteen, during a meeting featuring the Swiss
> evangelist Maurice Ray, I perceived God addressing me the
> question, "Are you willing to follow me?" I realized that the
> death and resurrection of Jesus were a gift to me and that God's
> commands and laws were good for the world. That day, I
> answered yes to God. At that moment a deep compassion for
> the world arose in me and I wanted to make his ways known to
> people close to me and far away (email: December 2004).

From that time on, her aim was to prepare for ministry. She studied theology and crosscultural communication and developed a love for languages. Upon completion of an M.A. in applied linguistics in Strasbourg, though advised by her professors to pursue a career as a translator, she headed to England to study linguistics with the Summer Institute of Linguistics. After that experience she would gladly have become a Bible translator. However, as she prayed to discover where she should serve, God changed her plans and she was back studying theology for the next two years in a Bible institute near Paris.

During these years she met a group of North African Muslim background Christians working with an organization called l'AMI and discovered that she could serve crossculturally right within France. This contact "embarked [her] in a journey that lasted over two decades" (ibid). She began to learn about Islam, North African society and Muslim worldview from these converts and became a part of l'AMI, learning experientially and serving alongside and under the North Africans. She adds,

> It is difficult to describe in a few lines my work at l'AMI. It touched all areas of the North African community: social, family and spiritual. I did everything from preparing hundreds of cups of coffee in a row for people who visited our homes, helping people find a job, organizing conferences for pastors from twenty two Arab countries, creating literature relevant to the Muslim context or developing training programs for new believers all over Europe. I traveled also extensively in North Africa and the Middle East and partnered with believers and churches throughout the Muslim world. I met and interacted with hundreds of believers who later started ministries all over the world. I saw thousands become followers of Jesus. These years provided me with a sense of connectedness with people from the Muslim world, and a better grasp of the issues that Christians and Muslims face when they interact (ibid).

In 1987, at a conference in Belgium, she first heard of Fuller's Islamics emphasis. The following summer, then, she enrolled in the summer intensive program in Islamic studies that we offered, seeking to learn more about Islamic theology. On her return to Paris, Evelyne found herself more eager to interact with Muslims on an academic level. Taking a sabbatical, she returned to Pasadena in 1994 and completed her M.A. in Intercultural Studies. Three years later, she came back to do her PhD, completing it in 2001. Her dissertation was

closely related to her work with l'AMI. It is a study of the ways
North African Muslim background Christians bond with the French
community. In the summer of 2001 Reisacher was invited to teach a
course on Women in Islam for us. She then spent the following year
doing postdoctoral research on "attachment" (bonding) in Los
Angeles. This led to her teaching a course in that area also.

Over the years, Evelyne has spent a lot of time shuttling back
and forth between Pasadena and Paris, continuing her ministry with
l'AMI while completing her studies and teaching adjunct courses.
When invited to join our faculty, then, she accepted for several
reasons.

> Firstly, I like Fuller's approach to Islamic studies. The
> Islamic department is deeply indebted to the work of Dudley
> Woodberry who has developed a well-built concentration with
> over twelve different courses on Islam. Fuller and its long
> history of research in Islam allows me to approach current
> issues in regard to Muslim and Christian relations within a
> multidisciplinary framework in the School of Intercultural
> Studies. Interactions between workers from all over the world
> who come to Fuller for research allow me to reflect on the
> various models and approaches with the Muslim world.
> Secondly, Fuller offers me the possibility to continue research
> on intercultural attachment and develop courses in this area.
> The emphasis in attachment research these days is on the
> importance of affect regulation and right brain. I believe it is
> important to integrate findings in this area with the field of
> Missiology. . . . And finally, I also want to share experiences of
> twenty-five years of ministry with students who prepare to serve
> cross-culturally or those who come to Fuller to reflect on their
> work (ibid).

Reisacher, in considering whether to accept Fuller's offer to
join the faculty, was concerned over whether or not she would be able
to keep up her contacts in Paris, North Africa and the Middle East. A
glance at the traveling that we all do, however, set her mind at ease.
She is grateful for the opportunities she has to regularly return to
France to teach and train and also to teach and minister in many other
places, thus keeping the connection between the classroom and the
global situation.

As for publication, Evelyne is just at the beginning of this part
of her academic career. Already published, however, is a chapter in
the book *Christian Reflection: Christianity and Islam*, entitled
"Beyond the Veil" (2005). Two other chapters of books have been

accepted and will likely be published in 2006. These are entitled, "Muslim Women and Law," and "Muslim Women and Conversion." She is also editing her dissertation for publication under the title, "Bonds between North African French Christians."

David Bundy (1948—)
At Fuller: 2002—

The last faculty member to be hired before SWM/SIS turns 40 was David Bundy. He was hired by Provost Lingenfelter to be the FTS Librarian and, since administrators hired at faculty level are also appointed to one of our three schools, Bundy chose SIS. Thus, though he spends most of his time running the library, his primary faculty relationships and whatever teaching he does are in our school. Bundy came to us after an extensive search from Christian Theological Seminary in Indianapolis where he had been Librarian for twelve years. Prior to that he had worked in various capacities at Asbury Theological Seminary (5 years) and the Catholic University of Louvain.

David was born in Longview, Washington in 1948, but attended junior and senior high school in a small town of 750 in the middle of Oregon (Madras, Oregon). And even then, he lived about 20 miles outside of town in the hills. But, he says,

> I liked to read and I think that teachers encouraged that because I was so socially inept that no other contact with me was possible. Thus, as a high school student, I found myself pouring over history, philosophy, social philosophy and economics texts imported from the universities of Minnesota, Washington, Hawaii and Ball State (email, May 2005:2).

His voluminous reading over the years led him on a philosophical roller coaster through Marxism and a variety of philosophical and theological viewpoints. But he had become a Christian and so enrolled in Seattle Pacific University, there majoring in both religion and history (most of which was done at the University of Washington). He received his B.A. cum laude in 1969. He then studied at the University of Washington and Western Evangelical Seminary (Portland, OR), eventually moving to Asbury and gaining an M.Div. (1972) and a Th.M. (1973) from Asbury. Though he began his career as a librarian during these years at Asbury, he spent a good bit of his time in Europe. He writes,

The years 1975-1985 were spent at the Universite Catholique de Louvain and at the (Pentecostal) Institute of University Ministry in Leuven, Belgium, where he served as Dean. During that decade in Europe, he catalogued Middle Eastern language manuscripts for numerous libraries across the Continent. He was active in European library and academic associations (email May 2005).

He received a Licentiate in Oriental Philology and History from the Universite Catholique de Louvain (1980) and has since become a doctoral candidate at the University of Uppsala in Sweden where only a dissertation remains between him and a Ph.D.

As can be seen, David has led a very colorful and academically productive life. He is much more than a librarian with speaking ability in five languages and what he calls "a passive knowledge" of 25 more! He is "a historian of early Asian Christianity (prior to 1400) and of the Methodist, Holiness and Pentecostal movements." He has published more than 300 scholarly essays and 200 book reviews, many of these in languages other than English. His publications are "in the areas of library science, American religious history, Pentecostalism (primarily outside North America), Pietism and the Wesleyan/Holiness traditions with a focus on the history of Christian mission . . . [and] Middle Eastern Christian studies, with a focus on Syriac, Armenian and Arabic sources" (Vitae 2005:4). Further, he is co-editor of a scholarly series *Pietist and Wesleyan Studies* (12 volumes published so far) and founding editor of EPTA Bulletin (now Journal of the European Pentecostal Theological Association) and of the *Bulletin d'arabe chretien* (a publication devoted to Christian Arabic studies).

After such a distinguished and varied career, David writes, partly in his Vitae and partly in a May email,

> Bundy chose to accept an invitation to Fuller Theological Seminary for a number of reasons. Fuller has a tradition of careful scholarly reflection and a strong commitment to the Church in its diverse manifestations around the world. The student body and faculty reflect that diversity.
>
> The library, with a competent staff having seventeen first languages, provides a base for interacting with churches and theologians from around the world. He chose to be part of the School of Intercultural Studies ... because of its history and present reality of relating to churches around the world and preparing leadership for those churches. . . .

Bundy comes to Fuller with personal history of involvement with churches around the world. He has extensive international experience, having served as invited lecturer in twenty-nine countries and having taught graduate level courses at institutions in sixteen countries. Part of that international experience is the decade spent studying and teaching in Belgium as well as significant periods spent living and teaching in Sweden and the United Kingdom.

We are happy to have David Bundy both in our library and on our SIS faculty. We look forward to learning a lot from him as the years go by.

Part III

Evaluation

Chapter 12

Retrospect and Prospect

One of McGavran's best presentations was entitled, "Sunset or Sunrise." In that presentation he made the point that when one looks at the sun when it is near the horizon, it is almost impossible to tell whether we are looking at a sunset or a sunrise. The sun can look very much the same at either end of the day. Likewise, McGavran held, when we look at the cause of Christian mission, we cannot always tell whether we are looking at a discouraging demise of the Christian cause or an encouraging "sunrise" of God-inspired activity destined to take the cause of Christ to new heights.

None of us who were here when McGavran was in his prime will ever forget that, beyond his keen research sense, he continually conveyed optimism concerning God's plan and program for winning the lost. Whatever doubts he may have had concerning SWM, and I'm sure he had some, were also covered by an air of hopefulness that what we were doing would be of benefit to the Kingdom. He did, however, insist that in all we did, we keep our focus on winning *panta ta ethne*.

In this final chapter I want to summarize and to evaluate what forty (actually 39) years has looked like, where we are now and what the future may hold. To do so, I will repeat some of what I've already presented in earlier chapters. My evaluations are, of course, my own. My colleagues may or may not agree.

In the preceding chapters, we have looked pretty carefully at the early years and at the aims and desires of the founders. We have, then, followed the growth and the changes that have occurred over these four decades and found that SWM/SIS in 2005 is quite a different place than it was in 1965. Let's take a look at what has happened over the years and come up with some tentative conclusions concerning our present and future.

It feels to me as though we've changed a lot. Whether this is for the better or for the worse remains to be seen. Given the large-scale changes that have taken place in the world, I feel we have had to change in response, especially since we believe so strongly in contextualization and receptor-oriented communication. Our change of name, for example, is a change in response to missiological reality. It is a change that had to be made and probably should have been made sooner.

So, change as change is not the issue. The issue is whether the changes we have undergone are appropriate or not—whether or not they enhance our mission or detract from it. Given the changes that have happened, can we be optimistic about the future?

Though I don't assume that everything McGavran put into place is better than whatever might have replaced or developed from it, I would like to ask a series of questions he might have asked concerning the changes. This will give us a convenient way to discuss the plusses and minuses of the changes that have taken place. But first, a discussion of the changes in the context within which we work today.

Today's Context

Change in our operation is demanded by changes in the context within which we function. Forty years ago much of the world was open to fairly traditional approaches to missionary work. Today, much of the world is more or less closed to such traditional approaches. True, at that time the Conciliar churches had become discouraged and were pulling back their missionaries. But Evangelicals rallied gladly around McGavran's optimistic assessment of missionary "possibility thinking" and evangelical mission boards recommended that their members come here to study how to be more effective than their predecessors.

Perhaps the greatest thing we did early on was to awaken many in the Christian world who had allowed their zeal for winning the lost to cool. The 1950s and 60s were a time of pessimism concerning Christian mission. The mistakes we missionaries had made loomed large in the Christian consciousness and we heard loud and clear the message coming from some of the national leaders in missionized lands that missionaries should go home. Not only had people in sending churches lost their vision, the missionaries themselves were often discouraged.

Into this world of discouragement and lack of zeal came Donald McGavran, a prophet with a dual passion for facts and for converts. McGavran himself had become discouraged but God had led him to look for facts—facts that indicated that people were coming to Christ, often in large numbers and facts that indicated that much of what missionaries were doing was counterproductive to bringing in the lost. Like the prophets of old, he seemed unbalanced and overboard. He antagonized many. But he awakened many both to our calling to win the lost and to the possibilities for doing so more effectively. Led by McGavran, then, SWM has served as a beacon to wake up missionaries and the church in general for missions, winning converts and church growth.

But that scene has changed a lot over forty years. In the world at large, the Cold War is over, the Muslim world has awakened, secularism and postmodernism have increased in Euro-America, immigration has increased the diversity in the United States and in many "limited access" countries Christians cannot get in on a missionary visa. Even where missionary work is allowed, missionaries are often much less welcome than 35-40 years ago.

Though many of the areas missionaries once worked in are virtually closed to ministry by outsiders, there are many encouraging movements to Christ occurring with little or no outside assistance. The "awakening" of the Muslim world and militant movements within Buddhism (e.g. the Dalai Lama) and Hinduism are new factors. There is, though, quite a bit of real creativity in certain sectors of the Christian population in getting witnesses into limited access countries, especially in the Muslim world.

Within the Christian context, then, mission thinkers have largely awakened to the need and possibility of becoming more effective through taking account of cultural and communicational factors. We have largely made our point with the thinkers and teachers. However, at the local church level, missionary giving is down and often only available for short-term assignments. A disturbing number of those concerned about crosscultural mission have opted for putting their resources into sending people out on short-term forays into other societies rather than encouraging long-term commitment.

In our ministry to crosscultural Christian workers and their concerns, we at SWM/SIS have welcomed growth, both in our operation and in the wider world of Christian witness. We have wanted to get the message across to the Christian world that people need Jesus and that many of the world's peoples are not responding due to ineffective approaches to winning them. To this end we have increased our faculty, expanded our approach to missiology, increased our course offerings, increased our student body, encouraged and engaged in research in numerous areas (not just Church Growth), developed extension programs and trained many who have gone into faculty positions in other institutions. But our central focus is still on ascertaining the relationships between the Gospel and the sociocultural contexts into which the Gospel message is to be communicated, and actively carrying out that communication.

These changes make for a very changed context at Fuller from the early days (prior to 1975) when there were just six of us faculty members focusing on five core areas of study with our students averaging 42 years of age and 14 years of field experience. Three of the areas most in demand among our students today, for example, weren't even in view prior to 1975. These are Leadership, Islamics and Spiritual Dynamics.

In addition, our student body is now much larger than in the mid-70s, with a much higher percentage of pre-field students and a larger, more diverse set of offerings with accompanying diversity of faculty. We have proportionately more doctoral students and proportionately fewer masters-level students. Perhaps this fact mirrors the attractiveness of our programs for those who plan to become professionals in missiology and the lesser concern for training of those who are only going out for short-term assignments.

In some ways, though, we have become victims of our own success. Many of our graduates are teaching in other institutions, many of which were either non-existent or small and struggling in the 60s and 70s. So there are now more training institutions for missionaries and international church leaders offering masters-level programs similar to ours. We are no longer "the only game in town." Arguably, then, there are a higher percentage of well-trained (as opposed to untrained) crosscultural witnesses in the field. There are far more books on mission subjects and far more concern that the methods we use are relevant to the people we seek to reach. Many who have come here have gone through paradigm shifts that have made them more effective in their ministries.

However, many who have studied with us have not gone back into the ministries they sought to learn about when they came to

SWM/SIS. They have taken other positions, often in teaching or administration that have kept them from applying what they have learned in field situations. And some, we suspect, have been more concerned to get a degree than to do ministry. These facts grieve us.

One of the most significant of the changes in the context today is that there are many more nonwestern missionaries serving crossculturally. Korean and Nigerian churches especially have taken up the cause of missions big time, sending out thousands. Though economic problems have kept the flow of Nigerians to SIS small, Koreans now constitute 25-35% of our student body. Adding other internationals to the Koreans, our student body is more than half non-American.

So the contexts in which we operate, whether in the world at large or here at home, have changed considerably. The word "mission" and its derivatives has become an impediment, so we felt compelled to change our name. As mentioned, the old name kept some students from coming and forced some of our graduates to try to hide the name of their *alma mater.*

Nor can we continue to assume either that our students have had genuine field experience before coming to us or that they were preparing for long-term crosscultural work. For many of our students and the churches that they attend, mission is a three-week or two-month foray into a place where they have no language facility to do something that, from a career missionary perspective, seems quite superficial.

And the challenges of crosscultural communicating have come right into our classrooms, with so many who don't have English as their first language. Nor do these have a western worldview as their basis for understanding what we're teaching, in spite of the westernizing influences of their schooling.

And, on top of these changes, we are in the midst of a generational shift. Though younger faculty may be able to handle the material just as well as we old-timers have, it may take several years before they have the kind of reputation and publications that draw students. The early pioneers are but a distant memory. But in the last few years Wagner left and Pierson and Gilliland have virtually wrapped up their teaching careers. Sogaard has already moved to Senior Professor (semi-retired) status. And within the next two years, Woodberry, Clinton, Shenk, Gibbs and myself move to Senior

Professor status. This "changing of the guard" makes for significant change in a very short period of time. We older faculty are, however, excited about what the younger ones are contributing. We are also happy that established people like Van Engen, Lingenfelter, Shaw and Brewster will continue for several more years with us Senior Professors still making contributions as well. Such a large-scale change may not be easy, however.

Retrospect

To recap our history a bit, let's look at the internal changes we have undergone. As we have grown and gained and lost faculty members, the internal makeup of our operation and the ways we function have of necessity changed.

SWM started as a training institute for career missionaries based on a radical change that had taken place in McGavran's perspective on missionary activity. McGavran had, during 30 years in India changed from a generalist and educational missionary to one with a radical concern first, last and always for winning people to Christ and enfolding them in churches. He played his one-string fiddle with great optimism that through research more effective ways could be found to bring in the lost. With this vision to research what makes churches grow and to train career missionaries to discover and take advantage of what they discover, he set up the Institute of Church Growth in Eugene, Oregon in 1960, moving it to Fuller in 1965.

I'd say we were true to McGavran's single-minded vision through the McGavran Era and into the Glasser Era, at least on the surface. Beneath the surface, however, even in the earliest years, there were indications that we were expanding our approach from McGavran's narrow focus on Church Growth into what could be called "Church Growth Missiology." I would point to at least four factors that led to this expansion.

First, Tippett was never as narrow as McGavran. His perspective was as broad and deep as biblical Christianity itself. While believing in and supporting McGavran's church growth emphasis, Tippett's fiddle had many strings on it. So did Winter's and mine. If McGavran led people to develop "Church Growth Eyes," Tippett, Winter and I brought to our approach an understanding of the cultural complexity in which churches are to be planted.

Secondly, Glasser, in bringing a more theological component to CG Missiology, expanded our concern from a fairly narrow focus on Church to a much broader focus on the Kingdom of God as the context within which the Church is to function. To the extent that McGavran took note of the Kingdom, it appeared that the Kingdom was to serve the Church. Glasser turned this around to correspond with the Scriptural emphasis on Kingdom as the end, with Church as the major means.

Thirdly, the professional society for missiologists, the American Society of Missiology was started with Winter thoroughly involved and Tippett the first editor of its journal, *Missiology*. This changed our publishing focus from the narrow focus of the *Church Growth Bulletin* that promoted a monolithic church growth perspective on missions, to a much broader approach to Missiology. The founding of the William Carey Library by Ralph and Roberta Winter also played a part in this broadening by publishing student theses and books by authors not a part of SWM/ICG that were not restricted to the narrow church growth focus.

The fourth factor, then, was Wagner's expansion of Church Growth theory and practice by applying it to the American scene. McGavran's focus was on the Church in non-western contexts, though he gave nodding recognition to the need for American churches to apply his principles. But Wagner took the principles and research method developed in non-western contexts to American churches. And it caught on in a big way. Though the rest of our perspectives were not taken up to any great extent in American contexts, the Church Growth emphasis soon became the "in thing" among American pastors so that at least that part of our little operation would never be the same again.

Undoubtedly additional factors were at work, but these are four of the more important ones.

During the beginning of the Glasser Era we continued the Church Growth Seminars for missionaries and mission executives. And we did a similar thing for the student orientations at Fuller. We each did lectures in these orientation events, highlighting our particular slants on missiology. And, though McGavran was still the "star" of our operation, the rest of us in the seminars and orientations were expanding our Missiology beyond the strong Church Growth emphasis that had characterized the McGavran era.

The Missiology of the journal *Missiology*, with which we were thoroughly involved, was even broader than what we were teaching. In addition, the presentations of Winter and McGavran at the 1974 Lausanne Congress had attracted so much attention in evangelical circles that this constituency began to look to SWM as a major fountain of missiological thinking. The days when Church Growth thinking was derided as too narrow, largely by World Council Protestants (McGavran's primary circle) were now replaced by an attitude of expectancy toward SWM on the part of evangelicals. Though this change of constituency kept McGavran slightly off-balance, we all felt we were privileged by God to be major players at a crucial point in mission history.

In the middle of the Glasser period we hired the Brewsters. Then Winter and Tippett left and were replaced by Hiebert and Gilliland. These changes, plus McGavran's decreasing participation in teaching and writing, also contributed to the move from strictly Church Growth to broader Missiology. Though Tippett's and my anthropology had always been a broadening element with its focus on the cultural context and the communicational elements of missiology, Hiebert's brilliant input opened up still more anthropological vistas to be considered. During the latter part of the seventies, evangelicals increasingly accepted contextualization theory. In 1978, the *Evangelical Missions Quarterly* devoted a whole issue to the subject and the important Willowbank Consultation was held. Then came the publication of my *Christianity in Culture* in 1979. Our participation in these events was significant, both outside and inside of SWM, and enhanced our position as a leader in the field.

A major change in SWM, beginning in 1976, was brought about by the starting of a pre-field program involving the Brewsters and Gilliland. Especially for pre-field people, the Brewsters added courses on language and culture learning to our curriculum. We also designated 1978 as "The Year of the Muslim" and began to turn our attention to Muslim evangelism. Other than these changes, we offered pretty much the same classes, throughout this period. We did, however, institute our first doctorate, the Doctor of Missiology, with the first graduate in 1971, and were eventually allowed to offer Ph.D.s.

During the Pierson years we expanded incredibly, adding first Clinton and the very popular Leadership program, then Shaw and the Translation program. Sogaard came, strengthening our offerings in Communication, Tan came to develop a Chinese program, Gibbs came to build up the Church Growth offerings after McGavran's retirement. Then we brought on Woodberry, adding Islamics. Next it was Elliston to add to our Leadership offerings and Van Engen to succeed Glasser and Wong to help with the Chinese program. We lost Hiebert and Tan with Gibbs moving to the School of Theology.

All of these faculty additions and the programs that came along with them made SWM a much bigger operation than it had ever been before. Student enrollment also grew. But probably the major event of this period was the 1982-5 controversy over the Signs and Wonders course and the movement of Wagner and myself into the area of spiritual power. This changed many lives (especially ours) and added important offerings to our curriculum. It also changed our reputation in many circles, turning many Pentecostals and charismatics more open to us and many traditional evangelicals more suspicious.

So, by 1992, the beginning of the Woodberry Era, we were well into a very broad definition of Missiology and a deep commitment to academic research and degrees. It was no longer accurate to speak of our approach as simply "Church Growth" or even "Church Growth Missiology." It was and still is Evangelical Missiology or, perhaps, "Incarnational Missiology," but no longer as narrow as it had been in the McGavran and Glasser eras. Our commitment to breadth continued through the Woodberry Era with the adding of Jude Tiersma-Watson to teach Urban Studies, Young Lee Hertig in Gender and Ethnicity, Wilbert Shenk in History and Mission to the West, Bob Freeman in Distance Learning, Tim Park to teach and run our Korean program, Pablo Deiros half-time in History and Spiritual Dynamics, Eddie Gibbs returning in Church Growth and Roberta King in Communication and Ethnomusicology. We lost only Elliston and Hertig.

In addition, Woodberry was able to attract four academic Chairs to add to the McGavran Chair of Church Growth. The new chairs are in Islamics, Theology of Mission, Global Mission and History. These are important, since they guarantee our future. During this period, then, there was further broadening and a definite turn toward stricter academics.

Under Lingenfelter we added Doug McConnell half-time in Leadership, Betsy Glanville to direct our doctoral programs and teach Leadership, Jehu Hanciles in History and Globalization and Stephanie Smith to teach on Spirituality and administer the masters-level degree programs.

McConnell brought on Ryan Bolger to assist in Distance Learning and to focus on postmodern influences and Evelyne Reisacher in Islamics. David Bundy, appointed by now Provost Lingenfelter as Fuller Librarian, then, chose our faculty as his academic home.

So, from six (seven counting Orr) faculty members in 1971 we have grown to 24 in 2004, several of whom are not full-time but are regular part-time. And we have moved from a narrow focus on Church Growth to a very broad Missiology. Such growth, of course, has positive and negative aspects to it. I wonder what McGavran would say if he could see us now!

What Would Our Founder Think?

Though I don't want to dwell on this very much, it is intriguing to wonder what McGavran would think of us now. He was such a driving force, so single-minded, so committed to winning and discipling the lost. And his passion was for an institution that would be just as committed as he was to extending the Kingdom of God. So, imagining what he would think can give us a way of measuring where we are at the 40 year mark.

As we have seen, McGavran's concern was to have a place where career missionaries could find the facts and develop "hard, bold plans" based on a dispassionate assessment of the facts and a willingness to change programs and patterns to bring about more effective evangelism and church growth. McGavran had one string on his fiddle—winning the lost and enfolding them in churches—and all that he did and stood for was, for him, to be evaluated in terms of that one aim. He was fond of contrasting all of the "good things" that missionaries do with the one "best thing"—bringing the lost to Christ and into congregational life.

So, McGavran would most likely evaluate SIS in terms of this one string on his fiddle. But SIS at forty is quite a different operation than was SWM in 1965-70. We are larger, more diverse, more academic. We have a far larger percentage of pre-field students than

McGavran envisaged, and the research we do covers far more territory than the church growth research that he was so passionate about. In addition, for better or worse, we are far more degree-oriented and we have proportionately less missionaries and more national church leaders and "would-be" leaders in our student body.

If McGavran came back, he would probably say we are too diverse and too academic. As one trained in education, he wanted to be a part of an operation that is able to offer graduate degrees. That's why he wanted his Institute of Church Growth to be based in an academic institution. But his heart was always for the practical application of academic insights, not for academics for its own sake. The academic rigor we now require and the fact that effective practitioners are sometimes excluded from degree programs because of their lack of academic credentials would disturb him greatly.

He would probably also question our diversity, asking if we really are as focused as we should be on reaching the lost and enfolding them in churches in which they can grow spiritually. He would ask this question of each of our specialty areas. Is our anthropology so focused? Our communication? Our leadership? Our Islamics? Our history? Our theology? Our contextualization? Our spiritual dynamics? Or have we turned to doing good things but forgetting the best thing?

McGavran would likely be quite disturbed to see the percentage of field experienced people in our student body dwindle and the percentage of pre-field people increase. He would, however, applaud the increase in the number of nonwestern students, many of whom have had significant experience. His commitment was to assisting missionaries and international church leaders who have worked hard but not seen much fruit to examine their approach and, if possible, to have more success. He tolerated a handful of pre-field people but his passion was to help the struggling mid-career missionaries and international church leaders whom he delighted in calling "Associates," rather than students. He loved to work with them one on one to seek answers to their problems. He had less time for those who were only theoretically involved in the issues they chose to research.

How Much Have We Changed?

The question about how much we have changed is a good one. Have we changed a lot? I think the answer is "Yes." The hidden question is, however, the important one: "Are the changes for the better or for the worse?" And the answer to that question is not so easy, for it has many parts, or sub-questions. I will discuss ten of these sub-questions.

1. Do we still have a driving concern for winning the lost and discipling them?

This would, I believe, be McGavran's first concern and probably should be ours as well. When he was here, his continual insistence that our primary concern had to be seeking the lost, kept us focused. It was impossible when McGavran was here to forget that winning and discipling the lost was to be our aim. He referred to *panta ta ethne* as our primary concern in just about every speech and conversation. He was often tiresome and predictable, but he kept us focused.

We don't have any such "focus-forcer" with us today and probably can get lax in our concern for and emphasis on winning the lost. Nor do our students keep us focused in the same way the preponderance of mid-career people did during the McGavran and Glasser Eras. The questions asked by experienced people in and between classes are quite different from those of inexperienced people. In the McGavran and Glasser Eras, we had a larger percentage of students who were attracted by the Church Growth emphasis. These kept us focused on reaching the lost. Now our students come with a wide variety of interests. And many students are not quite sure why they are here. Indeed, they may be here simply because they are seeking to find something worth investing their lives in.

The change from having students with a well-defined agenda stemming from field experience to those whose agenda is to find something that might attract their interest is a major change. So is the change from each of us relating our particular focus to Church Growth Theory to the possibility that we are more concerned about the broader theoretical emphases of our disciplines.

2. What effect does the larger percentage of pre-field students have on our operation?

As mentioned, when our student body was made up largely of experienced field missionaries and international church leaders, we faculty were constantly being challenged with very practical questions concerning the applicability of what we were teaching. "How does this insight play out in such and such a situation?," was a typical kind of question we had to be ready to answer at any time. This kept us on our toes. Though many of the questions asked by experienced people deal with theory, learning theory was for them a very practical thing, easily related to their practice.

With inexperienced people the practical applications of our theories tend to be illustrated only from our own experiences since we have little experience to draw from our students. This puts theory in a more academic context, as something that might someday be relevant (if they can remember it long enough), rather than something they can experience as immediately relevant and applicable. The difference is enormous.

It is good to train people before they go to the field. We believe in this and do not resent the fact that pre-field people come to us to learn what they may have to face if and when they get to the field. But when inexperienced students are mixed with experienced students, their presence in our classes changes things. When we first began to attract significant numbers of pre-field students, we set up separate sections of the core courses for inexperienced and experienced students. But this overloaded those of us teaching the core courses since we had to do two sections of each course. And many of the inexperienced complained that they did not have the kind of classroom interaction with experienced people that attracted them to our school. So we abandoned the attempt to keep the groups separate.

Now, however, with a larger faculty, we have gone back to having separate sections in six areas: Theology, History, Anthropology, Communication, Leadership and Spirituality. This is a good move though it does not address the desire of the pre-field students to mix with the experienced ones.

A related issue is the fact that when we required field experience for entrance, it was three years of field experience plus the ability to minister in the field language. We have now so softened on this issue that, not only don't we require such a background for pre-field people, we don't always require it for those we consider to be experienced people or for those entering our doctoral programs. I am greatly concerned about the latter, since it means that there are some who have written dissertations and received doctorates in Missiology who have no practical involvement in mission. They can only write from a theoretical perspective.

3. Does the greater diversity of specializations among our faculty members betoken a lack of a central core concern?

In the McGavran and Glasser Eras, the number of areas of specialty was quite limited and quite focused on winning the lost. All of our students were exposed to each of what we called our core areas: Church Growth, Theology of Mission, Anthropology, Animism and History. They could also do a bit in TEE, Islam, Contextualization and a few other areas, but always with an evangelistic focus. Perhaps our smallness contributed to the singleness of our focus on winning the lost.

Now, however, we offer courses and specializations in areas such as Leadership, Islamics, Urban Mission, Translation, Spiritual Dynamics, Communication, Ethnomusicology, Mission to Contemporary Culture, Distance Learning, Children at Risk and others. This diversity is a positive thing, unless it takes us away from a primary focus on winning the lost and discipling them as believers. We now have around 24 faculty members with lots of expertise and lots of interests. This means that students with a wide variety of interests can come and specialize in a wide variety of areas. Though it is a positive thing to be able to offer such diversity of courses and specializations, can so many of us keep first things first or are we too diversified? Hopefully, each of us in our special areas will put as our top priority the winning of the lost and the enfolding of them in spiritually maturing churches. God forbid that we simply become academics.

In this regard it is heartening to listen to student comments concerning the faculty members' devotionals and prayers at the beginning of classes. Often they are as much or more impressed by such devotionals and prayers as they are with the faculty members' handling of the academic material. But being good at devotionals does not necessarily mean that we have a Great Commission focus.

We are all still deeply concerned for the winning of the lost and the growing of Christian communities. But there is not the singleness of focus that we experienced in the Church Growth days. There are different flags on our mastheads and no one pressing us as McGavran did to give top billing to a single concept.

In our early days we were known as the Church Growth School. I wonder what we are known for now—probably different things to different groups. For some it may be Church Growth. For others it may be spiritual power, or anthropology, or Islamics, or leadership. or history. Students already here might see the contextualization of the Gospel in human cultures as our core area. This is probably the concern that unites us more than any other. Or they might feel that communication or missional theology or leadership is central to all that we teach.

We may illustrate the problem with diagrams such as the following. If diversity of subjects with no clear focus is our major contribution, the arrows pointing out from a center would describe us. This was the problem we who did our studies at the old Kennedy School of Missions experienced. We entered their degree programs as Missionaries and came out as Anthropologists, Linguists or Area Specialists in African, Asian or Latin American Studies.

SWM/SIS has, however, attempted to reverse this process by making our students Missiologists—those who take the various subjects we teach and integrate their insights into a discipline that focuses on the communication of the Gospel to the world's peoples. The second of the diagrams below is intended to picture that approach.

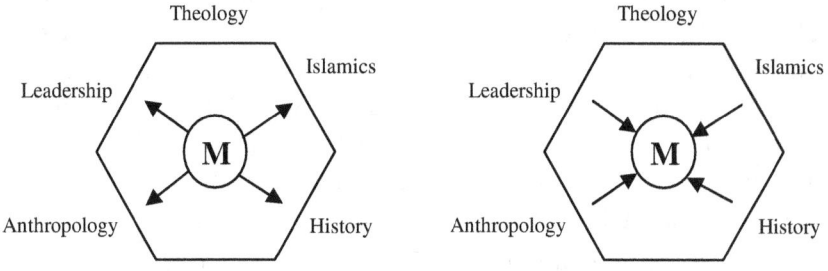

Figure 12.1   Diversified versus central focus. Note: The M in the center stands for Missionary/Missiology.

4. What about the greater focus on academics?

When our main degrees were an M.A. or a Th.M., and most of our students had field experience, we encouraged them to do very practical studies of their field situations with the aim of solving problems they had encountered in their ministries. These were the kind of studies we and the students felt were most helpful. As faculty, we felt we were helping people who had been struggling with their real problems. We felt the same when we introduced the Doctor of Missiology degree, since it is a practice-oriented degree. When, however, we began offering the Ph.D., we began to be more concerned with developing missiological theory, a very academic concern. And, especially during the Woodberry Era, when more rigorous procedures were instituted for entering the Ph.D. program, a focus on more academic concerns rather than largely practical ones increased.

Some of our faculty now face a dilemma because we really want our students to do their research and writing on something practical and meaningful in their ministries. This would motivate them toward the D.Miss. degree. We find the students, however, striving to get into the Ph.D. program that requires a theoretical dissertation because of its greater prestige, rather than doing a D.Miss. that would allow them to be more applicational.

What might be called "academicism" can be a tough thing to deal with for those of us who are seeking real life answers rather than simply theoretical musings. In academic institutions, especially at the Ph.D. level, schools are cranking out a large number of dissertations that have little relevance to real life. I remember being on a doctoral committee in a program other than ours and, after I had read the dissertation, I asked what it had to do with real life. Neither the chairman of the student's doctoral committee nor the student himself could answer me! It hadn't occurred to either of them that a real life payoff was important.

I'm afraid we are in danger of being seduced into putting academic excellence, as defined by the academic world, ahead of practical relevance. If so, I believe we are not fulfilling the purpose for which God has called SWM/SIS into existence. Has our focus changed from ministry to developing theory? If so, we've lost a lot more than we've gained.

5. What about the changes required because of the growth in our doctoral programs and lessening of the percentage of masters-level students?

Along with the preceding discussion comes the fact that our doctoral programs are attracting proportionately more students while our basic masters programs are attracting less. One reason for this is that there are several other institutions offering masters-level missiology programs, often with our graduates as faculty. So, more and more students are coming here with masters degrees already in hand looking only for a doctorate.

Many of these are well-instructed in what we consider the basics. Some, however, do not have adequate academic or experiential background. Many of the latter are international students who haven't fully understood the material, either because they were part of a poor masters program or because they took their courses in English but didn't understand enough of the language to really grasp the material.

Other than this problem, the larger number of applicants for doctorates puts pressure on us to admit more than we can reasonably handle. Each of us as faculty has more doctoral candidates than we should have and, if we do our job with them properly, they take more time than masters students. They require more one-on-one time and different kinds of seminars than masters students, since we don't do regular classes for doctoral-level people. They also take more administrative time and take longer to complete their programs. This latter fact has financial implications, since the bulk of the work with a doctoral student in finishing up his/her dissertation may come some time after all of his/her tuition money has come in (and been spent).

In recognition of the overloading problem, Dean McConnell has taken steps to cut down on the number of Ph.D. candidates admitted each year. To compensate, he is focussing on developing a major off-campus D.Miss. program and raising the number of D.Miss. students in a distance learning program patterned after our very successful M.A. in Global Leadership program.

6. How well do we control what students learn?

Each discipline has certain basic concepts that students need to master if they are to be considered experts in that discipline. Missiology is no different. In the early days, we defined these concepts in terms of five areas that we taught in five Core Courses.

These were the courses we felt everyone had to take and be examined on in order to assure that our students had the basics of what we felt to be our approach to Missiology. The courses were: Church Growth, Theology of Mission, Anthropology, History and Animism. The students would take these courses plus whatever electives they wanted and then pass Comprehensive Exams on these five areas before they could graduate. These exams served both as terminal exams for Masters degrees and as entrance exams for Doctoral programs.

The advantage of a Core Course approach is that a major part of the curriculum each student takes is what we as faculty determine to be basic to what we're all about. But as we expanded and added more and more subjects to our curriculum, it became increasingly difficult to contend that the five core areas we started with were the only ones that should be considered core. What about Leadership? What about Islamics? What about the specialty that a given student has come to focus on? Don't these qualify as core areas for certain students of equal standing with the five we started with?

Then we got confused and for a time had no required courses. We gave up the idea of Core Courses and Comprehensive Exams. So, for several generations of students we had no way of knowing how grounded they were in Missiology when they graduated. Everything was elective and there was no final check on what they had learned.

Eventually, though, we came back to a policy that requires certain basic courses of everyone who is to carry our degrees. We now require seven or eight basic courses for our M.A. programs and five for the Th.M. program[1]. In each of the Masters programs, further, the students take "Thinking Missiologically" as a kind of exit experience. This solidifying of the requirements is a welcome change from the day of all or nearly all electives.

I believe it is important that we control the basics of our programs, especially since many of our students will be teaching Missiology after they graduate. I applaud the efforts of our Masters

---

[1] The M.A. required courses are Biblical Foundations, History, Anthropology, Church Growth, Leadership, Communication and Thinking Missiologically with one M.A. program adding Spirituality and Mission to the list. The Th.M. students are required to take Theology of Mission, Anthropology or Communication, a choice of two from Church Growth, History, and Leadership, plus Thinking Missiologically.

and Doctoral Administrators to make sure that each of our graduates leaves us with as firm a control as possible of the basics of Missiology.

7. What is the impact of the greater number of internationals and the lower numbers of missionaries?

SWM was founded to train and equip missionaries. Those of us who have been here longest, then, originally geared our courses to that audience. Our concepts were designed to help Westerners who go to non-Western societies. Our illustrations tended to come from our own experiences as Western missionaries and we risked the possibility that they would not be as relevant to the problems of internationals as we would like them to be. Though the experience of many internationals has been such that the problems we deal with and the illustrations we use do apply to many of them, there may be some serious differences between our experience and theirs that reduce the relevance to internationals of some of what we teach.

Over half of our students in any given year come from other countries and do not speak English as their first language or share an American worldview. This has major implications for what they understand, especially since internationals are often loathe to ask questions when they don't understand. And many come from educational systems that teach them to memorize what the lecturer says, whether or not they understand.

Yet, as the number of international students has grown, we haven't always adjusted to their needs as fully as we should. Nor is adjusting easy, even when we recognize the need for it. For the international students come from a wide variety of places with a wide variety of needs and expectations. We cannot treat them all the same. And even though the majority of our internationals are from Korea, we cannot even treat all Koreans the same.

Supervising non-English speakers with their theses and dissertations is often a major challenge. It is here that we discover their misunderstandings. Fortunately, the internationals we have taught usually are lovely people and easy to work with, though they usually do take more time than Americans. We have an English as a Second Language program that helps internationals to learn English so that they can do better in our courses.

So many Koreans have come to us that we have started a Korean Studies program in SWM/SIS. We have one Korean professor (Tim Park) who supervises the program. But we need at least one more Korean faculty member to handle the numbers of students and the courses they require. The Korean program runs a full curriculum in Korean. This is a very good thing and much appreciated by the Koreans.

8. What can we do about tensions between the academic part of our concern and our concern for the Cause of winning people to Christ?

In dealing with potential and actual problems in SWM/SIS at 40, it may be instructive to ask the question, Where does the Cause we seek to serve fit into the demands of an academic program? This problem came into focus early in our experience and played a major part in the discussions leading up to Ralph Winter's leaving us in 1976. There were many such discussions.

Winter's perspective and passion were probably closer to McGavran's than the perspective and passion of any of the rest of us. His commitment to winning the lost and to seeking ways to do evangelism better were (and are) like trains running on McGavran's tracks.

One important implication of this is that both McGavran and Winter were extremely impatient with the slowness and hindrances of institutional processes. It is in a way surprising that McGavran so readily linked up with an institution like Fuller to pursue his desire for a research and training facility. Didn't he know that entanglement with an institution would tie him and his dream down? He probably did know this but felt it would be worth the price to legitimize his Institute. And, anyway, he was desperate since things were falling apart at Northwest Christian College. I wonder if he ever regretted his decision to come to Fuller.

To his credit, McGavran did insist that SWM be a separate school. He would not come if the arrangement was to be just a couple of faculty positions in the School of Theology. And for that we can be eternally grateful. We would never be anywhere near where we are now if we were simply a few faculty members on a theological faculty. The aims of theologians are seldom the aims of activist missiologists.

Though things are somewhat better now, there is still a tension between the missionary activism of most of us and the requirements of an academic institution. As noted, our early discussions led to

Ralph Winter establishing a U.S. Center for World Mission. But none of us felt we should leave Fuller to join him, though we have cooperated with the U.S. Center in various ways through the years.

So, we stayed at Fuller and have continued to this day to struggle with the tensions between our academic involvements and our activism. We were and are constantly challenged by the fact that the concerns of an academic program often do not coincide with the concern for winning a lost world for Christ. To try to deal with both the academic issues and the practical ones, several of us faculty members have resorted to starting our own ministry organizations to serve what we see as our part of the Cause without the encumbrances of academia.

9. Are we unbalanced or overboard in some direction?

Sometimes we are accused of being overboard or unbalanced. This accusation has happened primarily at two times over the course of our history. The first time, of course, was when the Church Growth emphasis was the focal point of our teaching and writing. The second time was when the Signs and Wonders course was attracting a lot of attention both on and off campus.

McGavran was an enthusiast, single-minded in his commitment to seeking and winning the lost. His commitment to evangelism was probably greater than it might have otherwise been, since he had undergone a sort of conversion from a "doing good works" sort of missiology to a "harvesting the lost" commitment that he called Church Growth. And it was this commitment that energized his desire to train and retrain missionaries and national church leaders.

McGavran's passion was what SWM was known for in the early years. As mentioned, however, we were broader than Church Growth, narrowly conceived, even from the early years. For Tippett and I were dealing with the cultural aspects of evangelism, conversion, the growth of Christian communities, the insights of anthropologists and communication specialists into all aspects of Christian witness, contextualization and the like. And Glasser's Kingdom Theology of Mission broadened the theological basis for the whole of Christian ministry, not just the planting and growth of churches. He taught on what he called the "cultural mandate" (i.e. Christian responsibility in social issues) as well as the "evangelistic mandate." Likewise, Winter's approach to the history of the Christian movement was far broader than simply dealing with the planting and growth of churches.

But we all agreed that winning the lost and assisting them in their growth toward maturity was central. So we happily supported McGavran in his central concern and the outside world had the impression that we were all of one mind. Our detractors often evaluated us by what McGavran said and wrote and considered us simplistic. Within SWM, however, we and those who got close to us knew that there was nothing simplistic about the approach Tippett, Glasser, Winter and I were taking. We were laying the foundations for the broader missiology of the 80s, 90s and following.

A later time when we were accused in some quarters of being unbalanced was in and after 1982 when the Signs and Wonders controversy was in full swing. Traditional evangelicals felt that we were becoming charismatic and that our most visible faculty member, Peter Wagner, had gone off the deep end.

We all do a lot of speaking and writing for a much wider audience than simply the students in our classes. Wagner, more that the rest of us, was widely known and widely influential outside of Fuller through his American Church Growth teaching and writing. When, then, he got into healing and spiritual warfare, the impression of many outside of Fuller was that he spoke for all of us. This meant that Fuller personnel who were not into charismatic things had to continually explain and defend what was going on at Fuller, whether or not they were happy about it (and many of them, especially School of Theology faculty members, were not). Many in the Schools of Theology and Psychology plus Hiebert and Glasser in SWM were very uncomfortable and even angry. Over the years, some have changed their minds (e.g. Glasser) and some have left (e.g. Hiebert and some School of Theology people) at least partly because of the reputation Wagner and I were giving the school.

The problem has continued for those in the other two schools who are critical of this emphasis. Some were happy when Wagner left to establish his own ministry in Colorado Springs and would like to see my teaching in this area discontinued. These see our emphasis on power ministry as bringing an unbalance.

When we move into this area, however, far from becoming unbalanced, we are seeking to bring Biblical balance into an unbalanced situation that secularizes healing and ignores deliverance.

If healing and deliverance from demons were as important to Jesus and His followers as the New Testament shows they were, any seminary that claims to be Biblical ought to be reprimanded for not giving power ministry a central place in its curriculum. I am, of course, biased, since moving into this dimension has transformed my life. But even when I try to be objective, it seems to me that a seminary is severely unbalanced if it ignores power ministry.

So, we were criticized earlier because of McGavran's high visibility when outsiders automatically assumed that whatever he said was supported by all of us. This was not the case, but many outsiders never figured it out. Nor was it the case that Wagner spoke for all of us in the Signs and Wonders emphasis, even for me, though I agree with him most of the way. But this kind of appearance of unbalance can be a major problem for an institution like ours.

I would contend that we were not really out of balance in the church growth area and we are not now out of balance in the spiritual power area. These were prominent and important emphases, noticed because they were/are unusual. The Church Growth emphasis was important in its day but that was far from our only emphasis. We dealt with culture, communication, theology of mission, theological education by extension and other important issues from the beginning.

And spiritual power is but one of our many emphases now. And, I am not the only one who contends that it is an important one to add to our list, since most of the world is spiritual power-oriented. We do not do justice to our students who go to the ends of the earth if we ignore this important feature of the world scene and of the Bible. In addition, if the problem for our detractors is that we appear charismatic, where better to deal in a balanced, sane way with charismatic emphases than at Fuller? There is so much distortion of these emphases in certain charismatic and Pentecostal circles that we can do and, I believe, are doing a great service to the cause of Christ by showing that spiritual power can be handled in a better way.

So, whether it be our contention, couched in the church growth emphasis, that evangelism be central to missions or our contention that missionaries are not well-trained if they ignore the spiritual power issues, we are seeking to rectify imbalance, not creating it. Our aim is for comprehensiveness and balance in faithful service to our Lord Jesus Christ.

10. What about our name change? Does this indicate that we have lost our vision and are becoming secular?

As recounted in Chapter 11, in 2003 we changed our name from School of World Mission to School of Intercultural Studies. Some have interpreted this change as indicating a softening of our concern for the winning of the lost and discipling those who come to Christ. There is, however, no softening. In fact, the change is an attempt to make it more possible for our graduates to get into positions in the modern world that will enable them to carry out the Great Commission.

We are told in Mark 16:15 to go into everyone's world to communicate the Good News. In today's world, this often means turning away from words that offend such as mission/missionary in order to be allowed to enter the world of those offended by such terms.

The unpleasant fact is that many of our graduates have found that having a degree from an institution with "mission" in its name has kept them from entering certain countries and/or being allowed to carry out their callings. We learn from communication theory that the meanings of words lie, not in the words themselves, but in the minds of those who use the words. Thus, words mean different things to different peoples and groups. The word "Christian," for example, though it may have positive connotations to us, is a very negative label in the Muslim world. For, in their minds, those they consider Christians are Euro-Americans and their lackeys who support Israel, sponsored the Crusades, foment immorality through Hollywood films and look down on the followers of Muhammad. A real breakthrough has come in winning Muslims to Christ in places where the converts are not required to call themselves by this hated name. They may call themselves "Muslims who follow Isa," or "Messianic Muslims," or "Isa followers," or some other name that has positive rather than negative connotations. And they are saved by following Jesus, not by wearing the name "Christian."

There is the same kind of problem with the word "mission" or "missionary." We might protest that either the name "Christian" or the word "mission" are being misinterpreted. But we have to live with the fact that we cannot change the impression these words have on people, especially on those who perceive Christians or missionaries negatively. The long-term association in people's minds of mission and missionary with colonialism, imperialism, cultural blunders and Christianity will not be changed soon, if at all.

So, our graduates, both internationals and Westerners, have for some time been asking us if we could give them degrees that did not have "mission" in their title. There are students who badly wanted to study with us but who did not enroll, since they work in parts of the world where a degree from a School of World *Mission* would prevent them from working freely or even from getting into certain countries. And we have graduates who have been expelled from a country or terminated in teaching positions once it has been discovered that they have studied here. This is especially true in Muslim and Communist lands. And graduates who have sought positions in secular universities in the States or in other countries have sometimes been turned down as well.

So, in response to those who experience such problems, we on the faculty seriously discussed a name change for about two years. We soon agreed that we had to make the change. But we could not agree on just what the name would be. After considerable discussion, then, we decided to go with the name that several other schools of mission are using—School of Intercultural Studies.

We have taken some flack for changing the name. There are those in our constituency (a minority, thankfully) who don't understand the communicational problems our students have been facing. These have been critical of our decision, often assuming that the change means compromise or, worse, a lessening of our concern to win the world to Christ. To us, it means neither. What it does mean is that many of our students will have greater opportunities in what have been called "limited access" countries to communicate the Gospel. To date, we have heard no complaints from the students. The only complaints have come from those few who don't understand the issues.

Suggestions for the Future

It's now been 36 years since I joined this faculty. There have been quite a few changes over these years. And, I think, quite a few lessons learned. But not all of us have been in on the changes and the lessons. So, lest we neglect the lessons of these years, perhaps it would be permitted for an "oldie" like me to record some of what I think we ought to take into the future.

From the above discussion, I would point to four crucial areas of concern: Students, Academics, Spirituality and Focus.

With regard to students, I believe we need to do our utmost to attract more mid-career, experienced people. Education works best when the students have had a body of experience to analyze as they are exposed to the emphases of the various classes. Schooling in our society has become much too unrelated to real life by encouraging people with too little life experience to spend their time simply collecting information. We must be aware of the danger of letting the same thing happen to us at SIS with the greater number of inexperienced students.

How much more educational is what is done in classrooms when those sitting there have a body of experience to analyze. Without sacrificing the needs of our inexperienced students, we need to give more attention to attracting experienced people. Indeed, the inexperienced people get more out of their time here when they get to regularly interact with those who have been in the thick of things.

I applaud the efforts of Dean McConnell, Bob Freeman and others in taking our teaching to the lands where church leaders are working through distance learning and a new emphasis on taking Doctor of Missiology courses to the fields. I pray that this will continue and increase.

Another concern is for the development of a greater *esprit de corps* among our students. The student government leaders have been doing well at sponsoring social events and the masters and doctoral specialty classes are helpful but there could be more. One custom from the early years that contributed to student relationships was a regular Friday evening gathering for fellowship and a presentation by one of the students of his/her ministry. This could be done again.

In addition, I believe we need to reinstitute a newsletter. For several years we had a good one named *Forwarding the Missionary Task*. It was available to students and alumni and contributed greatly to the sense of oneness of our student's with each other and with the alumni. It contained reports of faculty and student activities plus alumni news and profiles of alumni in their ministries.

Secondly, I am very leery of what I consider the over-academicization of our programs. Whether in the increasing regulation of our courses, the tendency toward emphasizing theory rather than practice, or the rigor of the procedures we put our doctoral students through, I believe we would do well to subject everything we do to questions concerning their relationship to the Cause we are committed to. If we faculty members simply become academics with our classes and programs high on theory and academic process at the expense of practicality and inspiration, we've lost what we're called to do. Assuming that it is the Cause of communicating Christ that we are called to, no amount of academically respectable teaching, research and writing can make up for a lack of hands-on applicability in real life missional situations.

I believe a fair amount of the tendency toward an overly academic approach to our teaching and research may come from insecurity. When I was teaching at Michigan State University, I remember some discussions with students and faculty members who had had experience at first-rate universities such as Harvard and Notre Dame. They all held that our requirements for doctoral degrees at MSU were considerably more rigorous than those at the more prestigious institutions. We concluded that the reason was that without the prestige those institutions had, we at MSU made our people work harder because of our insecurity.

I wonder if we at SIS might be exhibiting a similar kind of insecurity by overemphasizing academics and theory. Our purpose for existence is not to develop missiological theory but to contribute to the fulfillment of the Great Commission. I would warn us to always keep this in mind and to resist the "slippery slope" of sliding into mere academics that so many other schools have fallen into.

Another of my concerns in the academic area is that we never slack in our control of the basics of a missiological curriculum. Whether it be through requiring a set of Core Courses and exams or in some other way, we dare not return to the "everything is elective" stage of our history. I think our missiological integration course is a good idea, but one course is not enough.

A third concern of mine is for the spiritual tenor of our school and of what we teach and model. I think we do fairly well at this in the area of our class devotionals. Most of our faculty members are careful to emphasize devotionals and to tie them in with the subject-matter of the classes. We should never let down in this area.

It is, however, easy to neglect the spiritual dimensions of the subject-matter we spend the rest of our class time on. We need to never forget that there is an evil spirit world out there spending full time trying to compromise our efforts. Too much of the Christianity missionaries practice and have taken to the rest of the world is secular and powerless. We have taken secular medicine, secular schools, secular agriculture, secular development, secular church governing procedures, secular communication practices, secular ways of identifying and choosing leaders, secular counseling, even secular, information-based theology. Our teaching and advising should be characterized by full-scale integration of the activity of the Holy Spirit in such activities. We dare not simply perpetuate the kind of mission that has been called "the most secularizing force in history." Ours is intended to be a primarily spiritual activity. When we neglect this fact we do injustice to our calling, our students and our Lord.

The fourth area I'd like to highlight is our need of a focal concept that we can use to keep us on task. In the McGavran days, the concept of Church Growth was constantly before us. We sometimes got tired of being reminded that we stand for church growth. But we could never forget it. We were focused, constantly relating whatever we were teaching to that central concept. It provided for us a kind of motto, a theme by which we were identified both among ourselves and outside.

We could and, I think, should lift up a similar focus today. The day of the Church Growth focus is past, though we still believe what God wants is that people be brought into the Kingdom and enfolded in groups we call churches. There is, however, another concept around which we could rally, something that we all deal with from our various perspectives that might be the flag we could raise. We all believe in and teach the contextualization of Christianity. The term "contextualization" is, however, too technical to serve well as a motto. I would, therefore, suggest *Incarnational Ministry* or something similar. Some have suggested *Communicating Christ in a Complex World*. A more technical possibility would be *Great Commission Missiology*.

The point would be to consciously identify in motto form something we all deal with, something we all believe in, all teach and all try to practice. Without making such a theme conscious, I'm afraid we may each be going off in our own direction, focusing on what McGavran used to term "many good things" without constantly reminding ourselves of the "one best thing." Not that we have been forgetting our commitment individually to the Great Commission. But there is value in highlighting corporately a joint commitment in motto form. This could well be the theme of the missiological integration class. And we could require that each of us state in our course outlines the relationship of our course material to this central theme. My desire is that we be just as overt about our commitment to ministry as modeled by Jesus as we are to the academic procedure.

Here's a diagram that's intended to show the diverse fields represented in our urriculum, all related to Incarnational Ministry:

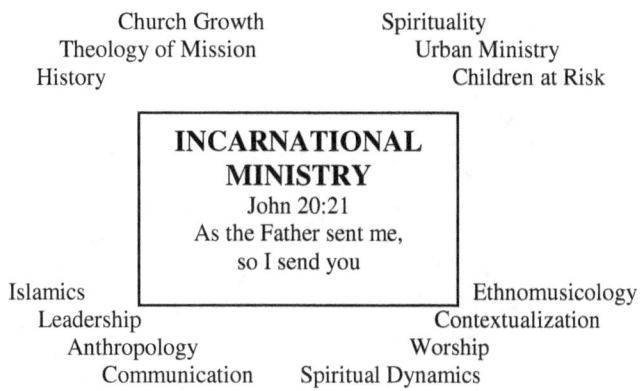

Figure 12.2 Incarnational Ministry as our central focus.

Though it is a positive thing to be able to offer such diversity of courses and specializations, I think we do need to articulate a central core theme such as Incarnational Ministry. Such a motto would show our concern to imitate Jesus in contextualizing His message plus our commitment to minister to the people He loves in their home contexts.

Conclusion

I have attempted here to raise some of the issues that confront us as we turn forty. Again, these are my comments, coming from my perspective. They may not be shared by all of my colleagues, though I have attempted to get their feedback and take it seriously.

We have changed over the years. A more comprehensive evaluation of the changes will have to await the insights of some future historian with a longer view than mine. Personally, I can live with the changes, though I'm not keen on some of them. But the faculty and administration of SIS are committed to Christ and Incarnational Ministry. And they are trustworthy. This institution, so continually blessed by God, is in good hands. So, to quote Adoniram Judson, a missionary of yesteryear, "the future is as bright as the promises of God."

Appendix A
Timeline

I. PREHISTORY

1940s:

    A. Charles E. Fuller, radio preacher on the Old Fashioned Revival Hour, envisioned a new school to train preachers and missionaries.

    B. Harold John Ockenga, pastor of Park Street Congregational Church in Boston advises Fuller to instead start a seminary.

        1. Such a school would prove to the Liberal Theological Establishment that Evangelical scholars could do acceptable scholarly work.

        2. A seminary that would be a "Princeton of the West."

1947—Fuller Theological Seminary started classes at Lake Avenue Congregational Church.

Early 1960s:

    A. A sizeable gift was made available by the Weyerhaeuser Foundation toward the starting of a school of psychology as a part of FTS.

    B. At around the same time discussions were initiated toward the founding of a school of mission.

    C. A committee set up to work toward the school of mission. On the committee were Dan Fuller, Wm LaSor, Kenneth Strachan (of Latin American Mission), Carlton Booth.

1964—Kenneth Strachan Brought in to Teach a Course on Mission. Came back to teach it again in 1965 but died in February.

Question: Who Would Lead the School of Mission?

A. As President David Hubbard searched, one name kept being brought to his attention: Donald A. McGavran.
   1. McGavran, though 65 years old, a bundle of energy and vision.
   2. Very perceptive—had a knack for seeing the broad picture.
   3. Very committed to Christ and the Church.
   4. Had come from a liberal background into a very evangelical, even fundamentalistic, faith.
   5. Very compelling speaker.
B. McGavran had started the Church Growth Institute at Northwest Christian College in Eugene, Oregon in1960.
C. In his Institute, McGavran hand-picked seasoned missionaries.
   1. To study how and why churches grew or did not grow around the world.
   2. Since its founding, more than 50 missionaries had engaged in research at the Institute.
D. Among those early students at ICG was Alan R. Tippett.
   1. A long-term (1941-61) Australian Wesleyan missionary to Fiji.
   2. Tippett had studied history and anthropology at American University and become interested in history of Christianity in the South Pacific.
   3. During his time at ICG Tippett was asked by McGavran to teach on culture and encouraged to enroll in a doctoral program at the nearby University of Oregon in anthropology.
   4. Tippett received his Ph.D. in anthropology from the University of Oregon in June of 1964.

5. Tippett was invited to join the faculty of ICG starting in the fall 1965.

E. But support for the Institute of Church Growth became uncertain.

1. Becoming more costly for Northwest Christian College to support.

2. ICG had been strongly supported by NCC President Ross Griffeth.

3. But Griffeth was due to retire.

4. Not sure a new president would be as committed as Griffeth was to the Institute.

1964-1965—Hubbard-McGavran Discussions

A. McGavran willing to move and received the blessing of President Griffeth for the move.

B. Certain conditions.

1. FTS had to hire Tippett also.

2. Had to keep the name Institute of Church Growth. The full name was to be School of World Mission and Institute of Church Growth.

3. The Church Growth library moves to Fuller.

4. The Church Growth Bulletin, the Institute's journal, started in September 1964 moves to Fuller.

5. Fuller takes over certain publishing arrangements.

6. A Lilly grant to ICG would get transferred to Fuller.

C. Two problems with regard to Tippett.

1. Tippett had returned to Australia and thence to do research in the Solomon Islands.

2. He knew virtually nothing about these arrangements until contacted by McGavran after the arrangements had already been made.

3. Couldn't get Tippett a visa to come to America to teach until Billy Graham (an FTS Board member) was contacted and appealed to President Lyndon Johnson. Visa granted.

4. Tippett came, arriving the very day of the start of classes in Fall 1965. Taught a class his first day.

II   THE McGAVRAN ERA (1965-1971)

1965—Started Classes Fall 1965

A. McGavran (Dean) & Tippett were the whole faculty.
   1. McGavran (Ph.D. Columbia University) had served in India from 1923-54 in education, administration and church planting.
   2. He had written three major books on church growth: *The Bridges of God* (1955), *How Churches Grow* (1959) and *Church Growth and Christian Mission* (1965).
   3. Brought with him the Institute of Church Growth including Church Growth Bulletin, Church Growth Seminars and several publishing commitments.
   4. Tippett (Ph.D. University of Oregon 1964) had served in Fiji from 1941-61, and done research in the Solomon Islands (published as *Solomon Islands Christianity* in 1967).
B. Twelve students.
   1. Students were granted fellowships of $1,000 to $3,000.
   2. Applicants for these fellowships "must be able men now in responsible positions . . . must have the backing of the Churches and missions [and the] problems they propose to attack must be significant" (CGB II, 1:14, 1965).
C. The announcement of the new school in the Church Growth Bulletin stated:

> "The School of World Mission at Fuller envisages a faculty of six and a student body made up of missionaries on furlough and missionary candidates under appointment. Graduate fellows from younger Churches in Asia, Africa and Latin America will strengthen the research arm of the

School. It is expected that an International House will be affiliated with the new School. Initially the School will offer the Master of Theology and Master of Arts degrees to experienced missionaries" (CGB I, 5: special news release, June 9, 1965).

1967—Hired Ralph Winter (Ph.D. Cornell) to Teach Theological Education by Extension, Later Focused on History.

    A. Presbyterian missionary to Guatemala (1956-66).
        1. He and colleagues had initiated Theological Education by Extension in Guatemala.
        2. Though trained in anthropological linguistics, he developed a crosscultural approach to history— called it The Historical Development of the Christian Movement (he rejected the traditional split between Church History and Mission History).

1967—McGavran Invited Edwin Orr to Teach a Course on Revival.

    A. A specialist on revivals.
        1. Taught just one or two courses per year.
        2. Didn't always agree with McGavran's analyses.
    B. Taught as an Adjunct till his untimely death in 1987.

1968—McGavran Had C. Peter Wagner (M.Div., M.A. Fuller) Teach as an Adjunct.

    A. A student 1966-67.
    B. Had returned to Bolivia to continue his work there.

1969—Hired Charles Kraft (Ph.D. Hartford Seminary) to Teach Anthropology and African Studies.

    A. To teach courses such as introductory anthropology, culture change, African studies and conversion.

B. Tippett was brilliant but often difficult for beginning students to understand, except when telling stories, so Kraft was given the introductory courses in anthropology.

C. Kraft had served as a missionary in Nigeria from 1957-60 and had been teaching African languages at Michigan State University (1963-1968) and UCLA (1968-1973).

D. An anthropologist who had specialized in linguistics but was happy to get back to his first love—anthropology.

Place—Our Building—An Old House on Campus that is now an Eating and Meeting Place Called "the Catalyst."

A. Across Oakland Avenue from the main campus.

B. Our offices encircled the central room in that house.

1969—Winter started William Carey Library.

A. To publish books on mission.

B. To do so cheaply and get them out fast.

By Now McGavran Going on 73 Years Old.

A. Under criticism for being weak on theology.

B. Looked for a new Dean, preferably a theologian.

1970—Brought on Arthur Glasser to Succeed Him as Dean.

A. Long term member of Overseas Missionary Fellowship, recently retired as Candidate Secretary.

B. Had worked in China (1947-51) and also had great interest in reaching Jews.

C. Glasser spent one year as an ordinary faculty member to get used to things.

D. Took over as Dean in 1971.

1971—Wagner (Ph.D. USC achieved after he was already on the faculty) hired to teach full time.

    A. A graduate of Fuller School of Theology (1952).

    B. Served 16 years as a missionary in Bolivia under Andes Evangelical Mission.

    C. Returned to Fuller to study Church Growth under McGavran in 1966-67.

    D. Taught Church Growth and Latin American subjects.

1971-1976—We operated with the six faculty envisioned in 1965.

    A. McGavran, Tippett, Winter, Kraft, Glasser, Wagner.

    B. Moved to newly built offices over the arch opening into the "Garth."

        1. This was expected to be temporary.

        2. Plans were made to build our own building where a small apartment building is to the West of the Union Street entrance to campus.

    C. Glen Schwartz hired as Glasser's Administrative Assistant.

1973—The American Society of Missiology started.

    A. Initiative of Ralph Winter and Gerald Anderson.

        1. To establish Missiology as a discipline.

        2. Tippett the first editor of the new journal of the Society: *Missiology.*

    B. Winter negotiated the incorporation of the journal *Practical Anthropology* into the journal *Missiology.*

1974—Started the "In Service Program" (Distance Education).

    A. One of our students, Alvin Martin, the Director.

　　B.　Recorded our classes on audio tape.

　　C.　Sent out materials so students overseas could take our courses without coming to campus.

1975—Started Cross-Cultural Studies Program (CCSP).

　　A.　Needed a program for the growing number of pre-service people.

　　B.　Hired students Phil Elkins and Bob Douglas to run it.

1976—Hired Tom Brewster (Ph.D. Arizona) and Betty Sue Brewster (Ph.D. Texas).

　　A.　Linguists working with Campus Crusade for Christ.

　　B.　Originally hired to start a Bible Translation program.

　　C.　But their major interest was in language acquisition.

　　D.　With the growing number of pre-field students, this fit nicely with our new pre-field program (CCSP).

1976—Ralph Winter Left to Start US Center for World Mission.

　　A.　Sought to provide an adjunct to SWM that would provide a center for missionary organizations to cluster to cooperate on missionary projects.

　　B.　Bought the campus of the former Pasadena Nazarene College.

1977—Alan Tippett Retired in Spring to Return to Australia.

　　A.　Intent on devoting his last years to Australia.

　　B.　Arranged with St. Mark's in Canberra to give him an office and house his library.

　　C.　Sadly, Australian missions and academia largely ignored him.

1977—Paul Hiebert (Ph.D. Minnesota) hired to teach Anthropology and Asian Studies.

    A. From teaching at the University of Washington.

    B. Missionary experience in India with Mennonite Brethren.

1977—Dean Gilliland (Ph.D. Hartford) hired to teach Contextualization, Theology, Islamics.

    A. Methodist missionary to Nigeria—18 years.

    B. First ever professor of contextualization in a theological Seminary.

    C. President Hubbard with help from Chuck Hunter of Asbury arranged for Methodist Board to support him for one and a half years.

    D. Also asked him to take over directing the CCSP.

    E. Took over Kraft's Africa courses.

1978—The Year of the Muslim.

    A. We focused on Islam in our teaching.

    B. Had Kenneth Bailey teach as an Adjunct.

1978—Don McCurry Hired as an Adjunct to Teach on Islam.

    A. Long term missionary in Pakistan.

    B. One of our students.

    C. Samuel Zwemer Institute started.

We Started Several New Programs While Glasser Was Dean

    A. Two-hour faculty prayer and discussion time on Wednesdays (now Tuesdays). Perhaps the most important decision we have made, since it brought us faculty all together weekly.

    B. SWM Summer Program—Gilliland administrating (1992).

C. Our publication—*Forwarding the Missionary Task* (unfortunately, discontinued in 1999 for financial reasons).

D. Extension program in cooperation with ACTS in Korea.

E. Wagner teaching Church Growth in D.Min. program.

F. Degree programs
   1. Th.M. Missiology (for mid-career people).
   2. M.A. CCSP (pre-field).
   3. M.Div. CCSP in School of Theology.
   4. Doctor of Missiology.
   5. Ph.D. Missiology (with SoT, now defunct).
   6. Ph.D. Intercultural Studies.

1980—Glasser turns 65, to retire as Dean but continue to teach.

A. Search Committee formed to find a new Dean.

B. Down to two final candidates.

C. Don McCurry asks, "Have we considered Paul Pierson?"

D. Suspended vote, checked out Pierson and invited him.

1980 (Fall)—Enrollment 162

1980—McGavran Retires from Teaching at Age of 83

A. Kept his office for several more years

B. Died in 1990,

IV THE PIERSON ERA (1980-1992)

1980—Started the SWM Partners.

A. An Organization of lay supporters of SWM.

B. Provided funds to start new programs and hire new faculty.

1981—Focus on Leadership.

    A. Several of us faculty had been dealing with leadership from our own perspectives.

    B. Decided to create a new field.

    C. Hired Bobby Clinton (D.Miss., Ph.D. Fuller), one of our graduates, to take what our faculty had been saying about leadership and develop a new field.

    D. Bobby had come as a student in 1979 and served as T.A. for Kraft and Wagner—impressed us greatly.

    E. Had served under West Indies Mission in Jamaica and Miami.

    F. New position financed with Partners money at first.

1981—Viggo Sogaard (Ph.D. Fuller) Hired to Teach Communication.

    A. Already a world class communication specialist.

    B. Danish, continuing to live in Denmark.

    C. Came to do a Ph.D. and teach half-time.

1982-85—"Signs and Wonders" Course (MC510).

    A. Wagner was the "Professor of Record" with Wimber as an Adjunct doing the teaching.

    B. The course experience was transforming for many students as well as for Wagner and Kraft.

    C. Generated controversy within and outside Fuller.

    D. School of Theology vocal in objections.

    E. Course suspended in 1985.

    F. Students put the course on for no credit in 1986.

    G. Course resurrected under Wagner and Kraft as MC550 in 1987.

    H. This plus other courses on healing in curriculum since that time.

1982—Bible Translation Program Started.

A. I had dreamed of a program in which we would offer degrees in Bible translation.
B. We had hired the Brewsters with this in mind but their focus was on language learning.
C. Hired R. Daniel Shaw (Ph.D. University of Papua New Guinea), a Wycliffe missionary in Papua New Guinea to initiate the program.
D. Shaw had taught for us as an Adjunct in 1980 and 1981.
E. New position partly financed at first by the Shaws continuing under Wycliffe support.

1982—Papua New Guinea Extension Program Started.

1982—Chinese Program Started.

A. Tan, Che Bin (Ph.D. Manchester) seconded from China Graduate School of Theology in Hong Kong to start a Chinese Program.
B. Ran the program for nine years. Closed in 1991 for lack of students.

1984—Eddie Gibbs (D.Min. Fuller) Hired as Second Church Growth Person.

A. British, with field experience in Chile.
B. Had completed a D.Min. under Wagner in 1982.

1985—Hired J. Dudley Woodberry (Ph.D. Harvard).

A. The foremost evangelical Islamicist.
B. Experience in several Islamic countries.
C. We had wanted Islamics for some time—special year 1978.
D. He had come to Pasadena to work with Don McCurry in the Zwemer Institute—left Zwemer to join our faculty.

1985—Hired Eddie Elliston (Ph.D. Michigan State) to teach Leadership.

    A. The concentration grew so rapidly that we needed a second person.

    B. He had done an M.A. here in the 60s, then a Ph.D. under Ted Ward at Michigan State.

    C. Several years in Ethiopia and Kenya.

1985—Tom Brewster Dies.

1987—Edwin Orr Dies.

1988—Brought on Chuck Van Engen (Ph.D. Free University, Amsterdam).

    A. Needed a Theologian to Succeed Glasser.

    B. Chuck was brought up and served in Mexico.

    C. Did an M.Div. in Fuller School of Theology, then Ph.D. in Dutch in Holland.

1988—Tippett Dies, Retired in Canberra, Australia.

1988—Start Program for Messianic Jews.

1988—Brought on Hoover Wong (DMin Fuller) to Assist in Chinese Program.

    A. An American Born Chinese who had served several pastorates in Chinese churches.

    B. His primary focus was to attract American born Chinese.

    C. Also asked to raise funds for the program including his own salary.

1988—School of Theology Needs Professor of Evangelism.

    A. Asked our Dean for Eddie Gibbs.

    B. Gibbs agrees to fill the Robert Boyd Munger Chair of Evangelism.

1990—McGavran Dies at Age 93.

1990—Paul Hiebert Leaves to go to Trinity Evangelical Divinity School.

1991—Tan, Che Bin Leaves to Pastor.

1990s—Partnership Programs Started in Nigeria, Denmark and some Teaching in Israel.

1992—Hired Jude Tiersma-Watson (Ph.D. Fuller) Half-Time for Urban Studies.

    A. One of our Ph.D. candidates.

    B. Living and ministering in inner city Los Angeles.

Summary of Programs at End of Pierson Era (1992).

    A. Bible Translation Ph.D.

    B. Programs in Chinese Studies and Jewish Studies.

    C. Concentrations Available in Missiology by end of this period:

       Anthropology, Bible Translation, Communication, Contextualization, Church Growth, Chinese Studies, Development, History, Leadership, Islamic Studies, Theology, Urban Studies.

Enrollments During This Period:
    1984 (Fall)—Enrollment 285
    1985 (Fall)—Enrollment 324

1986 (Fall)—Enrollment 368

1987 (Fall)—Enrollment 428

1988 (Fall)—Enrollment 417

1989 (Fall)—Enrollment 366

1990 (Fall)—Enrollment 343

1991 (Fall)—Enrollment 320

V THE WOODBERRY ERA (1992-1999)

1992-95—Hired Young Lee Hertig (Ph.D. Fuller) Part Time to Teach on Women's Issues, Korean Studies, Spirituality.

A. A Korean-American who had just completed her Ph.D.

B. Left to teach at General Seminary in Dayton, Ohio.

1994—Student Statistics Since 1965.

A. Approximately 4,500 have studied at SWM at least one quarter.

B. 827 theses and dissertations written.

C. 1,627 degrees granted by SWM.

Statistics for 1992-94.

A. 1992 (Fall)—Enrollment 358.

B. 1993 (Fall)—Enrollment 359.

C. Approximately 800 persons enrolled in 1993-94, including:

    1. Those in residence (4 terms).

    2. Active doctoral candidates.

    3. 44 students in 3 extension centers.

    4. 200 in distance learning program.

D. 65 nations represented in the student body.

E. 135 languages spoken by students and staff.

1995—Wilbert Shenk (Ph.D. 1978 Aberdeen) Joins SWM to Teach History and Mission to Western Cultures.

    A. A Mennonite with missionary experience in Indonesia.

    B. Also experienced at administration.

1995—FTS Hired Robert Freeman (EdD Nova Southeastern University) to Run Fuller's Extension and Distance Learning Programs.

    A. Had been in a similar position at Gordon-Conwell.

    B. Elects to be a member of SWM faculty.

    C. To teach on distance learning.

1996—Hired Pablo Deiros (Ph.D. Southwestern Baptist) Half-Time to Teach History and Latin American Studies.

    A. Pastor of a large Baptist church in Buenos Aires.

    B. Experienced in healing, so adds courses in this area.

1996—Timothy Park (Ph.D. Fuller) Hired to Run Korean Studies Program.

    A. A large number of Korean students in our programs.

    B. He was a Korean missionary to the Philippines.

1996—Eddie Gibbs, after a stint as a pastor, returns to SWM.

1998—Eddie Elliston leaves to become Provost at Hope International University.

1999—Roberta King (Ph.D. Fuller) hired to teach Communication and Ethnomusicology.

    A. Missionary experience in Kenya and Ivory Coast.

    B. World-class Africanist ethnomusicologist.

New Academic Chairs Attracted During This Era.

    A. [Mary Varker] Chair of Islamic Studies (Woodberry).
    B. Arthur Glasser Chair of Biblical Theology of Mission (VanEngen).
    C. Sun-Hee Kwak Chair of Global Mission (Kraft).
    D. Paul Pierson Chair of Mission History (Shenk).

VI THE LINGENFELTER ERA (1999-2003)

1999—After an Extensive Search, Sherwood Lingenfelter (Ph.D. Pittsburgh) was Brought on as Dean and Professor of Anthropology and Leadership.

    A. He was Provost at Biola.
    B. An Anthropologist with a strong desire to become a Missiologist.

1999—Glasser Retires

1999—Doug McConnell (Ph.D. Fuller) Hired to Teach Leadership half-time while continuing to direct Pioneers Mission.

    A. Missionary experience in Papua New Guinea.
    B. International Director of Pioneers Mission.
    C. Had taught Missiology at Wheaton previously.

1999—Wagner left to run Global Harvest Ministries in Colorado Springs.

2000—Jehu Hanciles (Ph.D. Edinburgh) Hired to Teach History and Globalization.

    A. Born and raised in Sierra Leone.

    B. Outstanding student of Andrew Walls.

2001—Elizabeth (Betsy) Glanville (Ph.D. Fuller) Hired to Direct Doctoral Programs and Teach Leadership.

    A. A student of Bobby Clinton.

    B. Had been teaching for us as an Adjunct.

2001—Lingenfelter appointed Provost of FTS.

    A. Resists the appointment but says, "If we can find someone better than me to be Dean of SWM, I'll step aside."

    B. Felt that McConnell could do the job.

    C. Carried both Dean's and Provost's jobs for nearly two years.

2002—Hired Stephanie Smith (Ph.D. St. Andrews) to teach on Spirituality and to Administer the Masters Programs.

    A. Served and taught with YWAM.

    B. Spirituality and mission an important new area for SIS.

VII THE McCONNELL ERA (2003—)

2002—McConnell Becomes Dean in September but Doesn't Arrive on the Scene Until March 2003 Due to His Commitment to Pioneers.

    A. Has been International Director of Partners Mission for five years.

    B. Moves from half-time faculty to full-time.

2002—Ryan Bolger (Ph.D. Fuller) hired to work with Bob Freeman on Distance Education.

    A. Appointed as Academic Director of the M.A. in Global Leadership.
    B. Focuses on postmodernity and emerging churches.

2002—Evelyne Reisacher (Ph.D. Fuller) Hired to Teach Islamics.

    A. Our first French faculty member.
    B. Has worked extensively with Muslims in Europe.

2003—Changed the Name of the School from SWM to School of Intercultural Studies (SIS).

2003—David Bundy (Ph.D. Candidate) hired by the Provost to run the Library, chooses to join SWM faculty.

Appendix B
Student Testimonials

I would estimate that at least 7,000 students have studied at SWM/SIS since its founding in 1965. Most would testify to having had a good, often life-changing experience. A very small sampling of student reactions has been collected and follows. They are arranged in chronological order.

Charles ("Chuck") Bennett
(M.A. 1971)

President and CEO of Mission Aviation Fellowship (1973-85), Executive VP of Food for the Hungry International for 5 1/2 years, CEO of Partners International for 8 years, CEO of Paraclete mission consulting group for 3 years, founder and Chairman of the Board for 10 years of AirServ International.

I first met Dr. McGavran and my wife in the same meeting in Costa Rica, back in 1961. I was working in a fast growing people movement in Mexico that I described to Dr. Mac. He later visited that area and included it in his book, *Church Growth in Mexico*, but I didn't see him then because I was on my honeymoon. But I did sign up to attend his Institute in Eugene, Oregon during my next furlough.

A couple of months before I was to leave for furlough, in 1965, I received a letter from Dr. McGavran telling me to go to Pasadena, not Oregon. I had lots and lots of credit hours from Moody Bible Institute, Wheaton College and Goshen College but didn't have an undergraduate degree. So I came to Fuller as a special student, "part of the package" when Dr. Mac began the SWM. I did the full M.A. program, and my thesis, *Tinder in Ṭabasco,* was published by Eerdmans, but I received no degree because I didn't have an undergraduate degree.

Two years later, I was assigned to our Mission Aviation Fellowship offices in Southern California and began to pursue a degree. With encouragement from the SWM faculty, I tested into an M.A. program in Latin American Studies at UCLA, completed one quarter of studies with straight A grades, then asked Fuller why I didn't qualify for a graduate degree there since I clearly did at UCLA.

So, after many more twists and turns, plus another 30 units of theological studies at Fuller, and in spite of opposition from the Fuller Librarian because my thesis had already been published, I finally gained my M.A. in Missiology in 1971. It was my unorthodox approach that opened the door for scores of international students who did not have standard American education to gain graduate degrees from Fuller. Later I earned another graduate degree in Management from the Peter Drucker School at Claremont Graduate University, but I still have no undergraduate degree.

Without question, my studies at Fuller opened the door for me to launch the Presbyterian Center for Mission Studies in 1972 (Ralph Winter's idea), then to become President and CEO of Mission Aviation Fellowship, serving from 1973 to 1985. Then I served 5 1/2 years as Executive V.P. of Food for the Hungry International, then CEO of Partners International for 8 years, then CEO of Paraclete mission consulting group for 3 years. Along the way I also founded AirServ International and chaired its board for 10 years.

Today I am basically retired, although I am still a paid advisor to a wealthy donor who has given more than $35 million to missions over the past 20 years. I also consult with The Seed Company, a creative new division of Wycliffe, and occasionally with other mission agencies. We live on the Mexican border in the southern tip of Texas.

I studied at Fuller during the 1965-66 school year and again in 1969 through 1971. The first class of the SWM had only two full-time faculty, Drs. McGavran and Tippett, and only 12 students—all males, including Harold Kurtz and others of similar future influence. We all sensed that we were part of something very new and special, but none of us dreamed that SWM/SIS would become as big or as influential as it rather quickly became.

Eddie and Donna Elliston
(Attended 1966-68—Eddie, M.A. 1971)

Eddie is a former faculty member of SWM now Director, Degree Completion Program William Jessup University

From ministry to student to ministry to teaching, administration and mentoring was my relational path with Fuller Seminary's SWM. Donna's path was from spouse, to ministry to staff to student to ministry.

Our interest in Fuller Theological Seminary began in 1964-65 with the formation of the then School of World Mission and the installation of Drs. Donald A. McGavran and Alan Tippett to form the school. We were new mission candidates who had had some pastoral experience and, though at that time SWM was not accepting pre-field students, Dr. McGavran allowed me to register. At Fuller, I was significantly influenced by the full time SWM faculty, especially Ralph Winter, but also faculty from the School of Theology such as George Eldon Ladd, William Harrison, Geoffrey Bromiley, and SWM adjunct faculty member J. Edwin Orr. Donna found Mary McGavran to be an encouraging mentor.

After completing all of the academic requirements for the M.A. Miss., Dr. McGavran would not allow me to graduate until I could preach in the field language where we were to work in Ethiopia. When that was accomplished, I received the degree in 1971.

The influence of McGavran and Tippett has permeated our whole Christian Missionary Fellowship mission in terms of expectations, strategies and commitments. Over the years our whole mission has been blessed by the Lord beyond our expectations in conversions, church planting, and social change through the application of the insights of SWM.

Returning to Fuller to teach and later work in administration was a great joy and honor for me. Donna worked for a short time at FTS as a staff member and then later completed her M.A. Miss. We had the privileged opportunity to become acquainted with and encourage students whose ministries are touching every section of the globe. Whether working with pre-service excited candidates or seasoned veterans from many countries, we continue to be amazed at what God has brought together for good and the strengthening of His Kingdom through SWM/SIS. We praise God for the opportunity to participate in a small way as students, staff, faculty and administration.

Paul Utley
(Student 1969-70)

Coordinator for Campus Crusade's Jesus Film Project in Southeast Asia

When I was a kid growing up in Marion, Illinois, we regularly listened to "The Old Fashioned Revival Hour" with Dr. Charles E. Fuller. I loved the singing, preaching and the inspirational music of Rudy Atwood (who was from my hometown). Fuller was always in my conscious radar scope as a good school for training for ministry.

I had the privilege of visiting 6 different Asian countries while I was a student in my college and seminary. As a result I could not get the missionfield out of my mind. I knew I should be a missionary— but where. After graduating from Asbury Theological Seminary, I took a position as a youth pastor in a church in Ft. Lauderdale, Florida. During that year a great desire took hold of me to go to the School of World Mission and Institute of Church Growth at Fuller Theological Seminary. I thought I could find some direction about where to invest my life strategically in this vast wide world. So I applied. I remember when my acceptance came in the mail. I literally jumped up and down for joy.

I was not disappointed in my short stay at Fuller. Circumstances were such (working at two part-time jobs and responsibility for a dependent family member) that I could not take advantage of what was being offered to the fullest. But I did receive what I had initially hoped for, plus more. I wanted a panoramic 3D view of missions. I got it. The "more" was seeing this through the eyes, experiences and lives of some of God's choice servants— McGavran, Winter, Tippett, Kraft, Wagner, et al. Little did I know that when I sat at the feet of Dr. McGavran listening to him talk about the people movements among the Karen in Burma, more than thirty years later I would be involved in getting the Jesus film produced into some of their dialects.

Right after my time at Fuller I joined the staff of Campus Cursade for Christ. After two years of learning how to make disciples on the campus of Kansas University, I went to the Philippines. That was the beginning of a 30 year stint here in Asia. It's been an incredible opportunity of service—teaching different courses in our Institutes of Biblical Studies in different countries, disciple-making, serving as liaison to the Far East Broadcasting Company, working in Cambodian Refugee camps in Thailand, managing an evangelistic music group traveling from Japan to Indonesia and Pakistan to Sri Lanka.

For the past eight years and presently I am serving as the field coordinator for the Jesus Film Project here in Southeast Asia. I live in Chiangmai, Thailand, and am part of the EPIC Partnership (IMB, YWAM, Wycliffe, TWR and CCC, Jesus Film Project) working together to help reach many Unreached People Groups with the Joyful Sound!

Doug Hayward
(Student 1971-72, 76-77; M.A. 1977)

Professor of Anthropology, Biola University

Walking home late one Sunday evening in the mid nineteen fifites after a long day in church I was reflecting on the shear joy of what it meant being "in Jesus." It was in the midst of these reflections that I realized, this joy that I had found needed to be shared with the world. It was a secret too great to be kept hidden from people everywhere. Later that night, by my bed, I committed myself to the task of taking the Good News of the Gospel anywhere in the world that God would choose to send me.

From that moment on, missions became my passion, and after graduating from high school I went on to study missions at one of the finest missionary training schools in the country, Moody Bible Institute, and by the mid-sixties found myself at last in Irian Jaya in the midst of a booming people movement to Christ. Bible translation teams were already at work and the great need of the hour was that of teaching believers and of organizing them into communities of believers worshipping in newly forming churches.

My missionary training program had instilled within me a deep love for Jesus, and I felt well equipped in the skills I needed to exegete the Scriptures. So I dived into my new assignments with all due enthusiasm, but by the end of my first term of service I was finding myself facing some of the harsh realities of cross-cultural ministry. My particular brand of the evangelical faith, during the middle years of the 20th Century, had taken a "Christ against culture" approach and as a result I had had virtually no training in how to understand cultures, or how to apply the Gospel to problems that might arise in cultural situations with which I had never been confronted before. Now, I was being confronted with the need to answer believers' questions about such things as bridewealth payments, incest regulations, mortuary practices and a host of other questions being raised by earnest believers who wanted to tranform their culture into one that honored Christ.

It was with unexpected delight, then, when I returned home for my first home leave, and was directed to SWM where I was told that a group of scholars were pioneering some of the most exciting new ideas in missions today. Dr. Art Glasser warmly welcomed me into his office and gave me the strongest encouragement that a year of study in SWM would send me back to the field re-equipped and re-energized to face the task before me. And indeed, a year of study with Alan Tippett, and Charles Kraft (among others) showed me how I could better understand the cultural practices and thought processes of the tribal people to whom I had been called. They also introduced me to a better understanding of how to examine the Word of God as a casebook for use in strange cultural situations.

I spent two of my furloughs as SWM, and in the intervening years used the insights of Christian anthropology to more deeply enter in the lives of the members of the Western Dani tribe. My training with SWM enabled me to become more sharply focused on the process of both personal and cultural transformation as we sought to "make disciples from every tribe and nation." The success of this venture and the personal fulfillment it brought to me, so prompted me to continue to pursue anthropological training for the sake of missions, that I went on to complete a Ph.D. in anthropology and now teach what I have learned to a whole new generation of candidates for missionary service at Biola University. Praise the Lord.

Fred and Margie Stock
(Student 1961-62, 1967-68, 1978-79; M.A. 1974)

Presbyterian Missionary to Pakistan for 49 years

The Fuller Seminary School of World Mission has had a profound influence on my ministry in Pakistan. Let me explain. In 1956 we went to Pakistan as evangelistic missionaries under the United Presbyterian Church of North America. We were full of enthusiasm and desired to see the church grow and reach out to others with Christ's love. Eleven years later, after two terms on the field, we returned to the U.S.A. discouraged. Church factionalism and lack of concern for sharing the Good News with non-Christians made us wonder what hope there was for the future of the church in Pakistan.

We felt that the "mass movement" of people to Christ at the turn of the century and the missionaries' mistakes in handling it was the reason for the great problems we saw in church. We wondered if the time had come when we should leave the task of evangelism to the nationals. I entered the School of World Mission and Institute of Church Growth in the fall of 1967. That year revolutionized our minstry!!

The faculty under Dr. Donald McGavran's leadership confronted us with the following questions which led us to fascinating and productive research: 1) What caused the dramatic church growth in the Punjab at the turn of the century? 2) Which missionary methods were effective and which were not? 3) What groups in society were responsive? 4) Are there any of these responsive groups present today?

As we studied the past we gained a great respect for the early missionaries and national leaders who worked faithfully to bring people to Christ and establish a viable church. We began to see where the roots of the problems lay. Solutions began to emerge. We gained new insights that led to major changes in our whole approach and opened up a new ministry in Pakistan. We became involved in a fruitful outreach to new unreached responsive people groups.

Because we stayed and are still working in Pakistan, our five children who were born and raised there formed friendships and gained insights into what mission work could do for people. We have served in Pakistan for 49 years. The last ten have been as Volunteers in Mission with the Presbyterian Church U.S.A. I received my M.A. in Missiology in 1974.

Three of our five children have studied at Fuller. Two of them have graduated with degrees. Paul Stock graduated from the School of Theology with an M.Div. degree in 1985. He also took courses in SWM while completing his degree in theology. He and his wife Pat and their four children have been missionaries under Interserve in Pakistan since 1989.

Our oldest daughter Ruth Stock Stoscher took courses for two years (1992-94) in Intercultural Studies. During that time she met and married Mark Stoscher who graduated with an M.A. in Intercultural Studies in 2002. He and Ruth and their four children are involved in church planting and a camping ministry in Albania since 1994 under the auspices of Alongside Ministries. Our youngest daughter Sara and her husband David Treece have just graduated June 11, 2005 with degrees of M.A. in Intercultural Studies. They first taught English in Korea for two years. Now, sponsored by Interserve, they are doing community development in Central Asia.

Our middle daughter Lois is married to Kyle Scott who has been in the new and exciting program of Global Leadership at Fuller, studying largely over the Internet. Previously they, with their three children, were missionaries to Bangladesh under World Mission Prayer League (Lutheran) for eight years. While working on his Global Leadership degree the family served in Albania so as to apply what he was learning to a real mission situation. He will be returning with his family to Bangladesh in July 2005 to direct the minstry of Habitat for Humanity. He received his degree of M.A. in Global Leadership on June 11, 2005. Kyle Scott's mother Karen Scott has also taken studies and received an M.A. in Intercultural Studies in 2003. She is at present studying for her Ph.D. in Intercultural Studies.

We wish to acknowledge our deep sense of gratitude to all the faculty of the School of World Mission and Institute of Church Growth for the wealth of research and experience they have shared with us. This has expanded our horizons, clarified our vision and equipped us with many practical tools for work on the mission field today. A very special vote of thanks goes to the late Dr. Donald McGavran whose deep insights into church growth principles and whose many years of experience on the Indian sub-continent have been invaluable to us in our study and ministry.

Clyde Cook
(D.Miss. 1974)

President Biola University

I am so grateful for my time at Fuller Theological Seminary's School of World Mission. Certainly, I would not be in my current position without having had the wonderful experience of being a graduate of SWM.

When I took the responsibilities for the missions program at Biola University, I was assured by the administration that I would not need any more than the Th.M. that I had. However, my position at Biola led me into contact with Ralph Winter and Donald McGavran, and both of them urged me to pursue a doctorate at SWM, and so I started giving it some serious thought.

However, every time I went to Fuller for a conference or some other event, the traffic-loaded commute quickly cooled any ardor I had for making this part of my daily regimen. After a couple of years, I realized that they were right and I needed to get the terminal degree, especially as I was hiring faculty who had doctorates. So I applied, and Dr. Arthur Glasser worked out a schedule that accommodated my continuing on in my full-time role as chair of the Missions Department at Biola.

Of particular help were Charles Kraft, Peter Wagner and Donald McGavran, who became my dissertation advisor. All of them, along with Dr. Glasser, played a crucial part in expanding my thinking and knowledge in helping me equip those at Biola who were planning on cross-cultural ministry.

Most of the projects I worked on in my classes became part of my teaching and I especially thank Dr. McGavran for allowing me to use his manuscripts so our students had the benefit of *Understanding Church Growth* before it was even published.

To top off the wonderful experience, I received my doctorate without which I never would have been appointed President of Biola University. All this to say, I am deeply indebted to SWM.

David Price
(Th.M. 1978, D.Miss. 1979)

Principal, Bible College of Victoria, Australia, Training & Leadership Consultant, Pioneers Mission

My years at SWM in 1978/79 were a watershed experience for me. After 8 years struggling to connect with Melanesian culture, the needs of the church, teaching the Bible with relevant application, and the process of growing leaders the way finally opened after consistent encouragement from Alan Tippett to come as a family after completing several core courses in the In Service Program. What was the impact?

Arthur Glasser helped me to root my missionary obedience in the Triune God and the fullness of the biblical revelation—with a strong dose of passion! Ralph Winter sharpened my historical perspectives in a way that history came alive, and actually became an important aspect of my missionary engagement today. Chuck Kraft and Paul Hiebert opened up the concept of culture, deconstructed many of my prejudices and misunderstandings, and provocatively laid the foundations for thinking more clearly about how culture works and changes, and how the process of critical contextualization provides biblical integrity and cultural engagement for the indigenous church. Chuck made me think hard about indigeneity in the Th.M. project.

Alan Tippett, in one of his last courses at Fuller, opened some great windows into Melanesian and Polynesian culture with his course on Power Encounter. Ed Dayton, Edwin Orr, Peter Wagner, and Dean Gilliland also stirred mind and spirit. Arthur Glasser's patient and demanding supervision of the D.Miss. dissertation embracing the historical, biblical and cultural dimensions of conversion made me examine my own and think about the implications for others. One also remembers the camaraderie of engaging with fellow missionaries and national leaders from around the world and the tremendous stimulation of the classroom and informal discussions—not to mention lifelong friendships that developed.

Through the goodness God our time at Fuller SWM equipped us for a far more effective ministry as we returned to the Christian Leaders Training College in Papua New Guinea, and then after 16 years there, for a further 21 years teaching missiology at the Bible College of Victoria. Now as we commence a special ministry role with Pioneers in July 2005, our SWM experience will continue to impact our encouragement and training of those at the cutting edge of the mission of God to the nations of the world. Thank you Lord for the SWM!

Phil Parshall
(Attended 1978-79, D.Miss. 1980)

Missionary to the Philippines with Society for International Ministries (SIM).

Impact! Where did it all begin? Probably in 1972-73 as a student at Trinity Evangelical Divinity School. My missiological classes were jam packed with books written by Fuller SWM professors. Radical? Well, just enough to peek my interest and cause me to dream about a church growth movement among Muslims in Bangladesh where we had been serving since 1962.

Next came "Lausanne 1974," one of the only productive conferences I have ever attended. My heart was stirred as I listened to Fuller professors set forth paradigms of ministry that could possibly revolutionize my fruitless involvement among Muslims.

And then came implementation: 1975 saw our SIM team of 21 missionaries begin to plow new ground with a contextualized methodology that almost immediately began to bear fruit. This laid the groundwork for the hundreds of thousands of Muslims who have come to Christ in Bangladesh in the past 30 years. Men like Kraft, McGavran, Glasser, and Gilliland have deeply impacted this church planting movement, even without physical presence.

What a delight to go to Fuller for study in 1978-79. Students from around the globe were a tremendous daily challenge, both in and out of the classroom. Professors pushed us out to the edges intellectually and theologically.

Without doubt, my Fuller "credentials" opened the door to a mind-stretching Fellowship at Harvard Divinity School in 1983. Each Wednesday we four Fellows met for lunch with a senior professor of HDS. On one memorable occasion Harvie Cox met with us. I garnered up my courage and asked him his opinion on the subject of evangelicalism and academia. Immediately he responded with enthusiasm, "Oh, the whole movement has come of age intellectually. Places like Fuller Seminary have set the pace for academic respectability." I beamed!

And now, after 44 years of ministry, my wife Julie and I are soon to leave our beloved Asia. We, along with Fuller SWM "originals" are passing on the baton to other competent folk. It's been a great ride, one that has been impacted by the Fuller SWM. I am eternally grateful.

Kevin and Glenys Hovey
(Students 1978-79, 1983; M.A. Kevin 1983, Glenys 1993)

Directors, Global Training Ministries;
(Kevin) Head of Missions Faculty, Southern Cross College;
Former AOG Australia National Director

In 1978, Fuller SWM was a long way financially and conceptually from the Sepik River of Papua New Guinea, and from the Assemblies of God missionary team there. So when Glenys and I came to Fuller that year, it seemed to us like a very big step. But at the end of the first quarter I felt that we had already received more benefit from our studies than we anticipated for the whole year. The following quarter, we did an individual subject that was a similar amount of beneft to us, not to mention the other generally helpful subjects that we were doing at the same time.

In addition to the benefit from the subject material, there was also the invaluable networking that took place with both faculty and fellow students. In summary, I rate my decision to go to Fuller as the third smartest decision I have made in my life—led only by my decision for Christ and my decision to marry Glenys. This sense of value was additionally multiplied in two ways: first with the generous scholarships we received that we did not anticipate when we first applied to Fuller. Additionally, the opportunity to take the studies we were doing for ministry benefit and have them flow into an M.A. in Missiology was again more than we had anticipated. Eventually, Kev graduated in 1983 and Glenys graduated in 1993 having done much of her work by extension on the field in Papua New Guinea.

After 36 years in a wide range of field and leadership roles with Assemblies of God World Missions, Australia, in August 2004 we formed a new training organization called Global Training Ministries.

This organization positions the training courses (World Harvest Institute and STINT) that we have developed over the years on a neutral platform to serve the body of Christ more broadly. At the same time, I have taken on a part-time faculty role with Southern Cross College, Sydney, to develop an Intercultural Studies faculty within their school. These training programs fuel each other with good symbiosis between them.

T. Cyprian Kia
(Attended 1981-86)

Previous to my Fuller experience I had been involved in leadership, evangelism, church planting, discipleship, and community development. At Fuller I learned the principles upon which these ministry expressions were based. Interacting with the multicultural, multi-denominational student body, faculty and administration I learned the meaning of deep relationship with Christ. This relationship calls me to be His companion in life, in work, in suffering and in glory. Consequently, I now understand ministry only as a radically inclusive table of fellowship.

My wife and I serve as missionaries among the Igala-speaking people of Nigeria and in Ghana. We function as heralds of good news, as evangelists calling all persons everywhere to be reconciled to God, as gardeners who are planting and growing churches, as wounded healers introducing the hurting world to the Great Physician and as prophets who warn of judgment.

Paul Grant
(Student 1986-88, M.A. 1987)

Former Principal of Australian Assemblies of God School of Ministries, Brisbane, now visiting lecturer to various Australian Bible Schools

My story starts with my son Ian at age 34 studying at Fuller SWM. I was 59, and at a major intersection experience after 38 years of ministry. "Come over here and study", Ian proposed. With Dulcie my wife, I went. It was a journey into new discoveries. It proved to be as transformational as it was revelational. The year was 1985.

Time frames cannot fully contain or define the dealings of God. They dissolve under the chemistry of the Word and the Spirit. In 2 years my odyssey was changed into a specific trajectory. I was to give what Dr. Clinton calls the "convergence" and "afterglow" phases of ministry to teaching and training of students of all ages and experiences.

In these past 17 years I have taught and trained perhaps 3,000 or more people. The SWM "baptism" immersed me into paradigms and perspectives of significant worth. I have been graced with 58 years of ministry that have come to peak effectiveness in this afterglow time significantly shaped and directed by SWM studies and ethos. My observation: SWM founded in 1965 was brought into being *"for such a time as this"* and has proved to be a Joshua/Caleb instrument in God's hands for entering and possessing new missiological ground.

For me the SWM was a place and influence of:

Unique atmospherics. Classes were laboratories of the Spirit. I underwent probings, surgery, healings, enlightenment and inspiration. Daily interface experience with people from so many other cultures was itself a learning curve.

Exposure to inspired seminal teaching. Godly men and women in teaching were possessors as well as professors. They were exemplars in Christian faith. Proven practitioners. They incarnated their teachings. I saw Jesus in them.

Redefining of faith. Combined with 47 years of discipleship and ministry new insights drove me towards reshaping and sharpening my gifts in teaching. Since those years I have written more than 45 courses and have taught them under fresh revelation and anointing.

Increased appreciation of scholarship, reading, and writing. Also the value and privilege of personally knowing people of stature and distinction in missiological thought. (I refrain from beginning to name the professors. Space is limited and I might overlook some).

The freedoms of the Spirit. As a Pentecostal I reveled in the openness of mind and heart to the sovereign work of the Spirit in coursework and research.

The furthering of God's will. Jesus, who *"began a good work"* in me has been carrying it on to completion (Phil.1;6).

At 79 years of age all these elements have played a very significant part in the fulfilling of the personal motto I have written : **I want to finish well with dignity, passion, and integrity**.

We could well mention Marilyn Clinton in such a tribute because you helped to bring about a warmth and acceptation in the SWM that was quite unique. Bobby has been singularly gifted in having you at his side.

Larry Caldwell
(Student 1982-90, Th.M. 1985, Ph.D. 1990)

Academic Dean of Asian Theological Seminary, Program Director of the Doctor of Missiology Program of the Asia Graduate School of Theology, Manila, Philippines

I can't begin to describe how wonderful my Fuller years were, and how beneficial they have been to my ministry in the years since my graduation! I was at Fuller from 1982 to 1990, completing both a Th.M. and a Ph.D. ICS, while I taught full-time at William Carey International University and the US Center for World Mission. After graduation in 1990 my wife and I returned to missionary service in the Philippines where I became Professor of Missions and Hermeneutics at Asian Theological Seminary in Manila. I have taught many missions courses over the years, with all of them influenced in some way by my coursework, and especially, my professors, from Fuller.

Everyone I had as teachers was so great in their particular area of expertise! Two stand out. Art Glasser, who was my Th.M. advisor, had a way to get people to see the big picture and to strive for clear and accurate writing. Art graciously wrote the Foreword to my book, Sent Out!, based on my Th.M. thesis. Chuck Kraft, my Ph.D. advisor, opened my eyes wide to the then relatively new discipline of Ethnotheology. I took his class on the topic in 1981 and my life has literally not been the same since. I remember hanging on every word and devouring his book *Christianity in Culture*. His views have had a deep impact on my own understanding of ethnohermeneutics, a course that I have taught as "Interpreting the Bible Cross-Culturally" many times at Fuller as an Adjunct Associate Professor of Mission Theology. I have published several articles on the topic of ethnohermeneutics and have been working on a book on the subject for many years.

Currently I am the Academic Dean of Asian Theological Seminary, the Program Director of the Doctor of Missiology Program of the Asia Graduate School of Theology—Philippines, and the Editor of the Asian Journal of Mission. None of these accomplishments would have been possible without my Fuller experience. Thank you dedicated faculty of SWM/SIS!!

Fletcher L. Tink
(M.A. 1984, Ph.D. 1994)

Adjunct Professor of Urban and Compassionate Ministries, Nazarene Theological Seminary; Executive Director of the Bresee Institute for Metro Ministries; Academic Dean for Rescue College, Director of Education, Nazarene Compassionate Ministries, International

In 1977, I was still a green missionary in a brown place— Cochabamba, Bolivia, where adobe walls and dusty streets reflected the somber tones of the encircling Andes, when a missionary friend of mine took me aside in the local Baptist Seminary, introducing me to the "In Service Program" of Fuller's School of World Mission. I lit up on learning about this innovative alternative, and quickly wrangled denominational support to start my studies under the mentorship of Dr. Alvin Martin.

In succession, Drs. Chuck Kraft, Peter Wagner, Paul Hiebert, Paul Pierson and Dan Shaw became my personal guides, trudging along with me through the winding and exhilarating paths of academia, suddenly made practical in the wrenching issues of establishing Christian ministry in a strange culture. Not only did they make sense, they ignited imagination and motivated policy.

Some time later, my missionary service fizzled in dramatic burn-out—with a series of personal family tragedies that left me alone and straining for meaning. God intervened in numerous ways to restore me, with the Fuller assignments nailing my feet to responsibility. Mission, I learned, often happens best in the midst of our brokenness.

I landed on Fuller's campus, ready to learn anew. Dr Hiebert adopted me, and married my urban passions with a program of studies that allowed me to examine not only the chaos of the city, but also the disorder of my own life. Indeed, Bobby Clinton magnified its potential by observing the guiding hand of God through the processes of it all. Fact and theory, personal angst and mission, all converged and, although Dr Hiebert disappeared elsewhere, Dr. Chuck Van Engen picked up the dissertation scraps and helped me rearrange it all for presentation. Indeed, I inherited two of the finest mentors for the price of one. Along the way, I and the Bresee Institute for Urban Training that I co-founded, became something of a conscience of urban concerns for the seminary as a whole.

Twenty years after my initial introduction to Fuller Seminary, I found myself teaching an intensive course at the same Baptist Seminary in Bolivia where I was first "Fullerized." In the memory of that, tears of gratitude engulfed me. Across the intervening years, I had been provoked, stimulated, empowered, and credentialized by SWM, in dimensions exceeding what I had ever anticipated. But more than that, I had joined a family, one of the most vibrant, comprehensive and durable found anywhere in God's Kingdom, that continues to secure and bless me on a daily basis.

When young, I had Joseph-type dreams, that crashed. But like Joseph, in Genesis 45:1-2, I've celebrated in latter years that "aha" moment when I've seen God's guiding hand working not so much in foresight as in hindsight, moving and motivating me across a range of purposes, unimaginable earlier.

Currently, I teach urban and compassionate ministries at Nazarene Theological Seminary, in Kansas City and direct the Bresee Institute for Metro Ministries that trains young people in a myriad of ways for city ministries. I also serve as Academic Dean for Rescue College, a product of the Association of Gospel Rescue Missions, direct the "Life Connection" program at Leavenworth Federal Penitentiary, teach graduate courses worldwide—in 27 countries as of last count, and write extensively.

In sum, Fuller's SWM indeed was just that for me, a "fuller" experience that mopped up the hurts from the past, and launched me into a gracious and unbounded future that I happily and confidently step through.

Peter Y. Rhee
(Student 1986-88, 1992-96; Th.M. 1988; Ph.D. 1996)

Missionary to Indoensia 1988-92; International Director of The Center for Church Renewal & Development; Senior Pastor of International Dream Celebration Church, Seoul, Korea

My studes at SWM have deeply influenced my life and ministry. When asked by Dr. Paul Pierson about my studies at Fuller, I replied, "I have had several conversion experiences." He smiled at me because really new what I meant by "conversion experiences." Before I joined Fuller, I considered myself a pure evangelical, who had a deep concern for evangelism and world mission primarily through discipleship ministry. However, during my years at SWM, I experienced two radical paradigm shifts. The first one is the realization of the importance of a Christian's social duty. This was largely ignored in my Christian life and ministry. The second one, which challenged me more than the first, is the commitment to "power evangelism," the extension of God's kingdom by means of power encounters (e.g. healing, deliverance and pray ministries) with the kingdom of Satan.

People often say that meeting people in life can bring abudant blessings to them. This is surely my case in encountering some professors at SWM in God's providence. I really thank God for allow me to study under some godly and world-mission-minded professors such as Dr. Peter Wagner and Dr. Charles Kraft. I am very proud to have them as my academic and spritual mentors because they have really shaped my life and ministry more than anyone else, especially in the area of power ministry and the work of the Holy Spirit.

Whenever I visit the school, I strongly feel that Fuller is the home of my spiritual and minsterial growth. I like SWM in the way that she has embraced diversity in unity and at the same time she has never lost the deep concern for world mission, through words, deeds and power.

Irving A. Whitt
(Student 1974-76, 1983-84; M.A. 1976, D.Miss. 1994)

Missions Education Coordinator, Pentecostal Assemblies of Canada, Former Missionary to Kenya and Missions Department Chairman, Tyndale Seminary, Toronto

I have a professor's normal library, I guess. As I peruse my shelves I see books with titles such as *Verdict Theology in Missionary Theory* by Alan Tippett; *Understanding Church* Growth by Donald McGavran; Contemporary Theologies of Mission by Donald McGavran and Arthur Glasser; Christianity in Culture by Charles Kraft and On the Crest of the Wave by Peter Wagner. Now these titles date me. I not only own these books but also studied with the authors in the mid 1970s. After serving as a missionary in Kenya for four years and being introduced to the work of Donald McGavran, I enrolled in the M.A. program in Mission in 1974. With my wife, Ruth, and two young daughters I journeyed from Eastern Canada to arrive in smoggy San Fernando Valley in September of that year.

Fuller, School of World Mission, was still establishing its reputation during those days. M.A. and Doctoral students alike were required to write extensive theses and dissertations. Church Growth was the missiological focus. Professors Kraft and Tippett rounded out the faculty with their anthropological contributions and cultural studies. I can still recall Kraft's explanation of "form, function and meaning," and how these concepts opened the windows of understanding in missionary experience. Kraft guided me through my first thesis on "Missionary, Culture and Communication."

We were the guinea pigs for some of the professors' writings. I recall Kraft having us go through his *Christianity in Culture* manuscript long before it was published. Dean, Arthur Glasser helped ground us in the biblical basis of mission, and keep our theological senses sharp and our doctrinal convictions sure. All the students were practitioners – three years cross-cultural experience was required before admittance. Such wealth of experience greatly enriched dialogue and interpersonal relationships.

Seven years after graduating and finishing another four years of service in Kenya I returned to Fuller in 1983 to work on a DMiss. Paul Pierson was now dean of SWM and he acted as mentor for my doctoral dissertation. The school was changing. McGavran was finishing his career. One of my early classes at this time was "Signs, Wonders and Church Growth." Wimber's influence on my life cannot be overestimated, even though I grew up in a Pentecostal Pastor's home. It was the welcoming atmosphere that attracted us. Students from a broad spectrum of evangelical persuasion interacted with each other. Faculty, versed in their areas of expertise created the "wow" moments that made learning a pleasure. Having experienced that learning environment in pursuing two degrees I can say with conviction that the story of Fuller's missiological contribution still has to be told.

Jayakumar Christian
(Student 1991-92; M.A. Missiology 1992, Ph.D. 2004)

National Director, World Vision India

My family and I came to Fuller in December 1990, after almost 14 years of experience in the field with World Vision. I found the Fuller experience a rich time of relearning and renewal. Reflecting on our time at Fuller SWM, there are three things that come to mind.

First, the faculty were not only passionate about missions, but were also deeply spiritual. I always went away blessed from a meeting with every faculty member. The conversations were rich. The engagement was enriching and I always found something to learn from their lives. They not only transferred knowledge but also invested their lives in my learning. They listened, prayed with me, enquired about my family sincerely and always blessed my family and me. This made my time at SWM spritually enriching.

In addition to the spiritual enrichment, I found the faculty always created space for me to pursue what I believed was God's call for my life. They never tried to manipulate my call or marginalize it. The times of discussion and input into my academic life always were a stretching experience. I came back wanting to learn more, read more and discover more. Through all this never did they once give me a feeling that maybe I needed to rethink my basic call. I came out of Fuller with greater conviction about God's particular call in my life. I felt truly affirmed.

Finally the student body of SWM and Fuller enabled me to discover the breadth of God's Kingdom mission. I learnt through my times with students from all over the world that the mission of the

Kingdom of God was much wider than my particular call no matter how intensely I felt about it. I learnt to appreciate the diversity of the Kingdom mission. I learnt to understand in a small way about the sovereignty of the God of the Kingdom of God.

It was truly a major step in my personal life. I always look back at my time at SWM and thank God for those years. I am grateful to God for Fuller and theSchool of World Mission.

Nick Venditti
(M.Div. SOT 1993, Ph.D. SWM 1998)

President, Institute of Theology by Extension, Spain

As a mid-career missionary, I felt the need for further education to be able to fulfill the calling of God on my life. My wife Leona and I talked about various possibilities. Fuller had the best School of World Mission in the world, so that's where we wanted to go.

Through some amazing God-appointed circumstances, we received double confirmation of the decision to apply to Fuller. We had enough money saved for one quarter of study. During my eight years of study, God supplied time after time in surprising ways, and I was able to finish my studies debt-free. It was a faith challenge, for we had made the commitment to not go into debt so that we could continue our work as missionaries.

What a privilege it was to study under some of the most renowned scholars in missions such as Charles Van Engen, Paul Pierson, Art Glasser, Bobby Clinton, and others. I grew in knowledge of the Scripture and in my relationship with the Lord. The School of World Mission helped me develop a biblical theology of missions.

Bobby Clinton greatly impacted my life in the area of leadership. That training is now reflected in our work with the Institute of Theology by Extension that my wife founded in Spain. Today we are working in over 30 countries in 10 languages. The core of what we teach in INSTE is what I learned at Fuller. I owe a great debt of gratitude to the Lord and to the professors of the School of World Mission who gave me a foundation on which to build.

David Johnston
(Th.M. 1988, Ph.D. 2001)

Research Affiliate at the Religious Studies Department
at Yale University

After nine years of service in Algeria, I spent a year at SWM to complete a ThM (1987-88). Then after two more terms of service (Egypt and West Bank), we came back in 1997 to begin work on a Ph.D.-four great years as TA for Dudley Woodberry, my mentor, with some teaching on the side. Charlotte worked as a secretary at SWM in 87-88 and we continued to be involved together as much as possible in our second stay.

We loved the teachers and the staff, and we forged many friendships with fellow students. Perhaps what stands out most for us is the passion faculty have for God and for his glory to shine throughout all the peoples of the earth, combined with an amazing love for students (sacrificing time to help them and pray with them). I was personally amazed at their scholarly work, not just as individuals publishing research, but also as a community of scholars who discussed (and argued about) new ideas among themselves and embarked on numerous common writing projects. That combination of spirituality and scholarly output has inspired me during my last four years at Yale as post-doctoral fellow and part-time lecturer.

Shelley Trebesh
(M.Div. 1996, Ph.D. 2001)

Assistant Professor of Leadership (1/2 time, SIS)
Director for Membership Development, OMF INternational

For me, FTS/SWM/SIS became a calling as well as a treasure. Before moving to California, I committed to the Lord a year of ministry-free activity. (While participating in campus ministry, I discovered I have the propensity toward drivenness. Therefore, I find it important to have sabbaticals!)

This first year at FTS plunged me into the depths of self-discovery and spiritual growth. Coming out of the sabbatical, I embraced a call to come alongside leaders and serve their development. By serving as an advisor, learner, mentor, and teacher,

I experienced the breadth and depth of the Kingdom and the richness of the nations. Many faculty invested in my growth bringing freedom and opportunity. In my own pilgrimage with Jehovah, I know that I'm to join Him in calling forth life and creating life-giving organizations.

Presently, I serve half time as SIS faculty, live in Singapore and mostly work all over Asia endeavoring to provide leader and organizational development.

Erich W. Baumgartner
(Ph.D. 1990)

Assistant Professor, Department of Leadership, Andrews University

The School of World Mission I knew was a creative and spiritual place. If I were to characterize the fruit of my studies at Fuller Seminary in one word—it is Transformation. What attracted me to the School of World Mission was its creative ways to challenge the Church to move forward and equip its leaders with tools to be innovators.

I came as a pastor from my narrow corner of the world with visions of church growth in my church. But what I received was not only a Ph.D., but a greater capacity to see God at work in manifold ways and a passion to join Him in His mission in the world.

In addition, Fuller gave me life-long friendships with some of the most outstanding mission leaders in the world that accompanied me through the valleys and mountain tops of life. Thank you for that legacy in my life.

Robert L. (Rob) Gallagher
(Attended 1990-98, M.A. Missiology 1992, M.A. Theology 1993, Ph.D. 1998)

Assistant Professor, Wheaton College

My family and I arrived in Pasadena from Australia in the fall of 1990 with four bags and a strong sense that God had called us to Fuller Seminary. Upon reflection I now realize that we had little idea what a Fuller education was about and absolutely no thought about what the future would bring. In the midst of an institution that had played such an important role in the second half of the 20th century in the history of American evangelicalism, both historically and missiologically it was an exciting and controversial place to be.

Fifteen years later I look back on the eight-year Fuller journey with deep appreciation. The professional training of a M.A. in Missiology and a M.A. in Theology together with a Ph.D. in Intercultural Studies, has enabled me to teach for the last seven years in the Intercultural Studies Department at Wheaton College Graduate School in Illinois. Yet my Fuller experience was much more than receiving three diplomas.

The School of World Mission was an amazing and unique institution with a strong commitment to the Bible and the Gospel, as well as being open to freely investigate all questions that needed inquiry. I felt at liberty to be myself and to say what I thought. I found the professors lively, godly and imaginative, curious about God and his world, and willing to partner with the students in the learning process. They were academic practitioners who were teaching not just to impart content, but sincerely desiring to allow the educational experience to affect who they were and how they lived. It was that infectious missiological passion that has most changed my life.

Sue Plumb Takamoto
(M.A. 1996, Ph.D. 2002)

Serving with Asian Access in Sanda, Japan, planting house churches and supervising short-term missionaries.

My years at Fuller School of World Mission are rich with memories, triumphs and defeats (thankfully more of the former than the latter), friendships, and holistic growth. Community at Fuller was not something that I took for granted; sometimes I needed to work towards its creation by pulling together several friends to form a prayer group; brainstorming with a few others to "make fun" (i.e. polyester proms in the Catalyst; camping trips to Joshua Tree); doing other spontaneous things on campus. These days were rich. My friends were not just my peers, but also my mentors, professors and their spouses. Nor were they all North Americans; SWM is unique in its blend of nationalities, ages, and ethnicities. Being mentored by Bobby Clinton contributed to my formation way beyond the academic. The opportunity at Fuller to learn the practical (leadership emergence really works!); the theological (understanding Jesus' death and justification makes a big difference as a missionary); the way things really are (we are often talking with other missionaries about capital "R" Reality). The classroom of Fuller is still being transported into our everyday lives here in Japan.

It was at Fuller that I met my husband, Eric Takamoto. It was fun to begin dating and then to get married with the support and encouragement of our Fuller community. We are now serving with Asian Access in Sanda, Japan, where we are planting house churches and supervising short-term missionaries. Last year (2004) I taught a class at Fuller on "Transitions and Transformation of the Christian Leader", and I am working on creating a practicum that will be implemented here in Japan hopefully this next year.

Luis Bush
(Ph.D. 2002)

International Facilitator, Transform World Connections
Previously, International Director, AD2000 & Beyond,
International President, Partners International and
International President, COMIBAM

The Fuller Intercultural Studies faculty was a continuous source of inspiration through their writings, their witness and their friendliness. The incorporation of the cognitive, affective, volitional, and experiential learning domains in private and public interchange challenged me.

My doctoral committee provided timely, necessary advice and guidance throughout the entire process. Out of the dissertation emerged a Fuller-sponsored World Inquiry that compressed the reflective process into a practical instrument. With the encouragement of the faculty of the School of Intercultural Studies and the President's Cabinet, I was advised at various stages of the process on the research design and the inquiry process.

This Inquiry became a tool for listening to voices to help construct a missiology capable of empowering the global church for participation in God's mission for the twenty-first century with expectation of both a deepening and extending of our witness through the gospel. Several from the faculty and administration donated time and travel costs to support the Inquiry.

Appendix C
Church Growth/Missiology Lectures

From the beginning, Dr. McGavran instituted an annual Church Growth lectureship, continuing the series started when ICG was in Oregon. Over the years, starting in 1966, we have had 35 of these at Fuller. The list of lecturers is like a Who's Who of Church Growth and Missiology. Many of the lectures have been outstanding and several of them have resulted in publications.

I include the ICG Oregon lectures to give a complete picture of this lectureship. Though the lectureship was named Church Growth Lectures for many years, it was broadened and renamed Missiology Lectures somewhere along the line. The resulting publications are listed along with the titles of the lectures. They are also listed in the Bibliography.

Church Growth Lectures at ICG, Eugene, Oregon:

1961   J. Waskom Pickett, "The Dynamics of Church Growth." Published as *The Dynamics of Church Growth*, Abingdon Press, 1963.

1962   Calvin Guy, Melvin Hodges, Eugene Nida, and Donald McGavran, "A Symposium on Church Growth and Christian Mission." Published as *Church Growth and Christian Mission* by Harper and Row, 1965.

Church Growth/Missiology Lectures at SWM/SIS Fuller (publication data in parentheses):

1966   Harold Lindsell—Barriers to Church Growth.

1967   David Stowe—Ecumenicity and Evangelism (Grand Rapids: Eerdmans, 1970).

1969   Harold Cook—Historic Patterns of Church Growth (Chicago: Moody Press, 1971).

1971   John H. Sinclair—Congregational Life as a Factor in Church Growth.

1972   Peter Beyerhous—Shaken Foundations: Theological
        Foundations for Mission (Grand Rapids: Zondervan,
        1972).

1973   J. Robertson McQuilkin—How Biblical is the Church
        Growth Movement? (Chicago: Moody Press, 1973).

1974   Louis J. Luzbetak—Cross-Cultural Sensitivity and
        Evangelism.

1975   Donald R. Jacobs—Socio-Religious Change in Post-
        Conversion Experience.

1976   Kenneth E. Nolin—A Christian Witness to the Muslims.

1977   Wendell Belew—Children in the Marketplace.

1978   Stephen Neill—Biblical Sights and Insights on Church
        Growth.

1979   Charles L. Chaney—Church Planting at the End of the
        Twentieth Century (Wheaton: Tyndale, 1982).

1980   Harvie M. Conn—Eternal Word and Changing Worlds:
        Theology, Anthropology, and Mission in Trialogue
        (Grand Rapids: Zondervan, 1984).

1981   David L. Rambo—Third World Leadership Training: An
        Urgent Missiological Priority.

1982   Oscar I. Romo—Evangelizing Ethnic America.

1984   David Yonggi Cho—Dynamic Church Growth: Growing
        and Leading the Multiple Staff Church.

1985   Tom Houston—Great Commandment—Great
        Commission: A Whole Gospel for Growing Churches.

1986   Leighton F. S. Ford—A Vision Pursued—The Lausanne
        Movement 1974 – 1986.

1987   Jonathan Tiien-en Chao—"The Church in China:
        Dynamics of Contemporary Growth and Ministry.

1988   Timothy M. Warner—Spiritual Warfare (Wheaton:
        Crossway Books, 1991).

1989   George G. Hunter III—How to Reach Secular People
        (Nashville: Abingdon, 1992).

1990   Vinson Synan—The Spirit Said Grow (Monrovia: MARC,
        1992).

1991   Jack W. Hayford—Invading the Invisible: Spiritual
        Warfare in Effective Evangelism.

1992   Eva Burrows—Church Growth: A Denominational
        Dynamic.

1993   William F. Kumuyi—Basic Issues in Church Growth: An
        African Perspective.

1994   Lamin Sanneh—Pentecost or Hijra: Translation in Comparative Reflection.

1995   Dana Robert—American Women in Mission.

1996   Andrew F. Walls—A Cultural History of the Christian Faith: Eusebius Revisited and Latourette Reconsidered.

1997-98 Scholars from Six Continents—Christian History in Global Perspective. An international consultation with 45 scholars from six continents. Keynote speakers were Philip Yuen-Sang Leung, A.M. Mundadan, Gerald J. Pillay, Lamin Sanneh and Andrew F. Walls. Published as *Enlarging the Story: Perspectives on Writing World Christian History* (Orbis 2002).

1999   Juan Samuel Escobar—Mission from Below: Evangelical Missiology Toward the 21st Century.

2000   Symposium—Making Christian History. A symposium organized in conjunction with inauguration of the Paul E. Pierson Chair in Mission History and Contemporary Culture with Wilbert R. Shenk as first incumbent. Speakers were David Daniel, C.M. Robeck and Wilbert R. Shenk. Four doctoral students reported on their historical research-in-progress: Katherine Lee Ahn, Beate Eulenhoeffer-Mann, Paul Tsuchido Shew and Elaine Vaden.

2001   Eugene A. Nida—Culture, Communication, and Christianity.

2002   Jonathan S. Campbell and Alan J. Roxburgh—Church and Culture in a Postmodern World.

2003   Miriam Adeney—Making Disciples Through Appropriate Media.

2004   Baroness Caroline Cox—The Church at the Margins: Persecution, Women and Children.

Bibliography

Bolger, Ryan
   1998   "Dwelling, Distinctiveness, and Dialogue: The Missiological Triad of John Howard Yoder," in *Mission Focus: Annual Review*, vol. 6.

   2003   *Jesus for and Against Modernity*. Ph.D. dissertation, Fuller Theological Seminary.

   2004   (with Gibbs) "Tracking the Emerging Church," in *Journal of the American Society for Church Growth* 15:3-10.

   2005   (with Gibbs) *Emerging Churches: Creating Christian Community in Postmodern Cultures*. Grand Rapids:Baker.

Brewster, Dan
   1997   *Only Paralyzed From the Neck Down*. Pasadena, CA: Wm Carey Library.

Brewster, Elizabeth (Betty Sue)
   1995   "Preparing Life-Long Learners," in *Helping the Missionary Language Learner Succeed*, pp. 9-33. Edited by Lonna Dickerson. Colorado Springs, CO: Missionary Training International.

Brewster, Tom and Elizabeth Brewster
   1976   *Language Acquisition Made Practical*. Pasadena, CA: Lingua House.

   1981   *Bonding and the Missionary Task*. Pasadena, CA: Lingua House.

   1982   "Language Learning is Communication—is Ministry," in *International Bulletin of Missionary Research*.

   1986 (ed.) *Community is My Language Classroom*. Pasadena, CA: Lingua House.

Bundy, David
1989— (co-editor) *Pietist and Wesleyan Studies.* Serial
publication: Monographic series. Metuchen, NJ:
Scarecrow Press.

Clinton, J. Robert
1988   *The Making of a Leader.* Colorado Springs, CO:NavPress.

1992   (with P.D. Stanley) *Connecting: The Mentoring
Relationships You Need to Succeed in Life.* Colorado
Springs, CO: NavPress.

1995   *Focused Lives—Inspirational Life Changing Lessons From
Eight Effective Christian Leaders Who Finished Well.*
Altadena, CA: Barnabas.

1998   *Strategic Concepts—That Clarify a Focused Life.*
Altadena, CA: Barnabas.

2004   *Clinton's Biblical Leadership Commentary CD, vol. II (1,2
Ti; 1,2 Co; Php; Phe; Jn; Da; Tit; Hag; Hab; Neh; Jon.*
Altadena, CA: Barnabas.

Coe, Shoki
1973/1976 "Contextualizing Theology," in *Mission Trends No. 3.*
Edited by Gerald Anderson and Thomas Stransky. New
York: Paulist Press and Grand Rapids, MI: Eerdmans,
1976.

Deiros, Pablo
1986   *Los Evangelicos Y el Poder Politico en America Latina.*
Grand Rapids: Nueva Creacion.

1991   "Protestant Fundamentalsim in Latin America." In
Fundamentalisms Observed. Martin E. Marty and R. Scott
Appleby, eds. Chicago: University of Chicago Press.

1992   *Historia del Christianismo en America Latina.* Buenos
Aires: Fraternidad Teologica LatinoAmericanan.

1994   *LatinoAmerica en Llamas.* Miami: Caribe.

1997   *Protestantismo en America Latina.* Miami: Caribe.

1998　*La Accion del Espiritu Santo en la Historia*. Miami: Caribe.

2001　"Hispanic Pentecostalism in the Americas." In *The Century of the Holy Spirit*. Vinson Synan, ed. Nashville: Thomas Nelson.

Dundon, Colin
2001　"A Post Colonial Missiology: The Pilgrim Mind of Rev. Dr. AR Tippett," unpublished paper.

Elliston, Eddie
1993　*Home Grown Leaders*, Pasadena, CA: Wm Carey.

1998　*Christian Relief and Development: Developing Workers for Effective Ministry*, Irving, TX: Word.

2000　*Developing Leaders for Urban Ministry* (with J. Timothy Kauffman) NewYork: Peter Lang.

Gibbs, Edmund
1981, 1985, 1990　*I Believe in Church Growth*. Grand Rapids, MI: Eerdmans and London: Hodder & Stoughton.

1985　*The God Who Communicates*. London: Hodder & Stoughton.

1987　*Followed or Pushed?* MARC Europe.

1994　*In Name Only—Tackling the Problem of Nominal Christianity*. Bridgepoint.

2000　*Church Next.* Downers Grove, IL: InterVarsity.

2005　*Leadership Next.* Downers Grove, IL: InterVarsity.

2005　(with Ryan Bolger) *Emerging Churches*. Grand Rapids, MI: Baker.

Gilliland, Dean S.
1983　*Pauline Theology and Mission Practice*. Grand Rapids, MI: Baker.

1985　*African Religion Meets Islam*. Lanham, MD: University Press of America.

1989   *The Word Among Us*. Irving, TX: Word. Reprinted
        Eugene, OR: Wipf & Stock 2001.

1991   "First Conversion and Second Conversion in Nigeria,"
        Journal of Asian and African Studies 26:131-150.

2000   "Modeling the Incarnation for Muslim Peoples,"
        Missiology 38:329-38.

2001   "My Pilgrimage in Mission" in International Bulletin of
        Missionary Research 24:119-22.

2004   "For Missionaries and Leaders: Paul's Farewell to the
        Ephesian Elders," in R. Gallagher & P. Hertig, Missions in
        Acts, Maryknoll, NY: Orbis, pp 257-83.

2005   "The Incarnation as Matrix for Appropriate Theologies."
        In *Appropriate Christianity*. C. Kraft, ed. Pasadena, CA:
        Wm Carey.

Glanville, Elizabeth
    2000   *Leadership Development for Women in Christian Ministry*,
            Ph.D. dissertation, Fuller Theological Seminary.

Glasser, Arthur F.
    1973   "Church Growth and Theology." In *God, Man and Church
            Growth*. A.R. Tippett, ed. Grand Rapids, MI:Eerdmans,
            pp 52-68.

    1974   "What is 'Mission' Today? Two Views," *Mission Trends
            No. 1*, G. H. Anderson and T. Stransky, eds. NY: Paulist
            and Grand Rapids, MI: Eerdmans, pp. 5-11.

    1983   (with D.A. McGavran) *Contemporary Theologies of
            Mission*. Grand Rapids, MI: Eerdmans.

    1985   "The Evolution of Evangelical Mission Theology Since
            World War II," *International Bulletin of Missionary
            Research* 9:9-13. Reprinted in *Practical Theology and the
            Ministry of the Church, 1952-1984*, H.M. Conn editor.
            Phillipsburg, N.J.: Presbyterian and Reformed, pp 235-52.

    1989   "Old Testament Contextualization: Revelation and its
            Environment" *The Word Among Us*, D. Gilliland editor.
            Waco, TX: Word, pp 32-51.

Bibliography 335

1990 "My Pilgrimage in Mission" in *International Bulletin of Missionary Research*, 14:112-15.

1991-1992 Four articles on "Evangelical Objections to Jewish Evangelism," *Missionary Monthly*, December, January, February, March.

2003 *Announcing the Kingdom*. Edited by C. Van Engen, D. Gilliland and S. Redford. Grand Rapids, MI: Baker.

Grimley, John and Gordon Robinson
1966 *Church Growth in Central and Southern Nigeria*. Grand Rapids: Eerdmans.

Hamilton, Keith
1962 *Church Growth in the High Andes*. Lucknow, India.

Hanciles, Jehu
2001 "Anatomy of an Experiment: The Sierra Leone Native Pastorate," *Missiology* 29:63-82.

2002 *Euthanasia of a Mission: African Church Autonomy in a Colonial Context*. Westport, CT: Praeger.

2003 "Mission and Migration: Some Implications for the Twenty-first Century Church," *International Bulletin of Missionary Research* 27:146-153.

2004 "Conversion and Social Change: A Review of the Unfinished Task in West Africa." In *Christianity Reborn: The Global Expansion of Evangelicalism in the Twentieth Century*. Donald Lewis, ed. Grand Rapids, MI: Eerdmans, pp 157-180.

2004 "Missionaries and Revolutionaries: Elements of Transformation in the Emergence of Modern African Christianity," *International Bulletin of Missionary Research* 28:146-152.

2005 "Back to Africa: White Abolitionists and Black Missionaries." In *African Christianity: An African Story*. Ogbu Kalu, ed. Pretoria, South Africa: Univ of Pretoria Press.

Hertig, Young Lee

1993   (with Paul G. Hiebert) "Asian Immigrants in American Cities," in *Urban Mission,* March 1993.

1996   "Asian-American Women in the Workplace and the Church." In *People On The Way: Asian North Americans Discovering Christ, Culture, and Community.* David Ng, ed. Valley Forge, PA: Judson Press.

1998   "The Asian-American Alternative to Feminism: A *Yinist* Paradigm," in *Missiology: An International Review,* 26:15-22.

2001   *Cultural Tug of War: The Korean Immigrant Family and Church in Transition,* Nashville, TN: Abingdon.

Hiebert, Paul G.

1976/1983   *Cultural Anthropology.* Grand Rapids: Baker.

1982   "The Flaw of the Excluded Middle," in *Missiology* 10:35-47.

1984/1987   "Critical Contextualization," *Missiology* 12:287-96 and *International Bulletin of Missionay Research* 11:104-112.

1985   *Anthropological Insights for Missionaries.* Grand Rapids: Baker.

1987   (with Frances F. Hiebert) *Case Studies in Missions.* Grand Rapids: Baker.

1994   *Anthropological Reflections on Missiological Issues.* Grand Rapids: Baker.

1995   (with Eloise Meneses) *Incarnational Ministry.* Grand Rapids: Baker.

1999   (with R. D. Shaw and T. Tienou) *Understanding Folk Religion.* Grand Rapids, MI: Baker.

Huegel, John, Jack Taylor and Donald McGavran

1963   *Church Growth in Mexico.* Grand Rapids: Eerdmans.

King, Roberta R.

1989   *Pathways in Christian Music Communication: The Case of the Senufo of Cote d'Ivoire.* Ph.D. dissertation, Fuller Theological Seminary. Ann Arbor, MI: University Microfilms.

1990   "The Role of Music in Theological Education." *Africa Journal of Evangelical Theology* 9:35-41.

1999   *A Time to Sing: A Manual for the African Church.* Nairobi, Kenya: Evangel Publishing House.

2004   "Towards a Discipline of Christian Ethnomusicology: A Missiological Paradigm, in *Missiology* 32:293-307.

2005   "Variations on a Theme of Contextualization: Music Lessons from Africa," in *Appropriate Christianity*, C. Kraft editor. Pasadena, CA: Wm Carey.

Kraft, Charles H.

1994   *A Study of Hausa Syntax.* Hartford, CT: Hartford Seminary.

1963   "Conversion: Cultural or Christian?" in *Practical Anthropology* 10:179-87.

1971   "Younger Churches—Missionaries and Indigeneity" in *Church Growth Bulletin* VII, 6, reprinted in *Church Growth Bulletin: Second Consolidated Volume,* Wm Carey Library 1977:159-61.

1978   "The Contextualization of Theology" in *Evangelical Missions Quarterly*, 14:311-36.

1979/2005   (revised edition 2005) *Christianity in Culture.* Maryknoll, NY: Orbis.

1983/1991   (revised edition 1991) *Communication Theory for Christian Witness.* Maryknoll, NY: Orbis.

1989   *Christianity with Power.* Ann Arbor, MI: Servant.

1994   "Alan R. Tippett" in *Australian Dictionary of Evangelical Biography*, Sydney: Evangelical History Association.

1996   *Anthropology for Christian Witness*. Maryknoll, NY: Orbis.

1998   "My Pilgrimage in Mission" in *International Bulletin of Missionary Research*, 22:162-64.

2001   *Culture, Communication and Christianity*. Pasadena, CA: Wm Carey.

2002   *Confronting Powerless Christianity*. Grand Rapids, MI: Chosen/Baker.

2005 (ed.)   *Appropriate Christianity*. Pasadena, CA: Wm Carey.

Latourette, Kenneth Scott
1938   A History of the Expansion of Christianity. NY: Harper.

Lingenfelter, Sherwood
1986/2003   *Ministering Cross-Culturally: An Incarnational Model for Personal Relationships*. Co-authored with Marvin K. Mayers. Revised edition 2003. Grand Rapids, MI: Baker.

1992/1998   *Transforming Culture: Challenge for Christian Mission*. (Revised edition 1998.) Grand Rapids, MI: Baker.

1996   *Agents of Transformation: A Guide for Effective Cross-Cultural Ministry*. Grand Rapids, MI: Baker.

2003   Teaching Cross-Culturally: An Incarnational Model of Learning and Teaching. Co-authored with Judith E. Lingenfelter. Grand Rapids, MI: Baker.

McConnell, C. Douglas
1996   *The Holy Spirit and Mission Dynamics*. Pasadena, CA: Wm Carey.

2005   (With M. Pocock and G. Van Rheenen.) *The Changing Face of World Missions: Engaging Contemporary Issues and Trends*. Grand Rapids: Baker Books.

McCurry, Don
1979   *The Gospel and Islam*. Monrovia, CA: MARC (World Vision).

McGavran, Donald A.

1928   *How to Teach Religion in Mission Schools.*

1955   *Bridges of God.* NY: Friendship Press.

1959   *How Churches Grow.* London: World Dominion Press.

1962   *Church Growth in Jamaica.* Lucknow, India.

1965   *Church Growth and Christian Mission.* N.Y.: Harper & Row.

1970   *Understanding Church Growth.* Grand Rapids: Eerdmans.

1986   "My Pilgrimage in Mission" in *International Bulletin of Missionary Research*, 10:53-58.

1990   *Understanding Church Growth*, 3rd edition revised and edited by C. Peter Wagner. Grand Rapids: Eerdmans.

Middleton, Vernon James

1989   *The Development of a Missiologist: The Life and Thought of Donald Anderson McGavran 1897-1965.* Ph.D. dissertation, Fuller Theological Seminary.

Mulholland, Kenneth

2000   "Winter, Ralph D." In *Evangelical Dictionary of World Missions.* A. Scott Moreau, ed. Grand Rapids, MI: Baker.

Nketia, J.H.K.

1975   *The Music of Africa.* London: Victor Gollanz.

Orr, J. Edwin

1964   *The Second Evangelical Awakening in America.* London: Marshall, Morgan and Scott.

1965   *The Light of the Nations: Evangelical Renewal and Advance in the Nineteenth Century.* Grand Rapids: Eerdmans.

1976   *Evangelical Awakenings in the South Seas.* Minneapolis: Bethany.

1978   *Evangelical Awakenings in Latin America.* Minneapolis: Bethany.

1978   *Evangelical Awakenings in Southern Asia.* Minneapolis:
        Bethany.

Park, Timothy
1983   "Missionary Orientation," in *Sweat and Tears of Korean
        Missionaries* edited by Han'guk Paul Son'gyohoe. Seoul:
        Tul Sorisa, pp 50-61.

1992   "Trends of World Mission Toward A.D. 2,000 and the
        Mission of the Korean Church," in *Bit Kwa Sokum* (The
        Salt and Light). Seoul: Tyrannus Books, pp 173-79.

1996   "Mission Cooperation of Korean Missionaries in the
        Philippines,"in *The Vision and Cooperation for World
        Mission,* edited by Korean World Mission Council. Seoul:
        Hae-Bul, pp 11-16.

1999   *Missionary Movement of the Korean Church.* Seoul:
        Institute for Asian Mission.

Forthcoming   *Mission History of the Presbyterian Church in
        Korea During Japanese Colonial Rule.*

Pickett, J. Waskom
1933   *Christian Mass Movements in India.* NY: Abingdon.

1963   *The Dynamics of Church Growth.* Nashville: Abingdon.

Pierson, Paul E.
1974   *A Younger Church in Search of Maturity: Presbyterianism
        in Brazil 1910-1959.* San Antonio, TX: Trinity University
        Press.

1982   *Themes From Acts.* Ventura, CA: Regal.

1993   "Arthur F. Glasser: Citizen of the Kingdom" in *The Good
        News of the Kingdom*, C. Van Engen, D. Gilliland and P.
        Pierson, editors. Maryknoll NY: Orbis.

2005   "Renewal, Revival and Contextualization." In *Appropriate
        Christianity.* C.H. Kraft ed. Pasadena, CA: Wm. Carey.

2005   *Transformation from the Periphery: Emerging Streams of
        Church and Mission.* Pasadena, CA: Wm. Carey.

Read, William
   1965   *New Patterns of Church Growth in Brazil*. Grand Rapids:
           Eerdmans.

Reisacher, Evelyne
   2006   "Beyond the Veil" in *Christian Reflection: Christianity
           and Islam.* Waco, TX: Baylor University.

Sharp, J. Lauriston
   1952   "Steel Axes for Stone Age Australians," in *Human
           Organization* 11 (reprinted in *Practical Anthropology*
           7:62-73).

Shaw, R. Daniel
   1988   *Transculturation: The Cultural Factor in Translation.*
           Pasadena, CA: Wm Carey.

   1990   *Kandila: Samo Ceremonialism and Interpersonal
           Relationships.* Ann Arbor, MI: Univ of Michigan Press.

   1996   *From Longhouse to Village: Samo Social Change.* In Case
           Studies in Anthropology Series. George & Louise
           Spindler, eds. Fort Worth, TX: Harcourt Brace.

   1998   *Understanding Folk Religion.* See Hiebert.

   2003   (with Van Engen) *Communicating God's Word in a
           Complex World.* NY: Roman & Littlefield.

Shearer, Roy
   1966   *Wildfire: The Growth of the Church in Korea.* Grand
           Rapids: Eerdmans.

Shenk, Wilbert
   1973(ed.) *The Challenge of Church Growth.* Elkhart, IN: Institute
           of Mennonite Studies.

   1983   *Exploring Church Growth.* Grand Rapids, MI: Eerdmans.

   1983   *Henry Venn: Missionary Statesman.* Maryknoll, NY:
           Orbis.

   1987   *American Society of Missiology, 1972-1987.* Elkhart, IN:
           American Society of Missiology.

1996   "The Role of Theory in Mission Studies," *Missiology*
        24:31-45.

1997   (with G.R. Hunsberger) *The American Society of
        Missiology: The First Quarter Century*. Decatur, GA:
        ASM.

1999   *Changing Frontiers of Mission*. Maryknoll, NY: Orbis.

2000   *By Faith They Went Out: Mennonite Missions, 1850-1999*.
        Elkhart, IN: Institute of Mennonite Studies.

2001   "Recasting Theology of Mission: Impulses from the Non-
        Western World" in *International Bulletin of Missionary
        Research* 25:98-107.

2002(ed.)   *Enlarging the Story: Perspectives on Writing World
        Christian History*. Maryknoll, NY: Orbis.

2003   "Missiology." In *Encyclopedia of Protestantism*. Hans J.
        Hillerbrand, ed. NY: Routledge.

2004   *North American Foreign Missions, 1810-1914: Theology,
        Theory and Policy*. Grand Rapids, MI: Eerdmans.

2004 Articles   "Missiology," "John R. Mott," "World Council of
        Churches," and "World Missionary Conference" in
        Encyclopedia of Protestantism. London: Routledge.

Smalley, William
    1958   "Cultural Implications of an Indigenous Church," in
           Practical Anthropology, 5:61-65. Reprinted in *Readings in
           Missionary Anthropology II*. Smalley, W. ed. Pasadena,
           CA: Wm Carey 1978.

Smedes, Louis B.
    1987   *Ministry and the Miraculous*. Pasadena, CA: Fuller
           Seminary.

Sogaard, Viggo
    1975   *Everything You Need to Know for a Cassette Ministry*.
           Minneapolis: Bethany.

    1990   *Audio Scriptures Handbook*. Reading, UK: United Bible
           Societies.

1993   *Media in Church and Mission.* Pasadena: Wm Carey.

1996   *Research in Church and Mission.* Pasadena: Wm Carey.

2002   *Communicating Scriptures.* Reading, UK: United Bible Societies.

Stott, John R. and Robert T. Coote, editors
1979   *Gospel and Culture.* Pasadena, CA: Wm Carey.

Sunda, James
1963   *Church Growth in West New Guinea.* Lucknow, India.

Tiersma, Jude (see Watson)

Taylor, Jack
1962   *God's Messengers to Mexico's Masses.* Lucknow, India.

Tippett, Alan R.
1960   "Probing Missionary Inadequacies at the Popular Level", in *International Review of Missions*, 49:411-19.

1965-1967   "The Biblical Basis of Church Growth," in *Church Growth Bulletin.*

1967   *Solomon Islands Christianity.* London: Lutterworth.

1969/1973 (revised edition 1973)   *Verdict Theology in Missionary Theory.* Pasadena, CA: Wm Carey.

1970   *Church Growth and the Word of God.* Grand Rapids, MI: Eerdmans.

1971   *People Movements in Southern Polynesia.* Chicago: Moody.

1973(ed.)   *God, Man and Church Growth.* Grand Rapids: Eerdmans.

1985   *No Continuing City*, unpublished autobiography.

1987   *Introduction to Missiology.* Pasadena, CA: Wm Carey.

Van Engen, Charles

1981   *The Growth of the True Church.* Amsterdam: Rodopi (reprinted by University Microfilms, Ann Arbor, MI in 1995).

1985   *Hijos del Pacto: Conversion y Mision en el Bautismo.* Grand Rapids, MI: Tell.

1991   *God's Missionary People: Rethinking the Purpose of the Local Church.* Grand Rapids, MI: Baker.

1992   *You Are My Witnesses: Drawing From Your Spiritual Journey to Evangelize Your Neighbors.* Grand Rapids, MI: RCA Publications.

1993   *Good News of the Kingdom.* Maryknoll, NY: Orbis.

1994   (with Jude Tiersma) *God So Loves the City.* Monrovia, CA: MARC.

1996   *Mission on the Way: Issues in Mission Theology.* Grand Rapids: Baker.

1996   (ed with Pierson and Elliston) *Missiological Education in the 21st Century.* Maryknoll, NY: Orbis.

Wagner, C. Peter

1976, 1984   *Your Church Can Grow: Seven Vital Signs of a Healthy Church.* Ventura, CA: Regal.

1997   *The Ethical Dimensions of the Homogeneous Unit Principle of Church Growth.* Doctoral dissertation: Univ. of Southern California.

1979   *Our Kind of People.* John Knox Press.

1979   (Revised 1994, 2005) *Your Spiritual Gifts Can Help Your Church Grow.* Ventura, CA: Regal.

1990   (revision of McGavran) *Understanding Church Growth.* Grand Rapids, MI: Eerdmans.

1996   *Confronting the Powers*, Ventura, CA: Regal.

1999 *Churchquake! How the New Apostolic Reformation is Shaking up the Church as We Know It.* Ventura, CA: Regal.

2000 *Acts of the Holy Spirit: A Modern Commentary on the Book of Acts*, Ventura, CA: Regal.

2000 "My Pilgrimage in Mission" in *International Bulletin of Missionary Research* 23:164-67.

Wallace, Anthony F.C.
1956 "Revitalization Movements," in *American Anthropologist* 58:264-81.

Watson, Jude Tiersma and Charles Van Engen
1994 *God So Loves the City.* Monrovia, CA: MARC.

Weld, Wayne C. and Donald A. McGavran
1971/1974 *Principles of Church Growth.* Pasadena, CA: Wm Carey.

1970/1974 *Principios del Crecimiento de la Iglesia.* Pasadena, CA: Wm Carey.

Whiteman, Darrell
2005 "Wilbert Shenk and the American Society of Missiology." In *Evangelical, Ecumenical and Anabaptist Missiologies in Conversation.* Walter Sawatsky, James Krabill and Charles Van Engen, eds. Maryknoll, NY: Orbis.

Winter, Ralph D.
1969 (ed.) *Theological Education by Extension.* Pasadena, CA: Wm Carey.

1970 (ed.) *Warp and Woof: Organizing for Christian Mission.* Pasadena, CA: Wm Carey.

1970 *The Twenty Five Unbelievable Years 1945-1969.* Pasadena, CA: Wm Carey.

1973 "Planting of Younger Missions." In *Church/Mission Tensions Today.* C. Peter Wagner, ed. Chicago: Moody Press.

1974   "The Decade Past and the Decade to Come: Seeing the
        Task Geographically" in *Evangelical Missions Quarterly*
        10:1:11-25.

1975   "The Highest Priority: Cross-Cultural Evangelism." In *Let
        the Earth Hear His Voice: International Congress on
        World Evangelsim.* J. D. Douglas, ed. Minneapolis, MN:
        Kirk House.

1995   "My Pilgrimage in Mission" in *International Bulletin of
        Missionary Research* vol. 19:56-60.

2005   *Frontiers in Mission.* Pasadena, CA: Wm Carey.

Winter, Ralph D. and Steven C. Hawthorne, eds.
1999   *Perspectives on the World Christian Movement* (3rd
        edition). Pasadena: Wm Carey.

Wold, Joseph
1968   *God's Impatience in Liberia.* Grand Rapids: Eerdmans.

Wong, Hoover
1998   *Coming Together or Coming Apart.* Kearney, NE: Morris
        Publishing.

2003   *How to do Church.* Kearney, NE: Morris Publishing.

Woodberry, Dudley
1989(ed.)   *Muslims and Christians on the Emmaus Road.*
        Monrovia, CA: MARC.

1989(ed.)   *Where Muslims and Christians Meet.* Pasadena, CA:
        Zwemer Institute.

1996   (with Van Engen and Elliston) see Van Engen.

1997   *Dimensions of Witness among Muslims.* Seoul: Chongshin
        University.

1999(ed.)   *Reaching the Resistant: Barriers and Bridges for
        Mission.* Pasadena, CA: Wm Carey.

2002   "My Pilgrimage in Mission," in *International Bulletin of
        Missionary Research* 26:24-28.

2005   (with Osman Zumrut and Mustafa Koylu) *Muslim and Christian Reflections on Peace—Divine and Human Dimensions*. Lanham, MD: University Press.

Works, Herbert M., Jr.

1974   *The Church Growth Movement to 1965*. D.Miss. dissertation, Fuller Theological Seminary.

Index

AD2000 and Beyond Movement, 126, 325

Adeney, Miriam, 329

Afghanistan, 55, 179, 180

Africa University, 229

Africa/African, 9, 11, 60, 63, 65, 70, 73, 77, 98-99, 101-103, 117, 122-123, 138-139, 141, 146, 176, 184, 209, 212-213, 215, 217, 227, 229-231, 234-235, 243-245, 265, 284-286, 289, 328, 333-335, 337, 339

Ahn, Katherine Lee, 329

Air Force Academy, 203

All Saints' Episcopal Church, 174

American Anthropological Association (AAA), 81

American Bible Society, 22, 96, 100

American Born Chinese (ABC), 189-190, 293

American Society of Missiology (ASM), 96, 122, 200, 202, 217, 257, 287, 341-342, 345

American University, 17, 39, 44, 46, 179, 282

Anderson, Gerald, 95-96, 122, 287, 332, 334, 339

Anglican Church Missionary Society, 71

Animism, 86, 116, 120, 137, 264, 268

anthropology, 13, 17, 32, 35-36, 38-39, 41-42, 44-45, 61, 83, 86, 90, 93, 99-100, 103, 116-117, 120-121, 134-135, 137, 144, 161-162, 164, 195-196, 220-221, 234, 258, 261, 263-265, 268, 282, 285-286, 289, 294, 297, 305-306, 328, 336, 338, 341-342

anti-Pentecostal, 112, 168

applied knowledge, 70

Argentina, 205, 207

Arthur Glasser Chair of Biblical Theology of Mission, 297

Asbury Theological Seminary, 46, 84, 134, 245, 289, 304

Asia, 35, 60, 63, 65, 70, 98, 193, 209, 217, 225-226, 284, 304-305, 308, 312, 315-316, 323, 340

Asia Pacific Christian Mission (APCM), 225-226

Asian Center for Theology and Mission (ACTS), 144, 175, 208, 290

Asian Institute of Christian Communication (AICC), 159-160, 176

Assemblies of God, 20-22, 312-313

Associated Mennonite Biblical Seminary, 200

Association of Professors of Mission, 217

Australia, 14, 16, 27, 29, 31-32, 34, 36-41, 44, 46-49, 63, 65, 80-81, 133-134, 225-226, 283, 288, 293, 310, 312, 323

Azusa Pacific University, 200

Bailey, Ken, 124, 181, 289

Baptist, 20-21, 71, 97, 150-151, 155, 206-207, 211, 213, 296, 316-317

Baptist General Conference, 211

Barker, Glen, 146-149, 153

www.ingramcontent.com/pod-product-compliance
Lightning Source LLC
Chambersburg PA
CBHW051044060526
44539CB00047B/1497